The Jews in Old Poland, 1000–1795

The Jews in Old Poland
1000–1795

Edited by

Antony Polonsky, Jakub Basista and
Andrzej Link-Lenczowski

BLOOMSBURY ACADEMIC
LONDON • NEW YORK • OXFORD • NEW DELHI • SYDNEY

BLOOMSBURY ACADEMIC
Bloomsbury Publishing Plc
50 Bedford Square, London, WC1B 3DP, UK
1385 Broadway, New York, NY 10018, USA
29 Earlsfort Terrace, Dublin 2, Ireland

BLOOMSBURY, BLOOMSBURY ACADEMIC and the Diana logo
are trademarks of Bloomsbury Publishing Plc

First published in 1993 by I.B. Tauris & Co Ltd
In Association with the Institute for Polish-Jewish Studies, Oxford

This paperback edition published by Bloomsbury Academic in 2022

Copyright © I.B. Tauris & Co Ltd, 1993

All rights reserved. No part of this publication may be reproduced or
transmitted in any form or by any means, electronic or mechanical,
including photocopying, recording, or any information storage or retrieval
system, without prior permission in writing from the publishers.

Bloomsbury Publishing Plc does not have any control over, or responsibility for,
any third-party websites referred to or in this book. All internet addresses given
in this book were correct at the time of going to press. The author and publisher
regret any inconvenience caused if addresses have changed or sites have
ceased to exist, but can accept no responsibility for any such changes.

A catalogue record for this book is available from the British Library.

A catalog record for this book is available from the Library of Congress.

ISBN: PB: 978-1-3501-8596-8

To find out more about our authors and books visit
www.bloomsbury.com and sign up for our newsletters.

Contents

List of contributors vii
Introduction by Antony Polonsky 1

I *Society*

1 Jerzy Wyrozumski, Jews in Medieval Poland 13
2 Zdzisław Pietrzyk, Judaizers in Poland in the Second Half of the Sixteenth Century 23
3 Andrezej Link-Lenczowski, The Jewish Population in the Light of the Resolutions of the Dietines in the Sixteenth to the Eighteenth Centuries 36
4 Daniel Tollet, The Private Life of Polish Jews in the Vasa Period 45
5 Krystyn Matwijowski, Jews and Armenians in the Polish-Lithuanian Commonwealth in the Sixteenth and Seventeenth Centuries 63
6 Artur Eisenbach, The Four Years' Sejm and the Jews 73

II *Institutions*

7 Shmul Ettinger, The Council of the Four Lands 93
8 Israel Bartal, The *Pinkas* of the Council of the Four Lands 110
9 Moshé Altbauer, The Language of Documents Relating to Jewish Autonomy in Poland 119
10 Anatol Leszczyński, The Terminology of the Bodies of Jewish Self-Government 132
11 Jacob Goldberg, The Jewish Sejm: Its Origins and Functions 147
12 Mordekhai Nadav, Regional Aspects of the Autonomy of Polish Jews: The History of the Tykocin *Kehilla*, 1670–1782 166

13	Gershon David Hundert, The *Kehilla* and the Municipality in Private Towns at the End of the Early Modern Period	174
14	Chone Shmeruk, Hasidism and the *Kehilla*	186

III *Legal Status*

15	Stanisław Grodziski, The Kraków *Voivode*'s Jurisdiction over Jews: A Study of the Historical Records of the Kraków *Voivode*'s Administration of Justice to Jews	199
16	Shmuel Shilo, The Individual versus the Community in Jewish Law in pre-Eighteenth-Century Poland	219
17	Jacek Sobczak, The Condition of the Jewish Population of Wschowa in the Mid Eighteenth Century	235

IV *The Economy*

18	Maurycy Horn, The Chronology and Distribution of Jewish Craft Guilds in Old Poland, 1613–1795	249
19	Jan M. Małecki, Jewish Trade at the End of the Sixteenth Century and in the First Half of the Seventeenth Century	267
20	Janina Bieniarzówna, Jewish Trade in the Century of Kraków's Decline	282

V *Population*

21	Antoni Podraza, Jews and the Village in the Polish Commonwealth	299
22	Zenon Guldon and Karol Krzystanek, The Jewish Population in the Towns on the West Bank of the Vistula in the Sandomierz Province from the Sixteenth to the Eighteenth Centuries	322

Glossary	340
Chronology	346
Index	353

List of Contributors

MOSHÉ ALTBAUER is Emeritus Professor of Philology at the Hebrew University of Jerusalem.
ISRAEL BARTAL is Senior in Modern Jewish History at the Hebrew University of Jerusalem.
JAKUB BASISTA is Lecturer in History at the Jagiellonian University in Kraków.
JANINA BIENIARZÓWNA is Professor at the Pontifical Theological Academy in Krakow.
ARTUR EISENBACH is Emeritus Professor of Social History at the Histerial Institute of the Polish Academy of Sciences in Warsaw.
SHMUL ETTINGER was Professor of Jewish History at the Hebrew University of Jerusalem. He died in 1989.
JACOB GOLDBERG is Professor of History at the Hebrew University of Jerusalem.
STANISŁAW GRODZISKI is Professor of the History of Law at the Jagiellonian University in Kraków.
ZENON GULDON is Professor at the Higher Pedagogical School in Kielce.
MAURYCY HORN is Professor of History at the Jewish Historical Institute in Warsaw.
GERSHON DAVID HUNDERT is Professor of History at McGill University, Montreal.
ANATOL LESZCZYŃSKI is a research worker at the Jewish Historical Institute in Warsaw.
ANDRZEJ LINK-LENCZOWSKI is a Docent in History at the Jagiellonian University in Kraków.
JAN M. MAŁECKI is a Professor at the Economic Academy in Kraków.
KRYSTYN MATWIJOWSKI is Professor of History at the University of Wrocław.
MORDEKHAI NADAV was formerly Head of the Manuscript Department at the Library of the Hebrew University of Jerusalem. He is now retired.

LIST OF CONTRIBUTORS

ZDZISŁAW PIETRZYK works in the Library of the Jagiellonian University, Kraków.

ANTONI PODRAZA is Professor of History at the Jagiellonian University, Kraków.

ANTONY POLONSKY was until 1991 Professor of International History at the London School of Economics and Political Science. At present he is Professor of East European Jewish History, Brandeis University, Waltham, MA, and is Editor of *POLIN: Studies in Polish Jewry* and Vice-President of the American Institute for Polish-Jewish Studies.

SHMUEL SHILO is Professor of Law at the Hebrew University of Jerusalem.

CHONE SHMERUK is Profesor of Yiddish at the Hebrew University of Jerusalem.

JACEK SOBCZAK is Professor of History at the Adam Mickiewicz University in Poznań.

DANIEL TOLLET is Secretary-General of the Centre for the Jewish Studies at the University of Paris.

JERZY WYROZUMSKI is Professor of History at the Jagiellonian University, Kraków.

Introduction

Antony Polonsky

In the second half of sixteenth century, the Polish-Lithuanian Commonwealth, formed by the union in 1569 of the Kingdom of Poland and the Grand Duchy of Lithuania, was one of the largest and most powerful states in Europe. Its prosperity rested on the development of the grain trade down the Vistula river through Danzig to Western Europe. Politically it had been able to destroy the strength of the redoubtable Teutonic Knights and in the early seventeenth century it was even able to place its candidate on the throne of the Grand Duchy of Muscovy. Yet the power of this remarkable state, with its Renaissance culture and impressive flourishing of cultural life in the sixteenth century, rested on shaky foundations. Early modern Europe saw the development of a new system of government, which was based on the centralization of political authority through bureaucratic techniques. In states such as England, France, Prussia and even the Tsarist Empire, this new system of administration allowed the creation of new administrative methods which made it possible to organize and mobilize resources in a way that was previously inconceivable.

This process did not occur in the Polish-Lithuanian Commonwealth. As Fedorowicz has written:

> Poland . . . alone of all the great powers in Europe, failed to create the stable bureaucracy which could centralize political power within its sprawling domains and the price which it paid for this omission was political extinction once absolutism elsewhere had developed sufficiently to dismember the Commonwealth with impunity.[1]

The two principal weaknesses of the Polish-Lithuanian Commonwealth are well known. In the first place, its monarchy, which from 1572 was elected, was insufficiently powerful to administer the vast

---

[1] J.K. Fedorowicz, ed., *A Republic of Nobles: Studies in Polish History to 1864*, (Cambridge, 1982) p. 2.

domains of the state and failed to create a bureaucracy which could carry out these functions. This development was linked with the wide privileges acquired by the nobility or *szlachta* which enjoyed a monopoly of political power, which they exercised through the Sejm (Diet) or local *sejmiki* (dietines). The *szlachta* was able to use political power to reimpose serfdom on the peasantry and impose severe limitations on the power of the monarchy. Until the mid seventeenth century, the defects of the Polish political system were masked by the weakness of Poland's neighbours, the prosperity engendered by the developing grain trade and the persistence of a degree of royal power and authority. By the mid seventeenth century, however, the tensions created by the extension of the rule of Polish Catholic nobles over the largely Orthodox Ukraine came to the surface and led to violent upheavals between 1648 and 1657 as a result of which the left bank Ukraine and Kiev became linked with Muscovy.

The Commonwealth never fully recovered from this débacle. Partition was only narrowly averted in the 1660s and in the late seventeenth and early eighteenth centuries economic recession was accompanied by a further weakening of royal power. Within the *szlachta*, the great magnates became increasingly dominant. At the same time, the Republic became ever more dependent on foreign powers. Certainly, as a result of the Dumb Sejm of 1717, Poland became, in effect, a Russian protectorate. It was the attempt to end this Russian protectorate at the end of the eighteenth century which led to the extinction of Poland as a state.

The Polish-Lithuanian Commonwealth was a multi-national and multi-religious state. It included within its borders not only Poles but also Germans, Lithuanians, Byelorussians, Ukrainians, Jews, Armenians and many other national groups, as well as a large number of religious groupings. Toleration was the result both of the weakness of the central government and of the political values of the members of the *szlachta* who stressed the importance of political liberty. Both as a result of this toleration and of the economic expansion of Poland the country became by the early sixteenth century the home of one of the most important Jewish communities in the world. As Shimon Dubnow has pointed out, since the exile of the Jews to Babylon in the seventh century BC and the emergence of a Jewish diaspora, the history of the Jewish people has been characterized by the emergence of large centres of Jewish life and creativity which have enabled the Jews to preserve their separate identity. In the time of the Second Temple, such centres were to be found in Babylon and Alexandria, while in the Middle Ages Spain and the Rhineland played similar roles. With the persecution of the Jews of western Germany which followed the Black Death and the expulsion of the Jews from Spain in 1492, Poland became one of the major centres of Jewish life. As is described by Professor Wyrozumski (Chapter 1) Jews had settled in the lands which later made up the Polish State even before the formal establishment of a Polish kingdom. They emigrated to these areas from the Mediterranean, from the territories of the shortlived Khazar state in the Crimea and, above all, from the German-speaking lands. Arguments that the Jews of Poland were primarily derived from the Tartar-speaking converts of the Khazar kingdom are no longer widely accepted, although it is true that pockets of Tartar-speaking Jews could still be found in Poland until the seventeenth century. The Karaites, adherents of a heretical form of Judaism, preserved the use of the Tartar language for an even longer period. But the bulk of the community from the fourteenth century was clearly derived from the German-speaking lands. This was shown both in the fact that Yiddish, derived as it was from medieval high German, became the principal language of everyday life among the community and in the character of its constitutions. As Professor Wyrozumski demonstrates, the Jews were not, as has sometimes been argued, a 'caste', but a medieval corporation, with the rights and obligations of such a corporation. These rights and obligations were defined by charter, in particular, the Kalisz Statute granted by Boleslaw the Pious in 1264 and that of Kazimierz the Great in 1334. These charters had their origin in similar privileges granted to Jews in the German-speaking lands. Boleslaw the Pious's charter of 1264 was clearly modelled on the Austrian charter of 1240. Under these and other more local charters the Jews were given a specific legal position in the state. They were exempted from German (Magdeburg) law which governed the towns and were placed directly under jurisdiction of the *voivodes* or royal governors.

The Jews were welcomed by the monarchy as a means of facilitating trading and commercial contacts with the developing European world. They also performed a similar function for the more prosperous sections of the increasingly powerful nobility (*szlachta*). They aroused the hostility of the church, whose position on the Jews had finally been articulated at the Fourth Lateran

Council in 1215 and which, while prepared to tolerate the Jews, was determined to circumscribe Jewish influence and restrict Jewish industry to specific occupations – above all to trading and money-lending. The burghers in the towns, clearly alarmed by the prospect of Jewish competition, were also hostile to the Jews and their hostility sometimes manifested itself in anti-Jewish violence.

At the beginning of the sixteenth century, the Jewish population was still small. Indeed, it should be stressed (as is made clear in Part V), that all pre-modern population estimates must be treated with great caution. Considerable work has been done on this complex question and, although no definitive answers can be given, one can reasonably assume that at the end of the fifteenth century the Jewish community was still very small, numbering, according to Schipper, perhaps 18,000 in the Kingdom of Poland and 6,000 in Lithuania located in perhaps 85 towns.[2] This amounted to barely 0.6 per cent of the total population. Yet even these figures may be too high, as has been argued by Weinryb, who estimated the community at 10,000. By 1648, according to Weinryb, the Jewish community had probably increased in the Kingdom of Poland (excluding Lithuania) to nearly 170,000, the consequence both of natural growth and emigration from other centres of Jewish population. (A larger figure of 450,000 is given by Salo Baron, while Ettinger gives 300,000.) This population growth continued in the late seventeenth and eighteenth centuries and does not seem to have been greatly affected by the massacres during the Chmielnicki rebellion between 1648 and 1657 whose scale was probably exaggerated by contemporary commentators, as has been argued by Shmuel Ettinger and others. By 1764, with the accession of the last Polish king, Stanislaw August, the Jewish population had risen to perhaps 750,000, 549,000 in the Kingdom and 201,000 in the Grand Duchy of Lithuania, making up perhaps 8 per cent of the total population. The rate of Jewish population increase was clearly higher than that of the rest of the population. The reasons for this phenomenon have been variously assessed and include those provisions of the Jewish religion (above all ritual washing) which

---

[2] For different attempts to assess the Jewish population see I. Shipper in *Istoriya Evreyskogo Naroda*, vol. 11 (Moscow, 1915), pp. 107–15; Salo Baron, *A Social and Religious History of the Jews*, vols 2, 3 and 8 (Philadelphia, 1957 *et seq.*); B. Weinryb, *The Jews of Poland* (Philadelphia, 1976), pp. 308–20; Shaul Stampfer, 'The 1764 Census of Polish Jewry', *Studies on the History and Culture of the Jews of Eastern Europe*, 1985, pp. 141–7.

imposed tighter standards of hygiene, earlier Jewish marriage, religiously imposed celibacy among Christians and the fact that Jews did not perform military service. Certainly, by the mid eighteenth century, perhaps half the world's Jewish population lived within the Polish-Lithuanian Commonwealth.

This rapid expansion of the Jewish community in Poland coincided with the achievement by the nobility of its political monopoly of power and with the decline in the position of both the peasants, most of whom were reduced to serfdom, and of the burghers, whose political rights were now almost entirely done away with. In these conditions the nobles came to depend on the Jews to perform for them a large number of services including that of providing the craftsmen in the rural economy, of running their estates (the *arenda* system) and of acting as traders in the local, national and international areas. It was not without reason that this relationship was reflected in the wide currency of observations such as 'Every nobleman has his Jew' and 'Poland is heaven for the Jews, paradise for the nobles and hell for the serfs'.

Certainly in these years Jewish life flourished on the Polish lands – something which was reflected both in the increase in population (to which we have already alluded) and in the achievement of a wide degree of autonomy (which is described in Part II). Jewish religious and intellectual life also flourished. The Yeshivot (talmudic colleges) of Poland became models for talmudic study for the rest of Europe. They attracted students from Germany, Bohemia, Moravia, Hungary and even Italy. From the second half of the seventeenth century, most rabbis in Germany and Central Europe had obtained their rabbinic training in Poland. Polish masters of *halakha* (rabbinic law) became the dominant influence within the Jewish world. The critical glosses of the Krakow rabbi Moshe Isserles (Rama) to the rabbinic code of Joseph Karo established the mores of Ashkenazi Jews. The *novellae* on talmudic tractates by Shlomo Luria (Maharshal) and of Samuel Eidlish remain unsurpassed to the present day. The ascetic cabbalistic ethics of Isaiah Horowitz in his book *Shnei lukhot habrit* inspired both Ashkenazim and Sephardim alike, and for over two centuries his work remained the most widely distributed kabbalistic treatise. Indeed the mystical traditions of the Kabbalah flourished more in Poland than in any other Jewish community with the exception of Safed in Palestine. In Poland, cabbalistic study was widened from the domain of a small élite into a mass movement.

Secular learning also flourished, with Rabbis Moshe Isserles and Mordekhai Yaffe writing profound treatises on secular subjects, including philosophy and astronomy. Popular religious literature enjoyed wide diffusion. The most important work of this type was the *Tse'ena urena*, by Yakov of Janov, a Yiddish paraphrase of the Pentateuch. Women and unlearned men gained their knowledge of the Pentateuch by making use of a Hebrew-Yiddish glossary written in Poland (*Sefer Rav Anschel*, Krakow, 1534 and 1886), while many editions of the prayers were published in Hebrew and Yiddish. With the impact of the European Enlightenment further developments in secular literature took place. The later eighteenth century saw the publication in Poland of the first popular medical handbook (*Sefer ozer Yisrael*) as well as the translation of parts of the Bible into Yiddish by Mendel Lefin.

One of the most characteristic features of Jewish life in pre-partition Poland was the large degree of autonomy enjoyed by the community. Jewish autonomous institutions existed on three levels: local, provincial and national, with a sort of parliament, the Council of the Four Lands (*Va'ad arba aratso* – the four lands referred to the constituent parts of the Polish Kingdom; there was also a separate council for Lithuania). The Council, which generally met once a year, was responsible for negotiating with the Crown the level of Jewish taxation and for ensuring that the poll tax, the principal tax on Jews, was levied by local communities. In addition, it passed laws on internal educational and economic matters and other concerns of Jewish life. The principal characteristics of Jewish autonomy are extensively discussed in Part II. The autonomous institutions grew up essentially as a result of the interaction of two forces: the desire of the monarchy to ensure a secure form of tax revenue from the Jewish community and the universal diaspora Jewish aspiration to achieve as full a degree of internal self-government as possible. In this respect, the various Jewish autonomous institutions were similar in their origin to other parliamentary bodies in Europe. Indeed, it is a matter for further investigation how far the development of Polish parliamentarianism influenced the nature of Jewish autonomy. Certainly, Jews achieved in the Rzeczpospolita a degree of self-government which went considerably beyond that enjoyed by their co-religionists anywhere else in Europe. What eventually undermined the Council of the Four Lands was growing Jewish impoverishment and indebtedness, which made the levying of the poll tax more difficult. Local autonomous bodies, however, survived the partition of the Polish-

Lithuanian Commonwealth.

Yet the position of the Jews was by no means as secure as it appeared. As we have seen, one of the main features of the Polish-Lithuanian Commonwealth was its inability to create modern political institutions, above all a centralized and effective state bureaucracy under the control of the Crown. The resulting weakness of royal power meant that the Jews were increasingly dependent on the great magnate families who consolidated their hold over social and political life from the seventeenth century onwards. The larger royal-controlled towns declined and Jews in private (non-royal) towns were now subject to the jurisdiction of their aristocratic owners. As Podraza points out (Chapter 21), the centre of gravity of Jewish life shifted from the more developed western and central parts of Poland to the east, above all Polish Ukraine, where the magnates achieved enormous social and economic power at this time. The Jews were thus inevitably a target of Orthodox and Cossack resentment at Polish rule, being seen as the agents of the magnates. They suffered appallingly in the Chmielnicki revolt of 1648–57 which was the product of the social, religious and national resentment which Polish rule provoked in the west bank Ukraine. As we mentioned, recent research has tended to cast doubt on the casualty figures in the rebellion given, for instance, by such Jewish chroniclers as Nathan of Hannover. But even under revised estimates, as many as 20 per cent of the Jewish population may have lost their lives in the upheaval.[3]

No less disastrous was the effect of these events on the Polish-Lithuanian Commonwealth as a whole. Its economic and political decline was made manifest by the success of the rebellion and the loss of an important part of the Ukraine and the later years of the seventeenth century were marked by further economic recession and political weakness. These developments inevitably had an adverse effect on the position of the Jewish community which had become so impoverished and indebted that its difficulties in paying taxes led to the abolition in 1764 of the Council of the Four Lands. Within the Rzeczpospolita the power of the king declined still further, and with the growth of magnate influence there came too growing foreign interference in political life. This culminated in the Polish defeat in the Great Northern War and the Dumb Diet of 1717 which

---

[3] S. Ettinger, 'Khelkam shel hayehudim bekolonizatsiya shel Ukraina (1569–1648)', *Tsion* 11, pp. 107–42.

effectively made Poland a Russian satellite. The economic and political retrogression was also accompanied by growing intolerance and the strengthening of obscurantist and xenophobic tendencies, above all in the Catholic Church.

Within the Jewish community these years also saw an increase in mystical and obscurantist forms of religious practice, a reaction both to the deteriorating material and political position of the community and to what was perceived as the excessively dry and rationalistic character of rabbinic Judaism. This reaction took a number of forms, ranging from the mass following acquired by the false messiah, Shabtai Tsvi of Smyrna in the aftermath of the Chmielnicki rebellion, to the Frankist movement, named after its founded Jacob Frank, most of whose followers converted to Christianity. Its most lasting and significant manifestation was the hasidic movement, founded by Rabbi Israel of Miedybóz, the Besht or Baal Shem Tov, which sought direct union with God through various means, including singing and dancing and communion with nature. Originally opposed by the bulk of the religious establishment in Poland, the movement soon became particularly strong in the central and southern parts of the country and in the Ukraine. A genuine religious mass movement, it is still very alive in the Jewish world today.

The first partition of Poland demonstrated to the Polish political élite the defects of the country's archaic constitution and social structure and led to a series of proposals for their reform. These culminated in the Four Year Sejm (1788–92) which sought both to end Russian hegemony over Poland and to modernize social and political life. The Polish reformers also sought to transform the Jewish community, in line with the ideas of the Enlightenment, to 'productivize' and 'modernize' its members and convert them into 'useful' citizens. Some of these proposals are described by Artur Eisenbach in Chapter 6. Yet in spite of extensive discussion, the Four Year Sejm did not introduce any legislation improving the position of the Jews or doing away with Jewish disabilities. Indeed, by strengthening the position of the Christian burghers, it probably made more difficult the situation of their fellow-Jewish town-dwellers. The reforming activities of the Four Year Sejm provoked the hostility of the Tsarist monarchy and led to the Second and ultimately the Third Partition of Poland in 1792 and 1795. It was thus left to the partitioning powers, often in co-operation with local Polish political forces to carry out the emancipation of the Jews on the Poland lands, a process which, with the exception of those territories directly annexed into the Russian Empire was formally completed in 1862, although its full realization had still to be accomplished.

This collection of essays aims at providing an up-to-date account of the state of our knowledge on the Jews in the Polish-Lithuanian Commonwealth. It is not, of course, comprehensive; and it attempts to provide an analytical rather than a chronological account of the problems it discusses. It also does not provide any detailed description of the religious and intellectual life of the Jewish community. Its aim is, above all, to describe the place of this large and important group in the political and social life of the Rzeczpospolita. Its five Parts investigate the position of the Jews in the wider society of the Polish-Lithuanian Commonwealth, the nature of Jewish autonomy, the legal status of the Jews, the Jewish role in the economy and population growth and distribution. The essays are written by both Polish and Jewish scholars and are a product of the collaboration between the Centre for the Study of the History and Culture of Polish Jews at the Hebrew University in Jerusalem, the Research Centre for Jewish History and Culture in Poland at the Jagiellonian University in Krakow, the Institute for Polish-Jewish Studies in Oxford, and the American Association for Polish-Jewish Studies, Cambridge, Massachusetts. It is our hope that this volume will stimulate many more detailed studies on the Jewish community in the Polish-Lithuanian Commonwealth. We are also grateful for the assistance of Mrs Janina Haubenstock in bringing out this book in order to commemorate her husband, Dr Józef Haubenstock, a Cracovian and graduate of the Jagiellonian University, whose heart was committed to Polish-Jewish reconciliation.

Part I

Society

1 · Jews in Medieval Poland

Jerzy Wyrozumski

If, in a volume devoted to Jews in pre-partition Poland, I concentrate on the question of the Jewish population of medieval Poland, it is to give an idea of their status in law and practice during that period which foreshadowed and determined its future development. Many significant features of Jewish autonomy in the Nobles' Commonwealth can be traced back to the situation it faced in this earlier period and the problems it had to tackle.

I shall confine myself to several old questions and try to answer them through rereading well-known sources. The first question is: Where, when and in what circumstances did Jews move to Poland? The second refers to the size and spread of Jewish population in medieval Poland; the third to its professional activity; the fourth to Christian reaction to its presence; the fifth to the attitude of the Polish Church, as an institution, towards Jewish communities and individuals; and the last very fundamental question concerns the relationship between the Jews and the authorities. These are but a few of the many questions concerning Jews in medieval Poland, but attention to them will provide an all-round picture.

I

The earliest reference to a Jewish community within today's Polish boundaries is assumed to relate to Przemyśl in the third decade of the eleventh century. This information comes from the lost work of a learned rabbi, Yehud-ha-Kohen,[1] who lived in the first half of the eleventh century and probably had some ties with Mainz. Although it refers to the Polish-Ruthenian border, and thus suggests eastern, Chazar, origin for these Jews, the information about them found in the Rhineland shows that this cannot be the case. The information of

---

[1] F. Kupfer and T. Lewicki, eds, *Źródła hebrajskie do dziejów Słowian i niektórych ludów środkowej i wschodniej Europy* (Hebrew sources for the history of Slavs and some other peoples of Central and Eastern Europe), Wrocław/Warsaw, 1956, pp. 36–7.

the Czech chronicler Cosmas about the persecution of Jews in Prague and their flight to Poland and Hungary points rather to the west as the source of Jewish migration to Polish territory.[2]

The evidence of the tombstone, dated 1203, of Rabbi David, son of Sar Shalom, in Breslau,[3] is of prime importance here. Found in 1917 near Breslau Cathedral, its technique and lettering are characteristic of the regions of Worms and Mainz in the Rhineland. Jews who settled in Breslau must, therefore, have arrived from there. We can no longer link the topographic name Kawiory, found in medieval Kraków and Sandomierz,[4] with the Chazar, or, in other words, eastern Jews, for – as has been demonstrated by Professor Moshé Altbauer – this name comes from the Hebrew *kevarim* (cemetery).[5]

The explanation, favoured in Poland, that as these Jews were farmers they must have been the Chazar Jews who were known to be farmers in the east is, to my mind, doubtful. Besides, these farmers were found near Breslau and on the border with Lusatia, not in the eastern but western medieval Poland, which further diminishes the probability of their eastern descent.[6] Finally the use of Yiddish by Polish Jews points to their migration coming primarily from German-speaking areas.

Jewish movement to Poland started during the reign of the first rulers of the Piast dynasty and continued throughout the Middle Ages. We have precise information that Jews sought refuge in Poland against the oppression they met in the west,[7] but of course this was not the only reason that drove them towards Poland: there must have been others. Jewish merchants, who had long travelled back and forth through Europe, cleared the way, by supplying information about the possibilities of settling and the chances of continuing with preferred Jewish professional activities.

---

[2] H. Bretholz, ed., *Die Chronik der Böhmen des Cosmas von Prag*, MGH n.s. II, Berlin, 1923, p. 166.

[3] M. Brann, 'Ein Breslauer Grabdenkmal aus dem Jahre 1203' *Schlesische Geschichtsblätter* 1, 1919, pp. 11–16.

[4] F. Piekosiński, ed., *Kodeks dyplomatyczny Małopolski* (Diplomatic code of Little Poland) I, Kraków, 1879, no. 49; J. Długosz, *Liber beneficiorum dioecesis Cracoviensis*, ed. A. Przeździecki, I, p. 387.

[5] M. Altbauer, 'Jeszcze o rzekomych "chazarskich" nazwach miejscowych na ziemiach polskich' (More about the presumed 'Chazar' place names on Polish territory), *Onomastica* 13 (1968), pp. 120–8.

[6] G.A. Stenzel, ed., *Urkunden zur Geschichte des Bisthums Breslau im Mittelalter*, Wrocław, 1845, no. 2.

[7] Quoted by Cosmas – see note 2 above.

II

We do not, unfortunately, have a detailed map of Jewish settlement in medieval Poland. It could be created, especially if it were based on a thorough investigation of the history of Polish towns. Today, nevertheless, we can only list some of the towns in which Jewish population is mentioned by the authorities.

We can also assume a methodological clue: that at first Jews never settled individually but in smaller or bigger groups, thus enabling themselves to establish communities, as required by religion and custom. Only some years later do Jews appear as innkeepers and publicans, living and working in isolation yet always maintaining their ties with the neighbouring community. During the period when the Polish State was fragmented, we find Jews living mainly in the princely capitals, that is in Kraków, Kalisz, Breslau, Gniezno, Sandomierz, Płock, Legnica and Głogów.[8] Already in about the mid twelfth century, Jews owned the village of Tyniec in Silesia and, at the beginning of the thirteenth century, the village of Sokolniki.[9] In the castellan's domain, with its main fortress in Bytom on the Odra River, we find Jewish farmers.[10]

In the year 1262, Prince Bolesław Wstydliwy (the Chaste), in allowing the Cistercian Order to incorporate town communities in Koprzywica and Jasło, excluded Jews as potential settlers.[11] This was in accord with the wishes of the Order. This fact is worth mentioning as it shows that Jews, like others, were probably tending even then to settle in small towns. In the fourteenth century Jews lived in Lwów,[12] and, without any doubt, in other towns of Halicz and Włodzimierz Ruthenia, which then was linked to Poland. In the fifteenth century Jewish communities must already have existed in Lublin and Bochnia.[13] In fact, there were probably many other Jewish communities in Poland at this time.

Difficult though it is to establish a full tally of them, it is still harder

---

[8] See notes 4, 15, 17, 33.
[9] K. Maleczyński, ed., *Kodeks dyplomatyczny Śląska* (Diplomatic code of Śląsk) I, Wrocław, 1956, nos 68, 103, 107; II, Wrocław, 1959, nos 130, 193.
[10] See note 6.
[11] *Kodeks dyplomatyczny Małopolski* I, no. 60.
[12] *Akta Grodzkie i Ziemskie* (Town and Land Acts), III, Lwów, 1872, no. 5.
[13] *Dzieje Lublina. Próba syntezy* (History of Lublin. An attempt at a synthesis) I, Lublin, 1965, p. 72; A. Z. Helcel, ed., *Starodawne prawa polskiego pomniki* (Ancient memorials of Polish Laws) II, Kraków, 1870, no. 3230.

to make even the most sketchy estimate of the total number of Jews on Polish territory. This applies both to the absolute numbers and as a proportion against the Christian population. We can only give examples. In fifteenth century Kraków, we know by name about twenty Jewish families.[14] Płock sources testify to a special Jewish well in the year 1237.[15] In the Lwów incorporation charter from the year 1356, officials of King Kazimierz Wielki (the Great) named Jews, beside Armenians, Ruthenians and Saracens, as those who could keep their own religion and jurisdiction. Other nationalities were not excluded, but the ones mentioned were specified as more significant.[16]

III

The field of Jewish professional activity in medieval Poland was very wide. At the beginning, their preoccupation was undoubtedly trade – on a large scale as well as local peddling. We have already mentioned Jewish farmers. Early traces exist of Jews buying estates, even comprising whole villages, as a good investment. We cannot exclude the possibility that, before they were closed to them by the guild system, the Jews took up crafts, especially those needing qualifications. In princely service, mintage was their trade. A clear trace of this is found from the reign of Prince Mieszko Stary (the Old), when coins with Hebrew lettering were issued.[17]

As the importance of money grew, Jews engaged in usury, which was forbidden to Christians by the church. Jews managed to obtain the tenancy of many toll houses and various enterprises, including the largest state enterprise, the Kraków salt mine.[18] Estates also passed into Jewish hands by way of mortgage, which caused

---

[14] *Starodawne prawa polskiego pomniki* II, nos 1922, 1935, 1942, 1982, 3070, 3117, 3805, 4192, 4351, 4353, 4438, 4439. See also E. Muller, *Żydzi w Krakowie w drugiej połowie XIV wieku* (Jews in Kraków in the second half of the fourteenth century), Kraków, 1906, p. 11.

[15] J. K. Kochanowski, ed., *Zbiór ogólny przywilejów i spominków mazowieckich* (A general collection of Mazowsze privileges and memorials), Warsaw, 1919, no. 362.

[16] See note 12.

[17] Z. Zakrzewski, *O brakteatach z napisami hebrajskimi* (About bracteates with Hebrew lettering), Kraków, 1909.

[18] A. Z. Helcel, ed., *Starodawne prawa polskiego pomniki* I, Kraków, 1956, p. 218; see also J. Schipper, *Studia nad stosunkami gospodarczymi Żydów w Polsce podczas średniowiecza* (Studia on Jewish economic relations in medieval Poland), Lwów, 1911, ch. 13.

serious legal and practical complications. The church prohibition on allowing Jews to discharge public functions, as well as state laws forbidding loans secured on land,[19] prove that this was a real problem.

IV

Personal relations between native Poles and immigrant Jews are very hard to trace in the sources. The problem is further complicated by the fact that from the beginning of the thirteenth century we find German settlers in towns where Jews usually settled; they even sometimes played the principal role in the town's life. Therefore we have to rephrase the question and ask how relations were formed between the Christian population of a town and its Jewish settlers. This question covers the Ruthenian population of Lwów and other towns of Halicz and Włodzimierz Ruthenia as well.

In general, one has to admit that Jews rarely yielded to assimilative processes. They learned the language of their home country, yet – at least in Poland – kept their native language. They had their own faith and religious rituals, their customs with a centuries-old cultural tradition. On top of that, they engaged in usury, which sometimes had serious material consequences. Such were the early roots of antipathy, nurtured by prejudice and personal hostility which, as time went by, grew through gossip into myth, creating an unjust and highly harmful atmosphere around the Jewish population. Accusations of the ritual murder of Christian children, of the stealing of the host from churches to profane it, of the poisoning of water and food to harm Christians, and of arson were the stereotyped charges made against Jews, following them from state to state, from town to town, from one generation to the next. All of them reached Poland and their traces are found in the sources; they sometimes had drastic results.

The Polish chronicler Wincenty Kadłubek (Master Vincenty) mentions the enforcing, by Prince Mieszko Stary, of the heaviest penalty when Kraków students beat or wounded a Jew.[20] We do not comment here on the prince's protection of the Jewish population,

---

[19] See notes 28-30; beginning with the legal statutes of King Kazimierz Wielki, Polish law forbade borrowing money from Jews secured on land.
[20] A. Bielowski, ed., *Monumenta Poloniae Historica* II, Lwów, 1872, p.381.

but observe that even the twelfth century must have witnessed skirmishes between Christians and Jews. Riots and pogroms of Jews did happen. The Chronicle of Oliwa describes the 1349 pogrom, which took place 'in tota Germania et Almania et fere in tota Polonia'.[21] Yet the sources from that period, though relatively numerous, give us no concrete information. A well known anti-Jewish riot took place in Kraków in 1407.[22] When in the year 1447 in Poznań – as the 'Short (Silesian) Chronicle' has it – a fire broke out, some Jews were burned at the stake because of the accusation of arson.[23] Similarly, according to the Poznań annals, many Jews were killed in town in 1464, owing to the plague that broke out.[24]

The biggest Jewish pogrom was possibly the one which took place in the year 1453 following John Capistrano's preaching in Breslau, a town that was then no longer in Poland.[25] When John Capistrano was due to arrive in Kraków, Jews were panic-stricken. They even obtained a new confirmation of their immunity from King Kazimierz Jagiellończyk.[26] Yet, despite several months' preaching by John Capistrano in Kraków, there was no anti-Jewish outbreak. It was not until 1496 that an anti-Turkish crusade, organized partly in Kraków, caused the murder of Jews, as a consequence of which the Jews moved from Kraków to Kazimierz.[27]

It would be hard to obtain from these examples a clear picture of the size and range of these riots and pogroms. An even more difficult task would await us if we tried to compare them with similar happenings in Western Europe. But if the Jewish people did not emigrate from Poland but, on the contrary, immigrated to it, then medieval Poland cannot have been among the countries most hostile to them.

V

We shall now concentrate on the attitude of the Polish Church

---

[21] Ibid. VI, Kraków, 1893, p. 347.
[22] J. Długosz, *Historia Poloniae* bk 10, in *Opera omnia* XII, Kraków, 1876, pp. 567–8; Schipper, *Studia*, pp. 327–34.
[23] *Monumenta Poloniae Historica* III, Lwów, 1878, p. 722.
[24] Ibid. V, Lwów, 1888, p. 884.
[25] Ibid. III, p. 785–9; IV, Lwów, 1884, pp. 1–5.
[26] O. Balzer, 'Corpus iuris Polonici', *Kwartalnik Historyczny*, 1891, p. 332 (no. 154).
[27] *Monumenta Poloniae Historica* V, pp. 285–6.

towards the Jews. We shall consider the church as an institution, not as individual priests who were sometimes driven by religious fanaticism and initiated passive, or even active, hostility against the Jewish people. Let us stress at the beginning that the Polish Church was a part of the Universal (Catholic) Church and, as such, generally fell in line with the restrictions which were widely employed.

The Jewish problem was discussed at the Fourth Lateran Council in the year 1215. Its resolutions stated that Jews were to pay tithes from properties they acquired, to wear clothes that would distinguish them from Christians and to stay at home during Holy Week and the Easter holiday so as not to abuse the Christian cult. The prohibition on Jews holding public office, referring back to a similar law from the Council of Toledo of 589, was also among the resolutions passed.[28] The Polish Church did not try to put these resolutions into effect at once. Only over half a century later, in the year 1267, did the Breslau Synod introduce a number of restrictions concerning the coexistence of Christians with Jews. Christians were forbidden to invite Jews to weddings and other feasts, to share meals with them, dance with them, buy their food, go to the baths or attend inns with them. Also certain precautions were enforced to limit money-lending at interest by Jews and Jews were forced to move house in order to establish isolated quarters, separate from Christians.

These resolutions were motivated by fear of Polish Christian families adopting Jewish customs. Jews were permitted only one synagogue within each town. The local custom of Jews wearing horned or tapering hats, to distinguish them from Christians, was ordered to be revived. Jews were obliged to meet customary land services in favour of the parishes in which they lived and were prohibited from employing Christian servants, wet-nurses and so on. They were told to stay at home, even to close doors and windows, if the Holy Sacrament was to be carried by. Finally, they were prohibited from holding public office, especially the tenancy of toll houses.[29]

As the resolutions of the Budzin Synod from the year 1279 show, few of these orders and prohibitions found their way into Polish life.

---

[28] A. Garcia y Garcia, ed., *Constitutiones Concilii quarti Lateranensis una cum commentariis glossarum*, in *Monumenta Juris Canonici 2*, Vatican, 1981, nos 68, 69.
[29] *Kodeks dyplomatyczny Wielkopolski* (Diplomatic code of Great Poland) I, Poznań, 1877, no. 423.

Horned hats did not come back, as by now the obligatory sign was a red cloth circle sewn on to outer garments on the left breast. Great importance was attached to these signs. It was forbidden to give Jews fire and water if they did not agree to wear them.[30] But in reality Jews were not isolated, mutual relations continued, and they fulfilled public functions.

Mikołaj Trąba's Synodal Statute of 1420 again took up the subject of Jews. It repeated almost word for word the resolutions of the 1267 Breslau Synod, except that instead of the horned hats it ordered red circles on outer garments.[31] The repeating of those orders and prohibitions testifies that they were not observed. Anyway, for over a century, those matters did not occupy the Polish Church at all. It is known that Jews, even though they lived close together, did not form ghettos. For example, in Kraków, Christian property, the church of St Anna and Collegium Maius, stood next to what was then called Żydowska (Jewry) Street (today St Anna's Street). In the fifteenth century there were at least two synagogues there.[32] Despite the prohibitions, Jews were entrusted with toll houses and even the Kraków salt mine. Thus the church restrictions were implemented on only a small scale.

VI

Jews in Poland were protected by public law. This was exercised long before any adequate guarantee in this domain – whether from Emperor Henry V, Frederick Barbarossa or other rulers in the Empire – found its expression in written codes. Important testimony in this field is supplied by Wincenty Kadłubek, who even felt indignant at the fact that beating a Jew qualified as high treason. The practice dates from the second half of the twelfth century. The thirteenth century sees some Polish duchies introducing written law for Jews, first in the Duchy of Kalisz in 1264 by Prince Bolesław Pobożny (the Pious); next, soon after the year 1273, by Prince Henryk IV Prawy (the Righteous) for the Duchy of Breslau and, at about the same time, by Prince Henryk of Legnica for the Duchy of

---

[30] *Starodawne prawa polskiego pomniki* I, pp. 426–7 (113, 114).
[31] J. Fijałek and A. Vetulani, eds, *Statuty synodalne wieluńsko-kaliskie Mikołaja Trąby z r. 1420* (The Wielun and Kalisz Synodal statutes of Mikołaj Trąba from the year 1420), Kraków, 1915–20/1951, pp. 91–3.
[32] *Codex diplomaticus Studii Generalis Cracoviensis*, part 2, Kraków, 1873, no. 223, year 1469.

Legnica. In the last decade of the thirteenth century similar statutes were granted for the Duchies of Legnica and Breslau, whose boundaries had now changed, and for the Duchy of Głogów.[33] The statute of Bolesław Pobożny is the most important one for us, as it became the standard formula of the 'Jewish Law' in the united Polish kingdom. It was confirmed by King Kazimierz Wielki, later by King Kazimierz Jagiellończyk and, lastly, became part of the Jan Łaski's 'Legal Statutes' of 1506.[34]

The essence of 'Jewish Law' in medieval Poland was to secure the status of 'Servants of the King's Treasury' for the Jews. It assured them the protection of state jurisdiction, while at the same time granting them self-jurisdiction in cases concerning Jews only. As a result, a Jew could be accused only in front of a Jewish witness. The law also exonerated the Jewish people from the charge of using human blood in their rituals; a specific charge could be made only by three Christians and three Jews.[35]

I leave open the problem of 'Jewish Law', or even the special privileges granted by King Kazimierz Wielki,[36] as a subject requiring further investigation. We must nevertheless admit that even those laws which raise no doubts as to their authenticity caused antipathy on the part of nobles and burghers. Its background was, above all, usury and, linked with it, mortgages. We have the famous complaint of a Kraków burgher from the year 1369,[37] in a resolution put to the nobles' assemblies, with such invectives as: 'Judaica pravitas, perversa Judaica perfidia, Judei fidei nostre veri inimici, deceptiones

---

[33] *Kodeks dyplomatyczny Wielkopolski* I, no. 605; F. W. de Sommersberg, ed., *Silesiacarum rerum scriptores*, Leipzig, 1730, part 2, nos 84, 105; see also R. Grodecki, *Dzieje Żydów w Polsce do końca XIV w.* (History of Jews in Poland to the end of the fourteenth century), in his works edited by J. Wyrozumski and published after his death – *Polska piastowska* (Piast Poland), Warsaw, 1969, pp. 665–7.

[34] S. Kutrzeba, 'Przywileje Kazimierza Wielkiego dla Żydów' (Kazimierz Wielki's privileges for Jews), *Sprawozdania PAU* 27:10 (1922), pp. 4–5.

[35] *Kodeks dyplomatyczny Wielkopolski* I, no. 605, 31.

[36] J. Długosz, *Annales seu chronicae incliti Regni Poloniae* bk 9, Warsaw, 1978, p. 285 claimed that the privilege was granted because of the influence of the King's Jewish mistress, Ester, which is not confirmed by the sources. We know that King Kazimierz Wielki asked the town council to take special care of two Jews, Lewek and Kosma: K. Estreicher ed., *Najstarszy zbiór przewilejów i wilkierzy miasta Krakowa* (The oldest collection of Kraków's privileges and regulations), Kraków, 1936, pt 1, no. 7.

[37] F. Piekosiński and J. Szujski, eds, *Najstarsze księgi i rachunki miasta Krakowa* (The oldest register and bills of the town of Kraków), pt 2, Kraków, 1877, pp. 23–4.

Judeorum', and so on.[38] The confirmation of King Kazimierz Jagiellończyk's statute in a longer version – often regarded today as a forgery – had the following heading in the Sędziwój of Czechło's Code: *Jura maledicta Judeorum illegitime per regem concessa*.[39] In the opinion of some, a serious fire documented by Jan Długosz in the year 1455 was God's punishment for granting liberties to the Jews.[40]

---

[38] L. Łysiak, ed., *Statuty Kazimierza Wielkiego. Statuty wielkopolskie* (Kazimierz Wielki's statutes. Great Poland statutes), Warsaw, Poznań, 1982, art. 42; O. Balzer, ed., *Statuty Kazimierza Wielkiego*, Poznań, 1947, art. 18; J. V. Bandtkie, ed., *Jus Polonicum*, Warsaw, 1831, pp. 212–13, art. 19 of the Warcki Statute from the year 1423.
[39] Biblioteka Czartoryskich, Kraków, MS 1310, ff. 614–20.
[40] J. Długosz, *Historia Poloniae* bk 12, in *Opera omnia* XIV, Kraków, 1878, pp. 204–5.

2 · Judaizers in Poland in the Second Half of the Sixteenth Century

Zdzisław Pietrzyk

Andrzej Lubieniecki wrote that in the last decade of King Zygmunt August's rule many different religions and tens of sects, which he described as heretical, lived in Poland.[1] Among these heretics, he picked out in particular a group now known as Judaizers, who aimed to provide a bridge between Judaism and Christianity. Judaizing as a religious doctrine with wide appeal in Poland stemmed from three root causes: (1) the propagation of Judaism in Poland by Jews; (2) the influx into the tolerant Commonwealth of various peoples considered heretics in their own countries; and (3) the radical religious beliefs of heterodox intellectuals based on the principles of the anti-Trinitarian communities.

The propagation of Judaism undertaken by Jews in Poland has, unfortunately, not yet received sufficient scrutiny.[2] The upheavals and religious confusion of the Reformation led to a fundamental examination of the principles of faith. The sharing of a common language by the Jewish community and the burghers of German descent in Polish towns simplified mutual understanding and made it possible to hold disputes on religious matters. Numerous conversions to Judaism in Poland in the first half of the sixteenth century serve as evidence of this. Ambroży (Broży), a barber-surgeon, was an active missionary for Judaism in Mława, and in Sierpiec in the 1560s another barber-surgeon, Maciej, was engaged in similar work. Płock clergy investigating mutual relations between Jews and Christians in 1551 noted that both nobles and burghers lived in close

---

[1] A. Lubieniecki, *Poloneutychia*, quoted in I. Chrzanowski and S. Kot, eds, *Humanizm i reformacja w Polsce* (Humanism and the Reformation in Poland), Warsaw/Kraków, 1927, p. 420.
[2] W. Sobieski, 'Propaganda żydowska w 1539–1540' (Jewish propaganda 1539–1540), *Przegląd Narodowy* 21:1, 1921, pp. 24–42.

harmony with the Jews, though without keeping common feasts.[3] Marcin Bielski wrote of many Christians 'led into the Jewish faith',[4] who emigrated to the Ottoman Empire and were to be found among the merchants of Constantinople. Hans Dernschwamm, in his description of a journey to Turkey in 1553–5 mentions a Constantinople merchant's employee, Samuel from Kraków, who had converted to Judaism.[5] Resolutions of the 1644 and 1647 meetings of Jewish communities in Lithuania show that steps to propagate Judaism among Christians had been undertaken. It was then decided not to accept proselytes nor to promote Judaization. These resolutions were taken at the time of the Counter-Reformation's victory and the decline of the Reformation movement in Poland.[6] It should, however, be stressed that the propagation of Judaism was not carried out on an organized basis but was supported by individual speakers and apologists such as Jakub of Bełżyce or the Karaite Izaak ben Abraham of Troki.

The best-known case of apostasy to Judaism was that of Katarzyna Weiglowa, widow of a Kraków merchant, Melchior Weigl. Weiglowa was sentenced to death and burned at the stake on 19 April 1539, in the Mały Rynek (Small Market Square) of Kraków. She refused to believe Jesus Christ was the Son of God. The burning of Weiglowa took place at a time of fierce competition between the Kraków merchants and Jewish merchants from Kazimierz, as well as a looming Turkish threat after the Turks' success in Hungary. Jews were believed to be Suleiman's allies and this, when linked to the trade war in Kraków, makes the sentence passed on Weiglowa, who was known to have been inclining towards Judaism for many years, come as no surprise; it was the sad consequence of the situation in Kraków at that time. She had probably renounced her Christian faith because of the advocacy of Judaism by her husband's Jewish trading partners.[7] On the basis of Bielski's and Górnicki's laconic

---

[3] W. Budka, 'Przejawy reformacji na Mazowszu w latach 1548–1572' (Signs of Reformation in Mazowsze 1548–1571), in W. Urban, ed., *Odrodzenie i Reformacja w Polsce* vol. 30, 1985, p. 146.
[4] M. Bielski, *Kronika polska* (Polish Chronicle), Sanok, 1856, p. 1082.
[5] M. Mieses, 'Judaizanci we wschodniej Europie' (Judaizers in Eastern Europe), *Miesięcznik żydowski* 4, 1934, p. 254.
[6] Ibid., pp. 258–9.
[7] M. Bałaban, *Dzieje Żydów w Krakowie i na Kazimierzu 1304–1868* (History of Jews in Kraków and Kazimierz 1304–1868), Kraków, 1912, pp. 77–8.

accounts,[8] it is hard to determine Weiglowa's actual religious beliefs, but by the beginning of the seventeenth century she was already recognized as a Reformation martyr.

Another example of the propagation of Judaism comes from Jakub Nachman of Bełżyce's polemical exchange with Marcin Czechowic, and also the Karaite Izaak ben Abraham of Troki's work *The Consolidation of Faith*, which was not published till 1681, but is proof of the existence of converts to Judaism from Christianity and the fight against such conversions.[9] Works by Marcin Czechowic, of Lublin, a member of a radical sect, the Arians – *Rozmowy Chrystyjańskie* (Christian Discourses) and the subsequent *Odpis Jakóba Żyda z Bełżyc na Dyjalogi Marcina Czechowica, na który zaś odpowiada Jakóbowi Żydowi tenże Marcin Czechowic* (Response by Jakob of Bełżyce the Jew to Marcin Czechowic's Dialogues, to which, in turn, an answer is given to the Jew Jakob by Marcin Czechowic)[10] – provide solid evidence of the opposition to the propagation of Judaism as well as of Judaizing.

The second root of judaizing in Poland was, without any doubt, the flow of heretics from neighbouring countries to the tolerant Commonwealth, such as Judaizers from Muscovy. Among the first were the Novogrod-Moscow heretics. In 1471 Michał Olelkowicz and Sacharia (Zachariasz) came to Great Novogrod and began their Judaist propaganda, converting, among others, Orthodox parish priests. The Bishops' Council of the Moscow metropolis delivered a verdict on Judaizers in 1490, which clearly reveals a religious movement tending towards Judaism. The Judaizers were accused of celebrating Saturdays, performing Jewish rituals and, by way of explanation to the assembly, the Council informed it that 'they approve the Old Testament and cultivate the Jewish faith'.[11]

The Russian historian A. J. Nikitsky considered Judaizing to be a native Russian movement which developed out of Christianity

---

[8] M. Bielski, *Kronika polska*, p. 1080; Ł. Górnicki, *Dzieje w Koronie polskiej* (History of the Polish Crown), Sanok, 1855, p. 5.

[9] W. Zajączkowski, 'Izaak z Trok' (Izaak of Troki), *Polski Słownik Biograficzny* X, Warsaw, 1962–4, pp. 193–4; A. Geiger, *Izaak von Troki: Ein Apologet des Judenthum am Ende des sechszehnten Jahrhundert*, Breslau, 1853; M. Wajsblum, 'Izaak of Troki and Christian Controversy in the Sixteenth Century', *Journal of Jewish Studies* 3:2, 1952, pp. 62–77.

[10] Published by A. Rodecki's publishing house in Kraków, 1575 and 1581.

[11] J. Juszczyk, 'O badaniach nad judaizantyzmem' (On investigations into Judaizing) *Kwartalnik Historyczny* 86 (1969), p. 143; W. Urban in a review of I. J. Budownic, 'Russkaja publicystika XVI wieka', Moscow/Leningrad, 1947, in *Odrodzenie i Reformacja w Polsce* 2 (1957), pp. 228–9.

entirely without Jewish influence. In fact, most Russian historians deny any Jewish influence on the Moscow heresies and do not refer to their adherents as Judaizers.[12] But during the reign of Ivan III, there was an explosion of Judaizing; then came the persecutions of the mid-sixteenth century, following which refugees from Moscow appeared in eastern Lithuania, among them Teodozy Kosy and his companion Ignacy. Kosy rejected the Trinity, stressed the existence of one God and propounded the supremacy of the Old Testament over the New, thus renouncing Christian beliefs. On social matters, he preached utopian views. His activities in Lithuania and Wołyń around 1575 were certainly facilitated by the fact that he operated in a linguistic and cultural environment close to his own, and where the ground had been prepared by the Reformation, in particular by the anti-Trinitarians, who had much in common with the Judaizers. Among the followers he gained was Anna Korecka who, beginning with Calvinism, worked her way through anti-Trinitarianism to Judaizing and, finally, became Orthodox. Kosy's companion and disciple Ignacy was active in Polesie, where he gained followers for his sect.[13] It is quite possible that through their propaganda they influenced the extreme radicalism of Szymon Budny, the foremost exponent of religious heterodoxy.

In the 1560s, an Orthodox priest, Esayash, fled from Moscow, later to become a minister in Siewierz, an area controlled by Wołozko, the Chełm cup-bearer.[14] According to a synodalrecord, he was infected with Judaizing by Walenty Krawiec; this seems unlikely, given that Esayash and his colleagues had fled from Moscow as heretics, probably already charged with Judaizing. Esayash was received in Lublin by a rich wine merchant, Walenty Krawiec, the member of an anti-Trinitarian community. Together they preached the rejection of Jesus as Son of God and the celebration of the Jewish Sabbath and observance of Jewish ceremonies. As long as the spiritual leader of the Lublin community, Stanisław Paklepka, was alive, their activity stayed within bounds. But after Paklepka's death

---

[12] J. Juszczyk, 'O badaniach', pp. 142, 149.
[13] O. Lewicki, 'Socynianie na Rusi' (Socinians in Ruthenia), *Reformacja w Polsce* 2, 1922, p. 215; A. Kossowski, 'Zarys dziejów protestantyzmu na Wołyniu w XVI–XVII w' (Brief History of Protestantism in Volhynia in the sixteenth and seventeenth centuries), *Rocznik Wołyński* 3 (1934), p. 245; W. Urban, 'Kosy Teodozy', *Polski Słownik Biograficzny* XIV, Warsaw, 1968–9, p. 369.
[14] 'Najstarsze synody arian polskich' (The oldest synods of Polish Arians), ed. S. Zachorowski, *Reformacja w Polsce* 1 1921, p. 232.

in 1567, the growth of Judaizing appeared dangerous for the community itself.[15]

During the 1567 Kraków Synod, the anti-Trinitarians reprimanded and warned their Lublin brothers through their representative, the Lublin master carver Jakub Ostrowski, not to be deceived by false prophets and to remain in their faith.[16] As our sources testify, the synodal reprimand did not have much effect. In 1581 Marcin Czechowic wrote about 'numerous uncircumcised Jews in Lublin'.[17] Besides Walenty Krawiec, an unknown colleague, Eliasz,[18] was active in Lublin, possibly the same Esayash already mentioned or some other fugitive from Muscovy. Walenty Krawiec kept wide contacts with his co-religionists and corresponded with members of the Non-Adorationist and Sabbatarian sects which were emerging in Transylvania.[19] Possibly he had personally travelled to Transylvania as a merchant. His end was tragic and casts doubt on his moral rectitude. During the convocation of 1572 he was caught possessing false seals of various monarchs. After his arrest he committed suicide in gaol.[20] Yet he was effective in spreading his beliefs, as the Arians had to fight with Judaizing tendencies in the bosom of their community for a long time.

Among the most zealous in the fight against Judaism and Judaizing was Marcin Czechowic, the Lublin minister, who, in his *Rozmowy Chrystyjańskie*, besides upholding the banner of Unitarianism, fought decisively against Judaizers and the radical Christological ideas of Szymon Budny the leader of the non-Adorationists in Lithuania.[21]

The third root of Judaizing in Poland was genuine heterodox beliefs of both native and foreign origin, whose followers lived in the Polish Commonwealth. In the Judaizers' biographies, which are often based

---

[15] S. Tworek, *Zbór lubelski i jego rola w ruchu ariańskim w Polsce XVI i XVII wieku* (The Lublin community and its role in the Arian movement in sixteenth and seventeenth-century Poland), Lublin, 1966, p. 34.
[16] 'Najstarsze synody', p. 232.
[17] M. Czechowic, *Odpis Jakóba Żyda z Bełżyc na Dialogi Marcina Czechowica, na który odpowieda tenże Marcin Czechowic*, Kraków, 1581, p. 7.
[18] 'Najstarsze synody' p. 232.
[19] S. Lubieniecki, *Historia reformationis Poloniae*, Freistadt, 1685, pp. 228–31.
[20] A. Kossowski, *Protestantyzm w Lublinie i w lubelskiem w XVI–XVII w.* (Protestantism in Lublin and Lublin Province in the sixteenth and seventeenth centuries), Lublin, 1933, p. 34.
[21] L. Szczucki, *Marcin Czechowic. Studium z dziejów antytrynitaryzmu polskiego XVI w.* (Marcin Czechowic: On the history of Polish sixteenth-century Anti-Trinitarianism), Warsaw, 1964, pp. 89–100.

on very poor source material, we can trace the evolution of their religious views. They moved from Catholicism, through Calvinism and anti-Trinitarianism to Judaizing. For some of these 'dogmatic radicals' – Daniel Bieliński or Chrystian Francken, for example, men who often changed confessions – Judaizing was merely a passing phase.[22] This is the least-known route to Judaizing, since no research on how reformed Christian views were modified by specific individuals in Poland generally has been carried out. In the case of Judaizing, such investigations are extremely difficult, as the writings of Polish Judaizers have not, in the main, survived.

Marcin Czechowic's *Rozmowy Chrystyjańskie*, mentioned earlier, is a work which ranks among the most valuable sources for those who wish to become familiar with the religious doctrine of Judaizers. In *Rozmowy Chrystyjańskie*, Czechowic does not give the name of the author of a work on discrepancies in the New Testament, a work which includes the Judaizers' Catechism, but calls him simply *herst* (probably meaning today's *herszt* or leader).[23] From the later published works of Czechowic, Szymon Budny and Kasper Wilkowski, however, we learn that Daniel Bieliński was the *herst pogano-żydów* (leader of the pagan-Jews).[24] He was probably the descendant of a noble family settled in the Opole and Racibórz Duchy in Śląsk. Born around 1530, he began his studies in the Kraków Academy in 1554. A year later, we find him as a Catholic priest accused of heresy. In 1558 he was already a Protestant minister, often moving around in his work. His religious evolution in a radical direction proceeded fast. In 1563 he was an anti-Trinitarian and Anabaptist sympathizer; in 1569 we find him as a Unitarian and one of the founders of the Arian community in Raków. In the early 1570s, his theological radicalism reached its peak. Some time before 17 March 1574, he wrote a treatise, probably never printed, entitled *Przedstawienie kilkuset błędów w Nowym Testamencie* (Presentation of a Few Hundred

---

[22] L. Szczucki, *W kręgu myślicieli heretyckich* (In the circle of heretic thinkers), Wrocław, 1972, pp. 122–95; W. Urban, *Bieliński Daniel, Bibliotheca dissidentium*, Baden-Baden (in press).

[23] M. Czechowic, *Rozmowy chrystiańskie*, Łódź/Warsaw, 1979, p. 111.

[24] Czechowic, *Odpis Jakóba*, pp. 49, 285; K. Wilkowski, *Przyczyny nawrócenia do wiary powszechnej od sekty nowokrzczeńców samosatenskich* (Reasons for conversion to universal faith by the sect of Samos-Athens New-Baptisers) Wilno, 1583, p. 82; S. Budny, *O przedniejszych wiary chrystiańskiej artykułach* (On the foremost articles of Christian faith), Łosk, 1576, pp. N4r, Z4r: see L. Szczucki and J. Tazbir (eds), *Literatura ariańska w Polsce* (Arian Literature in Poland), Warsaw, 1959, p. 327).

Mistakes in the New Testament).[25] Czechowic's note about Bieliński's close contacts with Jakub Nachman from Bełżyce, an apologist and defender of Judaism, tells us yet more about the foundations of his Judaizing.[26] In his treatise, he argues that the New Testament lacks validity, citing as proof 45 quotations from the Old Testament about Jesus as Messiah which were wrongly interpreted by the Apostles, and 145 examples in the New Testament in which there are inconsistencies in the Evangelists' accounts.[27] According to Czechowic, these inconsistencies and the whole of the Judaizers' doctrine were the result of the fact that 'in the Order nothing other than the letter is observed'.[28] Bieliński's work was probably printed as, according to the testimony of Stanisław Budziński, the author handed the text over to a bookseller, Michał Królik.[29] We do not know the later fate of Bieliński's work except that in 1603 it was put on the Catholic Index.[30]

The catechism of the Judaizers' *herst*, mentioned by Czechowic, but of which we have no further information in our sources, is more mysterious. We can assume that Daniel Bieliński was its author. The teaching of this catechism is summed up by Czechowic:

> according to their own words, which their foremost *herst* uses in his catechism, I see that they consider of primary importance the legal statutes, penalizing themselves for offences against them. The greatest and first of these is what was put in the Ark of the Covenant, that is, the Ten Commandments. As secondary they consider circumcision, the church, various sacrifices, consuming the lamb, reclining and many other things.[31]

Further, attacking them for disloyalty, Czechowic wrote that: 'new uncircumcised Jews' divided the commandments of the Scripture 'so

---

[25] Urban, 'Kosy Teodozy'.
[26] W. Urban, *Chłopi wobec reformacji w Małopolsce w drugiej połowie XVI w.* (Peasants in the face of Reformation in Little Poland in the second half of the sixteenth century), Kraków, 1959, p. 201; L. Szczucki, *Marcin Czechowic*, p. 276; J. Goldberg, 'Żydowscy konwertyci w społeczeństwie staropolskim' (Jewish converts in old Polish society), in *Społeczeństwo staropolskie* (Old Polish society) IV, Warsaw, 1986, p. 202.
[27] K. Landsteiner, *Jacobus Palaeologus, Separat-Abdruck aus dem Programmedes Josefsstadter Gymnasiums*, Vienna, 1873, pp. 38–9 - a letter from Stanisław Budziński to Jakub Paleolog dated 17 March 1574; see also L. Szczucki, *Marcin Czechowic*, pp. 258–9.
[28] Czechowic, *Rozmowy chrystiańskie*, p. 112.
[29] K. Landsteiner, *Jacobus Palaeologus*, p. 38.
[30] *Index librorum prohibitorum*, Kraków, 1603, p. H^{10}.
[31] Czechowic, p. 111.

as to give themselves some freedom in following Moses' commandments in those matters which they prefer and find easier to accomplish, and to set aside what they cannot fulfil and keep'.[32] He added that they rejected circumcision as linked with physical pain, but accepted the Sabbath, as 'they found it easier to laze on Saturdays, as they are sluggards'.[33] Czechowic's remarks should of course be read sceptically, as they were written by an experienced and determined polemicist.

Similar opinions to those of the Judaizers' leading *hersts* were shared by Marcin Seidel from Oława, who fled from persecution to Poland. In 1584, we find him teaching in Lublin in the house of the anti-Trinitarian Aleksander Witrelin, and hoping to obtain a minister's or teacher's post in the community of the Polish Brothers.[34] In a letter to the Kraków community he presented his views: he considered the Decalogue as the everlasting and unchanging will of God, implanted in his brain by God, and remaining his eternal duty. This natural Decalogue, implanted in humanity by God, had been corrupted by human nature, and this is why man accepted the 'supplementary' Decalogue given to Israel by God, which Seidel considered identical to natural law; they complemented each other, together with Moses's written law, and form the basis of our behaviour.[35] Seidel also questioned the existence of Christ's divine kingdom and attempted to prove from biblical quotations that only a secular kingdom is meant. He rejected Jesus as the Messiah as well as the New Testament. He set out his views in a polemical exchange with Faust Socyn who tried unsuccessfully to convert him to Unitarianism. When he lost all hope of obtaining a post in the Unitarian community, he left Poland, wishing the Unitarians as lovers of truth success in turning all Christians to Unitarianism.[36] It appears from his debate with Socyn that apart from the Decalogue, which he treated as fundamental, Seidel considered the Old Testament as the root of faith, from which he drew his arguments.

Marcin Czechowic accused the Judaizers of rejecting the New Testament and the redeeming Passion of Jesus Christ, and of pretending to lead the faithful to God and the Old Testament, while

---

[32] Ibid.
[33] Ibid.
[34] L. Chmaj, *Bracia Polscy: Ludzie, Idee, Wpływy* (Polish Brothers: people, ideas, influence), Warsaw, 1957, p. 32.
[35] *Bibliotheca Fratrum Polonorum*, Amsterdam 1656, II, p. 806.
[36] Ibid., pp. 807–12.

in reality rejecting everything except the Decalogue, which they interpreted as reflecting ancient pagan philosophy. They also rejected the outer forms of religious observance.[37] Lech Szczucki advanced the hypothesis that the most extreme ideological trends of Judaizing treated religion as an irreligious moral doctrine.[38] Such a doctrine transcended all limits of religion, including Judaizing. These radical ideas had no chance of survival in any organized and open form, since Judaizers were opposed by all groups from Catholics to Unitarians, the latter feeling threatened as a small and barely tolerated religious group.

The Unitarians fought the Judaizers with their best theologians, among them Faust Socyn, who has already been mentioned and who later became the leader of the Polish Unitarians. In March 1584 he held a disputation in Pawlikowice with an ex-Jesuit, Chrystian Francken. Francken, at that time rector of a Unitarian school in Chmielnik, took part on condition that the debate was held without reference to the Bible. He insisted that the arguments be based on philosophy and rationality. He maintained that Jesus Christ as a human being cannot be worshipped, and attempted to prove his position through analysing the range of Christ's intellect and will and his function in the church; he argued that Christ's will was limited, stressed the differences between God and man, and pointed out that Christ was a person like Moses and Muhammad, who are not worshipped.[39] After the disputation, the community elders Jerzy Szoman and Szymon Ronemberg demanded his resignation as school rector in Chmielnik.[40] Following his polemics with Marcin Seidel and Chrystian Francken, Faust Socyn was convinced that Judaizing was widespread in Poland and gaining more ground, thereby threatening in particular the anti-Trinitarian community. He prepared a special paper for the community to use in their fight against Judaizing and thus prevent its further spread. In it he wrote that those who are neither Jews nor accept Judaism as an entity, and moreover reject the worship of Jesus Christ, have no hope of salvation and eternal life, especially as there is no promise of this in the Jewish religion. He argued, in opposition to Judaizing beliefs, that Christ's divine kingdom exists on earth, and that he should be worshipped, even if

---

[37] Czechowic, p. 7.
[38] Szczucki, *Marcin Czechowic*, p. 89.
[39] Szczucki, *W kręgu myślicieli*, pp. 173–6; L. Chmaj, *Faust Socyn 1539–1604*, Warsaw, 1963, pp. 231–3.
[40] F. S. Bock, *Historia Antitrinitariorum* I, part 2, Regiomontani 1774, pp. 360–4; L. Szczucki, *W kręgu myślicieli*, p. 174.

he were not the Messiah.[41] Moreover, Faust Socyn addressed a letter to a synod due to meet in Węgrów to discuss, among other things, the case of Chrystian Francken, in which he pointed to the dangers of Judaizing and its infamous 'atheism and epicureanism'.[42]

The 1570s and early 1580s saw the peak of Judaizing influence in Poland. Some time after 1579 Matias Vehe-Glirius, a German follower and propagator of Judaizing, came to stay in Poland. Glirius had been deacon of a Calvinist church in Kaiserslautern and was later arrested, along with Sylwanus and Neuser, on the suspicion of spreading Arianism. After leaving gaol, Glirius at once fled to Transylvania where, from 1574, he was rector of the Unitarian school in Koloszvar. It was probably under his influence that many Transylvanian Unitarians started to incline towards Judaizing. After the trial of Franciszek Davidis Glirius, known as the 'Jewish doctor', he was forced to leave Transylvania as one of those found guilty of spreading heresy. He probably settled first in Lithuania,[43] where he was in contact with Szymon Budny.

Budny, with his radical beliefs and especially his Non-Adorationism, was instrumental in preparing the way for the activity and arguments of the propagators of Judaizing, and was himself suspected by his contemporaries of being one of their number. Budny rejected the eternality of Christ and, in the notes to his translation of the New Testament, denied the Virgin birth, assenting that Jesus was Joseph's son. Even among heretical leaders Szymon Budny was considered a heretic and they would have nothing to do with him.[44] There has been no satisfactory explanation given for Szymon Budny's excommunication by the Unitarian community – whether it was simply on account of his notes to the translation of the New Testament, on some of which he later changed his mind, or his

---

[41] *Bibliotheca Fratrum* II, pp. 804–6.
[42] F. Socyn, *Listy* (Letters), ed. L. Chmaj, Warsaw, 1959, I, pp. 419–23; L. Chmaj, *Faust Socyn*, pp. 236–7.
[43] J. Tazbir, 'Maciej Vehe-Glirius. Z dziejów propagandy judaizantyzmu w XVI w.' (Maciej Vehe-Glirius: On the history of the propagation of Judaizing in the sixteenth century), in *Wieki średnie – Medium Aevum. Praca ofiarowane T. Manteufflowi* (Middle Ages – Medium Aevum: Works offered to T. Manteuffel), Warsaw, 1962, p. 291; see R. Dan, *Matthias Vehe-Glirius, Life and Work of a Radical Anti-Trinitarian with his Collected Writings*, 1982.
[44] J. Niemojewski, *Okazanie iż kościół rzymski papieski nie jest apostolski ani święty ani jeden ani powszechny* (Demonstrating that the Roman Papal Church is neither apostolic, nor holy, nor unique, nor universal), 1583, pp. 182, 204.

favouring of Judaizing.[45] In answer to Szymon Ronemberg's charges, Budny attempted in his work *O urzędzie miecza używającem* (About an office using a sword) to distance himself from Glirius and the Judaizers.[46]

Glirius actively engaged in quasi-Judaizing agitation on a wide scale in the Polish Commonwealth, at first mainly in Lithuania and later, as Janusz Tazbir has shown, in Lewartów, in the estates of the Lublin *voivode*, Mikołaj Firlej. After the death of his patron on 5 September 1588, we lose track of him in Poland. In 1590 he appeared in Germany, and was at once arrested and put in prison, where he soon died. He denied Mary's virginity, and proclaimed that she had two sons with Joseph, Jesus being the first-born. He claimed that God is one being as one nature, and that Jesus, as born of man and woman, cannot be worshipped or treated as a saviour or mediator between God and man. Jesus, being human, did not succeed in building an earthly kingdom, in which goal he was obstructed by the Jews, but according to Glirius a divine kingdom will be built in Jerusalem and will last a thousand years.[47] Kasper Wilkowski maintained that Glirius adopted some Jewish customs, having himself circumcised and accepting only kosher food.[48] Due to the lack of sources, it is hard to determine how effective Glirius's propagation of Judaizing was, but in Lithuania Judaizing and Non-Adorationism struck deep roots. The struggle against these tendencies of the Reformation was undertaken by a young member of the Polish Brothers of German origin, Walenty Smalc who, accompanied by K. Rudnicki and K. Lubieniecki, held a disputation at the synod of Nowogródek in 1600. After this they compelled the gathering to agree to the excommunication of Domanowski who, after Szymon Budny's death, had become the leading Non-Adorationist.[49]

The names of other followers of Judaizing such as Hieronim Piekarski, Garliński, Wasyl Tapiński, Maciej Albinus and Jan Baptysta Święcicki are known to us. Of some of them, like Hieronim Piekarski, we know when he was a Judaizer, and that this confession

---

[45] S. Kot, 'Szymon Budny. Der grösste Häretiker Litauens im 16. Jahrhundert', offprint from: *Wiener Archiv für Geschichte des Slawentums und Osteuropas* II, Graz/Cologne, 1956, pp. 102–4.
[46] S. Budny, *O urzędzie miecza używającem*, ed. S. Kot, Warsaw, 1932, p. 220.
[47] J. Tazbir, 'Maciej Vehe-Glirius', pp. 295–6.
[48] Wilkowski, *Przyczyny*, pp. 87–8 (see note 24).
[49] W. Smalc, 'Diarium vitae', in G. G. Zeltner, *Historia Crypto-Socinismi Altorfinae*, Leipzig, 1729, p. 1172.

represented an extreme form of theological radicalism, which he later abandoned.[50] We have no sources for the views of some of the other followers of Judaizing nor in what periods they adopted it.

Judaizing in Poland developed at the point where three major religions met: pre-Reformation Catholicism, Orthodoxy and Judaism, and, having much in common with Anti-Trinitarianism, it was intellectually enriched – usually only in the short term – by Arian thinkers impressed by its similarity to their own views. On the basis of Mateusz Mieses's thesis, Jan Juszczyk maintained that 'the Judaizing-Anti-Trinitarian movement on the eastern borderlands of the old Commonwealth was prepared by Ruthenian Judaizing, and conversely, that Arianism intensified the Judaizing movement which, in the second half of the sixteenth century, recurred in connection with Reformation unrest as a further consequence of Arianism'.[51] This thesis appears to be correct and explains the rich development of Judaizing in the bosom of Anti-Trinitarianism.

By Judaizing, we understand here the radical religious beliefs which worked back from the Christian faith towards its roots in Judaism, above all through rejection of the Trinity and the New Testament, the denial of the divine nature of Christ and the refusal of his adoration, the adoption of some of the laws of Judaism such as celebrating the Sabbath, circumcision and eating kosher food, the treating of the Old Testament and the Decalogue as the foundations of belief in one God. While preserving some elements of Christianity, the Judaizers put the Old Testament before the New, as it was granted directly by God; they addressed God directly, rejecting Jesus as Mediator or Saviour. By rejecting various ceremonial forms and simplifying religious observance, the Judaizers felt they were brought closer to God, without such useless mediators as priests.

As Marcin Czechowic wrote, the more radical trend of Judaizing went much further in its beliefs. It rejected the Holy Scripture entirely and all ritual, transcending in principle the limits of Judaizing and all contemporary religion. It recognized only the Decalogue inborn in human nature and granted in writing to Moses alone on the tablets of stone. It was no longer a religion but an 'irreligious moral doctrine' and, at the same time, a paganizing of both Christianity and Judaism. On the basis of an observation written by Iwaszko Czarny,

---

[50] W. Urgan, 'Hieronim Piekarski', *Polski Słownik Biograficany* XXVI, Warsaw, 1981, pp. 65–6.
[51] Juszczyk, 'O badaniach', p. 147; M. Mieses, 'Judaizanci', p. 255 (see note 5).

who worked at Tsar Ivan III's court, in which he says that the love of one's neighbour is the root of eternal joy and the principal moral obligation,[52] we can conclude that for the radical Judaizers the Decalogue had two essential points: love of God and of one's neighbour, the simplest formula for living according to God's commandments. Yet, although one can formulate its views in this way, it must be confessed that much remains speculation given our scant source material and the meagre knowledge we of this confession.[53]

---

[52] Juszczyk, 'O badaniach', p. 150.
[53] J. Tazbir, *Świat panów Pasków* (The world of the Lords Paseks), Łódź 1986, p. 196.

3 · The Jewish Population in the Light of the Dietines of the Sixteenth to Eighteenth Centuries

Andrzej Link-Lenczowski

In his excellent work *La Peur en Occident (XIVe-XVIIIe siècles)* Jean Delumeau paints an apocalyptic image of a Jew – a tool in Satan's hands rousing fear and terror in all social milieux in Western Europe. Pointing to the religious and economic reasons, which made legislatures multiply resolutions restricting Jews, he stresses the phenomenon, which he calls *peur idéologique*. This fear dictates the only radical and effective solution: the final breaking of all ties between Christians and Jews, which can be achieved only through their expulsion (one of the municipal resolutions of 1593). From this perspective, the most fundamental attitude towards the Jewish population aimed at the maximal isolation of this hostile and alien element and, in consequence, at its total elimination from social life. In attempting to provide a synthesis, such a formulation affords a very convenient and effective starting point. Yet even if we accept this point of view as a basis for research, when examining so complicated a problem as attitudes towards the Jewish population, it carries a great danger of over-simplification.

This danger was not avoided over a hundred years ago by Adolf Pawiński, who presented a gloomy picture of Polish Jewry in *Rządy sejmikowe w Polsce* (Dietine government in Poland). According to him, the Jewish community was 'systematically ill-treated, trampled, presented in [dietine] instructions as an easy and necessary object of financial robbery on behalf of the Commonwealth' by the *szlachta*. Similar opinions may be found in many more recent works devoted to the organization and functioning of the *szlachta*'s self-government.

Attempting to characterize the essential features determining the attitude of the *szlachta* towards Jews, as these found expression in the resolutions of dietines, we should first note the fact that the Jews were always treated as a separate community, ruling itself with its own laws. This fact was accepted as obvious, and all deviations from the generally accepted, legal principles of the functioning of the Jewish community, no matter who initiated them, were condemned. Many times, and for various reasons, the opinion was expressed, that Jews should not be 'required to submit to laws other than their own or to respect *in toto* laws passed against them'. Such statements are to be found especially in the first half of the seventeenth century. In the eighteenth century this view is put forth less often, and usually linked with criticism of attempts by Jews to broaden their economic activity in towns and villages. The above view was, moreover, formulated without use of any pejorative terms, in most cases treating Jews like other national groups, such as Scots or Armenians, and, less often Wallachians and Hungarians, groups which were seen mainly as merchants. The problem of liability in cases of individual or collective crimes was treated similarly. First steps against the guilty were always to be taken by the 'Jewish elders' and further, stricter actions were reserved for the future. Many times the problem of *podwojewodziński* jurisdiction was raised, always confirming that only this court was qualified to examine the appropriate matters, and all other steps, including those taken by the *szlachta* itself, were illegal. What is more, Jews were to be protected against such actions. The Wiszeński pre-Diet instruction from the year 1659 put it clearly: the Jews 'should remain with their jurisdiction; various other jurisdictions seeking to exercise authority over them and [the] various people . . . used to imprison the Jews and enforce justice *privata authoritate* in various ways are acting against the law'. Such examples may be multiplied, although it would be hard to quote as many in the eighteenth century.

The principle of non-interference in conflicts within the Jewish community, which usually broke out in towns and concerned the distribution of taxes, was stressed with equal determination. What, at the most, was done was to lay down means by which Jews should reach agreement among themselves to eliminate future conflicts. The eighteenth century brought somewhat more precision. The Halicz April dietine of 1734 stated that 'assessment of Jews in the Halicz region was unjustly conducted by a Jew, against [the recommendations of] Marek Rabinowicz, the Jewish general scribe', owing to which the distribution of taxes had to be carried out again, sworn and passed to Halicz and Trembowla. In the whole affair, the background of which remains obscure, it was Rabinowicz who was the principal 'prosecuting' party. On the occasion in 1622 when there was an accusation of counterfeiting money the Kraków dietine ordained that 'the principal perpetrators should be handed over to be impaled' to those 'whom they know best among themselves'.

In cases of danger threatening the state, no matter of what origins, a principle was held that no one could be exempted from rendering services. The attitude presented in 1616 by the Wiszeński pre-Diet dietine, which recommended deputies that 'when in the Diet a way to conduct military defence shall be sought no men and no estate *cuiuscuque conditionis* should be exempt from this obligation, which has to be borne for the Commonwealth's defence' appears to be typical. These opinions were usually reissued when it was necessary to pay the country's troops. This is why the second half of the seventeenth century and years of chaos during the Great Northern War resulted in frequent repetition of similar recommendations, always invoking the common destiny of all inhabitants of the Commonwealth. What was possibly stressed more in the eighteenth century, was the fact that the Jews, of the non-*szlachta* groups, had relatively greater financial resources. Nevertheless, Jews were hardly ever named separately (that is, without the Christian and Armenian merchants) as potential contributors. The example of the Halicz region, where in 1716 a tax without exception was imposed on Jews and rabbis, is rather isolated. This was done to satisfy 'warriors', when a confederated army division entered the region, led by Crown Field Scribe Michał Potocki, whose career in the army left no doubt about his ability to reach into the pockets of inhabitants of the region through which he passed.

Many more demands were addressed to Jewish inhabitants of towns. Let us just recall Kraków, Lwów or the small but important town of Przemyśl to note how often (probably also under the pressure of the town authorities) the duty to defend town against the enemy, mainly through participation in reinforcing fortifications was reiterated. It should be added that such demands were often accompanied by complaints, sometimes very strong that the Jews did not help in the town's defence. In the resolution of the Wiszeński pre-Diet dietine of 1625 it was stated: 'There are more

Jews in Przemyśl than Christians, and they purchase houses virtually in the market square, yet in times of danger you cannot find [them] to mount defence with proper help, [and] neither with their powder, nor with shotguns, nor with their persons do they wish to participate in such action.' The Wiszeński dietine returned to this problem a number of times, always stressing the necessity of participating in the town's defence through handing over appropriate sums of money or equipment. In 1656 it was clearly laid down that 'in such a pressing need of the Commonwealth, when all of us struggle hard, it would be right also that Jews, who profit in Commonwealth, contribute some considerable sum to relieve the burden of the Commonwealth'. The Proszów dietine in 1667 similarly acknowledged the receipt of a sum paid by Jews '*pro sustentatione praesidii* of the Kraków castle', adding the comment that this took place in the interest of all the town's inhabitants. A certain feeling of helplessness and consciousness of inefficiency of the whole fiscal system in emergency situations calling for the efforts of the whole country, was familiar to the *szlachta*. When, to this end, they considered the possibility of raising the Jewish poll tax, the *szlachta* declared that

> in such great dangers, when the Commonwealth is exhausted by unceasing wars, levies and taxes, it is the Commonwealth's concern that defence be thoroughly discussed, as the poor peoples' burden is great partly because we cannot find a way out of trouble, but further, because we [the Commonwealth] need more; *impossibilitas summa* brought us to this situation, where it is impossible to give more, when the people have nothing.

It was then that establishing an annual Jewish poll tax of 100,000 złoty was proposed as a way out of the difficulty, with the proviso that it should not create a new legal situation.

The problem of taxing the Jewish population, most frequently touched upon in the dietine acts, is somewhat more complicated. The sixteenth- and seventeenth-century *lauda* include a large number of complaints that Jews do not pay a high enough poll tax. Even if it is confirmed, that they do pay an adequate sum, accepted by appropriate resolution, it is pointed out that an attempt should be made to introduce additional services. This resulted from the *szlachta*'s conviction that, generally, Jewish payments to the treasury were below their fiscal abilities. The most often proposed system of enlarging the system of poll tax was that of paying 'in capita, not buying oneself with some sum'. The problem of Jewish poll tax was linked with the problem of the inefficiency of the whole system, which did not secure sufficient income to the treasury. The pre-Diet instruction from the Wiszeński dietine from the year 1635, in which it was asserted that 'the *szlachta* estate sees that so many subjects do not contribute taxes and Jews add but a small sum to the treasury' was typical. In face of this situation, a poll tax yield of at least 100,000 złoty yearly was proposed.

The Radziejów dietine, in which, according to Pawiński, resolutions of anti-Jewish character were frequently passed, in reality proposed the raising of the poll tax in 1672, in a moment when special danger threatened the Commonwealth. Yet this was done without expressing negative opinions on the Jewish community, and a year later, in 1673, it was stated, rather generally, that Jews were to pay taxes like other nationalities.

The pre-Diet Kiev instruction of 1698 stated that the

> great collapse of the *szlachta*'s fortunes, in the Polish Kingdom, in cities and in small towns [is] sufficient reason also to impoverish Jews . . . Various citizens complain of aggravation and injury from assignators, who travel with assignations of Jewish poll tax; and supplications from Jews arrive, since Jews pay if there is need, in provinces and regions for taxes *in supplementum*.

Similar statements may be multiplied and at the end of the sixteenth century and throughout the seventeenth century there was no dietine that did not put forward a similarly formulated demand. Nevertheless, it is hard to point to any special period of intensification of the *szlachta*'s demands concerning poll tax and its assessment. They appear in similar number in the eighteenth century, with the tone of demands visibly stronger; clearly this was linked with more negative opinions about Jews than the generalizations of a century earlier; but above all there were criticisms of organizational defects. The Halicz dietine of 1712 complained that 'Jewish poll tax is paid with resistance, and is not paid according to assessments of the Jews' own *kehilla* elders.' Also the 1718, 1720 and 1724 pre-Diet instructions devoted some space to the poll tax auction, with the proposition that the eventual sum be used to repair artillery. Much attention was devoted to this problem, when the levying of taxes for the army, one of the fundamental problems of the first years of King August III's reign, was considered. For example, in 1736 a raising of the Jewish poll tax, as a means of enlarging the army, was proposed, and linked with the demand that 'Jewry not grow through marriage, and every one marrying at young age be compelled to contribute a sum *in subsidium* to the army.' Similar demand, even somewhat sharper in form, were repeated in many later pre-Diet instructions.

Problems connected with the economic activity of the Jewish population roused more emotion than the question of poll tax. The *szlachta* fought trade monopolies with determination, namely 'all legal restrictions of free competition on behalf of a guild, a whole town, or a national group', and Jews were no exception here. Mention was sometimes made of Jewish losses resulting from the legal ban on their trading in Turkish goods. Peremptory demands were addressed to the Lwów furriers, who had prohibited Jews from trading in furs. The 1640 pre-Diet instruction stated that 'the *szlachta* estate understands it to be a main task for itself to ensure that only furriers are allowed to sell furs . . . deputies are to agree amongst themselves that this be enforced . . . and that not only furriers but also Jews be permitted to sell furs and sables, to make purchase cheaper.' A similar attitude was taken in cases of limited Jewish trade in some goods, although it was conceded that the eventual changes 'should not harm agreements which Jews had signed with towns'. However, no concrete means to offset these changes were suggested. This could have resulted from disbelief in the possibility of implementing those laws, and the awareness that it could result in harm to the merchants of other nationalities. At the same time, it was stressed that Jews in towns should enjoy the same rights as others, as 'they also build walls and participate in the defence with other merchants.'

The rights of the Jewish population to carry on its trading activities were recognized, but it was nevertheless demanded that Jews also pay taxes imposed on other groups of the town population. Such provisions are to be found over the whole period discussed, with more or less the same intensity. The demand that Jews pay 'land tax and other taxes on crafts' was constantly formulated. Also set forth were demands that Jews should not trade in saltpetre (a strategic merchandise), oxen, horses, salt or Hungarian wines (in this last case the prohibition applied to all merchants, assuming that the growing demand would result in the raising of prices by Hungarian merchants). The end of the sixteenth and the first half of the seventeenth centuries was a period when the provisions cited above were formulated in a very moderate manner, without any terms which suggest the existence of common and established pejorative stereotypes of the Jew, attributing to him a set of particularly negative features.

The second half of the seventeenth and the eighteenth centuries saw noticeable changes. Consciousness of helplessness in the face of the current political events, the impoverishing of the country and growth of the Jewish population did, undoubtedly, influence this change. The general Nowokorczyn dietine stated in February 1669 that 'this income, which could be *cedere in sustamentum* of poor people, Jews with their trades take away, and thus they should not interfere with them'. In the pre-Diet Halicz instructions of 1740 and 1746 the normalization of measurements is recommended 'in which there is disorder and dishonesty in sale both of liquors and cloth and materials which was introduced by Jewish impudence'. Finally in the 1752 pre-Diet instruction we come across the most uncommon demand: that Jews be forbidden to trade, as they 'cause great harm to merchants in trade and merchandise, due to which our royal towns remain in great ruin and desolation, thus they should be expelled from all trades and merchandise, with freedom to take their goods from them in any place'. But this was an isolated opinion.

The whole group of problems arising from employment of Christians by Jews was presented in a similar context. But while in the sixteenth and seventeenth centuries it was usually limited to pointing out that Jews should be prohibited from employing Christian servants, in the eighteenth century we often come across a negative image of a Jew being invoked in argumentation. At first the emphasis was on 'the slighting of Christian faith', or simply the authority of the church, which maintained that Jews should not keep Christian servants, was invoked. Judging by the number of times this problem comes up, any steps taken against it must have been as effective as the attempts to forbid Jews to trade. The Halicz *szlachta* in 1710 even adduced the argument that the hiring of Christian servants by Jews resulted in a situation where 'no lord nor simple person can obtain household hands, cooks, as all those mentioned servants in Jewry's *servitutem* seek light bread'. Thus a certain competition is noticed here, which is regretted but in practice accepted.

Finally let us pass to the decidedly negative and prejudiced opinions, which are attitudes thoroughly hostile to Jews. The list of these is much shorter than it would appear when one studies the literature of the *szlachta*'s self-government. Opinions referring to the religious differences, to their classification with other alien nationalities are, in fact, not to be observed in the seventeenth century, save for the term *'infidelis Judaeorum'* which was used rather seldom. Equally rare are opinions that Jews were the cause of all evil. But when such opinions are found, it is in the context of accusing them of counterfeiting money, which at this time meant export of good money from the country. Here it was those Jews not settled in the Commonwealth who were blamed and treated suspiciously – as were all outsiders. This opinion intensifies especially in the eighteenth century. In addition, the ruling that Jews should wear distinguishing clothing or marks was never enacted (the case of the Kraków dietine of 1622, when it was demanded that they wear yellow caps is exceptional). The thesis that Jews were concerned only with their own interest to the detriment of the Commonwealth's concerns is not often found although the Halicz instruction for the Warsaw general council of 1710 claimed: 'that Jews, *gens perfida* always seek *more lucrum sui* than *commodum* of the States of our Commonwealth.' This is worth attention, as it was connected with accusations that during the Great Northern War some Jews made a fortune in trade 'with the enemy, auxiliary army and bandits'.

Equally rare and sporadic are denunciations of Jews as enemies of Christianity, although we do come across statements of the type: 'Jews who God's Majesty *cruciatur*'. Though not found often, it appears that stressing of Jewish hostility towards all Christians was sometimes used by non-Catholics as a means of stressing the principle of toleration of the various Christian denominations to improve their own position. In this light we should read the Arian supplication to the pre-Diet Proszowice dietine of February 1659, which stated:

> struck with the lightning of a sharp constitution, we beg help that you would *occurrere* our final ruin, and God shall honour this and gift our country with fiscal and flourishing peace, when you tolerate so many Jews, pagans and other open blasphemers of God Son with patience, us . . . you shall not expel.

Equally rare pejorative opinions on Jews are linked to the

information about various riots and demonstrations in towns. Without going here into the complicated matter of the 'religious hatred of the masses' let us recall that in all cases of unrest in towns, in which in some way Jews participated, and which were reported in the dietines' *lauda*, resolutions calling for the maintenance of order and the punishing of rioters were formulated without any statements which stressed in a general manner the Jews' negative features. An example from Lwów, where in 1641 the confiscation was demanded of property from the Jew Boruch, who was involved in trade in stolen goods, testifies to this. So does another one from Kraków. And so, the Proszowice pre-Diet dietine of April 1678 stated:

> Great tumults multiply in Kraków, as well as in Kazimierz, in the Jewish town and in the suburbs . . . We demand of the Kraków *deputy-starosta* that these tumults whether initiated in Kraków or in Kazimierz or in the Jewish town, *manu forti reprimat*, and that he order the arrest of those who, stopping Jews and their wagons in Kleparz and the Wesoła district, as well as in the fields the public roads, *securitatem violate* . . . And no *szlachta*'s or clergy's house or cellar and no *libertationem pretext* must hide such hooligans from execution.

The eighteenth century brought no change in the character of such recorded statements. For example in the Bracław *laudum* of 1720 the *szlachta* demands the stopping of the artisans' frolics 'which take to various tumults and violations on Jews.'

Indeed, despite the more or less strong pronouncements and restrictions mainly concerning Jewish economic activity in the Commonwealth, Jews were in fact regarded as a permanent and necessary element of the social reality. This type of attitude can, of course, be supported and found much more easily in letters than in formal registers. Therefore, in concluding this chapter, let us quote the testimony of Stanisław Mateusz Rzewuski who, in a letter to the Łuck priest Kaszewski, defended the Jewish right to have Christian helpers, to organize independent education and to build and restore synagogues. 'Jews,' he wrote, 'cannot exist without the synagogue, as our towns cannot exist without them.' And this was not just one magnate's opinion.

4 · The Private Life of Polish Jews in the Vasa Period

Daniel Tollet

Modern historical research on the Jewish communities of Poland has largely concentrated on economic relations between Jews and Christians, on the political balance within the Jewish communities, and on political relations between them and the Christian authorities.[1] Although historians have not neglected the material basis of Jewish life nor their religious values and outlook on everyday life, no one has yet undertaken a systematic study of their private life.[2] The aim of this paper is not to present a complete picture of their private life but to point to possible lines of further research.

Right from the start, the Jewish communities faced the question of how their members could remain Jewish without being wanderers, poor or offending Christian sensibilities. To understand how the Jews lived, one has to understand the nature and principle of the ghetto. The principle of isolating Jews and Christians was formulated at the Lateran Council in 1215, yet it was only in 1564 that Zygmunt August, King of Poland, prohibited Kraków's Christian citizens from settling in Jewish towns.[3] The Jewish communal authorities, for their part, also enforced isolation. In the statute issued by the Kraków community in 1595, Jews were not allowed to leave the ghetto on Sundays without special permission

---

[1] D. Tollet, 'Les Juifs de la République nobilitaire polonaise (XVIe-XVIIIe siècles) dans l'historiographie de la Pologne Populaire (1950–85)', in M. M. Drozdowski, ed., *Między Historią a Teorią*, (Between History and Theory), Warsaw, 1988, pp. 322–37.

[2] The notion of private life, which should not be confused with everyday life, was defined by Georges Duby in his work *Histoire de la vie privée*, Paris, 1985, I, pp. 9–11.

[3] M. Bałaban, *Historia i literatura żydowska ze szczególnym uwzględnieniem historii Żydów w Polsce* (Jewish history and literature with special reference to Jewish history in Poland) III, Lwów, 1925, p. 227; L. Poliakov, *Histoire de l'antisémitisme*, Paris, 1981, I, pp. 332f., notices, that the separation of Jewish and Christian populations is a sixteenth-century phenomenon in the whole of Europe.

from the senior *mensis*.⁴ Moreover, the town gates were firmly locked every evening, with the result that life fluctuated between the two poles of home and town-gate.⁵ This found expression in the geographical framework of the ghetto: in Kazimierz, Lwów, Lublin and Wilno, Jewish administrative and religious centres were concentrated in a narrow area,⁶ and as the towns released little territory for Jews, Polish ghettos appeared overcrowded.

Unrest in ghettos was rarely the result of internal causes, of which I have found only minor traces,⁷ but of attacks from outside; this is why the Łuck Jews in 1626, and other communities later, were granted privileges by the monarch, including the right to fortify synagogues.⁸ Jewish towns also lived under the constant threat of fire, which often forced out of the town those made homeless. Fierce fires raged in Kazimierz in 1597 and again in 1604, and the 1643 fire destroyed almost all wooden houses, resulting in a mass panic.⁹ Similar disasters took place in Poznań in 1590, 1633 and 1662. After the fire of 1662, the town council

---

[4] M. Bałaban, 'Die Krakauer Judengemeindeordnung aus dem Jahre 1595 und ihre Nachträge', *Jahrbuch der Jüdischen Literaturgesellschaft in Frankfurt a. M.* 10, 1913, p. 231. A permission cost 2 grzywnas, while a penalty 4 grzywnas.
[5] M. Bałaban, 'Obyczajowość i zycie prywatne w dawnej Rzeczypospolitej' (Customs and private life in Old Polish Republic) in *Żydzi w Polsce odrodzonej* (Jews in reborn Poland), Warsaw, 1933, 1, p. 347.
[6] There were three synagogues and a cemetery in Kazimierz, on Szeroka Street. In Lwów all the buildings of public use – synagogue, baths, court, *kehilla* and school – were concentrated on the intersection of Żydowska and Nowożydowska Streets. In Wilno there were fourteen synagogues, a community library and baths on one street. See Bałaban, *Historia i literatura*, p. 229; G. D. Hundert, 'Jewish urban residence in the Polish Commonwealth in the early modern period', *Jewish Journal of Sociology* 26:1 (1984), pp. 25–34.
[7] I have found only one case of a conflict between Jews in the sources concerning Kraków and Poznań in the period under discussion. In 1646 Jakub Pinkus satisfied David Zysselow for an insult in Kraków. (Acta Grodzkie i Ziemskie (AGZ), *Varia 12*, ff. 955, 956). Relations between Jews were not idyllic, yet it is hard to learn all about them owing to the scarcity of sources.
[8] '... that Jews made their synagogue capable of withstanding an enemy, with provision for shooting from all four sides so it was possible to defend it, and paid to fashion a cannon, and create a defence force from among themselves according to the needs of that place'. The flat roof of Łuck synagogue enabled the Jews to place defenders there. Similar buildings appeared in Lublin, Lwów suburbs, Brody, Lesznogród, Tarnopol, Szaro, Żółkiew, and elsewhere. Cf. Bałaban, *Historia i literatura*, pp. 229, 230.
[9] M. Bałaban, *Historia Żydów w Krakowie i na Kazimierzu 1304–1868* (History of Jews in Kraków and Kazimierz, 1304–1868; 2nd rev. edn of *Dzieje Żydów* (1912) – see ch. 18, n. 3), Kraków, 1931, I, pp. 207 and 409.

threatened Jews with expulsion if their authorities did not order all fires to be extinguished at night.[10]

Another common hazard was plague. The 1595 Kraków community statute laid down that if plague broke out in any house, its inhabitants should alert the *kehilla*. The elders then sent an alderman (an official) to investigate the possibility of isolating that house, whose inhabitants were forbidden to go out under penalty of a 50 *złoty* fine.[11] Poznań experienced an outbreak of plague in 1607–13;[12] in Lwów, 10,000 people, including large numbers of Jews, died of sickness following the siege of 1648.[13]

Plagues were said to have resulted from the Jews' filth. Narrow, small, overpopulated, dangerous and dirty, the ghettos were not an attractive place to live for any Jew of means. It was to escape this environment that the richest Jewish bankers tried to settle outside Jewish towns.[14] If the collective hygiene of the ghetto left much to be desired, nevertheless personal hygiene, especially for women, was a reality. The Jewish religion obliges its believers to take weekly ritual baths.[15] The Lwów community leased baths in 1608, and had its tenants build walls around it.[16] A Kraków tenant paid the community 1 thaler a week and had to supply hot water three times every fortnight, and women were obliged to attend the Jewish bath.[17]

---

[10] J. Perles, 'Die Geschichte der Juden in Posen, *Monatschrift für Geschichte und Wissenschaft des Judentums* 13 (1864), pp. 30, 56, and Acta Consularia Posn. ss. 1504, 1506.

[11] Bałaban, *Historia Żydów w Krakowie*, pp. 451–2. These orders were repeated and specified by the 1628 statute (Cf. Wettstein, *Devarim Atikim*, no. 6, quoted by M. Bałaban, pp. 453–4) and the 1631 statute (Wettstein, no. 7).

[12] Perles, *Juden in Posen*, p. 50.

[13] Bałaban, 'Obyczajowość', p. 348.

[14] J. S. Bystroń, *Dzieje obyczajów w dawnej Polsce. Wiek XVI–XVIII*. (History of customs in old Poland from the sixteenth to the eighteenth centuries, Warsaw, 1960, 1, pp. 61–2.

[15] J. Karo, *Shulkhan Arukh*, ed. Weil, Paris 1980. This work stresses the role of purifying baths (see pp. 548–53). The evidence presented, even if it applies to a later period, may be trusted concerning the most essential matters of Jewish life.

[16] M. Bałaban, *Żydzi lwowscy na przełomie XVI i XVII w.* (Lwów Jews at the turn of the sixteenth and seventeenth centuries) Lwów, 1906, pp. 74–5.

[17] M. Bałaban, 'Krakauer Judengemeindeordnung', §68, pp. 41b and 42. The baths in Kraków were very deep as they were fed by spring water. (See Bałaban, 'Obyczajowość', p. 348). Considerable progress in hygiene may be observed in seventeenth-century Poland. The popularity of baths grew with the development of sewerage systems. Yet a number of baths had to be closed owing to the spread of infectious mainly venereal diseases. Nobles in big towns made use of steam baths. Bath facilities were usually leased, and individual baths were rare. Cf. W. Hensel and

Continuing our investigation, let us try to look inside the home. Since houses were usually built of wood, and have therefore not survived, we are not familiar with them. Generally, a three-storey building was inhabited by 15 to 20 families, that is by 40 to 100 persons.[18] Only the richest had individual houses: the Bocian, Horowic and Jekeles families of Kraków, the Wahl family in Brześć, the Montalto family in Lublin, and the Nachmanowicz family in Lwów.[19] At the end of the sixteenth century, Izaak Nachmanowicz owned many houses with stone worked façades and large windows – the one at 19 Blacharska Street even had a ballroom with a wooden balcony.[20]

Izaak's fortune was exceptional; the average fortune of a Jewish merchant was doubtless much closer to that revealed by Eliasz Seliogowicz of Lwów's last will. Eliasz died in 1636, leaving his wife half a house, and the rest of his possessions to his brother. As for his mother-in-law, she was allowed to live in the house, at a rent of 1 złoty per month.[21]

There were other Jews with more than one house. In 1635 Moses Kalahora of Kraków and his partner Fajwisz bought as many as sixty-five houses in Kazimierz.[22] These were, of course, for use as tenement-houses or for resale at a profit. Studying last wills and testaments, one learns how merchants used their buildings, whether for personal use, or as tenement-houses, or as warehouses. As for their interior decoration and furnishings, research reveals that Jews lived modestly; even the richest houses pale beside the palaces of the Christian patricians.[23]

Some Jews, while not in the luxury class, nevertheless aimed at a high standard of living. The community authorities waged a constant battle against such tendencies, so as not to provoke Christian resentment. According to the 1595 Kraków community statute, Jews were forbidden to employ Christians without the prior consent of the *kehilla*, and on no account were they to put up any Christian for the night. M. Bałaban points out that the statute put

J. Pazdur, eds, *Historia kultury materialnej Polski w zarysie* (History of material culture in Poland) III, Warsaw, 1978, pp. 395–8.

[18] Bałaban, *Historia i literatura*, p. 228.
[19] Bałaban, 'Obyczajowość', p. 349.
[20] Bałaban, *Historia i literatura*, p. 228.
[21] Bałaban, *Żydzi lwowscy*, p. 301.
[22] A. G. Z., *Varia 11*, pp. 653–8.
[23] On the furnishings of Christian homes see *Historia kultury materialnej*, pp. 252–7.

into effect the demand both of the Catholic Church synods and the town's own prohibition of 1615, namely the ban on Jews employing Christian servants.[24]

In the same spirit, the statute of 1595 laid down a maximum sum a Jew could spend on a feast or holiday. We learn with surprise that this sum did not depend on the type of the feast or holiday, but was calculated by reference to tax rates. In this way, the community made some allowance for the rich to spend on luxury items.[25]

Clothing was also subject to regulations emanating from either Christian or Jewish sources. The 1538 Piotrków constitution made it obligatory for Jews to wear distinctive garments, which meant wearing a yellow hat.[26] Anyone caught disobeying the rule was subject to a fine of 1 Polish złoty.[27] But in practice, these regulations were never put into effect.[28]

On their side, the communities of Lithuania, Kraków, and Poznań introduced sumptuary laws but, during the seventeenth century, had to adapt them for the benefit of the rich. In 1643 the Council of the Four Lands reduced the number of clothing and feast controllers from seven to five, putting them under the authorities of the *kehilla*, not the elders.[29]

The various bodies of the Jewish community well understood that Jews needed an outlet for expenditure, yet without offending Christians. Even this approach failed to satisfy everyone. A mystic, Hirsz Kiejdanower, writing in 1665 about the problems caused by people's behaviour and criticizing the 'get rich' attitude, wrote:

> I have seen Jewish women out on the street, dressed not as Jews but as nobles. They question their husbands' opinions and

---

[24] Bałaban, *Historia Żydów w Krakowie*, pp. 203, 231.

[25] D. Teimanas, *L'autonomie des Communautés juives de Pologne*, Paris, 1933, pp. 141–2. If paying a tax of 10 groszy one could invite 25 men with wives and people whose presence was necessary according to the liturgical requirements. Paying 10–20 groszy – 40 men; 20 groszy–1 złoty – 50 men; 1–2 złoty – 60 men, and there were no limits above this level of tax.

[26] *Volumina Legum*, I, pp. 258–9. Cf. L. Poliakov, *Histoire de l'antisémitisme*, p. 260.

[27] T. Czacki, *O litewskich i polskich prawach, o ich duchu, źródłach, związku i o rzeczach zawartych w pierwszym Statucie dla Litwy w 1529 roku wydanym* (On the Lithuanian and Polish laws, on their spirit, roots, relations and on matters included in the first statute issued for Lithuania in the year 1529), Kraków, 1861, I. p. 116.

[28] Bałaban, 'Obyczajowość', p. 351.

[29] L. Lewin, *Neue Materialien zur Geschichte der Vierländersynode*, Frankfurt, 1905, notes 17, 21, 24 and ch. 9, pp. 241, 244.

bring Christian hatred and jealousy upon us . . . How many men suffer from their inability to buy their wives a rich fur? How many have to borrow to pay for it?[30]

What, then, was the scale of values in the ghetto? In looking at this question, one must take into account the religious basis of the whole of Jewish life and thought in Poland during the period of the Vasa dynasty since, as we are well aware, it is impossible to separate religious from other attitudes. As A. J. Gurewicz said:

> Theology represented the supreme generalisation of social life . . . it offered a system for interpreting the universe and the members of feudal society understood themselves, as well as the whole world, in theological terms. There they found the justification and explanation of this world.[31]

In looking at the social system, education deserves particular study. The seventeenth century undoubtedly saw the decline of learning among Polish Jews. This explains the comment of Abraham Ben Sabbatay Horowic of Kraków in his will:

> He who learns does not forget easily. That is why you should take your books to the synagogue and read them while the cantor prolongs his prayer . . . Coming back from a shop, or from a market, read for your wife and your children . . . Make your sons and daughters pray and respect the Order and moral rules . . . You know how much difficulty I had raising you, so do the same for your children and grandchildren . . .[32]

In presenting an idealized image, after describing the honours bestowed on the head of the *yeshiva* (religious school and college), Nathan Hannover points out 'the jealous zeal with which all the wise

---

[30] Hirsz Kiejdanower, *Kaw Hajaszar, Frankfurt a/M 1665*, Lublin, 1912, quoted by Bałaban, *Historia Żydów w Krakowie*, p. 426.
[31] A. Gurewicz, *Categories of Mediaeval Culture*.
[32] Bałaban, 'Obyczajowość', p. 370. Concerning reading habits, it should be added (Bałaban, p. 367) that men spent Saturday mornings in the synagogue and read the Talmud after meals, while women studied the Bible for women. Moreover, in the sixteenth and seventeenth centuries women read German romances about Theodoric from Verona or the knight Hildebrandt, translated and published in Kraków. It was opposed by the rabbis.

have studied, constantly seeking to attain that standard and become the head of the *yeshiva* in another community'.[33]

To participate in teaching the members of the community was not only an obligation on the rich but was everyone's duty. The Bible was the foundation-stone of education. Mordekchay Jaffe showed his interest in education with the following advice: 'When the child is small and starts to speak, he should be made to repeat verses from the Bible; when he is three, his father should teach him the Hebrew alphabet; and at seven he should be sent to school.'[34] We know the organization of Jewish schools, thanks to the 1551 regulation of the fraternity of the Hevrat Talmud Tora from Kraków, which was charged with their support,[35] and also to the regulations adopted in 1623 and 1637.[36] There were also private schools alongside the community schools. Their fees were fixed by the Kraków community's statute of 1595.

The educational system, whose basic aim was to maintain the cultural identity of the Jewish community and which honoured rabbis before even the richest of merchants, fell into decline during the course of the seventeenth century. At the beginning of the century, Salomon Efraim of Łęczyca was already criticizing the practice of racing through the texts. He proposed to concentrate on the *Mishna* (the first part of the Talmud) and certain biblical texts, studying them in depth.[37] The *kehilla* schools, which used to buy

---

[33] N. Hannover, *Yevein metsula*, Paris, 1982, p. 73.

[34] M. Jaffe, *Levush Ateret Zahav* 1, 246, art. 5, quoted by H. Glejzer 'Życie Żydów w Polsce w XVII wieku na podstawie responsów' (Jewish life in Poland in the sixteenth and seventeenth centuries on the basis of responses), AŻIH: Master's Dissertation no. 51, p. 38.

[35] M. Bałaban, 'Szkolnictwo żydowskie w dawnej Rzeczypospolitej' (Jewish education in the Old Commonwealth), in *Żydzi w Polsce odrodzonej*, Warsaw, 1933, I, p. 338. In the year 1622 Jakub ben Izaak from Janów published a Bible for women, but at the end of the seventeenth century numerous other publications concerning ideal religious life existed as well. Also in 1604, in Prague, Moses Sertels published a Biblical dictionary in Yiddish – the so-called Beer Moshe, which was a considerable success in Poland. (Cf. Bałaban, *Historia i literatura*, pp. 252–4). Concerning publications and publishers see M. Bałaban, 'Drukarnie żydowskie w Polsce w XVI w.' (Jewish publishing houses in Poland in the sixteenth century), in *Pamiętnik zjazdu naukowego im Jana Kochanowskiego w Krakowie* (A Diary of Jan Kochanowski's scientific conference in Kraków), Kraków, 1931, pp. 102–16; see also M. Steinschneider, *Die Geschichte Literatur der Juden in Druckwerken und Handschriften*, Frankfurt, 1905. This question should be further investigated.

[36] Because of a plague, the 1623 texts never became valid. Cf. Wettstein, *Kadmoniyot mipinkasiyot yeshanim*, Kraków, pp. 3–7.

[37] Salomon Efraim of Łęczyca, *Amudei Sheysh*, quoted by Bałaban, 'Obyczajowość', p. 340.

the services of rabbis, were by the mid-seventeenth-century nothing more than an asylum for the poor.[38] As for private teachers, they were mostly cheats. In the second half of the seventeenth century, a rich Jewish woman from Hamburg, Glückel of Hammeln, decided to send her son to be educated by a Polish teacher, but the venture was a failure.[39]

A fundamental feature of Jewish life is its view of the family as the basic unit of Judaism, centred on the father in accordance with Talmudic law. Our knowledge of family life derives from moralizing texts which were lamentations. Thus, at the end of the sixteenth century, Moses son of Henoch wrote in his book *Brantspiegel*:

> Today it is bad, and will become even worse, unless the Messiah comes, as we witness young girls flaunting themselves in front of men in the streets and at banquets, how loudly they speak and how shamelessly. Young married women dress in vivid colours – gold, silver, pearls – and one sees young women looking men straight in the eye, dancing. Married women praise the good points of their female servants, unconcerned about the presence of young men.[40]

Jewish boys traditionally had to be married by the age of eighteen, girls between the ages of twelve and fourteen. If they did not, the community could force them into marriage.[41] Economic insecurity made parents marry off their children although, as Mordekchay Jaffe recalled, the Talmud forbade marriages between minors.[42] Parents signed a contract before the marriage and paid a deposit.[43] If the engagement was broken off, the father of the party which

---

[38] Ibid. p. 343.
[39] Glückel vol Hammeln, *Mémoires*, Paris, 1971, p 183.
[40] Moses, son of Henoch, Brantspiegel, quoted by Bałaban, 'Obyczajowość', p. 364.
[41] Ibid. p. 356.
[42] Glejzer, 'Życie Żydów', p. 53.
[43] Samuel of Międzrzecze, *Naklat shiwha*, § 8, and M. Jaffe, *Responses Tsemakh Tsedek*, no. 22. Cf. H. Glejzer, 'Życie Żydów', p. 54.
[44] At the end of the sixteenth century Rabbi Józef Kac noted in Szejrit Jozef that he was asked to settle a conflict which broke out over a marriage not taking place. The bride's father from Kraków did not bring his daughter to a wedding in Prague, where her fiancé waited. The fiancé's father claimed compensation, yet the bride's father managed to prove that on that day he was summoned before the *voivode*'s court and was threatened with a prison sentence, should he not show up. In such a situation

A practice which was seen as threatening family stability was the purely formal marriage. It seems that this was regularly done within rich families.[45] Salomon Luria confirms that the marriage was fulfilled when the boy declared to the girl: 'I want you for my spouse', and when she accepted a present, even without her parents' consent.[46] Communal bodies fought against this practice on the grounds that it questioned the principle of parental authority.

Marriages were arranged through matchmakers, whose statutory fees were fixed by the 1583 Tyszowce Jewish Diet. The regulation was incorporated into the statute of the Kraków community in 1595 and later, in 1623, by the Jewish Diet of the Great Duchy of Lithuania.[47] Merchants' families arranged marriages at the Lublin and Jarosław fairs.

Tax was levied on weddings, which the families concerned paid to the community. They were often so lavish as to cause Christian resentment, as happened in Lwów in 1639.[48] The increasing ability to display lavishness is an important indication of the growing distinction between rich and poor among Polish Jewry.

Examining marriage means also examining the social status of Jewish women in the sixteenth and seventeenth century in Polish society. Women at that time did not have equality with men, either on a legal or a practical footing, and they suffered from specific discrimination. The 1595 Kraków statute prevented women from having access to the synagogue, exceptions being made for women guests for a short period of time, as well as for girls and daughters-in-law during the year of their weddings. *Gabaim* (beadles) were charged with the control of women's access to the place of worship.[49] A merchant's wife was allowed to help or take her

---

Kac put the Christian–Jewish relations before those between the members of the community, and released the girl's father from paying a fine. Cf. Responsa no. 72 quoted by Glejzer, 'Życie Żydów', p. 54.

[45] Ibid., p. 64.
[46] S. Luria, *Maharshal*, no. 21.
[47] Matchmakers acquired 2.5 per cent of the dowry paid in gold and silver, and 1.25 per cent of that paid in goods or pearls. The percentage rose to 3 per cent if fiancées lived more than 10 miles away from one another. Cf. Bałaban, *Historia Żydów w Krakowie*, pp. 433, 434; idem, 'Krakauer Judengemeindeordnung', § 82.
[48] Bałaban, *Żydzi lwowscy*, p. 532. Bałaban also quotes the case of the wedding of Jakub Rufel from Kamieniec, who on the 14 October 1630 spent 33 Polish złoty 15 groszy on fish alone: Bałaban, 'Obyczajowość', p. 360.
[49] Bałaban, 'Krakauer Judengemeindeordnung', § 67, p. 39b.

husband's place in his absence but not to make any decisions.[50]

A rich woman was judged to be so dangerous and provocative that the 1595 statute contained a specific ban: 'In the Jewish quarter, women can wear silver-and gold-decorated garments, but not outside. This prohibition also includes corsets and collars decorated with silver and gold, and lace decoration on lingerie.' Certain exceptions to these prohibitions were made in favour of fianceés one week before their engagement, one week before the wedding, and thirty days after it.[51] It is to be understood that a woman would have been admired for only a short period of her life; later she would have been a diligent wife, with coquetry forbidden. Yet as time went by and she grew older, tradition permitted her to wear modest ornaments within the community. In the same spirit of modesty, the 1595 Kraków statute forbade women supervising expectant mothers to play cards and dice.[52]

The fiancée's father transferred dowry to the future husband and also, according to Jewish custom, gave his daughter some money for her needs. The custom of giving half a male's portion (*shtar chatsi zachar*) was based on the fact that a daughter could not inherit from her father.[53] In Kraków, poor girls received their dowry from the *kehilla*, although a ruling in 1627 forbade collections to be taken on their behalf.[54] In 1623 the Jewish Diet of Lithuania fixed the maximum dowry from the community to poor girls at 40 Polish złoty; in 1628 this sum was lowered to 25 Polish złoty.[55] By way of charity, rich merchants often provided poor girls with a dowry, as did the General Senior of the Ruthenian Lands, Marek Izaakowicz, at the beginning of the seventeenth century.[56]

---

[50] Examples of merchants' wives acting on order of their husbands may be multiplied. Let me but recall an example of Bella, wife of a Kraków Jew, Jonas Lewek, who in the year 1633 had to find two witnesses to prove that her husband obliged her to take merchandise from Mr Ważnik (Acta *Consularia Crac.*, 465, pp. 397, 398).

[51] M. Bałaban, 'Umysłowość i moralność żydostwa polskiego' (Mentality and morality of Polish Jewry), in *Kultura staropolska*, Kraków, 1932, p. 631; idem, 'Obyczajowość', p. 352.

[52] Bałaban, 'Obyczajowość', pp. 352, 353, 354.

[53] Glejzer, 'Zycie Żydów' p. 57.

[54] Bałaban, *Historia Żydów w Krakowie*, p. 356.

[55] Bałaban, 'Obyczajowość', p. 356.

[56] Bałaban, *Żydzi lwowscy*, pp. 65–6. The custom of providing poor girls with a dowry was known all over Europe. Examples from Lyons are given by N. Z. Davis, *Les Cultures du peuple*, Paris, 1979, p. 82.

According to tradition, a daughter did not inherit from her father. But this practice was changed by the steep increase in bankruptcies. In 1624 the Jewish Ruthenian Dietine decided that girls should inherit a part of their father's estate in proportion to the amount of their dowry.[57] It was the problem of increasing bankruptcies which made the Council of the Four Lands revise the inheritance laws in 1624. On the one hand, the children and wife of a bankrupt merchant were to be taken care of by their family; on the other, documents signed by a married woman less than two years before the bankruptcy were invalid and their debts were annulled as worthless.[58] The principles became clear as the number of such cases grew. In 1644 the Council of the Four Lands decided that the widow of a bankrupt merchant had absolute priority in claiming her dowry over other creditors. If she had been a widow at the time of her marriage, she was entitled to 150 florins; if she had been unmarried, she had a right to 300 florins. It was, in effect, an insurance system.[59]

Women had considerable financial rights. If a woman became widowed and no bankruptcy was involved, she inherited from her husband, either as sole heir or as life tenant. In the case of separation or divorce of couples, the husband had to pay his wife compensation – the *Ktuba*[60] – as repayment for her dowry. This compensation varied according to region. Rabbi Majer of Lublin thought that the laws of the place of residence, not of marriage, were applicable.[61] The very high rate of compensation leads to the assumption that cases of divorce were extremely rare.

Remarriage after the loss of a husband was very common.[62] As Hannover points out, consent for a second marriage was often granted after the wars of the second half of the seventeenth

---

[57] With a dowry of 200 Polish złoty a woman could be given 200 złoty, with a dowry of 400 to 1000 Polish złoty, she received 600; with 1000 to 1500, a sum of 1000 or more, over 1500 they received 2000 Polish złoty. Bałaban, *Żydzi lwowscy*, p. 543.
[58] Ibid., p. 424–5.
[59] Ibid., pp. 30–302. It should be stressed, that fragments of Zygmunt III's decree of 27 May 1592 are to be found in those texts.
[60] Glejzer, 'Życie Żydów', p. 59.
[61] Majer of Lublin, *Response Mhaharam*, no. 45.
[62] The Jewess Jota, daughter of Moshe from Poznań, was allowed to marry 14 years after she lost her husband. She married the Jew Beniasz (*Acta Consularia Posn*. 33, p. 1015^v.).

century with the aim of enlarging the Jewish population.[63] The general picture of the Jewish woman is that of a good wife and mother looking after the family business, which she could run though she had to refrain from making any major decisions. In conforming to this pattern, she fulfilled the demands of her community, to which her children belonged. She was therefore entitled to respect which could take the shape of financial compensation in the case of divorce.

The coherence of the community was shown by the solidarity of its members, manifested as charity to the poor and help for widows and orphans. The sources for this attitude can be traced back to at least two places in the Bible, in Leviticus and Deuteronomy.[64]

The sixteenth-century Polish moralist Mordekchay Jaffe reformulated traditional ideas in his commentaries on the *Shulhan Arukh* in very practical terms:

> Make your charity match your income. You shall not be of an obdurate heart, you shall not close your mind so as not to help your brother. Israel may not have been founded on charity but charity alone can keep it alive. Do not be so selfish as to say, Why should I lose my month in giving it to the poor? Remember that the fortune you acquire is not really intended for you; you are only its depository and you should use it according to the will of the depositor, who is none other than God.[65]

Well-known cases of rich and philanthropic merchants are Marek Izaakowicz from Lwów,[66] Moses Jakubowicz[67] and David Teodor Kożuchowski from Kraków.[68] Charitable institutions also existed in the communities apart from individual initiatives, particularly in

---

[63] N. Hannover, *Jevein metsula*, trans. M. Bałaban, Lwów, 1913, p. 62. (See ch. 9, n. 87 for full details.)

[64] 'When reaping the harvest in your field, if you have overlooked a sheaf in that field, do not go back for it. Leave it for the stranger, the orphan and the widow, so that Yahweh, your God may bless you in all your undertakings', Deuteronomy, 24:19; Cf. also Leviticus, 19:9.

[65] Karo, *Shulkhan Aruch*, pp. 693–707.

[66] Bałaban, *Żydzi lwowscy*, p. 65.

[67] These foundations caused trouble for Moses, as they brought the Kazimierz *kehilla*'s anger on him. The text of the 1595 Kraków statute stated that the *kehilla* had at its disposal places in private foundations. A conciliation between parties took place in 1615. (See Bałaban, *Historia Żydów w Krakowie*, pp. 415–16, 453.) Moses, so it seems, did not act without personal interest, as he wanted to broaden his influence through the foundation.

[68] A. G. Z., *Varia 12*, pp. 1586–98.

Ostróg for the purpose of buying out captives and welcoming travellers,[69] in Poznań[70] and in Kraków[71] for maintaining a hospital.

Mordekchay Jaffe wrote in *Levukh*: 'Misfortune is like a wheel turning through the world; it can reach you – you or your descendants – and cause them to find themselves in a miserable situation, asking help from those who asked it from you today.' In any case, this author considers the ransoming of captives as being the highest *tsedaka* (charity): 'This duty comes before that of feeding the hungry or clothing the naked.[72] Giving aid in time of need was often the task of close relatives. Thus, in a bankruptcy, families were supposed to look after the unfortunate man's wife and children.[73] In making provision for their children's upbringing after their death, merchants appointed guardians for their children. If this was not done, the community administered the estate, transferring it to its treasury and paying interest every two years, and appointing guardians who were supervised by an annual commission.[74] Normally, the guardians chosen were close relatives or business associates, often with a view to clearing up unfinished commercial transactions.[75]

The *raison d'être* of the Jewish communities lay in their religious identity, which should be fully studied in its material and moral aspects. A synagogue was essential for members of the community to meet and hold services. Nevertheless, the construction of a synagogue was not an easy task. The 1542 Piotrków Synod of the Catholic Church pronounced that Jews could not build any new places of worship (prayer houses) but only renovate old ones.[76]

---

[69] The 1613 regulation printed by Wettstein, Kadmoniyot mipinkasiyot yeshenim; Cf. Teimanas, *L'autonomie*, p. 129.

[70] *Acta Advocatialia Posn.* I, 385, pp. 399ᵛ–400.

[71] Bałaban, *Historia Żydów w Krakowie*, pp. 145, 464; idem, 'Obyczajowość', p. 369.

[72] Karo, *Szulkhan Arukh*, pp. 694, 702.

[73] Bałaban, *Żydzi lwowscy*, pp. 424, 425.

[74] In Kraków the rate was 15 per cent up to 400 złoty, and 10 per cent above that sum. See Bałaban, 'Obyczajowość', p. 357.

[75] In Poznań I came across the case of Ząbella, the governor of the children of the deceased Międzywiedz. He defended their case in Gniezno in 1596. (*Acta Advocatialia Posn.* I, 386, pp. 436, 465ᵛ). In 1605 Moises Kalisz and Giecz Naumberek administered and sold goods of the inheritors of Lipman Lazar, who died (*Acta Advocatialia Posn.* 391, pp. 633–4). Similarly in 1625 Michał Lewek and Simon Szavla directed the interests of the dead Lewek Efraim's children (*A. A. Posn.* 398, p. 5).

[76] B. Ulanowski, *Materiały do historii ustawodawstwa synodalnego w Polsce w XVI w.* (Materials for the history of the Synodal legislation in sixteenth-century Poland), Kraków, 1895, IX, pp. 67–8.

The 1589 Gniezno Synod complained that: 'Jews in the royal towns have synagogues and houses, which are finer and more numerous than the churches and houses of Christians. There is need for the King to act fast to rectify the matter.[77] The confirmation of the General Privileges did not alter the position, which was subject to local variation. But one can be fairly certain that the Jewish communities wielded considerable influence at the turn of the sixteenth and seventeenth centuries, as this was the period when numerous prayer houses were built.

The scarcity of sources makes it impossible to discover the full value of Jewish merchants' donations to the synagogues. But it is known, for example, that in 1581 Isaac Nachmanowicz had a synagogue constructed at his own cost in Lwów,[78] and that in Kraków Wolf Bocian followed suit in 1620,[79] and Isaac Jakubowicz in 1638.[80] One might ask whether this use of their money was to satisfy their religious aspirations or merely a desire for ostentatious generosity.

Was this piety on the part of a few rich individuals shared by all Jews? To answer this question clearly, one must study the religious attitudes of the time. It seems that participation in services was motivated more by a desire to shine in public than by profound faith. Mordekchay Jaffe mentions in one of his answers (*responsa*) at the end of the sixteenth century that the elders had to wear their prayer costumes (during services) which consisted of a knee-length coat open at the front.[81] The same author mentions that in reciting *kaddish* (the prayer for the dead), members of the community had priority over guests in reading the passage even if the latter were members of the dead man's family.[82]

Mordekhay Jaffe justifies the privileges accorded to the rich, on account of the charitable use of their money,[83] yet even he has to admit that, in some communities, priority could have been given to betrothed men one week before their wedding (*anruf*), to the fathers of newborn children or to boys on the day of their confirmation (*barmitzvah*), if the wealthier members had agreed to

---

[77] Bałaban, *Żydzi lwowscy*, p. 54.
[78] Ibid., pp. 52, 53, 57 and Ulanowski, *Materiały*, p. 20.
[79] Bałaban, *Historia Żydów w Krakowie*, p. 413.
[80] Ibid., pp. 261, 412.
[81] Jaffe, *Levukh Hatkheylet* § 86; Cf. Glejzer, 'Życie Żydów'. p. 34.
[82] Jaffe, *Levukh Hatkheylet*, § 133, art. 11.
[83] Ibid., § 141, art. 2.

cede their places.⁸⁴ Mordekhay concludes that these changes took place at the beginning of the seventeenth century. If previously a synagogue seat was a sign of respectability in the community, now unfortunately they were being sold.⁸⁵ Indeed, the practice of buying seats, backed by a deed of sale, became common. The 1595 Kraków statute instituted a twice-yearly sale of honours in the synagogue, at Passover and New Year.⁸⁶

These sales, even if their introduction was due to a shortage of funds, inevitably contributed towards a decline in faith and religious practice. At the end of the sixteenth century, Luria regretted that: 'The number of people who know Talmud decreases more and more and . . . if one finds a good Talmudist, his actions do not go together with his knowledge . . . He cares not for the knowledge for its own sake but treats it as a tool for his mental development.'⁸⁷

In 1623, the Lithuanian *pinkas* (records) indicate, more modestly, that one should 'limit the number of songs at services, to diminish the number of secular ones'.⁸⁸ In a more general way, Efraim of Łęczyca complains about his co-religionists: 'You are at the synagogue, but your hearts are in the street, and you disturb the service endlessly; you are the butt of Christian ridicule.'⁸⁹ The Lublin prayer in memory of those murdered in the massacres of 1648 and 1656 was followed by a blessing for 'those who did not talk during the prayer, for those who spend their time studying the Torah, and for the benefactors of the community'.⁹⁰

The decline in Jewish religious fervour throughout the sixteenth and seventeenth centuries did not, however, express itself in a wave of conversions. Although there were some cases of apostasy, none of the individuals concerned was ennobled; they merely acquired citizens' rights.⁹¹ The community preserved the cohesion of the group more for economic than for religious reasons. But as Maurycy Horn observes, the Jewish communities of Eastern Poland did contribute to conversion by rejecting the poor of their communities during the Cossack persecutions.⁹² One should

---

⁸⁴ Ibid., § 202, art. 7.
⁸⁵ Ibid., § 150.
⁸⁶ Bałaban, 'Krakauer Judengemeindeordnung', § 67, p. 79; idem, *Historia Żydów w Krakowie*, p. 414.
⁸⁷ S. Luria, *Yam shel shlomo baba kama*, ch. 8, sector 45.
⁸⁸ Glejzer, 'Życie Żydów', p. 33.
⁸⁹ Ibid., p. 29.
⁹⁰ Nissenbaum, *Lekorot hayehudim b'Lublin*, 1920, p. 84.
⁹¹ Bałaban, *Żydzi lwowscy*, p. 527.
⁹² M. Horn, *Powinności wojenne Żydów w Rzeczypospolitej w XVI i XVII w.*

therefore be extremely cautious in accepting Nathan Hannover's account, with its idyllic picture of Jewish communities insisting on their dignified acceptance of martyrdom while awaiting the Messiah.[93]

In the same spirit of justifying good through suffering, rabbi Yezayash Horowic wrote, *circa* 1630: 'Man should remember that his place is not in this world, but in heaven from where his soul comes . . . In pleasure man should remember evil, in his riches, poverty.' In writing these verses, Horowic had in mind the horrors of the Kraków and Wilno pogroms, which reinforced the influence of Cabbalistic thought in Polish communities.[94] The long waiting, together with half a century of pogroms, found its inevitable conclusion in the coming of the Messiah. So when news spread in Poland of Shabatai Tsvi being proclaimed Messiah in the East, the propaganda in his favour, deftly directed by his 'prophet', Nathan of Gaza, gained him the support of the Jewish community in Europe and the Maghreb, as Jacob Sasportas's *Sisat-Nobel-Tsvi* testifies.[95] The movement became so widespread that in May 1666 King Jan Kazimierz threatened that 'every person who claims to announce the Messiah shall have his goods seized'.[96] Not until 1670 did the representatives of the Jewish community, gathered in Lublin, decide to condemn publicly Tsvi's deception.[97]

Religious evolution, moving slowly along two divergent paths, was hastened by the Cossack massacres and finally came to the parting of the ways for the Jewish communities. On the one hand, some wanted to reassert community ties by erasing the distinction between rich and the poor in the mystic Hasidic movement, which harked back to the old movements born in Germany. On the other hand, a less numerous, essentially rich, group detached itself from Judaism, partly because being Jewish was a hindrance to its economic activities. Such groups found themselves at the beginning of the eighteenth century in the Frankist movement, which led them to convert to Christianity.

The ghetto, the living quarters, their furnishings, the education system and religious practices: these form the quantifiable back-

(Military services of Jews in the Commonwealth in the sixteenth and seventeenth centuries), Warsaw, 1978, pp. 132, 169.

[93] N. Hannover, *Yevein metsula*, pp. 73, 76, 77.
[94] Y. Horowic, *Shney Lukhot*.
[95] G. Scholem, *Sabbataj Cwi, Le Messie mystique*, Paris, 1983.
[96] Jews were, among others, accused of stirring up demonstrations.
[97] M. Bałaban, 'Mistyka i myśl żydowska', p. 10.

ground to domestic life, which we have tried to recreate for the Jews of the Vasas' Poland. These elements do not exhaust the topic,[98] and the study of private life, its material framework, its vision of this and the next world, and its modes of conduct, can and should be continued. This work is essential for relating major world events, whether political or economic, to individual experience. Luckily, we are in possession of the abandoned sources embedded in the *Rabbinical Responsa* (*Sh'ailot u'Tshuvot*) which because of their linguistic difficulties have scarcely been researched. The texts are in rabbinic Hebrew and Aramaic, and a sound knowledge of rabbinic methods of commentary is also required. But the richness of these sources merits the combined efforts of historians, philosophers, theologians and linguists.

If, for example, one examines the *Tsemakh Tsedek* of Rabbi Mendel M. Krochmal, who lived in Lublin in the seventeenth century, which was published in 1675 in Amsterdam, one finds 128 questions.[99] Of these, 40 concern the family (31.3 per cent), 31 problems of food purity (24.3 per cent), 20 are concerned with work and economic relations (15.7 per cent), 11 with community life (8.5 per cent), 10 with religious practice (8.5 per cent), 8 with civil and criminal law cases (6.2 per cent) and the same number refer to ancient customs.

Rabbinic *responsa* have been subjected to computer analysis at the University of Bar Ilan in Israel: they come from 248 collections, which is about a quarter of all this sort of work ever published in the world. I have personally researched the *responsa* of the Polish rabbis. Without claiming to have exhausted the subject, I have found twelve collections of authors born in the sixteenth century, and seven from authors born in the seventeenth century.[100] One

---

[98] Cf. D. Tollet, *Marchands et hommes d'affairs juifs dans la Pologne des Wasa (1588–1668)*, Paris, Economica (in press).
[99] A. Cohen, 'Problematique des responsa en Pologne au XVIIe siècle, a travers le recueil du Tsemah Tsedek', paper presented in June 1986 at the University of Paris IV – Sorbonne.
[100] The authors of rabbis' *responsa* in Poland: Salomon B. Luria (1510–74), Józef Katz (1510–91), Moses ben Isserles (1525–72), Mordekchay Jaffe (1530–1612), Salomon Efraim ben Aaron of Łęczyca (1550–1619), Majer of Lublin (1558–1616), Joel Sirkes (1561–1640), Yom Tov Lipman Heller (1579–1654), Issacher Dov ben Israel Lazar (1570–1623), Abraham Rapaport (1584–1651), Jozue Falk Kohen (1592–1615), Jozue ben Isaak Halevi (+1590), Mendel Krochmal (1600–46), Aaron Samuel ben Israel Kajdonover (1614–48), Tsvi Hirsh ben Jakob Aszkenazi (1660–1718), Meir Eisenstadt (1670–1744), Moses Rywkes (+1671), Hirsz of Kiejdanower and Samuel of Międzyrzecz.

of the aims of the research group working on Rabbinic Responsa at the University of Paris IV – Sorbonne is to contribute towards the better understanding of Jewish domestic life in Poland and other countries through the study of these *Sh'ailot u'Tshuvot*.

5 · Jews and Armenians in the Polish-Lithuanian Commonwealth in the Sixteenth and Seventeenth Centuries

Krystyn Matwijowski

The relationship between Jews and Armenians in the Nobles' Commonwealth has not, so far, awakened the interest of historians,[1] although one can come across this subject in some scholarly dissertations. In this situation, I concentrate rather on the research that has already been done on the past of each nationality.

Armenian history is one of those subjects that have been particularly neglected in the last forty years in Poland. This fact was recently alluded to by the doyen of Polish historians in this field, Professor Juliusz Bardach, who, at the same time, pointed to some extremely interesting achievements by Armenian scholars.[2] Yet some of their works, despite their through research, based on original sources, have aroused criticism, particularly because of their over-emphasis on class conflict, thus creating a false image of Polish-Armenian relations. For example, according to an Armenian scholar, the period of the conflict with the Cossacks which culminated in Chmielnicki's Revolt saw the Poles standing alone against the Ruthenians, Armenians and representatives of the other nationalities oppressed by them.[3] This is a reproach which should

---

[1] Among the few, one can note L. Streit, *Ormianie a Żydzi w Stanisławowie, Szkic historyczny* (Armenians and Jews in Stanisławów: a historical sketch), Stanisławów, 1936.
[2] J. Bardach, *Ormianie na ziemiach dawnej Polski. Przegląd badań* (Armenians on the territory of old Poland: review of research). KH: R. XC: 1983, 1.
[3] B. R. Grigorian, *Istoria armianskich kolonii Ukrainy i Polshi. Armianie w Podolii* (History of Armenian settlements in Ukraine and Poland. Armenians in Podolia), Yerevan, 1980. A particularly over-simplified image is presented in the introductory chapter, which supplies the background to the whole dissertation.

not be levelled against the leading Polish historian of the history of Armenians in Poland, especially in the town of Zamość, Professor Zakrzewska-Dubas.[4] There are various reasons for the post-war neglect of Armenian history: the language barrier, the weakening, after the Second World War II of the Armenian community in Poland, the paucity of sources in Polish archives and, above all, the difficulties in reaching sources outside Poland. Nor did the distinct lack of interest of the state, by far the biggest patron of research work in Poland, fail to have its effect; the state did not want historians to concentrate on the history of the Polish Commonwealth's eastern borderlands.

Let us now take a look at the works on the history of the Jews in Poland. On many points the situation is analogous and goes further, as we owe the basis of our knowledge of Armenians and Jews alike to the scholars and amateur historians of both nationalities, including the Reverend Sadok Barącz and Professor Majer Bałaban. The debt of Polish historiography to these men would have been even greater but for the activity of the Jewish Historical Institute.

In relation to Jewish-Armenian links, the most important works are those of Maurycy and Elżbieta Horn.[5] It is they who have

---

[4] M. Zakrzewska-Dubas, *Ormianie zamojscy i ich rola w wymianie handlowej między Polską a Wschodem* (Zamość Armenians and their role in the trade exchange between Poland and the east), Lublin, 1965; idem, *Historia Armenii* (A history of Armenia), Wrocław, 1977; idem, *Ormianie w dawnej Polsce* (Armenians in old Poland), Lublin, 1980. Earlier some aspects of Armenian history have been investigated by B. Baranowski, who published, among others: *Stosunki polsko-tatarskie w latach 1632–1648* (Polish-Tartar relations in the years 1632–1648), Łódź, 1949; idem *Znajomość Wschodu w dawnej Polsce do XVIII w.* (Knowledge about the east in Old Poland to the eighteenth century), Łódź, 1950; idem,'Ormianie w służbie dyplomatycznej Rzeczypospolitej', (Armenians in the Commonwealth's diplomatic service), *Myśl karaimska* 1 (1945–6); I do not mention here the works of scholars undertaking oriental studies and later synthesizing works; the first have been discussed by M. Zakrzewska-Dubas, *Ormanie zamojscy*, and recently in the work of J. Galustian, *Kulturnaya zhizn armianskich kolonii srednovievkovy Polshi, XVI–XVII w.* (Cultural life of Armenians in medieval Poland in the sixteenth and seventeenth centuries), Yerevan, 1981.

[5] M. Horn, *Powinności wojenne Żydów w Rzeczypospolitej w XVI i XVII w.* (Military service of Jews in the Commonwealth in the sixteenth and seventeenth centuries), Warsaw, 1978; idem, *Żydzi na Rusi Czerwonej w XVI w. i pierwszej połowie XVII w.* (Jews in Red Ruthenia in the sixteenth and first half of the seventeenth centuries), Warsaw, 1975; E. Horn, 'Położenie prawno-ekonomiczne Żydów w miastach na ziemi halickiej na przełomie XVI i XVII w.' (Legal and economic status of Jews in towns of Halicz Land at the turn of the sixteenth and seventeenth centuries), *BŻIH* 40 (1961), pp. 3–36; M. Horn in his work *Żydzi na Rusi* has presented the state of research, and named the most important works about Jews in the east, including the works of M. Bałaban, M. Schorr, J. Morgensztern, M. Kremer and his own.

broadened and increased our knowledge of relations in the eastern borderlands. Living in Lwów until the 1950s, they were able to find and make use of sources which are almost inaccessible for Polish scholars. This does not mean that the topic was completely neglected in Poland. It was probably discussed in many postgraduate seminars, where quite a number of articles may have been written, only to be put away into archives.[6]

As already mentioned, the eastern borderlands of the Nobles' Commonwealth constitute our prime concern. This is where the Armenians settled and where there were also considerable Jewish centres. The population of the two groups differed in size, with far fewer Armenians. Professor Zakrzewska-Dubas has avoided firm judgements on their numbers, confining herself to repeating the estimates found in historical literature. She did firmly reject the view of the Reverend Sadok Barącz, who argued that, from the beginning of their colonization, there were tens of thousands of Armenians in Poland. At the same time, she cites Zachariasiewicz, who estimated their number as 6,000, and a missionary, Galan, who in the seventeenth century counted the community at 3,000.[7] Although there is a tendency to increase these estimates, it seems to me that, until more detailed calculations are made, we should accept the size of the Armenian population as being around 6,000. Such data should be set alongside the newer and more convincing calculations made by Maurycy Horn, who estimates the Jewish population of Ruthenia at about 54,000 – approximately 10 per cent of Poland's Jewish population. Armenians constituted about the same percentage of the Jewish population in that area. Even assuming a very high Armenian birth rate, if we take into account their later movements, they are unlikely to have changed their numbers relative to the Jewish population which, according to Horn, about tripled within a century.[8] The size of both groups must surely have had some influence on the role of each of them in the various centres as well as on mutual relations, although other factors were also significant.[9] Strong influence worked in both

---

[6] See, for instance, the works of Professor Z. Kwaśny from Wrocław University, which are based on dietine sources, as well as those dealing with demographic problems.
[7] Zakrzewska-Dubas, *Ormianie w dawnej Polsce*, p. 42.
[8] Horn, *Żydzi na Rusi*, pp. 42–75.
[9] As examples, one can cite such qualities as readiness to expand, and adaptability to changing circumstances.

directions, strengthening both groups, but also evoking reactions from other nationalities.

On that score, both groups had almost identical experiences, albeit in different periods. Professor L. Charewiczowa, a good though not entirely unbiased scholar and local historian of Lwów, made this point in the 1930s. She explained how the growing importance of the Armenians in Lwów during the sixteenth century led to the combined opposition of all the other nationalities. The result was that, despite the favourable attitude of the Crown, the Armenians were prevented from expanding their presence. The trouble started when they wanted to buy two new market stalls. The gap created when they did not get them was filled by the expanding Jewish population.[10]

The situation in the second half of the seventeenth century in the town of Stanisławów may serve as another example. After the fall of the fortress of Kamieniec, a number of Armenians moved to the town in several waves, grew in number and, with the backing of the owner of town, Jędrzej Potocki, and later of the king, Jan III Sobieski, tried to eliminate Jewish competition.[11]

This brings us to the problem of the attitude of the government towards both groups. Documents illustrating the attitude of Polish rulers towards Armenians have been compiled several times. Just before the Second World War, Professor L. Matwijowski concentrated on sources which regulated the functioning of the Armenian communities.[12] Professor Zakrzewska-Dubas has recently tackled the subject of the protective edicts concerning Armenians, stressing their number and variety in relation to their small number in Poland.[13] Similarly, the documentation illustrating the attitude of Polish monarchs towards Jews has been described a number of times. Perhaps the most complete presentation is that in Bałaban's work on the Jews of Lwów.[14]

There is no disguising the fact that most of these documents owe their existence to the skilful influence of Armenians and Jews on

---

[10] M. Charewiczowa, *Handel średniowiecznego Lwowa* (Trade in medieval Lwów), Lwów, 1925, pp. 115 and notes.

[11] C. Chowaniec, *Ormianie w Stanisławowie w XVII i XVIII w.* (Armenians in Stanisławów in the seventeenth and eighteenth centuries), Stanisławów, 1928.

[12] L. Matwijowski, *Prawo ormiańskie w dawnej Polsce* (Armenian law in Old Poland), Lwów, 1939, pp. 10–16.

[13] Zakrzewska-Dubas, *Ormianie w dawnej Polsce*, pp. 243 and notes.

[14] M. Bałaban, *Żydzi lwowscy na przełomie wieków XVI i XVII* (Lwów Jews at the turn of the sixteenth and seventeenth centuries), Lwów, 1906.

the state authorities – to put it euphemistically. After all, one had to pay to have one's privileges confirmed. One cannot escape the fact that there were laws restricting the economic privileges and autonomy of both nationalities.[15] Without going into detail, some general problems should be mentioned. Royal protection of which these privileges were an indication, was dictated mainly by economics. The authorities were interested in the growth of trade relations with the east, in which both groups actively participated. The contribution of Armenians to the development of crafts might also have been considered. After all, this was the era when fashions and even life-styles were dominated by eastern influences, and the expertise of the Armenian craftsmen could meet the needs of Polish nobles and aristocracy in this domain.[16] At the same time, one must not underestimate the role of Jewish craftsmen, especially in the production of everyday goods.[17]

The authorities were very well aware, not only of the direct benefits of the economic activity of both groups, but also of the profit they could yield to the state. Most important was the liability to taxation. It is sufficient to glance through the resolutions of the dietines even without looking into the treasury accounts, to realize how big were the sums involved.[18] In this area, Armenians, as a much smaller group, could not compete with the Jewish population.

Up to now, it seems, we have also undervalued the contribution of the two groups to the security of the state. Professor Horn's dissertation has shown us how big a role Jews played in helping to reinforce the fortifications of various towns, in defending them in case of direct threat, and also in forming, maintaining and serving in army regiments. They often distinguished themselves in the waging of military operations, for instance as Chrzanowski in the time of King Jan III Sobieski.[19] Similar examples could be cited from

---

[15] For example, a 1469 law removing the Armenian mayor in Lwów from participation in jurisdiction, L. Matwijowski, *Prawo ormiańskie*, p. 25.
[16] Recently this matter has been investigated by J. Galustian, *Kulturnaya zhizn*, pp. 44 and notes.
[17] Horn, *Żydzi na Rusi*, 3, 'Rozwój rzemiosł' (The developing of crafts), pp. 83 and notes.
[18] For example, A. Prochaska, ed., *Akta Grodzkie i Ziemskie (AGZ)* XXI, *Lauda wiszeńskie 1648–1673*, Lwów, 1911.
[19] Horn, *Powinności wojenne*, pp. 126–7; the author quotes the case of J. S. Chrzanowski, according the opinion of King Jan III Sobieski's courtier F. Dupont; he also describes Jewish participation in ensuring the state's security.

works on Armenian history, although they have received less attention.[20]

In addition, many representatives of both nationalities, especially Armenians, supplied extremely important information, which was not only confined to reconnaissance work. Finally, we can point to the loyalty of Armenians and Jews at the most difficult moments of Polish history, for example, during Bogdan Chmielnicki's Revolt. Let us recall the participation of Jews in the defence of Lwów, and the arms given to them from the town arsenal, thus showing how fully they are trusted.[21] The fact that this movement was also directed against some Jews, above all leaseholders and administrators of magnates' estates, does not diminish their role. At the same time, Armenian merchants gave unstintingly to pay ransoms.[22] Certainly members of both groups found themselves among the hostages.

This does not mean that the attitude of the state towards Armenians and Jews was unequivocally positive. Both groups had active and influential rivals and enemies. These included the representatives of the town authorities, representing the Catholic or Orthodox merchants and craftsmen as well as the church, though its role must not be overestimated. Professor Charewiczowa has noted that already during the reign of 'the most Catholic' King Zygmunt III, the Jews in Lwów were granted considerable privileges.[23] Some time earlier, a Jewish writer referred to the Polish State as 'a Mother in Israel'. On the other hand, Counter-Reformation propaganda had a very negative influence on the local community and, consequently, on the charters negotiated with the town authorities,[24] whose terms were often worse than earlier. This applied not only to Jews. Before the conclusion of the union in the 1730s, the worsening of attitudes was also felt by Armenians, from as early as the reign of King Zygmunt III. Yet, in the whole period under consideration, the situation of Armenians was obviously better than that of the Jews.

Representatives of both groups who managed to make a career

---

[20] Galustian, *Kulturnaya zhizn*, p. 27, where, among others, the author describes Armenian participation in reinforcing the Kamieniec fortifications.
[21] Horn, *Powinności wojenne*, pp. 98 and notes.
[22] They paid a ransom of 30,500 thalars, and 50 years later over 20,000. W. Łoziński, *Patrycjat i mieszczaństwo lwowskie w XVI i XVII w.* (Lwów authorities and burghers in the sixteenth and seventeenth centuries), Lwów, 1892, p. 306.
[23] Charewiczowa, *Handel Lwowa*, p. 118.
[24] Ibid, pp. 109–20.

and, for example, found themselves at court, had a much greater possibility of influencing the state authorities. There were a number of such individuals, although it would be difficult to prove they had any direct influence on the destiny of their kinsmen. We have to rely on guesswork as too few sources have survived; after all, all this happened in direct contact with the monarch and his entourage. Physicians, many of whom were Jews, clearly were in a good position to intervene with the king.[25] It might have been more difficult for lesser officials in the diplomatic service, many of whom were Armenian, especially in the field of relations with the east.[26] A very specific situation was that of bankers, among whom were found members of both groups and who, without even being close to the royal court, could influence its policy.[27]

Armenian influence was especially strong in the reign of King Jan III Sobieski, and here we come across another element, the role of state policy itself or, in an even broader sense, the effect of international events on the monarch's attitude. In this specific case, the Polish ruler, having withdrawn from his pro-French policy, devised plans for a broad anti-Turkish league with Persian co-operation. This led to the growth of Armenian influence, as they could have been very useful in the realization of the king's projects. In older historical literature, we even come across assertions that the king attempted to re-establish the Armenian kingdom, but it seems that this idea never went beyond the stage of being suggested through diplomatic channels.[28] Although King Sobieski's plans remained unrealized, this trend in foreign policy led to the presence of Armenians in the king's entourage to whom the monarch showed favours.[29]

Jews and Armenians could also, frequently, expect goodwill from Polish magnates and officials of high rank. This they acquired in the same way as they did the monarch's. After all, apart from trade, their principal occupation was lending money at interest, while the nobles were apt to suffer from chronic lack of funds. The tried and tested method of giving presents was also employed. Let us give a

---

[25] For example, the Jew Jonas, see Z. Wójcik, *Jan III Sobieski*, Warsaw, 1983, pp. 396, 483.
[26] Z. Wójcik, *Historia dyplomacji polskiej* (A history of Polish diplomacy) II, Warsaw, 1982, pp. 234, 275, 313; Łoziński, *Patrycjat*, p. 281; Baranowski, 'Ormianie w służbie'.
[27] K. A. Bernatowicz and S. Barącz, *Zarys dziejów ormiańskich* (Sketch of Armenian history), Tarnopol, 1869, p. 65.
[28] Ibid., p. 68.
[29] Chowaniec, *Ormianie w Stanisławowie*, Zakrzewska-Dubas, *Ormianie w dawnej Polsce*, p. 29 gives examples of resolutions.

few examples. During the reign of King Zygmunt III, the Lwów Jews were granted the protection of the Lwów governor, Mikołaj Herburt.[30] In the second half of the seventeenth century, Armenians in Stanisławów could rely completely on the owner of the town, Jędrzej Potocki. It was to him they were indebted for their privileges which, as we have mentioned above, were later confirmed by King Jan III Sobieski. Later, the Potocki family backed their efforts to monopolize trade with Muntenia.[31]

Of all the factors which contributed to the situation of both groups on the eastern borderlands, the most important was their autonomy. The Armenians attached great importance to their own laws. Their aim of achieving self-government was most fully accomplished in Kamieniec Podolski and also, temporarily, in Lwów where, despite the fact that after a long struggle they lost some of their prerogatives at the expense of the town council, they retained wide autonomy in the economic sphere. Some court cases were handled by their own jurisdiction. Even in the suburbs of Lwów, although they were dependent either on the *starosta* or, in the church's jurisdiction, on the dean, they managed to retain some of their immunities.[32]

For the Jews the situation was similar, and they governed themselves through the *kehilla*. Although Armenian and Jewish forms of self-government differed in their constitution and operation, there is no doubt that these institutions promoted many measures to obtain, and subsequently maintain, immunities or other advantages. The Jewish situation was probably better, as the Jews managed to organize a central representative body.[33]

The two communities sought to influence not only the state authorities and high officials but also the lower levels of the Commonwealth's constitutional structure in an effort to gain the nobles' goodwill and consequently get their demands backed in the dietines as well as in the Diet. As an example, one could adduce the Wiszeński dietine, which passed resolutions favouring an Armenian monopoly for trade with the east, and defending the interests of Jewish merchants. These resolutions must – we can only guess – have proved expensive.[34]

---

[30] Bałaban, *Żydzi lwowscy*, pp. 24, 44, 47, 417, 473.
[31] Chowaniec, *Ormianie w Stanisławowie*.
[32] Matwijowski, *Prawo ormiańskie*, pp. 21 and notes.
[33] I. Lewin, *Z historii i tradycji. Szkice z dziejów kultury żydowskiej* (From history and tradition: sketches from Jewish cultural history), Warsaw, 1983, pp. 35–81.
[34] *AGZ* XXI, *Lauda wiszeńskie*, pp. 146 (60 & 46), 396 (208 and 107).

Lastly let us look at the problem of mutual relations. Rivalry between the two groups was, it seems, mostly felt in trade, as Jewish and Armenian craftsmen occupied different niches, Armenians producing luxury goods, while Jews concentrated on the production of everyday articles. Despite these differences, Armenians and Jews often co-operated, and one can even detect something like a division of spheres of influence. Trade with the west was in Jewish hands, and was only occasionally undertaken by an Armenian, while Jews, in turn, owing to the unfavourable attitude of the Muscovite rulers – to put it mildly – plucked up the courage to cross the borders of that state only sporadically and then under the protection of Polish monarchs. Armenians, who found their situation in Turkey difficult, used Jewish brokers there to their advantage.[35] We also come across Armenians being hired by rich Jewish merchants, or even co-operation between representatives of the two groups.[36] All this took place despite the antagonism and rivalry to which it might lead. Clashes between Armenians and Jews probably occurred mainly in Wallachia and Muntenia, as only Armenians travelled on further to Persia. However, the state of mutual relations in this area is comparatively little researched. We can find few references to this subject, which makes it an important field for future research. We know about Armenian, Jewish and Ruthenian trade, as well as that carried out by Catholics, and trade in the Nobles' Commonwealth in general; yet our knowledge of the ties and relations between the merchants of different groups is very limited.

Finally, what of the differences between the two groups? Armenians settled mainly in towns. We do not have much information about Armenian nobles, especially in the early stage of their settlement in Poland, but in more recent times, their number was still not very high. Few Armenians settled in the countryside, and only the names of some towns and villages suggest that such settlement did occur.[37] Jewish settlers were in a different situation. According to the results obtained by Professor Horn, apart from the main group that settled in towns, almost 17 per cent chose to live in the countryside, probably in surroundings linked with magnates' and nobles' estates, tenancies, and with Jewish

---

[35] Zakrzewska-Dubas, *Ormianie w dawnej Polsce*, pp. 126 and notes; idem, *Ormianie zamojscy*, pp. 103, 113.
[36] Horn, *Żydzi na Rusi*, pp. 189 and notes; Bałaban, *Żydzi lwowscy*, pp. 87, 193, 191.
[37] J. Galustian, *Kulturnaya zhizn*, p. 15.

crafts. Though often poor, this group, along with the rich townsmen, provided those Jews who were baptized and ennobled. We may assume that the fate of their kinsmen was not a matter of indifference to them.

Let us stress once more that both in the case of the Jews as of the Armenians, self-government played the most important role. It united and integrated these communities and had a twofold influence. On the one hand, it made assimilation difficult, strengthened both groups internally and defended their economic activities and position in local society. On the other hand, it defended their place in the state system and, despite the very specific features of both groups, made it easier for them to function in Polish society. The process of acculturation was much faster among Armenians who, after the union of their church with Rome, had no religious barriers separating them from the Poles. Among Jewish communities, a comparable development was only beginning to take place in recent times and the majority of the group always maintained a high degree of self-identity and separateness.

6 · The Four Years' Sejm and the Jews

Artur Eisenbach

I

Let us start, in my brief sketch of this broad topic, by recalling that the Enlightenment – a European-wide movement of ideology and culture – inspired major reforms in many countries in the second half of the eighteenth century. The conviction that society could be so organized as to give every human being the chance to lead a happy life lay at the heart of the Enlightenment's teaching. The concepts of natural and indissoluble property rights and individual freedom were proclaimed; demands were put forth for religious tolerance, free speech, judicial independence, free economic activity and wider education. Such ideas called into question the whole system of social relationships and values, by demanding equality before the law and in the obligations imposed on people.

The contemporary ideological currents and the change of political systems in Europe, particularly the reforms of enlightened absolutism in Austria and Prussia, led to several reforms in Poland as well. Some writers and activists during the reign of King Stanisław August, inspired by the principles of the Enlightenment, demanded a reform of the government and its institutions and the enforcement of state government in the fields of administration, treasury and army; they pointed to the need for universal education and complete tolerance of other religions. An atmosphere was thereby created for the initiation of a discussion about the position of the Jewish population, the need to change its legal status, its education and its place in the estate (or class) structure of the state.

II

As in other European countries, the Jewish problem arose in Poland only with the beginning of the crisis of the feudal system. Owing to the size of the Jewish population and its various economic roles, its situation became an important problem in the process of society's reconstruction, especially in economic reforms and town organization.

During the Four Years' Sejm, the Jewish population numbered about 800,000, i.e. 6.3 per cent of the total population of approximately 14 million.[1] This number alone shows the extent of the problem. In the whole of the pre-partition Polish Commonwealth, two-thirds of all Jews lived in towns and one-third in the country;[2] on Crown Lands the proportion was 73.1 per cent in town as against 26.9 per cent in the country. In economically developed Great Poland, the percentage of Jews living in the country was relatively the lowest and usually below 5 per cent. Thus a considerable correlation can be observed between the development of various Polish provinces and the urbanization of Jews and their professional structure. As a general rule, the further east we go, into an ethnically more mixed population based mainly on the *folwark* (manor) economy, the higher the percentage of Jews living in villages.

In looking at the professional structure of the Jewish population of the time, we can base ourselves on R. Mahler's research to obtain the following picture. In towns: 35–38 per cent in trade, 31–33 per cent in crafts, 13–15 per cent as *arendors* and innkeepers, 2–3 per cent in transport and 16–18 per cent in other trades. Thus, Jews predominated in domestic and foreign trade and fulfilled certain functions in other branches of the town's economic life. In the organization of crafts, there were specific differences between Jews and Christians. About 70 per cent of Jewish craftsmen worked in the textiles and haberdashery trades and 17 per cent in food; the rest comprised goldsmiths, glaziers, coppersmiths, soap-makers and others. This situation was prin-

---

[1] A. Eisenbach, 'Liczebność i elementy struktury demograficznej i zawodowej Żydów' (The demographic and professional structure of the Jews), in *Z dziejów ludności Żydowskiej w Polsce w XVIII w.* (On the history of the Jewish population in Poland in the eighteenth century), Warsaw, 1983, pp. 14–16.
[2] Ibid., pp. 17–19.

cipally the result of the guild monopoly and the restrictions on work and residence that met the Jewish population.

Among the Jews in the country, *arendors*, innkeepers and taverners made up 80 per cent, distillers, brewers and wine-makers 4 per cent; all of them, in practice, acting as extra agents in the nobles' tavern monopoly. They would also buy farm crops and supply villages with 'industrial' products, trading between town and country. Jews were also factors, collecting various payments for others; they organized wood-cutting, exported farm produce and wood, leased out mills, nurseries, distilleries and breweries. The number of Jewish servants, both domestic and in businesses, Jewish farmhands and wagoners was again fairly high. In the free trades, Jews were found as doctors, teachers, barber-surgeons, synagogue servants, cantors, musicians and others.

Thus the Jewish population, like the other classes, was not a homogeneous community but covered a range of professional and social distinctions. The social conflicts which took place then between the poor and the *kehilla* oligarchy provide additional evidence of this situation.[3]

The legal aspect of the problem is very important to our subject, as all Polish-Jewish community affairs were governed by the law. Although Jews were free, lived principally in towns, with economic activities similar to those of Christian burghers, they were not granted the rights of that estate. The Jewish population was not in fact recognized as part of any of the existing contemporary estates. Its position was governed through the centuries by ducal and royal privileges; in practice, Jews were treated as another, separate estate.[4]

The legal distinction of Jews had serious consequences, above all for themselves. They were not granted the right of municipal citizenship, regardless of how assimilated a family or individual was. Following its feudal character, the judiciary limited Jewish legal prerogatives in court cases. Moreover, they were debarred from

---

[3] R. Mahler, *A History of Modern Jewry*, London, 1971, pp. 295–7; A. Eisenbach, 'Do kwestii walki klasowej w społeczeństwie żydowskim w Polsce w drugiej połowie XVIII w.' (On the question of class struggle in the Jewish community in Poland in the second half of the eighteenth century.), *BŻIH* 17–18, pp. 129–70, 19–20, pp. 60–113.

[4] A. Eisenbach, 'Elementy więzi stanowej społeczności żydowskiej' (Elements of class ties of the Jewish community), in *Z dziejów ludności* . . ., pp. 216–52.

many professions and all public office; they could not join any craftsmen's or traders' guild. The consequences for the state were no less serious, as the legal isolation of the Jews became institutionalized in numerous forms, thereby preventing the integration of the two groups of city population and resulting in the underdevelopment of the third estate in Poland. The class isolation of the Jewish population was also an important component in the feudal structure of Polish society before the partitions.

III

As changes in the economy of towns and *folwark* (farm) started to take place, the question of Jewish settlement in towns and villages became an important economic and social issue. Various limitations on Jewish settlement in towns had been in force in Poland over a long period of time. Most of the free (that is, royal) towns, practically all the clergy's towns and some private towns possessed royal privileges, edicts of assessor's and commissioner's courts, and resolutions of town councils. Many towns had privileges with the clause *de non tolerandis Judaeis*; others allowed them to settle only in specified districts. During the reforms of the Enlightenment, Jews were still in practice restricted to a limited, and small, number of free towns. In some towns, according to the recommendations of the 1768 Sejm, Jews entered into agreements with the town authorities, and gained limited rights to live and work, in return for an annual payment in cash or kind. The right of Jews to own property was equally limited. Only in private towns, and with the owner's consent, could Jews purchase houses and plots of land. In the country, there were laws prohibiting them from the purchase of real estate or other property.

All these issues were debated in contemporary publications, in the reports of the Sejm deputies and in the petitions of the town and craft guilds. Growing rivalry led to the spreading of rumours against the Jews: they were said to be economically harmful and cause towns to go into decline.[5] Moreover, the nobles, aiming to get rid of Jews as middlemen in their rural economy, started saying

---

[5] S. Staszic, *Przestrogi dla Polski* (Warnings for Poland), Warsaw, 1790, entitled 'Żydzi' (Jews).

that Jewish innkeepers, *arendors* and taverners were mainly responsible for peasant drunkenness, misery and ignorance. Without tackling the problems of villein service, the nobles' alcohol monopoly and tavern system, the expulsion of these particular Jews was demanded as the only way to improve the peasants' situation. Indeed, expulsion of Jews in some provinces did take place in the reign of King Stanisław August. This resulted in overcrowding in the poorer quarters of the less developed small towns. Along with the problem of the 'free people' (*ludzie luźni*), Jewish tramps and beggars appeared. Attempts were made to solve the problem by employing such people in newly established industries or by farm settlement.

IV

As fiercely clashing publications discussed which model to take as the basis for reorganizing the Jewish population in relation to the state – the Austrian, Prussian, or possibly some elements of both – an important question arose: What place in the Polish Commonwealth's estate society should be assigned to the Jewish population? Should it remain separate, outside the burghers' estate, or should it be recognized as an integral part of that estate and thus be granted its economic and even political and municipal rights?

Several years before the proceedings of the Four Years' Sejm, this problem had been discussed by an anonymous author in a pamphlet published in 1785: *Żydzi, czyli konieczna potrzeba reformowania Żydów w Rzeczypospolitej polskiej* (Jews, namely, the necessity to reform Jews in the Polish Commonwealth). Being an advocate of the doctrine of natural law, the author concentrated principally on the Jews' social position. He assumed that, apart from religious education and requirements, laws were a major factor in the shaping of an individual. He stressed the fact that Jews had not been considered as members of any of Poland's social estates. 'It was the national constitution's mistake, a defect in our legal system,' he wrote. Special taxes were enforced on Jews who had no 'citizen's title', their membership of craft guilds was made impossible, their right of residence in towns was restricted, they were called 'a foreign nation having no mother country with us'. In such a situation it was the duty of the state authorities to give Jews citizenship. 'In my opinion,' he writes, 'the middle estate, that is, the town estate, is the most appropriate for them.'

Responding to the call for economic development in towns and the state, the unknown author sought to broaden the social basis of recruitment and called for the removal of barriers to municipal citizenship. We must remember that, many years earlier, regulations on the granting of municipal rights to dissenter burghers had been modified, under pressure from the Russian and the Prussian governments. In 1768 the Sejm voted changes in the legal status of the dissenters: nobles were granted rights to various offices and could be elected as deputies to the Sejm; in 1775 burghers were granted municipal citizenship. The old limitations on Jews remained in force. The anonymous author demanded the abolition of these restrictions and the acceptance of the Jewish population into municipal citizenship. He explicitly states:

> To set Jews in the municipal estate is to grant them all freedoms and prerogatives, which our towns are proud of; it is to take them out from under any other power and put them under the government and the rule of the town authorities. In other words, to cancel all distinctions which exist between Jew and Christian in this day.[6]

This was the first call to recognize Jews as an integral part of the burghers' estate and grant them economic and political municipal rights.

The anonymous author campaigned against the current propaganda of the harm caused to the country by the Jews. This, he explained, was the result of age-old repression and yet another reason to regularize their legal status quickly. The incorporation of this group into the burghers' estate, accepting them into guilds, recruiting them to military service and, at the same time, reforming their customs and education, would change them and strengthen their links with Poland. The pamphlet struck a chord with 'enlightened' Jews,[7] while the Warsaw press, which observed the Jews' condition in other countries, and the results of their emancipation, rejected the idea of incorporating them into the burghers' estate.[8]

---

[6] A. Eisenbach, J. Michalski, E. Rostworowski and J. Woliński, eds, *Materiały do dziejów Sejmu Czteroletniego* (Sources for the history of the Four Years' Sejm), hereafter *MDSC*, Wrocław, 1969, VI, pp. 73–93.

[7] The anonymous pamphlet was translated into German by Eliasz Ackord: *Die Juden und die notwendige Reformation der Juden in der Republik Polen*, Warsaw, 1786.

[8] P. Świtkowski's article in *Pamiętnik Historyczno-Polityczny* (A historico-political diary) 5 (1785), pp. 414–23, and 1788, p. 515.

V

The Jewish question appeared during the first proceedings of the Four Years' Sejm, when questions of Jewish residence in towns and raising their poll tax came up. A sharp debate on the subject, lasting several years, which I have discussed elsewhere,[9] was conducted in the press, in other publications and in the Sejm. Here I should like just to indicate the main aspects of the matter and the views of the various parties.

Right from the start of debates in the Sejm, the community representatives and the 'enlightened' Jewish group realized the crucial relationship of the state to their own community. They presented a series of exact requirements to the Sejm and the state authorities. They knew that their emancipation was closely linked with the reform of the country' social system, which was under parliamentary debate. Generally speaking, they concentrated on efforts to obtain the following rights: residence in free towns, including the capital, unimpeded economic activity, removal of the formal barriers enforcing their isolation, and municipal citizenship. At the end of 1788, the representatives of the Warsaw Jews began presenting the monarch and the Sejm with petition after petition, recalling their historic rights and privileges granted by the Polish monarchs.[10] The debate over the condition of the whole Jewish population intensified from February 1789, as several publications appeared, discussing their economic, fiscal and educational concerns, as well as their social status. When, in the autumn of that year, the representatives of the burghers presented their political requests and their plan for a new system of municipal authority, delegates of the Jewish Crown communities arrived in Warsaw and addressed a *Pokorna prośba* (Humble Submission) to the Sejm, seeking to obtain new rights of residence in the royal towns.[11] The petition was not even read out in the Sejm.

The period between autumn 1789 and spring 1792 was a time of drastic efforts to reform Jewish status in Poland. When, on 18 December 1789, the Sejm appointed a commission to prepare a plan for free towns, it had already been agreed to abandon any idea

---

[9] A. Eisenbach, 'Sprawa żydowska w Polsce w okresie stanisławowskim' (The Jewish question during Stanisław August's reign) in *Z dziejów ludności*, p. 44.
[10] Ibid., pp. 44–5.
[11] *MDSC* VI, pp. 129–32.

of granting rights to the Jews. The Jewish population was not yet admitted to the struggle for national, political and social reform. Indeed, it was not to participate until 1848, the year of revolution. Conscious of their situation, Jewish community representatives limited their demands to the right of residence and freedom to participate in urban economic life.

VI

A special separate statute was to be issued for the Jewish population. But the law was a long time in the making. Only after the anti-Jewish riots in Warsaw in 1790 (on 22 March, 19 April and 16 May) which caused political repercussions, as the Russian and Prussian ambassadors became interested in the problem,[12] did the Sejm attempt to do something about it. On 19 June 1790, a *Deputacja do rozstrzygnięcia projektu reformy Żydów* (A Commission to Discuss a Plan for Jewish Reform) was established.[13] In August the plan was ready and even signed by the president of the Commission – Vice-Chancellor Maciej Garnysz.[14] Yet the opposition of several members of the commission ended in the plan not even being read out in the Sejm.[15]

The plan proclaimed religious tolerance, contained regulations on the organization of the Jewish communities and Jewish tax obligations, permitted Jews to undertake any trade and craft, but debarred them from selling liquor in country taverns. Thus it set down the main economic and residential rights in free towns but made no mention of Jewish rights to municipal citizenship. Jews were to bear all municipal obligations and be subject to the town authorities, but in the estate society they were placed right at the bottom. The commission aimed to establish a single rule for the Jewish population of the whole state. It was characteristic of the Enlightenment to do away with the hotchpotch of the feudal legal system, with its different applications of different laws (some of ancient standing) in different places, as in this case, and replace it

---

[12] W. Kalinka, W. Smoleński and J. Kitowicz wrote about the anti-Jewish riots and the Sejm debate; see A. Eisenbach, 'Ludność żydowska w Warszawie', (The Jewish population of Warsaw), in *Z dziejów ludności*, pp. 103–4.
[13] *MDSC* VI, p. 215, complete list of the Sejm Commission; W. Smoleński, *Ostatni rok sejmu Wielkiego*, (The last year of the Great Sejm), p. 329.
[14] *MDSC* VI, p. 215.
[15] AGAD, *Arch. Sejmu Czteroletniego* (Archive of the Four Years' Sejm), henceforth *ASC*, VIII. pp. 503, 518–19, 532–3, 546–7 – reports of various deputies.

with a single homogeneous system which would be enforced nationally. This trend was already under way in Austria and Prussia, with the patents granted to the peasants and Jews. There were similar plans under King Stanisław August to introduce a general law for the burghers and Jews, replacing the individual princely and royal privileges formerly in force in Poland.

The debate on the Jewish problem was closely followed by enlightened Jews in Poland and abroad, who soon entered the discussion. Nine publications, eight of them influenced by the Jewish Enlightenment and French Revolution, favouring the idea of reform of Jewish internal organization, were published during the Four Years' Sejm. The authors made various proposals for Jewish emancipation to the state authorities and the Sejm in the area of citizenship, reform of Jewish autonomy and educational system.[16] Their requirements testify to the wide range of social and cultural differences within the Jewish population and are evidence of newly awakened Jewish interest in the nation's political condition.

We should mention here the declaration by a group of enlightened Warsaw Jews who, in May 1790, addressed an open letter to the town delegates. It was from this group that the Jewish bourgeoisie in Poland emerged, and it was well acquainted with the preliminary middle-class concepts of human rights and freedom. The authors recall the towns' petition of December 1789, expressing appreciation of the efforts of the burghers' representatives, and hope that the natural rights which are cited in the struggle against feudalism will apply equally to the Jewish population. This group felt they had much in common with property-owning Christian citizens, if for no other reason than their common economic interests. This petition contains the first expression of the very idea of co-operation of the whole third estate which – should it become economically and politically strong enough – could stand up to the supremacy of the nobles.[17]

---

[16] These authors were A. Ackord, Zalkind Hurwitz, Mendel Lefin of Satanow (Satanower), Abraham Hirszowicz, Salomon Markuze, Szymel Wolfowicz, Jakub Kalmansohn and Salomon Polonus. I have discussed their works in *Z dziejów ludności*, pp. 62–4, 309–10.

[17] Petition reprinted in *MDSC* VI, pp. 188–90; see also Eisenbach, 'Sprawa żydowska', pp. 69–71.

VII

The Warsaw authorities had for many years waged a struggle against Jewish settlement in the capital. During the Four Years' Sejm they organized a national campaign in parliament with general publicity aimed, among other things, at preventing any concessions on Jewish settlement and citizenship.

In the second half of the eighteenth century, 80 per cent of the Christian population in all towns, especially private ones, made their living from farming, livestock and breweries. In these circumstances the Jewish community, engaged as it was in domestic and foreign trade, crafts, transport and other services, fulfilled a vital role in urban life. In the last decade of the Polish Commonwealth, the processes of urbanization, demographic growth and economic progress do appear in some provinces, but only scantily and, in general, the state remained economically and politically underdeveloped.[18] Townspeople were an estate without privileges, they were not represented in the Sejm, their powers to purchase and own land were limited, and the estate itself exercised no force in any political or economic sense.

Going back to the autumn of 1789, 300 deputies converged on Warsaw from various towns to sign an act of unification and organize the *Czarna procesja* (the Black Procession) on 25 November. They handed a long petition with the royal towns' requests to the monarch and to the marshal of the Sejm. On 18 December the Sejm formed a commission to prepare a town statute which – as stated above – had from the start decided in principle to exclude any consideration of the Jewish population's status. Indeed, every version of the planned municipal law, as prepared by the commission and Fr Piattoli, which has survived, contains a clause excluding Jews from municipal reform and the rights of this estate.[19] In the statute of 18 April and the constitution of 3 May 1791, this condition was dropped, but the first article, paragraph 10, explicitly stated that only Christians were entitled to municipal citizenship.

---

[18] J. Topolski, *Narodziny kapitalizmu w Europie w XIV–XVIII wieku* (The origins of capitalism in Europe in the fourteenth to the eighteenth centuries), Warsaw, 1965, p. 165.
[19] *MDSC* II, p. 388; III, pp. 211, 220; B. Leśnodorski, *Dzieło Sejmu Czteroletniego* (The work of the Four Years' Sejm), Wrocław, 1951, pp. 184, 197–9.

The Polish burgher estate was small in numbers, underdeveloped and preoccupied with its struggle against competitors from other religions. Additionally, the very success of Jewish enterprises led to the accusation that they brought recession to the towns and their citizens. Like most of the nobles, the leading burghers were way behind the times in their political thinking and unable to respond to the needs of the situation. For them, the best thing the Sejm could do would be to reconfirm the towns' medieval privileges. Their concern stopped short not only of the peasants' interests but also of other towns' inhabitants, since they limited their requests to free towns. They were also willing to see an intensification of Jewish isolation outside the third estate. Thus, while the struggle was going on to modify the outdated class system, the burghers' leaders could not see the pressing need to consolidate all groups of the third estate as an urgent condition of town and state development.

The burghers' political movement was not born from within its own estate but was initiated and influenced by a group of reformers from among the nobles who wanted to turn the third estate into its ally in the struggle for change in the political system. It was, after all, the vice-chancellor, Hugo Kołłątaj, who helped the towns' deputies to formulate their political programme which, in any case, had no chance of being accepted by the Sejm, given its composition and the social forces at work in Poland. The plan was in fact accepted but only on a limited scale: the burghers did not become a co-ruling estate, their representatives played no part in the legislative body, and only certain rights to obtain posts in the state administration and purchase land were granted to them. The nobles based their alliance with the burghers on the criterion of estate, not wealth: the latter was to be accepted only later in the constitutional monarchies.

Through the ennoblement of a few hundred burghers, the nobles creamed off for themselves young bourgeois – officials, lawyers, military officers. But at the same time this led to the weakening, the intellectual impoverishment, and even the demoralization of the middle classes, as it increased neither their political power nor their prestige. In fact, it had the opposite effect of reducing their interest in the estate's concerns, especially on the part of non-property owners, and weakened their struggle for the full emancipation of all burghers in the state.

VIII

The claims of the town representatives were supported by influential reformers, for example, Stanisław Staszic, one of the thinkers of the Enlightenment and a propagator of social reforms. He himself was against granting Jews municipal rights, but demanded that they be subject to the town authorities and municipal judiciary.[20] Nor did Hugo Kołłątaj, who inspired the national burghers' movement for political reform, see any possibility of granting municipal citizenship to Jews, even on a limited scale. Like Staszic, he demanded that Jews be subject to the local judiciary.[21] The opinion of the radical F. S. Jezierski did not differ much from the above, although he did admit that what were pointed to at the time as Jewish faults were really the result of the existing system.[22] In his view, only a complete reform of the social system and of aristocratic attitudes could change the condition and economic function fulfilled by Jews, thus enabling any start to be made in reforming their legal status.

In the light of the contemporary sources one can see that the majority of the nobles were conservative and opposed to any fundamental social and political change. They wanted to maintain the class separation of the Jews, and even the limitations on their right to work and trade or to settle in towns and villages. Thus they were against admitting Jews to any form of citizenship.

A different group of reforming nobles worked out liberal plans to change the status of the Jewish population. They insisted that a fundamental change in Jewish status was in the interests of the state and its development. An aristocratic deputy, M. Butrymowicz, gave the widest view of this issue in his pamphlet *Sposób uformowania Żydów polskich w pożytecznych krajowi obywateli* (A way of turning Polish Jews into citizens useful to the state).[23] The pamphlet, published in February 1789, was an altered version of the publication of the anonymous author mentioned earlier, which

---

[20] S. Staszic, *Pisma filozoficzne i społeczne* (Philosophical and Social works), Warsaw, 1954, I, pp. 298–303.
[21] H. Kołłątaj, *Listy anonima i prawo polityczne narodu polskiego* (Anonymous letters and the political rights of the Polish nation), Warsaw, 1954, II, pp. 329–33.
[22] F. S. Jezierski, *Wybór pism* (Selected works), Warsaw, 1952, p. 24.
[23] Reprinted in *MDSC* VI, pp. 79–93.

appeared in 1785. Butrymowicz demanded that the legal status and question of Jewish residence be settled and suggested setting up a Sejm commission to prepare a bill for presentation to the Sejm.

Following his own suggestion, he presented a bill for enactment to the marshal of the Sejm, a bill which was read in the Sejm on 30 November and presented to the monarch on 4 December 1789.[24] With the new situation in the state, and after the 'Black Procession' of the royal towns, Butrymowicz did not demand that Jews be included in the third estate. Yet they were to be granted economic rights in free towns and access to the guilds: they were to be subject to general administrative and court laws, and not be forced to pay any special taxes. The author refrained from proposing the recruitment of Jews to military service, explaining that this was premature.

Józef Pawlikowski, another radical, expressed similar views in an anonymously published pamphlet.[25] On the whole, he was against any class separation of Jews and proposed that they should be on an equal footing with the Polish burghers, both in economic rights and in duties – payment of taxes and military service.

The most radical idea came from T. Czacki, who worked in Warsaw in the Commission of the Crown Treasury during the proceedings of the Sejm. Probably influenced by Russian class structure, he proposed the division of the Jewish population into three classes: peasant farmers, craftsmen and merchants. Their rights and duties were to be identical with those laid down for the corresponding classes of the national population. Thus, following his proposals, Jews in towns were to obtain full citizens' rights – the right to vote, and access to all offices and honours appropriate for their class. They could then become members of guilds and fraternities, buy houses and, when farming in the country, buy land as well.[26]

The views of the castellan, J. Jezierski, are also worth looking at. When the municipal delegates opposed the regularizing of Jewish residential rights, he pointed to the economic aspect of the whole

---

[24] *Chronicle of Debates on 30 Nov. and 4 Dec. 1789, ASC* IV, p. 399; V, p. 43; *MDSC* VI, pp. 119–28.
[25] J. Pawlikowski, *Myśli polityczne dla Polski* (Political thoughts for Poland), Warsaw, 1789.
[26] This detailed plan was published only in T. Czacki's *O Żydach* (On the Jews), Wilno, 1807.

opposition. Moreover, he stressed that it was a much broader state issue and thus, when the Sejm was discussing the status of various groups of people, the Jewish position should be cleared up as well.[27]

IX

The Four Years' Sejm introduced a number of political and constitutional reforms into Poland: it strengthened the military forces and defence of the state, abolished the institution of *liberum veto*, as well as the Rada Nieustająca (Permanent Council) and the Russian guarantee, established a new form of government, reorganized the highest state authorities, especially in the educational and financial spheres, and settled the problem of royal inheritance. But the constitution of 3 May was a result of a *coup d'état*, not of a revolution, and this had serious consequences. It did not change the differences resulting from birth, nor did it make people equal before the law, but it did maintain the division into estates, thus allowing the nobility to retain all privileges and rights and the Catholic religion to remain the state religion.

In effect, no basic social changes were introduced. The Sejm voted a new organization and form of government in only in royal towns, (about 15 per cent). The political wishes of the burghers were completely disregarded and it was still only the representatives of the nobles who sat in the Sejm. The burghers did not become a partner in ruling the state, its representatives were not admitted to the 'Sejm and the legislative body'. The municipal delegates allowed to enter the Sejm had none of the rights of deputies and no access to the operations of government. The new town rights were a compromise and, as they applied only to the royal towns, they did not violate the time-honoured principle of the owner's sole authority in his hereditary estates, including municipal areas. The municipal statute retained the ban on residential town rights for Jews and this was confirmed by the Grodno Sejm in 1793. Nor did the reforms of the Four Years' Sejm bring about any basic changes in the peasants' condition. Their serfdom and villein service were retained and they were granted only the illusory 'care of law and state government'.

---

[27] *MDSC* VI, p. 492; *ASC* IX, p. 819; W. Smoleński, *Stan i sprawa żydów polskich* (Status and problem of the Polish Jews), p. 279.

X

The Jewish question was back on the Sejm's agenda in the second half of May 1791 and was the subject of quarrels and sharp conflicts over the next twelve months. On 24 May, Butrymowicz asked the Sejm to vote without further ado for the bill as presented by the commission. It was tabled.[28] On 4 June 1791, the representatives of the Jewish community from the whole country addressed a petition, Żądania Żydów (Jewish Claims), to the Sejm which included a request for wealthy Jews to be granted municipal rights in all free towns.[29] Analysis of this document shows that the idea of making these claims came from the French Jews.

In September, Jewish delegates from towns in Great Poland, Little Poland and Lithuania arrived in Warsaw, where they held a meeting with several people chosen by the monarch: Fr Piattoli, Kołłątaj, Linowski and also with the members of the Sejm commission. Having reached an agreement with the Jewish representatives, Piattoli prepared several petitions, plans for 'Jews' reform' and fiscal calculations, and he proceeded with correspondence on the subject with the monarch and others.[30] The problem was to agree upon a bill for enactment which would normalize the Jews' position, on condition that they agreed to make a substantial contribution to the king, the state treasury or even the towns. Piattoli managed to win over several influential members of the commission and prepared the final version which even gained the king's approval. Yet the project was not even discussed at the Sejm, owing to objections by the Sejm marshal Małachowski.[31] At the same time, the town representatives waged a strong campaign against any statute affecting the status of the Jewish population.

Piattoli, aware of the importance of the vice-chancellor, Kołłątaj became president of the commission, which had been increased by several deputies and even by town delegates. Yet because of the objections of the latter to all versions, no single plan was ever put forward. To make it quite clear, let us remember that the limited version of Piattoli's project was accepted by the representatives of

---

[28] *AGAD, ASC* XIX pp. 324–6: reports of Butrymowicz, Potocki, Chołoniewski; *MDSC* VI, pp. 269, 271.
[29] *MDSC* VI, pp. 276–8; various Latin *Desideria Judaeorum* have survived and were known to the deputies. See *MDSC* VI, p. 263.
[30] *MDSC* VI, pp. 347–55, 358–73.
[31] Eisenbach, 'Sprawa żydowska', pp. 82–3.

the Jewish population and had the king's assent. According to this plan, Jews were to be granted the right of residence in free towns and the right to work and trade, in return for a 5 million złoty annual payment to the monarch, the state treasury and the army.[32]

Under pressure from various sources, the next plan was prepared by the Sejm commission and a motion was tabled. This was the *Urządzenie ludności żydowskiej w całym narodzie polskim* (The settling of the Jewish population within the Polish nation),[33] which was a compromise between the strong opposition of the municipal delegates to granting Jews any municipal rights, the programme of the nobles' reforms and the Jewish struggle to gain municipal rights. According to the *Urządzenie*, Jews could settle in those free towns where they already possessed such rights by virtue of ancient privileges or agreement with the town authorities and they were also granted the right of economic activity. Wealthy Jews were granted economic municipal rights, that is, they were accepted into town councils without the right to vote.

As he wrote to the monarch in a letter of 4 April 1792, Piattoli hoped to win the support of the majority of the commission's members to read and discuss the proposed bill at the Sejm. With these hopes, the king himself asked Małachowski for 'help on 2 May, so that the marshal gives aid in the progress of this matter in the Sejm'.[34] Both Piattoli and Kołłątaj approached the marshal. The first stressed the importance of the social and the fiscal aspects of the problem, insisting that the acceptance of the statute was an important issue for both state and royal interests. The second, knowing that the bill stood little chance of being voted for in the Sejm, suggested to Małachowski that it at least be read. Should it be rejected, explained Kołłątaj, 'It will be no fault of ours.'[35] These precautions were not without reason. On 29 May, the castellan J. Jezierski brought the commission's document to the Sejm, but he was not even allowed to read it.[36] It was the last day of the parliament's proceedings.

The Jewish representatives, knowing that owing to the balance of parliamentary power, there was little chance of putting their modest claims into effect, turned first to the Commission of the Police and

---

[32] Ibid., pp. 84–7; *MDSC* VI, pp. 391–6.
[33] *MDSC* VI, pp. 492–515.
[34] Ibid., pp. 335.
[35] Ibid., pp. 336–7.
[36] W. Smoleński, *Ostatni rok Sejmu Wielkiego*, p. 406.

then to the monarch with petitions on behalf of Jews in free towns. These efforts had no obvious results.[37]

All attempts at a solution to settling the condition of Jews in the Polish Commonwealth had been rejected by the municipal representatives, backed by a majority of the noble deputies. The reforms of the Four Years' Sejm, although they did, to a certain extent, modernize the state, brought about no fundamental change in the social system; class division was not removed. There could be no discussion of political or even civil equality of the Jewish population in a society where the old estate system survived.

The political activity and the range of proposals presented by the representatives of several hundred Jewish communities during the Four Years' Sejm, and their addresses to the monarch and Chamber of Deputies on behalf of their kinsmen call for attention. Their petitions testify that despite their religious and national separation, they were absolutely convinced that, as inhabitants of Polish soil for centuries, they formed an integral part of the third estate. They thus had a legal right to the privileges of that group as well as its corresponding obligations. We can also see that the revolutionary events of France and reforms in neighbouring countries strongly affected the nature and range of the wishes expressed by the representatives of the Jewish population.

---

[37] Eisenbach, 'Sprawa żydowska', pp. 90–9, 1.

Part II

Institutions

7 · The Council of the Four Lands

Shmul Ettinger

> 'The sceptre shall not depart from Judah' – these are the Exilarchs in Babylonia . . . 'nor a lawgiver from between his feet'* – these are the descendants of Hillel who teach Torah to the people.
> (Sanhedrin [Babylonian Talmud] 5a [commenting on Genesis 49, 10])

From the time that Judah lost its political independence it became one of the supreme aims of the Jews, wherever they were, to attain autonomy, the independent conduct of communal affairs. Apart from their strong desire to preserve their collective identity, external factors also operated here: chiefly the agreement of their rulers, especially the Roman authorities, to free them from the need for state protocol and the 'registries of the Gentiles', and to permit them to live 'according to their statutes'. Thus life in accordance with the Torah became a mark of recognition of every Jewish community that went by the name of *kehilla kedoshah* (holy congregation). The important decisions of the community were entrusted to its own leadership – *nesiim* (patriarchs, presidents), exilarchs, *geonim*, sages, *parnasim* (heads of communities), *rashim* (another name for heads of communities).

The Jewish *kehilla* as a unit achieved, in practice, an appreciable measure of autonomy in its internal affairs even in its relationship with the central Jewish leadership; only fundamental questions concerning the fulfilment of the Torah and rules for internal organization remained in the hands of sages who lived in the centres of Torah, first in Erets Israel and subsequently in Babylonia, and the great majority of Jewish communities submitted

---

* As in the Authorized Version. The Onkelow Targum renders it 'and a scholar from his descendants', as does the Talmud.

to their jurisdiction. This arrangement was preserved in the East for about a thousand years after the destruction of the Second Temple, and its impress was felt there even later.

The situation was otherwise in the communities which came into existence in Europe after the fall of the Roman Empire. The character of the new communities, their economic and social function in the life of their locality, and their status in the eyes of the authorities made it necessary for the individual community to adapt itself to the conditions peculiar to its own area and, in most matters, to act independently. There were European communities which entered into arrangements for co-operation on a regional or national scale, generally as a result of changes in external conditions. Such were the assemblies of the Rhineland communities – Speyer, Worms and Mainz – in the time of the Crusades in the twelfth and thirteenth centuries and the communities of Spain at the time of the persecutions in the fourteenth and fifteenth centuries. These assemblies took decisions and passed enactments but did not establish permanent central institutions operating continuously.

The unique character of the Council of the Four Lands (and the Council of the Land of Lithuania, which resembled it in its methods of operation and was a partner and, indeed, at times a part of the Council of the Lands) lay in the fact that it created permanent central institutions, was continuously active over a period of about 200 years (from the sixteenth to the eighteenth centuries) and was accepted by the *kehillot* of Poland-Lithuania during the whole of that time as a supreme authority in communal matters. The Council of the Lands was recognized by the authorities as a Jewish representative body until its official disbandment in 1764. It retained the medieval form of assembly in which representatives of the regions (the 'lands') and *kehillot* came together in the senior institution. At the height of its success these assemblies were held twice a year. The Council also used to elect several office-bearers (*parnas* [head of the Council], *shtadlan* [who used his contacts with the authorities to defend Jewish interests], trustees) and officials who represented the Council between assemblies and preserved the continuity of its activities. No wonder, therefore, that the Council of the Lands was regarded as the greatest expression of Jewish aspirations towards self-rule since the institution of the Gaonate came to an end.

How was it that this autonomous institution, the Council, came into being? It was largely due to the conditions which prevailed in the kingdom of Poland and the ways in which the Jewish community developed in that country during the period when the Council of the Lands was taking shape. For the Jewish community in Poland, in its early days – as far back as we have information on organized Jewish communities in the thirteenth century – was similar to its neighbours in German lands. Jewish settlement in the towns of Poland took place against the background of a stream of German immigration, when German townspeople were coming to settle in the devastated land after the incursions of the Mongols. At a time when in Western Europe, in the thirteenth to the fifteenth centuries, the centralizing aims of the rulers and the rising power of the townspeople led to expulsions and the liquidation of the Jewish communities; when, at the time of the Black Death, hundreds of Jewish communities in Central Europe were destroyed, and hatred of the Jews became an appreciable factor in the culture of the Germans, who oppressed and humiliated the remaining communities – Poland became a haven for refugees from all over Europe. At the height of her power in the fifteenth and sixteenth centuries and the first half of the seventeenth century, when she greatly extended her boundaries, her waste lands, especially those in the East and the Southern steppes, needed to be peopled and developed, and the kings of Poland recognized the Jews as an important colonizing element. To these influences were added fiscal considerations and the economic aims of the nobility (the magnates), the owners of the estates (who were also the holders of the most important offices in the state). It was the combination of these circumstances which was responsible for the fact that from about twenty to thirty thousand souls at the end of the fifteenth century, Polish Jewry increased to a community of about 300,000 in the middle of the seventeenth century.

The legal status of the Jews and the organization of their community also developed, in the first place, in accordance with patterns determined in the German states: the first writ authorizing residence on Polish soil – that which was granted in 1264 by Duke Bolesław Pobożny (the Pious) of Kalisz to the Jews under his rule – differs only in a few details from the charters issued not long before by the rulers in Central Europe. Now was there a departure from the traditional patterns in the confirmation of these writs in the middle of the fourteenth century by Kazimierz III (the Great) and in the middle of the fifteenth century by Kazimierz V, the Jagiellonian, both of whom extended the measure of self-rule accorded to the

Jews. The change occurred after the revocation of the expulsion of the Jews from Lithuania, in the first years of the sixteenth century, with the accession to the Polish throne of King Zygmunt I, who sought to strengthen his authority in the face of the growing demands of the nobility and, for this purpose, to carry out some constitutional and financial reforms. The king was anxious to raise and keep at his disposal an army of mercenary soldiers. He decided to apply to this object the taxes levied on the Jews, who were regarded as 'Servants of the Treasury', which is to say, subject to his authority and under his protection. With this in view he appointed, in 1512, a number of wealthy Jews as collectors of the Jews' taxes in the regions of Little Poland, Great Poland and Lithuania, and alongside them he installed chief rabbis (*rabbanei medinah* – province rabbis) for these regions, who by virtue of their authority and with the help of threats of *herem* (excommunication) would be able to oblige the Jews to pay the taxes and obey royal orders. To that end he granted the rabbis who were appointed extensive powers in regard to internal jurisdiction and the fulfillment of the law of the Torah.

The collection of the tax was hindered by conflicts of interest within the communities (*kehillot*), and especially by the disputes between the main communities in each province and the *sevivot* – the small communities which had been organized in their vicinity – as a result of the growth of the Jewish population by natural increase and migration. These *sevivot* aspired to set up their own communal institutions (synagogue, ritual bath, cemetery, *hekdesh* [a shelter for the poor, the sick and travellers], and so on) and to free themselves from the tutelage of the principal communities in regard to both taxation and jurisdiction. For these reasons the central collection of the tax ran into difficulties, and within a short time the administration gave up the system of chief collectors it had instituted, but not the aim of centralized collection. This meant that the communities, especially the smaller ones, in the various provinces had to meet in order to reach agreement on the share to be contributed by each of them to the royal taxes. This was apparently the principal spur to the establishment of the 'councils of the districts' as a permanent institution, and to their recognition by the authorities. Moreover, at about the same time it also became a practice among the members of the Polish nobility of each region to meet from time to time to voice their requests and take decisions. It is to be supposed that these dietines (*sejmiki*) served as a model for the Jews.

The communities also opposed the chief rabbis appointed by the Crown, even when these ranked as great Torah scholars; and in the middle of the sixteenth century they acquired the right to choose rabbis in accordance with the wishes of the whole *kehilla*. In this case, too, while the institution was abolished, the purpose remained – the rabbis chosen by the communities were similarly granted by the Crown powers of jurisdiction and punishment extending to the amputation of limbs and the imposition of the death penalty on 'one who transgresses against the laws of the Torah of Moses' (though the rabbis almost never availed themselves of these powers).

The development of Polish towns and the expansion in them of trade and crafts, the bitter struggle conducted by the townspeople against the aristocracy who had deprived them of their economic and political rights, their conflict with the Jews both as competitors and as the assistants and agents of the nobility, and the action taken by the Jews (most often with the help of institutions of the Crown and the great nobles) to defend themselves against this attack – these factors together brought about a situation in which many matters involving Jews from various places were not settled within a framework established in their own locality and community but required assemblies of the members of different communities in central situations for the purpose of investigation, consultation and action. The great fairs in Lublin and Jarosław served as convenient occasions for these assemblies. We know of assemblies of rabbis at the Lublin fair going back to the 1530s, who sat in judgment there on law suits between Jews from various communities, and we are told of a 'great *bath-din*' (court) which sat at the fair in the middle of the century and was composed of representatives of the communities. There were also some general social factors which contributed to the assemblies becoming regular features at the fairs: traders came there with their wares, information of importance to the whole Jewish community in Poland was passed on, agreements were concluded there and marriages arranged between the well-to-do members of the communities and their dignitaries, and small men found an opportunity there to earn a little as brokers or middlemen.

The *pinkas* (minute book) of the Council of the Four Lands has not been preserved, and so we cannot establish with certainty how matters developed. (All reference to the debates and decisions of the Council, in so far as they were known at the time of compilation, were gathered together with great diligence by Israel Halperin, whose monumental work is the nearest substitute we have for the original *pinkas*.) However, there is no doubt that these assemblies were the genesis of the Council.

It seems, nevertheless, that the main factor responsible for the assemblies developing into a permanent arrangement and for the recognition of the Council by the authorities was the question of taxation. As early as 1549 a poll tax of one złoty a year was imposed on all the Jews of Poland, but the government lacked any administrative machinery for assessing the number of Jews or raising the tax from them. The government therefore handed over responsibility for collecting the tax to the Jews themselves, who had to apportion the tax among themselves at their assemblies. The wars waged by Lithuania in the 1560s led to increased taxation (instead of one złoty per head, a tax of several złoty was levied in one year). The Council of the Land of Lithuania was organized at that time with, at its head, 'nine heads of provinces and three rabbis, and at every Lublin fair are to sit three heads and one rabbi with them, to see to the general welfare'. And also: 'At every fair in Lublin the aforesaid heads shall choose three judges to be ready to sit in judgment, to hear the cases between their brethren [Deut. 1: 16]; they shall hear the greater and the small alike [Deut. 1: 17] and their decisions shall be binding' (literally 'according to their mouth shall a matter be established' – a further allusion to Deuteronomy). In 1579, apparently because of the difficulties in collecting the poll tax on the basis of estimated numbers, the authorities fixed the tax at an inclusive total – 10,000 złoty for Poland and 3,000 for Lithuania. It is not surprising that the first document we have testifying 'that the heads and leaders of the Four Lands agreed' dates from 1580, for it was then, apparently, that the Council was recognized by the authorities and took responsibility for the payment of the tax.

Thus it was that a complex system of Jewish self-rule, headed by the Council of the Lands, took shape in the kingdom of Poland-Lithuania. The organization was carried on the shoulder of the local community (*kehilla*), which retained all its powers in the conduct of its internal affairs: it looked after the Jewish quarter and the associated administrative arrangements, relations with the townspeople and the local authorities, prevention of economic competition, supervision of business ethics and prices; it campaigned against luxuries, and at the same time it cared for children's education, the study of Torah and *yeshivot*, medical assistance, and support for the poor and the wayfarer. The leading institution of the *kehilla* was the *kahal* (congregation), which was a comprehensive name for the *rashim* (heads) or *parnasim* who were leaders of the *kehilla*, *tovim* (boni viri, elders) – deputies of the 'chosen of the congregation',* those who bore office alongside them (such as treasurers of various funds, judges – who in those days were chosen by the *kahal* and were not necessarily linked to the rabbi – and tax assessors); and the officials of the *kahal* (the rabbi, who in spite of his great authority in matters of law and in the life of the *kehilla*, was a paid official of the *kahal* and was generally appointed for a fixed period, the *maggid* or *darshan* (preachers), the scribe, the beadle, and, in the course of time, also the cantor and the ritual slaughterer). All these together used to carry on the traditional way of life, dealing with the collection of taxes and the apportionment of the tax burden, trying law suits between members of the *kehilla*, and serving as the authorized representative body of the whole *kehilla* in relation to the Jewish public in the province and the provincial Jewish institutions, as well as in regard to external affairs. There were also within the *kehilla* various societies, some of them of a socio-economic character, for example, societies of craftsmen or travellers to a particular fair; among them, too, were societies for Torah and prayer, including groups for the study of Mishnah (*hevrat Shas*) or psalms, and societies with philanthropic objects, such as the *hevrahkaddisha* which existed for the burial of the dead but also for mutual help among its members, societies for 'the practice of charity' (*gemilut hasadim*), visiting the sick, dowering the bride, and so on.

The level above the *kehilla* in the arrangements for Jewish autonomy in Poland-Lithuania was that of the councils of the districts of regions (*vaadei ha-gelilo*). They arose from the need to apportion the tax among the various *kehillot*. Sometimes what caused them to be set up was the splitting off of the *sevivot* (the small *kehillot*) from the main *kehilla*, as happened at Poznań at the beginning of the sixteenth century, where all the small communities in the area used to meet and decide on the apportionment of the tax among themselves, but the *kehilla* of Poznań did not take part in these assemblies. In other places, however, matters developed

---

* The expression in quotation marks comes from the book of Numbers, for example Num. 1: 16. The *tovim* were aides to the leaders of the community.

differently: in the environs of Lwów, for example, the 'Council of the District (*galil*) of (Red) Russia' was set up jointly by the main community and the small ones around it, though at first the main community had the controlling voice in its decisions. However, after the massacres of the Jews during the Chmielnicki rebellion the importance of the main community declined and that of the others increased greatly. But apart from fiscal matters the main communities kept their status, and their rabbis retained their authority in relation to the whole district; and their *beth-din*, too, served as the supreme rabbinic court of the district. In the case of 'the Province of Lithuania' ('the Council of the Provinces'), the Council was set up to mediate between some main communities from among whose leaders and rabbis the 'heads of the province' were elected to conduct the affairs of the Council. For a long time the Council of the Province was presided over by the *rav beth din* (head of the rabbinic court) of Brisk (Brest Litovsk), the most important of the main *kehillot* in Lithuania. In the sixteenth century there were only three main *kehillot* in Lithuania; in the course of time, after numerous efforts, two more were added and were likewise accorded representation in the council. But at the end of the seventeenth century and the beginning of the eighteenth century the rest of the Lithuanian *kehillot* began to rebel against this arrangement, and in 1721 they lodged an official complaint against the main *kehillot* before the Lithuanian state court. There were also districts, for example, Volhynia, which divided into secondary districts with a main *kehilla* at the head of each.

The number of districts was not fixed. At first the Council of the Lands was called 'the Council of Four Lands' or even 'the Council of Three Lands', the reference being to Great Poland (with the main *kehillot* of Poznań and Kalisz), Little Poland (with Kraków and Sandomierz), Russia ('Red Russia', with Lwów), and Volhynia (with Ostróg, Łuck, Włodzimierz and Krzemieniec), plus, at times, the Grand Duchy of Lithuania (making 'the Council of Five Lands'). But because of differences in economic and social development between the various regions of Poland, schisms and disputes broke out (especially after the 1648 massacres), and there was a great increase in the number of bodies represented on the Council of the Lands, among them individual main *kehillot* as well as councils of districts whose territorial limits changed from time to time. 'The Province of Lithuania' retained an appreciable measure of independence until the dissolution of the Council of the Lands in 1764, when the authorities revoked their recognition of the Council as a body representing the whole Jewish community of the state. In central matters Lithuania was part of the Council of the Lands, which on not a few occasions made financial demands on it, but at the same time it was a province in its own right, 'the Province of Lithuania'.

In the early days of the Councils, as has been said, the assemblies took place twice a year, in spring and autumn, at the great fairs. The 'heads of the provinces', that is to say the representatives of the constituent bodies of the Council (altogether some tens of representatives) met there and considered matters to do with taxation to meet liabilities and relations with the authorities. They made regulations with regard to economic activity and the administrative arrangements of Jewish society. Separately from them but side by side with them, 'the judges of the Lands' met. These were the rabbis of the main *kehillot* and the districts, and sometimes judges specially elected for the purpose of adjudicating according to the law of the Torah on the various claims and disputes between the leaders, the districts and the *kehillot*, and also between individuals and one or other of these bodies. Sometimes the judges of the Lands would lend the support of their authority to the decisions of the 'heads of the provinces' and their ordinances. Between assemblies the Council was represented by office-bearers: the '*parnas* of the Four Lands' – not a rabbi but one of the lay leaders – who presided over the assemblies and acted with the authority of the Council in both external and internal affairs; and the 'trustee of the Four Lands', who was treasurer and secretary of the Council, a post to which it was also possible to appoint a rabbi. Later on, when the accounts of the Council of the Lands ran into difficulties and debts mounted, several 'trustees' were elected at the assemblies. The most important official of the Council was the *shtadlan*, a man well rooted in the life of the province and on terms of friendship with its influential people. His mission was to represent and protect Jewish interests at the royal court, in the Sejm and before the Ministry of Finance. The Council also had a 'writer' (*kotev*), who fulfilled the function of an administrator, assisted by other officials. After the 1648 massacres the frequency of the assemblies was affected, and in the eighteenth century they changed their character altogether, for state officials representing the Minister of Finance began taking part regularly in them in order to oversee the activities of the Councils, especially in the financial sphere. In the course of time the Council no longer met at the fairs but in the small towns owned by the Minister of Finance or under his control, and mostly when summoned by him. In this way the assemblies began to lose their character as independent Jewish delegations, and it is to be supposed that in addition to the official assemblies there were meetings, and perhaps decisions too, without the knowledge of the authorities.

The method of electing the 'heads of the province' who took part in the assemblies varied from place to place. Most often they were elected in the main *kehillot* at the time of the election for the heads of the *kahal*. Residents in the *sevivot* (the small communities) were not entitled to participate in this election at all, and even in the *kehillot* themselves a high minimum means test was set as the qualification for the right to vote, so that only a very small percentage of heads of households in Poland were voters. Hence public affairs were entrusted to a restricted class of rich people and scholars, the ties among whom were strengthened as a result of marriages and through the joint education of the rich and the scholars in the *yeshivot*. From the start the influence of the Jewish public as a whole on the affairs of the *kehillot* and the Councils was very small. With the expansion of the *sevivot* and the growth in social differentiation which followed the 1648 massacres, the situation described became ever more acute. This contrast between the social classes caused great unrest among the Jewish public in Poland at the end of the seventeenth century and in the eighteenth century and served as a background to the appearance of preachers and sermonizers who criticized the leaders of the *kahal*, to the production of a rich moralistic literature, and to the emergence of oppositional societies of craftsmen and groups of ascetic *hasidim* (pietists) imbued with a spirit of mysticism; from these groups, later on, the Hasidic movement developed.

The authorities did not bestow specific powers on the Council of the Lands; in their eyes it was only the supreme Jewish body to which the collection of the tax had been farmed out and which was responsible for its payment, but the wide powers granted to the general Jewish community and the various *kehillot* in their charters (writs authorizing residence) served as a legal basis for the Council's activities. Because of the situation which existed in Poland-Lithuania in the sixteenth century, – the spread of the Reformation and the war against it, and the intensification of the struggle between the weakened royal government and the aristocracy which was increasingly acquiring privileges (the *liberum* veto, the right of every individual noble in the Sejm to frustrate the passage of any resolution) – efforts to preserve the rights of Jews in Poland came to require activity on various levels. To the struggle of the townspeople against the Jews referred to above, which spawned a wide range of anti-semitic literature at the end of the sixteenth century and in the seventeenth century, there was added the enmity of the Catholic Church, which accused the Jews as well as the Protestants of responsibility for all the troubles which befell the kingdom. Hence the duty was laid upon the 'heads of the province' not only 'to be vigilant to inquire and examine for the benefit of the public and to punish transgressors and rebels and those who steal from and defraud Jews and Gentiles, lest the name of Heaven be profaned there (which Heaven forfend)', but also to take action against 'three notorious false accusations, namely *mamzer* (illegitimate children), abhorrent bread and proselytes', that is, the blood libels and the desecration of the host, and the charge of making converts to Judaism. The first two were widespread throughout Europe; the third matter became acute in Poland, for in 1539–40 the Jews of Lithuania were accused of having helped Christians to convert to Judaism and smuggled them to Turkey. As a result of that accusation there were attacks on the Jews until the Grand Duke of Lithuania found time to institute an inquiry and decided to intervene in favour of the Jews. In the eyes of churchmen these events were a particular reason for attacks on the Jews, especially in view of the trial and conviction, in the 1540s, of a woman in Kraków who was burnt at the stake inveighing against Christianity and Jesus. The case in question was connected with the penetration of Judaizing tendencies into Unitarian circles. The Unitarians, for their part, embarked on a sharp polemic against Judaism. These phenomena taken together brought the church once again to regard Judaism as a source of danger. In the 1560s the blood libel was renewed.

The battle against the libel involved heavy expenditure in order to induce government officials to come out in defence of the Jews. In addition the councils endeavoured to secure the punishment of non-Jewish criminals who murdered Jews or attacked their property.

The first ordinance of the Council of the Lands which has been preserved, dating from 1580, is against 'the men who are eager for profit and money in order to enrich themselves' and the farmers of the excise duty on spirits or of customs duty or the right to mint coins – functions which excited jealousy against those who performed them, brought them into conflict with the population, and, as a result, endangered not only these farmers but the whole of the Jewish community. These ordinances show that both the Council and the Jewish public regarded the defence of the interests of the Jewish community against attacks and intrigues as a task of the first importance (although, in regard to the danger to be expected from the farming of customs duties and government revenues, the various groups were not unanimous, and the heads of the Province of Lithuania, so far from threatening the tax-farmers with excommunication, actually saw their status as conferring a blessing on Jewry).

The other functions of the Council were to lay down rules of general application governing the conduct of the *kehillot* with respect to the sphere of authority of those bodies and the relation between *kehillot*, between the *kehilla* and the individual, and between the *kehilla* and the councils, supervision of economic activity, and observance of the laws of the Torah and study of the Torah. The Council also regulated charity in various spheres.

Apart from the prevention of crime, fraud and bankruptcy, the supervision of economic activity was concentrated on the prevention of competition, similarly to the work of the corporations (the guilds and the *cechy*) of the Christian townspeople. In order to settle in any *kehilla* a Jew had to pay an appreciable sum and undertake to accept the burden of the taxes and duties determined by the *kehilla*, not only because of the corporate principle which applied in the towns but also because the authorities and the Christian citizens regarded the Jews as 'sureties for each other'; that is to say, they held Jews collectively responsible for the acts of individuals. The aim of preventing competition which was pursued by the urban corporations, and concern for the general Jewish community and its individual members, combined in Poland to bring about a special development of the principle of *'hazakah'*, that is, the acquisition of authority by a Jew to compete with another Jew who rents an estate, an inn or any source of revenue, or even one who rents a house or shop for three years (a period after which, in Talmudic law, a person in undisputed possession acquired a right of possession – *hazakah*). A prominent feature of the activity of the Council was the prevention of competition in the printing of Hebrew books, in order to avoid harm to the printers. In addition, as has been said, the Councils determined the ways in which the tax was apportioned among the *kehillot* and the methods of collection.

The concern of the Councils for the observance of the Torah encompassed many walks of life. Many are the ordinances relating to the proper observance of the Sabbath, especially with regard to the conduct of business and the performance of work by non-Jews when complete estates or branches of estates were leased by Jews from the nobility. In some ordinances it was stated that it was forbidden to operate distilleries or flour mills on the Sabbath; and with reference to the work of the serfs the heads of the Council mentioned that 'when we were in exile and in slavery to the Egyptians our ancestors chose the Sabbath for themselves as a day of rest . . . how much more so in a place where the Gentile is in servitude' (Halperin, *Pinkas* of the Council of Four Lands, first edition, p. 486). When financial transactions became more extensive and varied the Council laid down rules on how to avoid any transgression of the laws against onerous interest charges without adversely affecting the economic activity of the Jews (1607). The Council also took action against the sale of rabbinical posts, in order to maintain public standards of morality, and took a strict view of questions of chastity and the purity of family life.

The study of the Torah, too, and support for its students, had various ramifications. The Councils exempted Torah scholars from liability to tax and passed ordinances requiring the *kehillot* to establish *yeshivot* and provide for the subsistence of the students (*bahurei ha-yeshivot*) and the boys. It seems that the chronicler Nathan Note Hannover was close to the truth, though he idealized the situation somewhat, when he declared that

> a *kehilla* of fifty householders would maintain not less than thirty students and boys, and there would be one student with his two boys in the home of one householder, and at least the student would always eat at his table like one of his sons, even though the student received financial support from the *kahal* (the congregation). (N. N. Hannover, *Yevein Metsulah*)

It need hardly be said that charitable activities extended over a wide range. The council legislated to cover support for poor scholars and assistance for itinerant preachers but, equally, provision to keep them under observation, collection of funds for Erets Israel and help for those who went there to settle.

In the history of the community for which it was responsible, the activity of the Council can be divided into two periods: the first lasting up to the 1648 massacres (with a break at the 1569 Union of Lublin, which led to the strengthening of the ties between Poland and Lithuania); and the second being from 1648 to the break-up of the Councils in 1764, which was followed by the first partition of Poland in 1772. In spite of all the stresses and struggles, the first period was one of growth and consolidation for the Jewish community in Poland-Lithuania and the instruments of its self-rule (and it was not for nothing that the enemies of the Jews at that time jeered that *'clarum regnum Polonorum est paradisum Judaeorum'*). At the same time the patterns of action, systems of administration and guiding principles of self-rule were being developed. It was also a time of progress for the spheres of economic and social activity specific to the Jews of Poland-Lithuania. The second period was one of persecutions, stagnation, disintegration and internal conflicts. True, the number of Jews and Jewish settlements continued to grow, but their situation grew steadily weaker. The causes of this decline were many. The increasingly feeble royal government became less and less able to offer protection and support to the Jews; its writs of authority were, indeed, reconfirmed, but they were almost worthless in practice. The magnates did take many Jews under their protection but were quick to harm the Jews of their fellow-aristocrats. The townspeople, who came to life, as it were, in the eighteenth century and fought for their rights, regarded the Jews as their principal enemies, and their spokesmen voiced sharply anti-Jewish allegations. The church launched a fresh attack on the Jews; the blood libels became a common occurrence. Meanwhile, within the Jewish *kehillot*, opposition grew, as we have said, between the governing class and the general public, and quarrels and struggles for influence and power intensified among the distinguished families of the community and the ambitious leaders drawn from their ranks. To these factors were added religious unrest, Messianic expectations in the period of the Shabbatean awakening and the disappointments that followed it, and groups of mystic 'Hasidim' who earned the sympathy of not a few young people. Neo-Shabbatean activity after the appearance of Jacob Frank in the 1750s, the tension which it generated, the religious disputes and the apostasy of the Frankists and the appearance of the Hasidism of the Baal Shem Tov which, shortly before the break-up of the Council, became a not inconsiderable factor – it was in these turbulent waters that the system of Jewish self-rule in Poland-Lithuania foundered.

The revolt of the Cossacks, led by Chmielnicki, against Polish rule in 1648–9 and the wars of Russia and Sweden against Poland which went on until 1660 led to mass murders of Jews, the flight of tens of thousands of refugees and the destruction or undermining of Jewish economic activity. The *kehillot* were constantly obliged to raise great and ever-increasing sums of money for the payment of war taxes and ransoms to conquerors and for the release of prisoners. The level of the tax paid to the government rose steadily from 15,000 złoty at the end of the sixteenth century to 60,000 from the Jews of Poland and 12,000 from Lithuanian Jewry in the middle of the seventeenth century, and to 220,000, plus 60,000 from Lithuania, at the beginning of the eighteenth century (1717). In spite of this, because of the increase in the Jewish population and the decline in the value of the currency, this tax ceased to be the principle financial concern of the Councils. The wars and the spread of anarchy necessitated new payments, some well-defined and overt, some ill-defined and secret, such as bribes and gifts of various kinds. These obliged the Jewish leaders to take loans from monasteries and aristocrats and the payment of the interest on these enormous sums became the greatest fiscal problem of the Councils. Jewish debt continued to increase and the financial situation of the Councils and the *kehillot* to deteriorate during the whole of the eighteenth century was a result of the uprisings of the peasants and the Cossacks in the east of the country. The uprisings, supported by Russian agents, were accompanied by highway robbery, murders of Jews and attacks on towns large and small (the most notorious of these massacres being that of 1768 in Uman in which thousands of Jews were killed). The intervention of the Powers, in particular Russia and France, in the internal affairs of Poland in support of rival parties led to the establishment of confederations of nobles at war with each other who plunged the whole country into chaos, a situation expressed in the saying 'Poland exists on anarchy'. The most vulnerable element in this state of affairs was the Jews; and their safety and their legal and economic position were rapidly undermined. The debts were so huge and the conditions applying to them so complicated as to occupy the attention of the state government and the committees for liquidation of the debts for a long time after the break-up of the councils.

This situation in the eighteenth century caused some government circles to form the opinion that there was no advantage in collecting the taxes through the agency of the Council, and voices were raised claiming that direct collection by government officials would increase the state revenues. However, opposition from interested parties among the nobility prevented any possibility of change. In the 1730s and 1740s rumours were even spread that it was the Jews who were responsible for the Sejms having risen without taking any decisions, in order that the position of the Jews should not be harmed. The abolition of the Councils was decided within the framework of the fiscal reforms introduced after the election to the throne of Stanisław August Poniatowski. After the break-up of the Councils, the tax was collected not from individuals but from *kehillot*, on the basis of a census of the Jewish population from which it emerged that in Poland-Lithuania there were some 600,000 Jews over one year old (the number of Jews at that time was estimated to have been about 750,000). In the first years after the Councils were abolished tax revenues did, indeed, increase, but subsequently they began to fall steeply.

The Council of the Lands is recognized as occupying a central place in the history of the Jews of Poland and in the history of the Jewish people as a whole. We have pointed out above its continuous existence and the great variety of the tasks which it performed. In the state of Poland, which during most of the existence of the Council was almost completely without a Christian urban class and a public administration worthy of the name, the Jews constituted the bulk of the middle class and played important parts in the development of the towns and the economy. And within this active community the Jews' own leadership established patterns of solidarity and mutual help, preserved the unique way of life and the values which unite Jewry, the study of Torah, and the maintenance of Torah law, and took decisions on matters emerging anew in changing circumstances. On account of the great authority of the Jewish scholars in Poland in questions of *halakha* (religious law) and their active participation in the Councils of the Lands, the influences of the Councils was enhanced and the German *kehillot* and their sages resorted to the Council of the Lands for advice or rulings, as, for example, in the time of the famous dispute between Rabbi Jonathan Eibenschütz and Rabbi Jacob Emden. The influence of a leadership extending continuously over many generations like that of the Councils in Poland-Lithuania is not to be measured by what is explicitly said in its enactments or what is told about things done directly by it. The way of life and the unity preserved among

Jews in Poland by its guidance lent strength to those faced with martyrdom, gave courage in times of crisis, and produced expressions of active Messianic longing in various forms, some of which were even such as to alarm the leadership itself.

In the eighteenth century the Jews of Poland, by natural increase, came to be the greater part of the Jewish nation, so that on the eve of the Second World War, according to Salo Baron, the descendants of the Jews who lived in Poland-Lithuania before the partitions – among them the great majority of the Jews of Russia and the USA – represented about 80 per cent of the world Jewish population. It is not surprising that their inheritance – their spiritual values, their ethical and intellectual concepts, their way of life – has preserved important elements, the form of which was determined in Poland during the active period of the Councils and has been absorbed into many spheres of Jewish activity in modern times.

8 · The *Pinkas* of the Council of the Four Lands

Israel Bartal

The *pinkas* (minute book, record book) of the Council of the Four Lands – the Jewish administrative body which presided over the affairs of the *gelilot* and *kehillot* (Jewish districts and communities) in the lands of the Polish Crown – has been lost, and only a few remnants of it have been preserved. Dov Beer of Bolechów recounts in his memoirs, dating from the second half of the eighteenth century, that

> for that which was not clearly explained in the works of the *posekim* [authorities on the application of Jewish law] the rabbis and the great scholars made books of the enactments of the lands in accordance with our holy Torah, and it was accepted as Torah by the whole congregation of the children of Israel, and they used to call them the books of ordinances of [the] Lands. And in my childhood I saw these books in print.

But whether the author of these memoirs was inaccurate in detail or whether, in his time, there really were printed books of ordinances of the Council of Four Lands, no such material has been preserved to us, apart from a few pages in manuscript which were in the possession of the historian Simon Dubnow as a gift from Rabbi Margolioth in Dubno and which were deposited by Dubnow in the archives of Yivo (Yiddisher Vissenschaftlicher Institut) in Wilno. These pages contain ordinances from the years 5431–32 (1671–2). The Council was empowered by the representatives of the principal *kehillot* in Poland to enact ordinances, sit in judgement in its court, and give effect to its decisions. From time to time it passed ordinances in regard to matters spiritual and material, and the heads of the provinces and the *kehillot* were expected to ensure that these were implemented, 'each one within his border, and let them carry out everything that has been enacted'. These powers, which were never recognized by the Polish Government, embraced many spheres vital to the whole Jewish community in the Kingdom of Poland and concerned matters in which the individual *kehillot* were unable to enforce their authority. Thus the Council of Four Lands dealt with the protection of the rights of printers, conferred its seal of approval on books, interceded with the authorities in regard to the affairs of the *kehillot* in times of trouble, and even accepted the responsibility of interceding with the kings of Poland on behalf of Jews from other countries. The Council was also called upon to exercise its authority in favour of one or other of the parties to disputes in Jewish communities far outside the borders of Poland, as it did in the affairs of the *kehillot* of Frankfurt-am-Main and Amsterdam. Additionally, it played a part in raising money for the benefit of Jews in Erets Israel, and was prominent in resistance to religious trends which threatened to destroy traditional Jewish society, notably the Shabbatean movement and its successors in the seventeenth and eighteenth centuries. But all these represented only one side of the activities of the Council, namely that which concerned the internal world of Ashkenazi Jewry.

The other side of the Council's activities related to the only one of its functions which was officially recognized by the Polish Government – the responsibility for collecting the taxes due from the whole Jewish community in the kingdom of Poland. It was the Council's financial activity which made possible everything else in which it engaged. When that responsibility was removed by the decision of the Polish Sejm in 1764 concerning the reform of the system of collecting the tax from the Jews, the basis for the Council's existence disappeared. These twin aspects of the fields in which the Council of Four Lands was active are brought out clearly in the documentary sources relating to it which still survive: on the one hand there is an extremely large amount of material in the archives of government bodies, organizations and Christian institutions which were concerned with the taxes of the Jews, with loans and with debts; on the other hand, testimony to activity in the domain of internal Jewish affairs has been preserved in the *pinkasim* of the *kehillot*, in rabbinic literature and in other Jewish sources. The main source document, the product of nearly 200 years of activity in the fields mentioned, evidently incorporated a considerable part of the material relating to the Council. It is true that it is not extant in its original form, but from copies in the *pinkasim* of the *kehillot*, in Polish Government records and in contemporary rabbinic literature, students of the history of Polish Jewry – Harkavy and Bershadski, Perles and Levin – have been able to attempt a reconstruction of parts of this mine of historical information.

The late Israel Halperin, by years of assiduous work, accomplished an enormous task: from manuscripts and printed books, from the scholarly and literary press and from the rich and varied research literature on the history of Poland, Prussia and Russia, he gathered every piece of information and every record relating to the Council, its links with *kehillot* and organizations, and its financial, juridical and administrative activities. He arranged all the material thus recovered in chronological order, cleared up many obscurities with regard to the identification of persons and events, drew up indexes of names, subjects and geographical locations and also drew a map of 'the House of Israel of the Four Lands'. Everyone familiar with historical research on the Jews of Eastern Europe at the end of the Middle Ages knows and acknowledges the outstanding value of this work of compilation and research undertaken by Halperin; once published, it became the basic source for every scientific study produced on Jewish self-rule in Poland. Halperin's *'Pinkas'* became a historical source in its own right, so as to obscure, as it were, the fact that it was not an original document of the sixteenth to eighteenth centuries but a skilfull reconstruction by an author of the present century.

Israel Halperin did not 'reconstruct' a *pinkas* of a council functioning above the level of the *kehillot* like the *Pinkas of the Province of Lithuania*. What is in question here is a huge work including actually everything pertaining to this Council, everything which issued from it, was sent to it, was said about it in non-Jewish authorities and Jewish communities and was written in Gentile and Jewish languages in printed books and records. While the *Pinkas of the Province of Lithuania* has been preserved in its original form and in several copies, the corresponding *pinkas* of the Council in Poland has been lost. Everything contained in Halperin's monumental work is not necessarily what was in the original *pinkas*; thus his book differs both in structure and content from what has come down to us from the Council of Lithuania. It may have chanced that some material has not been preserved while other matter which was found and included in the book was not necessarily in the *pinkas*. The words 'ordinances, writings and records' which Halperin used to describe the material in his book are certainly extremely general and permit the inclusion of an extremely wide range of topics; it is possible, indeed, that the Council of Four Lands had several sorts of *pinkas* and that Halperin's is a mixture of what was entered in the various sorts, each entry according to its subject matter. We know that the Council's ordinances, its rulings and some of the proceedings of its courts were recorded in official and binding form, as was customary in the Ashkenazi *kehilla*. Recording a document in this way served to validate it, as is shown by a statement in 5432 (1672) that a document was not valid unless 'it is written specifically in the *pinkas* of the Four Lands'. But there is no doubt that the Council had account books and that incoming and outgoing letters were kept in proper order. The '*pinkas* of the Four Lands' mentioned above, single pages of which have survived, was that which corresponded to the *pinkas* of the Council of Lithuania. Halperin's work perhaps ought to be called 'From the *pinkasim* of the Council of Four Lands'.

Halperin devoted eighteen years of his life to this undertaking, which was begun, according to his own testimony in his introduction to the '*Pinkas*', 'in the days of struggle for Jewish autonomy in Poland, when it seemed that there was a prospect of domestic Jewish government in the Diaspora' (after the First World War), when it was possible to carry out the work 'in Wilno, Warsaw, Berlin and Jerusalem'. It finished with the printing of the book, which took the whole of the Second World War, and its subsequent publication, when the magnitude of the human and spiritual destruction of the Polish Diaspora was becoming increasingly apparent to the survivors of the Holocaust.

Halperin began his great work while still a boy by copying the *pinkas* of the *kehilla* of Tiktin (Tykocin). Over the years he diligently gathered information as raw material for the task of reconstruction. His emigration to Erets Israel removed him from the places in which the majority of the sources for his undertaking still existed; in the years which followed, the work was hindered by the outbreak of the Second World War. The fact that, after 1939, the author was cut off from scholars in European countries and from the various archives has left its traces on the book: it was not possible to examine copies made by various scholars from *pinkasim* and manuscripts (and many of these documents, meanwhile, perished in the Holocaust); the author could not go and see for himself documents and source material in the cities of Western Europe and the USA. Even where it was possible to examine sources, as in the Bodleian Library in Oxford, this was not done, and defective references based on partial copies and fragmentary citations were left in the text. The publication of the book, too, suffered from wartime conditions: the *'Pinkas'* was printed on several kinds of paper.

From the moment the book appeared, the author took pains to note every correction, every addition and every piece of supplementary information which came to hand. In the private copy which he kept by his desk he wrote down in a tiny hand, often in abbreviations known only to him, allusions to supplementary matter; notes from books; references to files in his private archive; comments made orally by colleagues and opponents; surprises that occurred and doubts that arose in his mind as he went over the *'Pinkas'* again. And there was much to add and many comments to be made following the appearance of such an enormous work, based as it was on the meticulous collection of thousands of items from hundreds of sources.

First, Halperin revised his opinions on some of the dates he had fixed. This necessitated a change in the order of events as to both chronology and historical significance; it also affected the arrangement and structure of the *pinkas*.

Second, the destruction of European Jewry was accompanied by the removal of the archival treasures relating to Jewish history in Poland and their dispersal to other parts of the world, to say nothing of what was destroyed or was lost or damaged. Of the treasures of Yivo in Wilno, parts were transferred to Germany during the war years, and found their way to the cellars of the institute in New York. Other parts of the great collection were pulped for paper-making or stored on the orders of the Soviet authorities. On the other hand *pinkasim* or *kehillot* and rare documents such as the *pinkas* of the *kehilla* of Poznań reached Erets Israel; these had been known to Halperin, until then, only in incomplete and inaccurate copies.

Third, printing and photographic techniques had been improved, and such bodies as the Institute for the Photocopying of Hebrew Manuscripts (based in the National and University Library in Jerusalem) had been established. It was now possible to see in their original form documents and records which had previously been available only as copies, sometimes of doubtful reliability, made by scholars of earlier generations. Thus, for example, the present writer chanced to discover letters from an emissary of the Council of Four Lands to Rome in connection with the blood libel in Jampol in 1756; these were known to Halperin only in the copies of Berliner, Kaufmann and Marx which were published in periodicals at the end of the nineteenth century. And as they did not see fit to quote them in full, he was ignorant of important additional material contained in the original manuscripts.

Fourth, new publications were constantly appearing with the results of research by scholars in Jewish studies in Israel and abroad. These gradually added to existing knowledge, shedding further light on the links between the Council of Four Lands and Jewish communities in other countries, and revealing fresh details about well-known personalities among the leaders of the Council. In a study published in Dutch, for example, Fuks expanded what we knew about the controversy among the Ashkenazim in Amsterdam surrounding the rabbinate of R. David of Lida in the Polish *kehilla* in the city, and he added to the documents of the Council the material he found in the Bibliotheca Rosenthaliana in Amsterdam. Other new material was published from various archives, Polish and German, such as the articles of Brilling on the city of Breslau and its contacts with the Council of Four Lands on the supply of *etrogim* (citrons for the festival of *Sukkot*) for the Polish Jews, or on the fairs and the position of the functionary known as the '*shamash*'* of the fair on behalf of the organizations of the *kehillot* in Poland. Halperin did not live to see every research study published on the subject after the appearance of his first edition of the *Pinkas*. A wealth of new material continued to be published after his death, and was added to what the deceased scholar had been able to enter in the collection of addenda in his private copy. Some manuscripts appeared as books, with the addition of introductions, notes and indexes. The *pinkas ha-kesherim* (register of 'eligible arbitrators' – electors) of the *kehilla* of Poznań appeared in print, as did the memoirs of R. Pinhas Katzenellenbogen, rabbi of the *kehilla* of Boskovice in Moravia. Halperin, in his '*Pinkas*', had quoted only a short extract from these memoirs which had been included, with copying errors, in a work by another writer. And in Poland itself, in recent years, new documents connected with the Council have been found, some of them in the archives of government authorities which were concerned with the tax, and others which had found their way into various collections. It was only recently that Jacob

---

* See *Encyclopaedia Judaica*, vol. II, col. 1002.

Goldberg discovered further original documents in Hebrew and Polish which supplement our information on various topics and fit neatly together with the paragraphs of Halperin's *'Pinkas'*.

It was indeed untimely that the late Professor Israel Halperin's important research work had to be broken off. In 1965 he contracted a serious illness which made it difficult for him to carry on his creative activity. Nevertheless he did his best to go on with his research, and he continued to follow the changes and fresh discoveries in the study of Jewish autonomy in Eastern Europe. In the summer of 1971 he died, leaving behind him, among his other unfinished works, the partially revised *'Pinkas'*. The copy in which he wrote his notes and alterations was placed by his widow, Mrs Zipporah Halperin, at the disposal of a committee of scholars in the Institute for Jewish Studies in the Hebrew University in Jerusalem. The committee, which had undertaken to suggest ways in which the important works left behind by Halperin could be brought to completion, laid on the present writer the task of preparing a corrected and expanded second edition of the *Pinkas*. The Memorial Foundation for Jewish Culture allocated funds for the project.

Several decisions had to be made in connection with the preparation for printing of an enlarged second edition of a book which had become so central a source in scholarly research. The principal one was how to maintain a balance between the aim of introducing into the book all the new matter which had accumulated over the decades since the appearance of the first edition, and, on the other hand, the need to retain the 'original' chronological order of the *Pinkas* (that is, the order fixed by Halperin). The purpose of retaining that order was first and foremost to continue the use of the paragraph numbers[*] which, over the years, had become an accepted system in scientific literature. As already said, the author's revised conclusions sometimes involved the redating of a particular document, so that it became necessary to place it in an earlier or later position in the book and also to alter the whole set of notes and index references on it. The solution to the problem of adding new documents or altering the position of existing ones was found by *using the existing paragraph numbering* and adding a figure above the line to the new entry. Thus, for example, the reader will find, after paragraph *mem-bet* (42), paragraphs *mem-bet*[1] and *mem-*

---

[*] Using the letters of the Hebrew alphabet according to their numerical value.

*bet*². In any case it is evident that the user of the *'Pinkas'* will be able to locate the supplements which are not a *substitution of a corrected copy for an existing text or an addition of historical or bibliographical material* in an existing paragraph by the superior figures alongside the paragraph number. Moreover, the pagination of the first edition has been kept. The new material has been attached to the existing text or, where necessary, substituted for it. For this purpose the second edition has been divided into two volumes: the first contains the existing text, marked with indications of the new additions or textual corrections; in the second volume all the new documents are reproduced in full, whether in Hebrew or in another language, together with notes and explanatory comments. The numbering of the paragraphs in the first volume corresponds to their chronological order; in the second volume the Hebrew documents in the 'chapter of addenda' are given in the chronological order settled upon by Halperin for this chapter, and therefore their distinguishing letters do not run in alphabetical order.

A more difficult problem was presented by the copy of the book left by Halperin: he had not prepared it for printing but had written notes and corrections for his own use, phrasing his remarks with the utmost brevity, using initials for the title of a book, or recording the source of his information in the form, 'as my friend observed to me . . .' Often he relied on his memory and on his large bibliographical card-index, and generally contented himself with an allusion or the hint of an illusion. I will quote here two characteristic examples of this complex problem – a problem which was sometimes solved only after lengthy searches. In one case (paragraph *shin-samekh-bet* [362], page 159 in the *Pinkas*), there was a note about Simon of Poland, the agent of the Polish king Jan Sobieski in Holland: 'Compare Fuks, Simon de Pol'. The reference was to the article by L. Fuks: 'Simon de Pol, Agent un Faktor fun Kenig Yan Sobyeski in Holland', in the periodical *Bleter far Geshikhte* of 1956. Here it was possible to identify the article by the use of bibliographical indexes and common sense – for the Fuks who wrote about a Polish Jew in Holland was certainly Leib Fuks – and from that point it was but a short step to the solution. Or there was a note three words long referring to Katz and his explanation of the first document in the *Pinkas*, page 2 – the allusion being to the note by Professor Jacob Katz in his book *'Bein Yehudim le-Goyim'* ('Between Jews and Gentiles'), p. 152, note 35. Questions of this kind arose in almost every spot that Halperin dealt with in a note, and they were solved by searching through books and articles, or by the indefatigable help of expert colleagues who deciphered not a few of the secrets of these skeleton references.

Israel Halperin kept his supplementary entries up to date from the day that the book was published until he fell ill in 1965. Among other things he corrected in manuscript, most meticulously, the corrupt copies of the *pinkas* of Poznań, working from the original which, today, is kept in the Central Archive for the History of the Jewish People in Jerusalem. He was also able to insert, in manuscript, references and additions taken from the book by the scholar who lost her life in the Holocaust, Bella Mandelsberg, *Mekharim le-Toledot Yehudei Lublin* (Studies in the History of the Jews of Lublin), which was published in the same year. From then on his updating was only partial (for the years 1965–71). From 1971, the present writer did his best, with the aid of scholars in Israel and abroad, to add the new material which presented itself in learned journals in the various languages and in general research studies appearing after that time. The more that the work of preparing the book for the printers progressed, the more the number of additions and corrections increased. The last ones were added to the proof at the end of 1988.

Halperin's own words, written in the period up to 1965 and expressed in the first person, have been left unaltered. Where the reader might be in doubt who had written them, they have been noted with his initials in brackets, thus: (I.H.). Where I myself have added new material to additions made by Halperin before 1965 and the first person is used, the note 'I.B.' appears in brackets. Obviously additions and corrections connected with material which was published after 1971 relate to findings subsequent to Halperin's death.

The preparation of the revised volumes extended over long years. It will form a basic tool to any further study of the history of Jews in the Polish-Lithuanian Commonwealth and should greatly facilitate the work of scholars in this field.

---

* This article is a shortened version of the Hebrew introduction to Israel Bartal's new edition of Halperin's *Pinkas Vaad arba aracot*.

9 · The Language of Documents Relating to Jewish Autonomy in Poland

Moshé Altbauer

Co-operation between linguists and historians or pre-historians has a long tradition both in Polish and more recently in Israeli scholarship. This co-operation has provided us with many positive results. For example, let me recall an important book on the origins of the Slav motherland by my teacher, Professor Lehr-Spławiński.[1] This great Slavist combined the results of linguistic research into the historical dialectology of the Slavic languages with Professor Jozef Kostrzewski's archaeological investigations into Lusatian culture, as a result of which the location of the Slav 'pre-motherland' could, in contrast to the views of Russian scholars, be transferred a long way westwards. Numerous students of Professor Lehr-Spławiński, in Poland and abroad, have co-operated extensively with historians in such areas as editing older historical documents, re-polonizing Germanized names of towns and villages on Polish soil (especially after the Second World War), and in many other fields of linguo-historical research.

In my linguistic discussion of Jewish settlement on the eastern borderlands of historic Poland,[2] I sought to demonstrate that the hypothesis of the existence of Khazar place names is without basis. The aim of that hypothesis was to confirm the argument that the first Jewish settlers in Poland were the descendants of Judaized Khazars who arrived from the east. An Austro-Hungarian official, H. von Kutschera,[3] familiar with oriental languages, was the father

---

[1] T. Lehr-Spławiński, *O pochodzeniu i praojczyźnie Słowian* (On the origins of the Slav motherland), Poznań, 1946.
[2] M. Altbauer, 'Jeszcze o rzekomych "chazarskich" nazwach miejscowych na ziemiach polskich' (More about presumed Khazar place names on Polish territory), *Onomastica* 13, 1968, pp. 120–8.
[3] H. von Kutschera, *Die Chasaren*, Vienna, 1910.

of this toponomic hypothesis. It was uncritically accepted first by a sociologist, Maksymilian Gumplowicz,[4] and then by an outstanding student of the history of the Polish Jews, Ignacy Schipper.[5]

According to these authors, the 'Khazar' names of such places as *Kozary, Kozarka, Kozarowicze, Kozarowszczyzna, Kozarcy*, and so on,[6] were assumed to be based on the ethnic name of *Chazar*. Yet clearly none of these names begins with *ch*,[7] although in Polish the names for the country and its ethnic derivatives – *Chazaria, Chazarzy* – do have this initial sound.

The name *Kawiory* in the Czarna Wieś district (at present a street name in Kraków-Krowodrza), has also been placed on the list of assumed Khazar names, deriving from the name of the one of the Khazar tribes, known from the Byzantine sources as 'Ka apoi', which in early medieval Greek pronunciation would come out as *Kawari*. Even Schipper, who had access to the historical documents which enabled him to connect the name *Kawiory* with the Hebrew word for grave (*Kever*), considered this etymology valid. Kazimierz Nitsch alone, in a long appendix to my paper 'W sprawie *Kirkutu*' (On the question of the Jewish cemetery),[8] basing himself on such historic authorities as the *Kodeks dyplomatyczny miasta Kazimierza* (Diplomatic Codex of Kazimierz) and *Najstarsze Księgi miasta Krakowa* (The oldest records of Kraków), and others supplied to

---

[4] M. Gumplowicz, *Początki religii żydowskiej w Polsce* (The origins of the Jewish religion in the Polish Commonwealth), Warsaw, 1926.

[5] I. Schipper, *Di kultur geshikhte fun di yidn in povlin bisn mitalter*, Warsaw, 1926. Incidentally, one should add that Majer Bałaban, a historian who has greatly contributed to the history of Polish Jews, did at the beginning of the 1920s incline to accept the 'Khazar' theory of place names. In his three-volume *Historia i literatura żydowska ze szczególnym uwzględnieniem historii Żydów w Polsce* (Jewish history and literature with special reference to the Jewish history in Poland), Lwów/Kraków, Warsaw 1920–5, he wrote: 'from the Khazar Jews . . . are thought to originate the names of towns and villages in Red Ruthenia and Little Poland: . . . *Kozarze Kawiory*' (III, p. 257). But ten years later he definitely rejected the possibility of linking the name *Kawiory* with *Kabaroi*.

[6] I. Schipper, *Kultur geshikhte*, pp. 25–6.

[7] In the 1930s an Israeli historian, A. N. Polak, took up the problem of the Khazars (together with assumed Khazar place names on Polish territory) in his monograph *Kazaria: The History of a Jewish State in Europe*, Massada, Tel-Aviv, 1943 (in Hebrew). In an earlier work, 'The acceptance of the Jewish religion by the Khazars', *Tsion*, 1935, pp. 106–12, 160–80 and also published separately, the same author discusses the phonetic variations of the ethnic name of the Khazars: *Qazarija*, Italian *Gazaria* (also *Giriconda* and *Gerazonda*) and the Russian *Kozar*, which is incorrect.

[8] M. Altbauer, 'W sprawie *kirkutu*', (On the subject of the *kirkut*), *Język Polski* 34, 1954, pp. 202–4.

him by historian Roman Grodecki, demonstrated that Kraków's *Kawiory* is, in reality, *sepulturae Iudeorum*, deriving it from the Hebrew *Kavurym* (in Polish Ashkenazi pronunciation), meaning tombs or graves. Nitsch accepted my hypothesis that *Kirków* (*Kierków*) derives from the German *Kirchhof*; earlier it meant 'evangelical cemetery' and only later became the name of a Jewish cemetery. With the help of research centres in many universities, he looked into the meaning of the word *Kierków*, its many phonetic and morphological variations, and its geographical range.[9] After many years, it became clear that the results of our overlapping research during the 1950s was confirmed by the character of many of the privileges granted to the Jews in Polish towns.[10]

On the basis of the work done by the Polish toponomasts (placename specialists) of our century – among others Witold Taszycki, Mieczyslaw Karaś and Halina Safarewicz – I have attempted to demonstrate that all words considered Khazar by Kutschera, Gumplowicz and Schipper are indisputably Polish and have their parallels in the place names of other Slavonic countries.[11]

After this introduction, and with the aim of explaining the participation of a linguist in this *historical* collection, let me proceed with the main topic my chapter. When I first began to write on this theme, I did not realize that the lexical data of the Polish, Latin, Hebrew, Yiddish, Old Byelorussian (the bureaucratic language of the Grand Duchy of Lithuania) and German documents relating to Jewish autonomy in the Polish Commonwealth could form the basis of a long linguistic monograph. This monograph now awaits its author, who would have to master these languages and have

---

[9] K. Nitsch, 'Dopisek do artykułu M. Albtauera w sprawie *kirkutu*', (Supplement to M. Altbauer's article on the subject of the *kirkut*), *Język Polski* 34, 1954, pp. 204–6.
[10] J. Goldberg, ed., *Jewish Privileges in the Polish Commonwealth: Charters of Rights Granted to Jewish Communities in Poland-Lithuania in the 16th–18th Centuries*, Israeli Academy of Sciences and Humanities, Jerusalem, 1985, pp. 424, col. 1, (further quoted as Goldberg, *Privileges*); M. Schorr, *Żydzi w Przemyślu do końca XVIII wieku* (Jews in Przemyśl to the End of the eighteenth century), edition and publication of source records, Lwów, 1903, in the series *Monografie z historii Żydów w Polsce, Konkurs imienia A. H. Wawelberga* (Monographs on the History of the Jews in Poland. A H. Wawelberg Competition), further quoted as Schorr, *Żydzi*.
[11] Further details in M. Altbauer, 'Jeszcze o rzekomych "chazarskich" nazwach miejscowych'.

enough knowledge of the subject and a linguistic bent.[12] My aim is smaller in scope. Within the limited possibilities of this essay, I shall attempt to use a number of examples to expound the main features of this problem, which is central to linguistic studies of Polish–Jewish relations.

Perception of Polish (or Latino-Polish) Terms

Polish terms relating to Jewish autonomy in Poland were used by Jews in their Hebrew or Yiddish documents, and possibly in everyday usage, in three ways:

1. they adopted the Polish term without any changes and transliterated it into the letters of the Hebrew alphabet, which was also the alphabet of Yiddish and of the other languages of the Diaspora and still is today (with the exception of several oriental Jewish languages in the Soviet Union, which have had the Cyrillic alphabet introduced by the government);
2. they transliterated the Polish term adding a Hebrew or Yiddish translation;
3. they translated the Polish term into Hebrew or Yiddish, sometimes creating a semantic neologism. Similar semantic neologisms in administrative and political terminology were created in the other Ashkenazi centres in Europe.

Polish words incorporated into Hebrew and Yiddish and transliterated into Hebrew characters

The material under review covers about fifty terms of this type among which are: *ordynacja*, *arenda*, *otaki* (from the Turkish term for a fair on the borderlands of Valachia), *instygator*, *instrument* (the message contained in an official document), *elekcja*, *asygnacja*, *gabela* (from the term for a *kahal* food tax), *wojewoda*, *winnica* or

---

[12] Scholarly literature on the subject is very inadequate. There is I. Halperin's short article in Hebrew [A Collection of Words from the Cultural Field of the Ashkenazi Jewry], *Leshonenu* 15, 1947, pp. 190–7. The author discusses eight words and Hebrew phrases relating to Jewish autonomy in Poland, and in footnotes draws our attention to books and editions of historical sources where some Hebrew terms are described. In addition M. Gilon has described the Ro'e hahesbon' – 'Financiál Controller' in the Jewish System of Autonomy: Problems with the Hebrew term (in Hebrew), *Iyunim b vigoret hamadina* 38, 1984. See also the article in this volume by Dr A. Leszczyński.

winica (also in the sense of alcohol distillery), *talar, tynf, czopowe, marszałek, naród* (a general dietine), *suplika, podymne, powrotne, protestacja, berdon* (food tax), *faktor, komisja, konstytucja, kontentacja, kuna, komora, konwokacja, rata, reister, starosta, szpilkowe, żupa* and others.

A detailed analysis of transliteration shows that the pronunciation of some Polish terms was Yiddishized, for instance the Polish ending *-cja* turned into *-cie*, while some Polonisms passed through an 'integration' process: *sygnacje* turned into *asygnacja* (the initial *a-* being identified with the Yiddish indefinite article), *instygator* came from *stigator*, and so on.

This Yiddishized form of Polish does not, generally, prevent the correct understanding of Polish words transliterated into Hebrew characters. The problem becomes more difficult when we meet not single Polonisms in a Jewish text, but complete Polish documents transliterated into Hebrew characters by Jews with only a poor knowledge of Polish. (We meet similar practices in sources for the history of Jews in other countries, such as Germany.) Things become even more complicated when the original document is lost. This is what happened with a document containing the text of a privilege granted to the Wiłkowyszki Jews by King Jan III Sobieski in 1679 (ratified by King August II in 1700), which was transliterated into Hebrew characters in the Jewish *pinkas* (book) of that town in 1792 (See Goldberg, *Privileges*, pp. 359–66; with a photocopy of the transliteration and the text in Polish).

The author – a historian – did not analyse the principles of the Hebrew transliteration (possibly, he was not even aware of the problem) and did not identify the Yiddishized Polish elements put in by the Jewish translator, who originated from the north-east of historical Poland. Through a mechanical retransliteration back into the Polish alphabet, we obtain a text which in some parts has grammatical errors and clearly differs widely from the Polish of the original historical document. Thus a methodological question arises: should the historian, as editor of a historical document, transliterate back into the Polish alphabet the transliteration of the Polish text recorded in a foreign alphabet, or should he attempt to work out a reconstruction of the original Polish text?

Because of the limitations of space at my disposal, let me give just one example, leaving the discussion of the analysis of the reconstruction of the whole text from the Hebrew transliteration to another occasion:

każdy jednak i z pomienionych rzeźników co rok do dworu kamień łoju oddawać powinien będzie [each of the aforementioned butchers shall hand over each year a stone of tallow to the court]. (Goldberg, *Privileges*, p. 365, lines 78–81)

The conjunction *i* (and) before the words '*z* pomienionych rzeźników' is completely superfluous. The mistake in the reconstruction of the Polish original arises from the fact that the transliterator unwittingly incorporated certain characteristic features of the Polish spoken by Jews. In an article 'O błędach ortograficznych i gramatycznych w zadanich polskich Żydów przemyskich' [On spelling and grammatical mistakes made by the Przemyśl Polish Jews],[13] as well as in my doctoral thesis[14] I explained the appearance of anlaut vocal elements, such as *y* (sometimes also *u*) in the prepositions *w* [in] and *z* [with or from].[15] In the transliteration of the historical document made by the Wilkowyszki Jew we have '*iz* (Hebrew letters: alef + yid + zayin), which should be reconstructed as the preposition *z*. An identical Hebrew translation on page 366, line 100, suffers from a similar wrong reconstruction, *i z nich* [and from them], and in line 104 on the same page, *Żyd któryby miał sprawę i z Żydem*, [a Jew who would bring a case and with a Jew].[16] Incidentally, the almost identical phrase appears in a document published by M. Schorr in his work *Żydzi w Przemyślu* [Jews in Przemyśl], document no. 90, issued by the *voivode* Stefan Czarniecki for the Jews of Przemyśl on 17 March 1660, p. 167, para. 159: 'Żyd z Żydem sprawę mający'.

Transliteration of Polish words and their translation into Hebrew

Gród [fortress, castle]: transliteration + translation into Hebrew: *mivtśar* – 'a fortified place, fortress'. The word *mivts'ar* appears a

---

[13] M. Altbauer, 'O błędach ...'. *Język Polski* 19, 1928, pp. 105–10, 131–53.
[14] 'O polszczyźnie Żydów' (On the Polish language of the Jews), Wilno, 1931, a manuscript in the Institute of the Polish Language at the Jagiellonian University.
[15] Altbauer, 'O błędach', p. 134.
[16] The above notes about certain mistakes in the reconstruction of the Polish original do not in any way diminish the value and importance of Professor Goldberg's book. It has already taken its place along with the works of M. Schorr, M. Bałaban, L. Halperin, and S. Dubnow as one of the standard works on the history of Jews in the Polish Commonwealth. The enormously detailed index (108 pages altogether!) makes it more accessible, especially for readers who are not historians, and who wish to use this very important and rich edition of sources on the history of the Jews in Poland.

number of times in various books of the Bible, usually in a compound form *'ir-mivts'ar* singular, 'fortified town', *'arey-mivts'ar* plural, but also several times as an individual word. Fr Jakub Wujek in his well-known translation of the Bible rendered this word into various Polish equivalents: *zamek, obrony, płoty* [castle, defences, fences]. In the vocabulary of Jewish autonomy in Poland, *mivts'ar* developed a new meaning, '*iudicium*, site of the court'.[17] Similar new meanings are found in the *kahal* and guild *pinkasim* of other Ashkenazi centres elsewhere in Europe:

Hiberna (tax to support the army in winter): transliteration + Hebrew translation: *lehem-horef*, literally 'winter-bread';
Sejm and *sejmik* (Diet, dietine): transliteration + Hebrew translation: *va'ad, va'ada*, for example in the expression *va'ad 'arba 'aratsot* meaning 'Council of Four Lands';
skarb [treasury] and *podskarbi* [treasurer] also appear in transliteration and translation into Hebrew – the basis of transliteration for the latter being its everyday phonetic version, *pockarbi*.

Translation of Polish expressions into Hebrew and Yiddish

Opening the Kraków conference on Jewish autonomy, Professor Józef Gierowski observed: 'Autonomy to this extent, as experienced by the Jewish population of the old Polish Commonwealth, was an exceptional phenomenon in Christian Europe of the fifteenth to eighteenth centuries. It laid the foundation . . . for considerable demographic expansion among the Jews . . . and ensured their economic and *cultural* development.'[18] Language is an important social achievement and a useful indication of the state of cultural development. This section of my chapter and the preceding section illustrate this phenomenon. Through the introduction of Polish vocabulary dealing with Jewish autonomy, Hebrew, as a language of documents, became enriched with numerous semantic neologisms. Moreover, old biblical and post-biblical Hebrew terms were revived

[17] Cf. I. Halperin, ed., 'Pinkas vaad arba aratsot. Likutey taqanot ketavim uresumot', in *Acta Congressus Generalis Judaeorum Regni Poloniae (1580–1764)*, Bialik Institute, Jerusalem, 1945, further quoted as Halperin, *Acta*. See index under entry 'gród' (p. 538, col. 2), for data about the meaning of the Hebrew word *mivts'ar*, with numerous quotations.
[18] Quoted in *Tygodnik Powszechny*, 5 Oct. 1986, p.1.

and entered into this new vocabulary, as the following examples illustrate.

The Hebrew *ad'on* means master (*pan*), but in the context of Polish life it came to signify specifically 'power, owner of estate, squire', and so on.

The Hebrew *zah'uv* [gold] is also used for a Polish coin of that period, złoty, and was still so used until recently.

The Hebrew *zaq'uq* instead of the Polish *grzywna* (*moneta*, a monetary unit in Poland), from a biblical root meaning 'percolare, liquare, purgare'. Wujek translates this word variously as '*siedmiokroć przeczyszczone, szczere złoto, srebra najczystszego*' [seven times cleaned, pure gold, the purest silver].

The Hebrew *huts la' 'ir*, meaning literally 'outside town', in our context comes to be used for 'suburbs'.

Some translations of Polish terms retain their original biblical and post-biblical Hebrew sense. For example *mas-qulqol´et* literally meant 'skull tax, head tax' instead of the Polish *pogłówne* [poll tax]. In the Wujek translation of the Bible we find; 'gomor *na każdą głowę, według liczby dusz waszych, które mieszkają w namiecie*' [an omer per head, depending on the number of souls living in the tent] Exodus 16: 16, and: '*Weźmiesz po piąci syklów na każdą głowę*' [you shall take five shekels per head], Numbers 3: 47. But from the same biblical root *g-l-g-l* a new morphological formation was created, *gilgul* (a noun derived from the verbal form *galgel*) with the meaning 'poll-tax assessment', unknown in biblical or post-biblical Hebrew. Similarly another biblical word *migr'as*, kept its earlier meaning of 'suburbs' or land around the town, when used in connection with Jewish autonomy (see Halperin, *Acta*, Index, p. 547). Wujek gives a similar translation of *migr'as* in 'a miasta będą pośrodku, a za miasty *przedmieścia*' [the town lying in centre and outside the town], Numbers 35: 5.

It is fascinating to observe the semantic development of the Yiddish word *m'uk m* (also *Mokem*), derived from the Hebrew *mag'om*, 'place'. In this period, the term gained a new meaning – Catholic town as opposed to Jewish town or Jewish street or district. *M'uk m* in this meaning survived till the Second World War. It was the name for Warsaw's old city and the surrounding streets (I am indebted for this information to Dr Aleksander Guterman). We find numerous instances in documents from the last century and other Hebrew and Jewish sources (Halperin, *Acta*, pp. 546–7). Incidentally, Dutch Jews also use the word *m'uk m* in this way (for this information I am indebted to Mr Re'em of the Israeli Academy of Sciences).

I should mention that in the biblical story of the destruction of Sodom and Gomorrah, the Hebrew *mag'om* (locus) is used several times as a synonym for the Hebrew word *ir* (urbs, oppidum, civitas), as for example in Genesis 18: 26: 'Jeźli znajdę w Sodomie pięćdziesiąt sprawiedliwych w samem mieście [If at Sodom I find fifty just men in the town – in Hebrew: *bat'ox ha'ir*] odpuszczę wszystkiemu miejscu dla nich' [I will spare the whole place because of them – in Hebrew *Lax'ol hamag'om*].

Perhaps the reason for this semantic process was the parallel meaning of the Polish words *miasto* and *miejsce* [town and place]. They derive from the same pre-Slavonic root *mest-*, and their difference in meaning is based on phonological and morphological divergence. On the other hand we should take into account the fact that the Yiddish *stut* (with a long *u* in central Yiddish) means both 'town' and 'fixed synagogue seat' (which was purchased, often at a high price, for life and was handed down from father to son).

Close analysis of the administrative terms used in autonomy leads me towards a hypothesis based on the progress of such terms as they wandered through various European centres of Ashkenazi Jews. Let me illustrate this with the following examples:

In a document signed by Karol Odrowąż, a Sedlnicki count and Great Crown treasurer (Halperin, *Acta*, p. lxxii, 9 September 1752) we read: 'aby cała Generalność obrała sobie przez Kreski Czterech lub Pięciu Starszych Żydów *Rachmistrzami* nazwanych, przed któremi rachunki Swoje publiczne *Wiernicy* Generalni czynić mają' [that the whole leadership chose by ballot four or five Jewish elders to be called *Rachmistrz*, to whom public bills would be presented by the *wiernicy*].

Rachmistrz [calculator, reckoner], borrowed from the German *Rechenmeister*, means 'a person whose profession is to check financial records'. In the Hebrew translation of this document (Halperin, *Acta*, p. 387), the Polish word *rachmistrz* is turned into a Hebrew compound *ro'ey-hesbonot* (plural), 'those who see bills', the modern Hebrew term for an accountant, which is evidently not an exact translation of the Polish term. The same Hebrew expression appears in a bi-annual *pinkas* of the Jewish community of Verona, dated 1657 and therefore nearly a century older than the Polish document issued by Stefan Czarniecki in 1752. In the Italian text we read 'd'ellegier *quarto reuisidori di conti*', and in the Hebrew text 'livhor *d* (letter daleth = 4) *ro'ey-hesbonot*'. Dr Meir Gilon, an official in the State Comptroller's Department in Israel, the author of a book on the Hebrew term *ro'e hahesbon*,[19] considers it to be equivalent in sense and form to the Italian term *reuisidori di conti*. At that time there were two groups of Jews in Verona, the Ashkenazim who had fled from Germany to more tolerant northern Italy and the Sephardim, who had escaped the Spanish Inquisition. The new term probably reached Poland through the agency of German Jews.

Writers of Hebrew documents in Jewish autonomous Poland did not always borrow neologisms invented by their German colleagues. When such neologisms jarred with the feel of Hebrew, they preferred to introduce the Polish expression in its original form. This happened, for example, with the term *szpilkowe*, meaning 'annual gift' (or rather, forced tribute) to the ruler's wife (sometimes also to other dignitaries of the Polish Commonwealth) in the form of a hairpin decorated with precious stones. This gift was offered to the monarch by the representatives of the Kraków Jewish community but its cost was met by the representatives of all the Jewish communities who made up the Council of Four Lands, as we read in a macaronic Hebrew – Yiddish document: 'As this gift is for the prosperity and the good of all Jews living on the territories of Little Poland, Great Poland, Podole and the Ukraine' (Halperin, *Acta*, p. 454, no. 858).

In the Hebrew documents and *pinkasim* of the Jews in Germany, the word for this gift was translated by the Hebrew *m zig'a*, which means 'mixing, or blending' (for example of a drink). This lexical puzzle was solved by a famous Jewish philologist and lexicographer Eliyahu Barukh, known in the Christian world as Elihu the Levite.[20] The problem arose because in German and Yiddish the word *schenken* means both 'to give a present' and 'to pour a drink'. The German Jews mistakenly chose the second meaning, and thus arrived at the incorrect word *m zig'a* (mixing a drink), instead of the correct Hebrew term *matan'a* [gift]. Such mistakes in translation, caused by picking the wrong meaning when faced with a choice, are well known to linguists.[21] But the Jewish writer of Hebrew

---

[19] M. Gilon, 'Ro'e hahesbon', see n. 12.
[20] Quoted by E. Y. Kutscher, *The History of the Hebrew Language*, Jerusalem, 1982, p. 168.
[21] Cf. data from my article [On the Hebrew Name for the Book of Psalms] (in

documents in Poland was correct in rejecting the unfortunate Hebrew literal translation of the word *szpilkowe* (German *Nadelgeld* or pin-money).

In this section we should also include Polish words translated into Yiddish, for example:

cener instead of the Polish *dziesiątek* – 10 groszy (Halperin *Acta*, Index, p. 568);
siler-geld and *mu s-siler* (the first part of the latter is Hebrew, the second Yiddish) – a 'buying off' of students to keep them out of anti-Jewish riots (Halperin, *Acta*, Index, p. 565, four instances in Hebrew documents);
sok for *kopa* – sixty (Halperin, *Acta*, Index, p. 570);
zekser for Polish *szóstak* – grossus sex duplex or double six grossed (144) (Halperin, *Acta*, Index, p. 560).

Polish Linguistic Analysis

Polish linguistic analysis of documents written in Polish which are concerned with Jewish autonomy in pre-partition Poland contains apparently fewer problems, but still calls for the Polish language scholar's expertise in Hebrew and Yiddish and some awareness of Jewish culture, both material and spiritual, in that era.

Polish–Jewish relations at state administrative level resulted in the introduction of Hebrew words into Polish, sometimes through Yiddish. Such words are: *kahał, kahalny* (of the *kehilla*), *przykahałek* (branch *kehilla*), *koszerny, trefny, szkolnik*, and so on. What is more, some old Polish words changed their meanings from the sixteenth and seventeenth centuries, as a result of Polish–Jewish contacts.

The word *bożnica*, or *bóżnica*, in old Polish had the general sense of prayer house, that is, for all religions, including pagan.[22] From the sixteenth century until now *bożnica* (*bóżnica*) has meant a *Jewish* prayer house.

In Polish documents referring to Jewish autonomy, as well as in numerous privileges issued for Jews in Poland the word *szkoła* [school] means the same as *bożnica*. This is a direct copy from Yiddish. The word *sy: ł* (with a long *y*) in the central (that is,

Hebrew), *Leshonenu* 42, 1975, pp. 152–255. The article will also be published in English.
[22] Cf. *Słownik staropolski* I, Warsaw, 1953–5, p. 145.

Polish) dialect of Yiddish means only *bożnica*, but *sul* in the Lithuanian dialect of Yiddish means both a school and *bożnica*, prayer and study converging as they do in Jewish life.

Both words for the Jewish prayer house often appear in combination, as in a document, no. 138, of 20 July 1746, containing a complaint by the Jews of Przemyśl against the Jesuit college, regarding an attack on the synagogue and listing all the damage: 'Wszedłszy *do szkoły to jest bożnicy żydowskiej*' – having entered the *school, to wit, the Jewish prayer house* (Schorr, *Żydzi*, p. 299).

The synonyms *bożnica* and *szkoła* in the meaning of Jewish prayer house are not equivalent to the Hebrew expression *bet kneset* which means 'house of assembly'. The nearest translation of that phrase is the word *synagoga* (assembly), taken from Greek via Latin. But before *synagoga* became the word for Jewish prayer house, it too passed through a curious semantic process. In the relevant documents, *synagoga* means the whole Jewish community, as in 'Generalna *Synagoga* Koronna' (the General *Synagogue* of Royal Poland) in a Polish document, and similarly 'Congress *Synagogi* Koronney (the Congress of the *Synagogue* of Royal Poland) – (Halperin, *Acta*, pp. liv, lxv.) Another example appears in a document written in the official language of the Grand Duchy of Lithuania: 'starszie Żidy sboru Volodimerskago . . . i vsee *sinagogi* zidovskoe voevodstva Volynskago javne' [Jewish elders of the country of Vlodimir and all Jewish *synagogues* of Wolyn province] (Halperin, *Acta*, p. xxii, 28 August 1666).

With the passage of time, and until today, *synagoga* came to mean Jewish, and no other, house of prayer. In Latin documents, *synagoga* sometimes appears in conjunction with the word *schola* in the sense of Jewish prayer house: 'circa *synagogam vulgo scholam*' (Goldberg, *Privileges*, p. 90, line 36). *Synagogue* also appears in German documents as *Synagoge* (Halperin, *Acta*, p. xxxvii, no. 40). The word *Schul* appears next to it as well as separately in these documents: 'das wir allhier keine *Schul* halten sollen' (Halperin, *Acta*, p. xxxv, no. 38).

Doktor, originally meaning 'learned theologian, especially biblical specialist',[23] is another example of neo-semantization. In Latin and Polish documents connected with the Jewish self-government in

---

[23] Cf. *Słownik staropolski* II, Warsaw, 1956, p. 121, under the entry for *Doktor* (doctor): 'uczony, szczególnie znawca Biblii i teologii, w chrześcijaństwie niekiedy oficjalny tytuł pisarzy teologicznych, vir doctus, imprimis Scripturae sanctae et theologiae peritus, apud Christianos etiam scriptorum theologorum titulus'. Quotation from the fifteenth century.

Poland, the notion *doktor*, referring to Jews, also means a 'rabbi' (sometimes with Iudaeus added, and, moreover, 'the president of Jewish community'. So it is to be found in M. Schorr's work.[24]

Examples could be multiplied. Thus it is beyond any doubt that Polish scientists should read the appropriate historical documents, and broaden the range of their semantic inquiries to the specific and important group of words, which are being neo-semantized in relation to Jewish autonomy in Poland.

---

[21] M. Schorr, 'Organizacya Żydów w dawnej Polsce od najdawniejszych czasów aż do roku 1772' (The organization of the Jews in Old Poland from earliest times to 1772), *Kwartalnik Historyczny*, Lwów, I, 1899 p. 21.

10 · The Terminology of the Bodies of Jewish Self-Government

Anatol Leszczyński

Any student of the history of Jewish self-government in the old Polish Commonwealth will have noticed a bewildering variety in the terminology used in historical sources and in the secondary literature on the three levels of the Jewish autonomy.[1] This chapter expands on an earlier article,[2] and its aim is to discuss and systematize this problem, and to suggest suitable terms for these institutions, whether in English or in Polish.

The lowest level of Jewish autonomy in the Nobles' Commonwealth was composed of communities known in the sources as *kahały*[3] (Hebr. *Kehillot*), that is communities[4] (Pol. *zbory*) or 'synagogues'.[5] These were municipal, and very occasionally rural, administrative and religious associations of the Jewish population with their own administration (Hebr. *vaad hakehila*), which

---

[1] See for example J. Kleczyński and F. Kluczycki eds, *Liczba głów żydowskich w Koronie z taryf roku 1765* (The Number of Jewish heads in royal Poland according to the 1765 lists), Kraków, 1898, pp. 19–20. In this publication I have noticed the lack of consistency in using terminology of various categories of *kahały* – even within one province.
[2] A. Leszczyński, 'Sprawa nazewnictwa organów samorządu żydowskiego w dawnej Rzeczypospolitej' (The problem of the terminology of the organs of Jewish self-government in the Old Commonwealth), *BŻIH* 139, 1986 pp. 13–23.
[3] M. Horn, ed., *Regesty dokumentów i ekscerpty z Metryki Koronnej do historii Żydów w Polsce 1697–1795* (Summaries and excerpts from the Crown Registers for the history of the Jews in Poland 1697–1795), I, *Czasy Saskie* [Saxon Period] *1697–1763*, Wrocław/Warsaw/Kraków/Gdańsk/Łódź 1984, reg. 101, p. 18; on 27 June 1731 King August II passed jurisdiction of the *kahały* of the Ruthenian province to the Lwów castellan.
[4] AGAD, *Kapiciana*, 46, p. 340. The Great Crown Treasurer Marcin Zamojski's proclamation passed on 16 Dec. 1684 'for the Tykocin community' concerning the poll tax payment.
[5] AGAD, *Archiwum Gospodarcze Wilanów. Administracja Dóbr Opatowskich* (quoted further as *ADO*), I/109, p. 9. Extract from the Opatów synagogue elders' bills from 1752–3.

consisted of the *kahał*'s elders. The terms *kahał*, 'community' and 'synagogue' are used not only for this administration, but also for the whole population of the community. For instance, in a warning issued in 1622 in Lublin by the elders of three provinces (districts – *ziemstwa*) to the elders of the Grodno *kahał* and its rabbi we read: 'Our sincere greetings . . . to the leader of the holy flock of the holy Grodno *kahał*' (Hebr. *Kehilla kedosha*);[6] on 31 March 1698 the Poznań *voivode* Wojciech Breza addressed a proclamation to the 'elders, rabbi and the whole synagogue' in Poznań;[7] in a *mandamus* of 22 July 1702, the Ruthenian governor Jan Jabłonowski is quoted as 'considering the earnest petitions of the unbelieving elders and the whole Przemyśl synagogue'.[8]

In published works we find various interpretations of the term *kahał*. Majer Bałaban considers *kahał* as meaning only the administration.[9] The author of the entry *kahał* in the *Jewish Encyclopaedia* treats it as 'Jewish self-government and the community'.[10] According to Bałaban, one should distinguish between two closely related words: *kahał*' and *kohoł*'; the first meaning the community, the second only its administration.

In the surviving sources, communities were divided into 'synagogues of the main towns', *kahals* and *przykahałeks* (sub-kahals), according to their place in the administrative structure of Jewish self-government. This division is confirmed in King Jan III's proclamation of 6 May 1677, which states that Jews lived in 'main towns' and smaller towns, villages and estates, 'and so every Jew

---

[6] S. Dubnow, 'Akty yevrieyskogo koronnogo sieyma ili "Vaada Chetirokh Oblastiey", tykochinskaya kolektsia (1621–1699)', *Yevreyskaya Starina*, 4 1912, doc. 3, p. 73; this was also published by A. Leszczyński, 'Spór pomiedzy kahałami Grodna i Tykocina o hegemonię nad skupiskami żydowskim pogranicza Korony z Litwą w XVII w. w świetle dokumentów' (Dispute between the Grodno and the Tykocin *kahał* over supervision of Jewish centres on the Crown and Lithuanian border in the seventeenth century in the light of sources), part 2, *BŻIH* 129–30, (1984), doc. 3, pp. 139–40; I drew attention in nn. 4 and 5 to the variety of terminology concerning Jewish self-government.
[7] AP, Poznań (quoted henceforth as APP), *Poznańska Księga Grodzka* (Poznań Town Records), 1242, p. 751, a proclamation about *kahał* elections.
[8] M. Schorr, *Żydzi w Przemyślu do końca XVIII w., opracowanie i wydawnictwo materiału archiwalnego* (Jews in Przemyśl till the end of the eighteenth century, edition and publication of sources), Lwów, 1903, doc. 130, p. 208.
[9] M. Bałaban, 'Ustrój kahału w Polsce w XVI–XVIII w.' (The kahał system of government in Poland in the sixteenth to the eighteenth centuries (*Kwartalnik poświęcony badaniom przeszłości Żydów w Polsce* 1, 1912, fasc. 2, pp. 17, 12, 34; idem, *Żydzi lwowscy na przełomie XVI i XVII w.* (Lwów Jews at the turn of the sixteenth and seventeenth centuries), Lwów, 1906, p. 260.
[10] *Yevreyskaya Encyklopedia*, Petersburg, IX, p. 78.

singulariter is subject to the elders of the above-mentioned main towns and districts, to which old tradition and division of districts and synagogues he is obedient, in their jurisdiction and supervision'. In the same proclamation the king obliged 'the Jewish elders of the main towns' to divide state tax payments among 'lesser [lower] towns, villages and district estates'.[11] I will return to the term 'district town' referring to the intermediate layer of Jewish autonomous organization later in this chapter.

Similar categories of communities are found in the following sources: a confirmation by King August II on 14 July 1699, of a declaration of the 'deputies and senior judges to the community (*zbór*) and the Ołyka *kahał*';[12] August III created a commission on 7 November 1750 'to liquidate the debts of the whole leadership, as well as of the synagogues and *kahałs* of all unbelieving Jews of the province of Wołyń;[13] the same monarch, in a mandate of 9 July 1752 to meet the Przemyśl Jews' demand, called Jews *et omnes parochies ad synagogam Praemisliensiem pertinentes, civitates, oppida ac pagos* to meet their duties towards the 'head community';[14] the owner of the town of Wodzisław in his declaration of 18 November 1740 used the following terms: 'unbelieving Jewish elders and the whole commonalty of the synagogue of my hereditary town' and 'the long-owned parishes'.[15] As appears from the above quotations, 'communities' and 'synagogues' were communities of a higher category, and occur in the documents before the terms *kahałs* and 'parishes'.

Bałaban considered that the term 'parish' applied to those Jews who inhabited the region under the *kahał*'s administration; these were usually single families or *przykahałeks* subject to the *kahał*.[16] In a contemporary translation of a Hebrew resolution issued by the Council of the Four Lands in Jarosław in 1692, and confirmed in 1712, a 'general town' was called a *kahał* of this sort; to it were subject all 'those living up to two miles away in remote towns and

---

[11] AGAD, *Kapiciana* 45, pp. 168, 170–1, 174; A. Leszczyński, *BŻIH* 113, (1980, pp. 86–8 published the same document; R. Rybarski, *Skarb i pieniądz za Jana Kazimierza, Michała Korybuta i Jana III* (the Treasury and currency during the reign of Jan Kazimierz, Michał Korybut and Jan III), Warsaw, 1937, p. 224; the author has made use of the same document but from a different copy.

[12] Horn, *Regesty*, reg. 94, p. 17.

[13] Ibid., reg. 335, p. 72.

[14] Schorr, *Żydzi w Przemyślu*, doc. 140, pp. 233–5.

[15] AP, Kraków (quoted henceforth as APK), *Castrensia Cracoviensia*, vol. 165, B, rel., pp. 3247–8.

[16] M. Bałaban, *Żydzi lwowscy*, p. 257.

villages'.[17] In Bałaban's works, I have come across the term 'free town'. It signified those *kahals* which elected and sent delegates or envoys to the meetings of the Council of the Four Lands.[18] It also refers to the *kahal* around which Jews had settled, in surrounding villages and towns, and organized their own *kahals* or *przykahałeks*, as the 'capital (mother)' *kahal* (Pol. *stołeczny*).[19] A community which was granted financial independence and whose delegates were admitted to the Council of the Four Lands, and to its debates or to the debates of the district (*okręgowy*) dietines, is referred to by Bałaban as a completely 'emancipated' *kahał*.[20] The 'central' or 'land' *kahal* was, according to him, a community of this sort, whose authorities controlled and governed the surrounding *przykahałeks*.[21] Moses Schorr introduced a category of 'neighbouring' *kahals*, which were subordinate to the 'chief community'.[22] Simon Dubnow agrees with Bałaban in referring to a *przykahałek* as a community which paid its taxes indirectly through a superior *kahał*.[23]

Dubnow was one of the first in historical literature to introduce, at the end of the nineteenth century, the division of communities into three categories, regional, intermediate and small *kahals*. According to him, the regional (Hebr. *qalil*; Pol. *okręgowy*) *kahal* supervised 'smaller' communities situated over a 'considerable' geographical area. Jews living in small towns and villages were subject to the intermediate *kahals*. As small *kahals*, Dubnow considered those communities which attended to internal matters independently but 'officially' were subordinate to the authorities of a neighbouring, bigger *kahal*; this subordination was connected with tax collection and 'similar duties'.[24] In this division, Dubnow did

[17] I. Halperin, ed., 'Pinkas vaad arba aratsot', in *Acta Congressus Generalis Judaeorum Poloniae (1580–1764)*, Jerusalem, 1945, no. 45, p. xliii, in Hebrew, with Polish, German and Latin appendices.
[18] M. Bałaban, *Historia i literatura żydowska ze szczególnym uwzględnieniem historii Żydów w Polsce*, (Jewish History and Literature with special reference to Jewish History in Poland), III, Lwów/Warsaw/Kraków, 1925, pp. 220–1.
[19] M. Bałaban, 'Z zagadnień ustrojowych żydostwa polskiego, Lwów a ziemstwo rusko-bracławskie w XVIII w.' (On the problems of government of Polish Jewry, Lwów and the Ruthenian-Bracław district in the eighteenth century), *Studia lwowskie*, 1932, p. 41.
[20] M. Bałaban 'Kagal', in *Istoria yevreyskogo naroda* XI, Moscow, 1914, p. 160.
[21] Bałaban, *Żydzi lwowscy*, pp. 250, 252–4.
[22] Schorr, *Żydzi w Przemyślu*, doc. 140, p. 233.
[23] S. Dubnow, 'Istoricheskie oboshchenie, podgotovlienie raboty dla istori ruskikh yevreyev', *Voskhod* 4, 1894, pp. 16, 25; Bałaban, 'Kagal', p. 160.
[24] Dubnow, 'Istoricheskie', p. 25.

not take into consideration the importance of *kahał* representation at the higher levels of Jewish self-government although, as I have already mentioned, this was later taken into account by Bałaban. Israel Halperin, for his part, divided communities into main, independent (self-governing) and other.[25]

On the basis of earlier investigations, and taking into account newly available sources, I propose to follow Dubnow and Halperin and divide communities into three categories. The first would include 'main *kahałs*' and *kahałs* having land rights'. Main *kahałs* are those communities with the strongest economic base, which regularly sent delegates to two levels of meetings of Jewish self-government, that is to the district and to the central administration. *Kahały* with land rights were, in practice, the communities in the 'principal' towns (Kraków, Lublin, Lwów, Poznań), which sent their deputies directly to the meetings of the main organs, bypassing the second, district, level. The second category, that is 'intermediate' *kahały*, are those communities which usually sent delegates to the district or regional meetings and only sporadically to the highest levels, and also other independent communities subject to the authority (*seniorat*) of a district or region (*ziemstwo* or *okręg*). *Przykahałeks*, the third category, I take to be those communities whose self-governing prerogatives were limited by both of the superior types of *kahałs*. The first two categories of *kahał* exercised their authority over Jews inhabiting certain regions of the *kahał* administration (possibly some *przykahałeks* as well). On the basis of newly found sources, I have concluded that at the end of the seventeenth century, in many cases, the *przykahałek* authorities paid their taxes directly to the tax collectors,[26] not, as is maintained by Bałaban and Dubnow, through superior bodies.[27] This apportionment of tax was, to a certain extent, an index of the relative independence of *przykahałeks*.

---

[25] Halperin, 'Pinkas', app: Hebrew map – Jews of the Four Lands in Poland 1667–1764.

[26] It appears unequivocally from fiscal authorities, for example from an order of payment issued by the Crown Treasury on 13 Oct. 1696 for the 'district' Jews of Sandomierz-Kraków, where the sum to be paid by various small Jewish centres is specified for, for instance, Baranów, Iwaniska, Rozwadów, Rudniki: AGAD, *Archiwum Skarbu Koronnego* (Files of the Crown Treasury) (quoted henceforth as *ASK*), MS25, p. 225. In the apportionment of Jewish poll tax for the Crown Jews 1710–1711, we find small towns and single *arendors*, Czartoryski Library, Kraków (BCz), MS 2666, ff. 31–41.

[27] See n. 23.

Over the *kahały*, as the intermediate level of Jewish self-government in the sixteenth century, stood the provinces, lands or districts (Hebr. *medina, erets*; Pol. *ziemie, ziemstwa*) and, after the fragmentation of the territorial *kahał* administration following the wars of the second half of the seventeenth century, also the regions (Pol. *okręgi*). This terminology is frequently found in the sources. In his proclamation of 15 July 1750 King August III used the formula 'to the synagogues and *kahały* of the Ruthenian province'.[28] In using the word 'province', the king was recalling an earlier period before the wars of the second half of the seventeenth century, when the intermediate layer of Jewish self-government consisted of the four provinces of Great Poland, Little Poland, Ruthenia and, until 1623, the Great Duchy of Lithuania. In another document, a resolution of the rabbis of the Zamoyski *Ordynacja* (entailed estate) of 14 January 1700, we read: 'All orders of payment, which have been issued for towns and smaller towns from districts, we accept.'[29] The same terms are found in a 1702 protest 'against the same Jews living in large and smaller towns in the Kalisz-Poznań district',[30] and in Queen Maria Kazimiera's privilege issued to the Jews of Olesko between the years 1665 and 1698: 'We permit appeals to the Jewish district court in serious cases.'[31] A different term is found in the title of a document: 'Security of the deputy of elders from the district *kahały* of the Wołyń province (*województwo*) of 10 February 1700'.[32] Basing himself on this document, Dubnow gave the provincial body the name of the 'Wołyń Synagogue'. This body, he claimed, had authority over all Wołyń *kahały*, and as the 'regional *kahał* diet' was the central organ of the area.[33] Like Dubnow, Bałaban used the name 'Wołyń synagogue' or 'synagogue of Wołyń province'.[34]

[28] Horn, *Reqesty*, reg. 380, p. 79.
[29] AP, Lublin (quoted henceforth as APL), Sąd Komisarski w Zamościu, (Zamość Commissioner's Court), no. 6, p. 23; see also T. Opas, 'Sytuacja ludności żydowskiej w miastach szlacheckich województwa lubelskiego w X VIII w.' (The situation of the Jewish population in the Nobles' towns in Lublin province in the eighteenth century), *BŻIH* 1968, 64, p. 24.
[30] APP, Poznańska Księga Grodzka, 1236, p. 91.
[31] Jacob Goldberg, ed., *Jewish Privileges in the Polish Commonwealth; Charters of Rights Granted to the Jewish Communities in Poland-Lithuania in the 16th-18th Centuries*, Israeli Academy of Sciences and Humanities, Jerusalem, 1985, p. 234.
[32] *ASK*, MS 25, f. 356, 'Security concerning the scribe of Wołyń province', the term 'district' (*powiatowe*) *kahały*' applies to communities situated within the borders of the province.
[33] Dubnow, 'Istoricheskie', p. 28.
[34] M. Bałaban, 'Yevreyskii seym, v Polshe ili vaad Korony i seymiki ili vaady okrugov', in *Istoria* XI, p. 166. (See n. 20.)

Similarly, the Jewish population of Lithuania living in the provinces of Witebsk and Mścisław was subject to the authority (*sendirat*) of the 'White Ruthenian Synagogue'.[35]

The Sandomierz governor, Jan Tarło, in a document issued on 7 June 1742, used the phrase 'Sandomierz district [Jewish] elders'.[36] It is clear that the term *ziemscy* (district elders) originates from the Polish for district (*ziemia*), not from the Hebrew word for land (*erets*) and, in addition, in the old Polish administration, most districts formed part of a province. *Erets* should thus not be translated literally as land but as district.

Roman Rybarski noticed that in the assessment of Jewish poll tax, 'districts' are mentioned, but not in the literal meaning of this term. A Jewish district often included more than one district – often a whole province.[37] This matter is clearly illustrated by an order of payment issued by the Crown Treasury on 7 August 1692, for 'the Jewish elders of the Ruthenian district', ordering them to pay 610 Polish złoty in poll tax. From a receipt adjoined to the document, it appears that the sum was paid 'for public expenses by the Jewish district elders of the province of Ruthenia'.[38] Bałaban has quoted a poll tax assessment from the year 1691 referring to Jews of the 'Kraków and Sandomierz district',[39] but he failed to explain the essential meaning of the phrase, namely that it applied to the Jewish population of the Kraków-Sandomierz district. When discussing above the *kahał* categories, I have mentioned 'district town' which, linked with notion 'district Jews' referred to – as is clear from the sources – a district or regional *kahał*, which itself was, in the terms of my classification, a main *kahał*. Because of the difference in the meaning of the term district (*powiat*) in the old

---

[35] M. Marek, 'Administrativnoye dielenie yevreyskikh posielieni v litovskoy oblasti', in *Istoria* XI, p. 208.

[36] APK, *Castrensia Cracoviensis*, vol. 166, pp. 1960–1, on the disobedience towards the rabbi appointed by the governor. See also M. Strzemski, 'Obraz Żydów polskich' (Image of Polish Jews), *Znak*, 25, 1983, 339–40, p. 564. Strzemski holds that *ziemstwo* (district) is an administrative unit but in fact in the expression 'Diet of Four Lands' it is used to mean 'lands' or 'countries'.

[37] Rybarski, *Skarb i pieniądz*, p. 222.

[38] *ASK* 24, p. 609.

[39] M. Bałaban, *Historia Żydów w Krakowie i na Kazimierzu 1304–1868*, (History of Jews in Kraków and Kazimierz, 1304–1868; 2nd rev. edn of *Dzieje Żydów* (1912) – see ch. 18, n. 3), Kraków, 1936, p. 191; see 'Sandomierz, Wołyń, Chełm, Lublin and Przemyśl district Jews' in a poll tax assessment 1710–11, BCz, MS 1079, ff. 176–93. See also n. 26.

Commonwealth, it is inconvenient to use the word *powiat* for a Jewish district in historical writing.

Ignacy Schipper introduced a uniform terminology for the intermediate level of Jewish self-government. He called a district (*ziemstwo*) and region (*okręg*) those units which sent four and two representatives respectively to meetings of the Council of the Four Lands.[40] Halperin, in his work, made only a very general division into districts and regions.[41] Both of them do attempt to provide numbers. Thus, Schipper arrives at six districts, six regions and four independent *kahals* in royal Poland (*Korona*) in 1717; and fifteen districts, three regions and four independent *kahals* in 1762. Halperin, on the other hand, notes five districts and three regions down to 1764.[42] The determination of the exact number of middle-level units of Jewish self-government under the Crown is the aim of my further research.

A similar situation obtained in Lithuania, where only five main *kahals* (Brześć, Grodno, Pińsk, Słuck, and Wilno) representing the relevant districts and regions had the right to send delegates to the meetings of the Council of Lithuania (*Vaad medinat Lita*).[43] The separate Sephardic superkahał organization in Poland has been described by Salo Baron as a 'super-community'.[44]

Regular assemblies of the district and regional *kahals* were called meetings (*zjazdy*),[45] congresses[46] and dietines. During such meetings, delegates elected a district and regional seniorat (Hebr. *vaad hemedina, qalil*), which functioned permanently under an

---

[40] I. Schipper, 'Der tsuzamenshtel funem vaad arba aratsos', *Historishe Shriftn* 1, 1929, p. 86.
[41] Halperin, 'Pinkas', map.
[42] I. Shipper, 'Der tsuzamenshtel', pp. 76, 80; Halperin, 'Pinkas', map.
[43] M. Marek, 'Administrativnoye dielenie', p. 7; see Bałaban, *Historia i literatura* III, p. 212.
[44] Salo Baron, *The Jewish Community: Its History and Structure to the American Revolution*, I, Philadelphia, 1942, pp. 283–347. The author devotes a whole chapter to the problem under discussion. My information comes from a review: J. Shatzky, 'A geshikhte fun der yidisher kehile', *Yivo Bleter* 23:2 1944, p. 221.
[45] M. Kramer, 'Dzieje Żydów przemyskich na przełomie XVII i XVIII w.' (A history of Przemyśl Jews at the turn of the seventeenth and eighteenth centuries), Warsaw, 1934, Master's dissertation, Archive of the Jewish Historical Institute, Warsaw; quoted further as AŻIH, no. 24, p. 87.
[46] Ossoliński Library in Wrocław (quoted henceforth as BOs), MS 303, f. 223. Commissioner's court sentence of 6 September 1754; M. Bałaban, *Z zagadnień*, p. 9.

elected marshal who presided at the meetings.[47] The delegates were a legislative body for the Jews they represented, dealing with, among other things, financial matters (tax assessment) and electing deputies to the highest body of Jewish autonomy, who were then given their instructions before leaving. The analogous organization and similar functions to those of the nobles' dietines (*sejmiki*) resulted in the Jewish district and regional meetings being called 'dietines'. For example, on an order of payment issued by the Great Crown Treasurer on 12 April 1677, the tax collector noted: 'at the Jewish dietine, before the Lwów fair'.[48] In a deputies' instruction prepared for the Kiev delegates in Włodzimierz on 26 March 1698 the term 'Jewish dietine' was used;[49] in the security of 10 February 1700 already mentioned, we read: 'We, the undersigned deputy elders . . . as we have once supplied a security on ourselves at our last Jewish dietine called in Łokacze on the 5th of the month July 1699'.[50] Rabbis of the Zamoyski *Ordynacja* decided on 14 January 1700 that 'all judgement shall belong to the dietine's edict . . . Any rabbi or elder shall have the power to judge . . . only as the dietine indicated.'[51] In the Ołyka *kahał*'s syndic's protest of 17 April 1703, the word 'dietine' is used a number of times.[52] In the decision issued at Jarosław in the year 1670 in Hebrew, the highest body of Jewish self-government allowed the authorities of the Tykocin *kahał* to pay from the 'meeting's treasury' for dietine expenses (Hebr. *hotsaot seymiks*), for each dietine 100 Polish złoty.[53] Mojżesz Schorr has worked out from

---

[47] In 1752 the Kraków-Sandomierz district, the Jews' marshal was Nokhem of Wodzisław, BCz, MS 1079, f. 251. The allocation of poll tax in 1752 and 1753; see also I. Lewin, 'Dzieje sejmików Żydów Wielkopolskich' (The history of the Jews of Greater Poland's dietines), in idem, *Z historii i tradycji, szkice z dziejów kultury żydowskiej* (From history and tradition, sketches from Jewish culture), Warsaw, 1983, pp. 64–75.

[48] *ASK* VI, MS 20, f. 288; see also s. 22, p. 118.

[49] *Arkhiv Yugo-Zapadnoy Rossii izdavaymi komiseyu dla rozbora drievnikh aktov sostayashchey pri kiyevskom, podolskom i volynskom general gubernatore* III, part II. *Postanovlenia provintzonyalnykh seymikov Yugo-Zapadnoy Rossiji 1698–1726 godach*, Kiev, 1910, p. 11. Deputies were instructed to propose the abolition of the middle and lowest levels of Jewish self-government.

[50] *ASK* MS 24, f. 356, a copy.

[51] APL, Commissioner's court in Zamość, s. 6. p. 24v.

[52] *Arkhiv Yugo-Zapadnoy Rossii izdavaymi vremenoyu komiseyu dla rozbora drevnykh aktov*, I, part II, *Akty o gorodakh*, Kiev, 1869, doc. 68, p. 207. Protest against the authorities of Jewish self-government for not calling a meeting of the (Jewish) dietines of Wołyń province of Ołyka.

[53] Dubnow, 'Akty', doc. 13, pp. 81–2; see n. 6. Resolution issued by demand of the *kahał* authorities.

the sources that the dietines between the *kahał* and the general meetings were called 'comitalia'.⁵⁴ Bałaban used the terms 'meetings' (*zjazdy*) and 'dietines',⁵⁵ and Schipper 'dietines' and 'small vaad'.⁵⁶ Thus the use of the expression 'Jewish dietines' or 'Jewish sejmiki' in historical literature is justified.

At the head of Jewish self-government from 1580 until its abolition in 1764 was the highest autonomous body – the Board or Council of the Four Lands (Hebr. *vaad arba aratsot*). Although, as is known, in 1623 the Jews of Lithuania separated from the Crown Jews and organized their own top body (Hebr. *vaad medinat Lita*, or *vaad Lita*),⁵⁷ as appears from source materials, until the end of its existence, the Crown Jews called their central representation the *'vaad arba aratsot'*,⁵⁸ even though there were many more districts and regions. The Council of the Four Lands consisted of deputies,⁵⁹ chief leaders (*starsi generalni*)⁶⁰ and seniors (delegates) of various districts and regions, and of *kahałs* having land rights. The basic functions of the Council of the Four Lands, as the main representative body of the Jewish population, were attending to fiscal matters (tax assessment), secular legislation and intervention with the appropriate state authorities. Meetings were presided over by a marshal,⁶¹ who also presided at the permanent *seniorat*, which was formed of trustees (*wiernicy*),⁶² rabbis and scribes.⁶³

---

[54] M. Schorr, 'Organizacya Żydów w dawnej Polsce od najdawniejszych czasów az do r. 1772 – głównie na podstawie źródeł archiwalnych' (The organization of the Jews in Old Poland from earliest times to 1772 – based mainly on archival sources), *Kwartalnik Historyczny*, 13, 1899, I, p. 757.
[55] Bałaban, 'Z zagadnień', p. 8.
[56] Schipper, 'Der Tsuzamenshtel', p. 73.
[57] The reasons for the Lithuanian Jews' breakaway from the Crown Jews are discussed by A. Leszczyński, 'Spór', *BŻIH* 126-7, 1983, pp. 89 ff.
[58] See for example, a letter of 1725 from the Lublin *kahał* elders to the scribes of the Crown Jews' diet, on poll tax, in 'Dokumentn tsu der geshikhte fun "Vaadi haglilot" in Poyln', *Historishe Shriftn fun Yivo* 2, 1937, doc. II, pp. 641-2.
[59] 'Posłowie od kahałów delegowani' (Envoys delegated by kahałs), BOs, MS 303, ff. 223. A copy of a sentence of commissioner's court from the year 1754.
[60] 'Z pogłównego żydowskiego podług podziału starszych generalnych uczyniona' (Consisting of the poll tax assessment according to the leading elders), *ASK* VI, MS 16, ff. 335; order of payment, 12 Oct. 1674.
[61] 'Marszałek starszy generalności Żydów Majorek (Mejer) z Dubna', (Marshal of the Jewish leadership, Majorek (Meyer) from Dubno), BOs, MS 13705/III, f. 131; land court sentence from Sandomierz province, 2 May 1765, about a case in 1758.
[62] 'Wiernicy generalni Żydów Koronnych' (General Trustees of the Crown Jews), BCz, MS 746, f. 896; poll tax assessment for 1763/4.
[63] 'Z podania Starszych koronnych pisarzy' (From a petition of the scribes of the Crown elders), BCz, MS 1079, f. 171; assessment for 1737.

142   INSTITUTIONS

In the sources, this body is referred to as 'General Congress',[64] 'General Jewish Congress',[65] 'Jewish Congress',[66] *'Congressus Judaicus'*,[67] 'General Jewish Meeting',[68] 'Meeting (*Zjazd*)',[69] 'Leadership (*Generalność*) of the Crown Synagogue',[70] and 'Leadership'.[71] I have come across an interesting expression in a document prepared in the royal offices. On 19 November 1669, Michał Korybut Wiśniowiecki granted leave to the Zamość Jews, in order that they might 'sit in *consyliis* with other Crown Jews'.[72] The phrase 'Jewish Crown elders'[73] also referred to the Council and its representatives spoke 'in the name of all elders as well as the commonalty of our whole Jewish nation living under the Polish Crown'.[74]

This body is also referred to in the sources as a 'Diet' (*Sejm*). From a letter of 23 May 1687 written by the Zabłudów *starosta* and Wilno *łowczy* Tobiasz Pękalski to the *conciliators*, we learn that in Zabłudów 'now, according to the Jews' will, their general meeting takes place, which they call their diet, and all of the Duchy [of Lithuania] rabbis are to arrive here'.[75] In the instructions for the Kiev deputies of 26 March 1698 the phrase 'Jewish Diets' is

[64] *ASK* VI, MS 6, p. 64. The congress took place in Pinczów in 1659.
[65] Horn, *Regesty*, reg. 120, p. 22.
[66] Halperin, 'Pinkas', doc. 57, p. lv.
[67] Schorr, 'Organizacja', p. 486.
[68] Bałaban, *Historia Żydów w Krakowie* II, pp. 267–8; Halperin, 'Pinkas', doc. 60, p. lxi.
[69] 'Podział na zjeździe w Pinczowie przez starszych Żydów uczyniony' (Assessment made by the Jewish elders during a meeting in Pinczow), *ASK* VI, s. 16, p. 21; payment order of 9 Sept. 1673; 'Zjazd lwowski' (The Lwów meeting), ibid., p. 357, payment order of 2 Oct. 1674. The place of meeting was also denoted by the term 'fair', for example, 'The fair of St Agnes' in Lwów in 1651, *ASK* VI, MS 4, ff. 344, 348, payment order of 16 Apr. 1652; 'Jarmark Jarosławski' (Jarosław Fair), *Kapiciana* 45, p. 173, King Jan III's proclamation of 6 May 1677.
[70] BCz, MS 1079, f. 281, poll tax assessment for 1756.
[71] *ADO*, I/109, p. 25, *Kahał* bill 1759–60.
[72] AGAD, *Sigillaty* 11, f. 29, p. 58; see J. Morgensztern, 'Regesty dokumentów Metryki Koronnej i Sigillat do historii Żydów w Polsce 1669–1696', *BŻIH* 69, 1969, reg. 7, p. 73, in the summary 'w Żydowskim Sejmie Koronnym' (in the Jewish Crown diet).
[73] AGAD, *Metryka Koronna* (Crown Registers) quoted further as *MK*, 136, ff. 132–3, King Zygmunt III introduced poll tax on 14 Mar. 1591; see Morgensztern, 'Regesty (1588–1632)', *BŻIH* 51, 1964, reg., p. 60.
[74] *MK*, 205, ff. 54–7, and *MK*, 369, ff. 235–8, Authentication of an act of 18 May 1666; see Morgensztern, 'Regesty (1660–1688)', *BŻIH* 67, 1968, reg. 133, p. 89, in the summary 'w imieniu sejmu żydowskiego' (in the name of the Jewish diet).
[75] AGAD, Archiwum Radziwiłłów, sec. V, tekxa 264, no. 11560/III. I should like to thank Professor Tadeusz Wasilewski for pointing it out to me. The diet meeting of Lithuanian Jews in Zabłudów in 1687 is discussed in M. Bersztejn, *Zabłudowe, Yizkor Bukh*, ed. S. Cesler, J. Reznik and I. Cesler, Buenos Aires, 1961, p. 74.

used.[76] Stanisław Grodziski, the Great Crown *vice-instigator* and Kraków deputy, demanded 'the annulment of the Jewish Diet' during the 1748 General Diet.[77] In his regulation of 2 November 1747 for the Jews of Kraków, the Kraków *voivode* Jan Klemens Branicki noted that 'they should elect for the Jewish Diet two district (land) elders'.[78] In the Włodzimierz *kahał*'s elders' testimony of 28 August 1666, I have come across the statement 'Jewish Diet' several times.[79] In a *laudum* of the Crown Jews' elders of 8 November 1718, 'Jewish Diet' is used and, at the conclusion of the document, we read: 'translated from Hebrew in the General Jewish Diet during which the generous Master Great Crown Treasurer Jan Przebendowski gave his approval'.[80] In a copy of a court verdict, 'translated from the Jewish writing', in a case between the Krzemieniec *kahał* authorities and 'the elders of the Crown Synagogue', it is stated that sentence was 'passed by the rabbinic elders at a Diet in Jarosław 9 Septembris 1724'.[81] The term 'Jewish Diet' also appears in a summons of 10 September 1740 of 'the noble Jan Jakub Szydłowski', who was a convert.[82] The expression 'General Diet in Jarosław' is used in an agreement entered into on 29 September 1740 by the Lwów Jews' elders and the elders of the district of the Ruthenian province.[83]

'The Great Court' (Hebr. *Bet Din Hagadol*),[84] which functioned under the presidency of the marshal of the diet, was an integral element of the central body of Jewish self-government. In a 1698 source, it is called 'the Jewish Tribunal'[85] or 'the Jewish Land Court'.[86]

---

[76] *Arkhiv Yugo-Zapadnoy Rossii* III, part II, p. 11.
[77] W. Konopczyński, ed., *Dyaryusze Sejmowe z XVIII w., Dyaryuisz Sejmu 1748 r.* (Diet diaries from the eighteenth century 1748 Diet diary), 1911, p. 253.
[78] 'Zbiór aktów do historii ustroju sądów prawa polskiego i kancelarii województwa krakowskiego z. wieku XVI–XVIII' (A collection of sources for the history of courts of Polish law and the Kraków Court Offices in the sixteenth to the eighteenth centuries), S. Kutrzeba, ed., *Archiwum Komisji Prawniczej Akademii Umiejętności w Krakowie* (Archive of the Law Commission of the Academy of Letters and Humanities in Kraków) VIII, part 2, Kraków, 1909, pp. 224–5.
[79] Halperin, 'Pinkas', doc. 21, p. xxii.
[80] Ibid., doc. 44, pp. xli–xlii.
[81] Ibid., doc. 50, p. xlviii–xlix.
[82] Ibid., doc. 60, p. lxi.
[83] Ibid., doc. 61, p. lxii.
[84] Schipper, 'Der tsuzamenshtel', p. 78; Bałaban, 'Yevreyskii', p. 171.
[85] *Arkhiv Yugo-Zapadnoy Rossii* III, part II, p. 11.
[86] This court functioned during 'the meeting in Przeworsk' in 1726, Kapiciana, 27, pp. 233–4. This document was published by A. Leszczyński, 'Żydzi ziemi bielskiej w dokumentach XVII–XVIII wieku' (Jews of the Bielsko district in the sources of the seventeenth to eighteenth centuries), *BŻIH* 116, 1980, doc. 8, p. 122.

These sources also show that the representatives of the Jewish population endeavoured to raise the standing of their administrative bodies in Poland. They considered that the '*vaad arba aratsot* is the continuation of the Jerusalem *Sanhedrin*'.[87] The use of the terms 'Diet' and 'tribunal' resulted from the same reasons already noted as for the use in sources of the phrase 'dietines'. So far I have found only one document originating from the royal offices in which 'Jewish Diet' is used. In King Jan III's rescript from 23 December 1681 concerning the termination of inter-*kahał* conflict, the king twice uses the expression 'the Diet of the unbelieving' Jews of the Great Duchy of Lithuania' and '[that] in their forthcoming Diet [the Jews] examine the conflict'.[88]

Ludwik Gumplowicz, in 1867, was one of the first historians to introduce the term 'Jewish Diet' referring to 'the meeting of rabbis and learned men from all over the country [which forms] the so-called Jewish Diet'.[89] Bałaban uses various terms in his works to name the highest body of Jewish autonomy: 'Jewish Diet', 'General Jewish Diet', 'Council of the Four Lands', [90] 'Crown Jews' Diet', 'Leadership (*Generalność*),[91] 'Jewish Diet in Lithuania'[92] and 'der Judenreichstag in Lublin'.[93] The same author uses the phrase 'Jewish Diet in Poland or the Crown *Vaad*' as a title of one of his works,[94] thus explaining the essence of the highest body of Jewish self-government. Similarly, Dubnow uses the title 'Acts of the Jewish Crown Diet or the *Vaad* of the Four Districts (lands)'.[95] Schorr uses 'the Diet of the Four Countries' and 'general meeting'.[96] Schipper makes use of such terms as 'Diet of Four Lands (*Sejm czterech*

---

[87] *Yevein Metsula, tj. Bagno Głębokie, kronika zdarzeń z lat 1648–1652, napisana przez Natana Hanowera z Zastawia i wydana po raz pierwszy w r. 1653 w Wenecji* (Yaveyn Metsula or the Deep Morass, a chronicle of events from 1648–1652, written by Natan Hanower of Zasław and first published in 1653 in Venice), tr. from the Hebrew original by M. Bałaban, Lwów, 1913, p. 75.

[88] *Akty izdavayemie Vilenskoyu Komiseyu dla rozbora drevnikh aktov*, XIX, *Akty o yevreyakh*, ed. F. Dobrianskii, I. Glebow, I. Sprogis and A. Turcewicz, Wilno, 1902, doc. 75, p. 122.

[89] L. Gumplowicz, *Prawodawstwo polskie względem Żydów* (Polish judicature in regard to the Jews), Kraków, 1867, pp. 115–16.

[90] Bałaban, *Żydzi lwowscy*, pp. xviii–xxi, 257.

[91] Bałaban, *Historia Żydów w Krakowie* II, pp. 20, 126, 255.

[92] Bałaban, *Historia i literatura* III, p. 224.

[93] Bałaban, *Die Judenstadt von Lublin*, Berlin, 1919, p. 35; '*Vier-Städte-Synode*' called '*Vaad arba aratsot*', J. Perles, 'Die Geschichte der Juden in Posen', *Monatschrift für Geschichte und Wissenschaft des Judenthums* 13, 1864, p. 365.

[94] Bałaban, 'Yevreyskii', p. 166; see n. 34.

[95] Dubnow, 'Akty', doc. 3; see n. 6.

[96] Schorr, *Żydzi w Przemyślu*, pp. 10, 60; idem, 'Organizacja', p. 486.

ziem)', 'General Jewish Diet', 'Diet of Jewish lands (districts-*ziem*)', 'Jewish leadership (*generalność*)' and 'the great *vaad*'.[97] Heinrich Graetz applies the term 'synod' (*Vierländersynode*),[98] and thus compares the highest body of Jewish autonomy with the Jewish synods in Germany. Dubnow used the same term, but only in the early period of his research.[99] Schorr insists that the German synods cannot be compared with the meetings of Polish Jews. The former were meetings of the clergy (rabbis), and community leaders; the latter, according to him, constituted a communal representation of a more secular and political character.[100] Michał Strzemski compromises with the term 'diet-synod' (*sejmosynod*),[101] and Izaak Lewin uses both 'Synod of the Four Lands' and 'Council of the Four Lands'.[102] Bałaban calls the court of the highest body of Jewish self-government a 'Diet Tribunal', as he maintains that it functioned like the Crown Tribunal,[103] while Abram Gawurin speaks of 'the highest Jewish court of the Four Lands'.[104] Stanisław Kutrzeba uses the term 'synod, that is, Jewish Diet' and '*vaad*', in which 'deputies elected by dietines' participated'.[105].

In post-war historical writing, the term 'Jewish Diets' is generally used,[106] with only occasional use of 'Jewish Diets called *vaad*'.[107] In the same period, works on the history of law use the term

---

[97] I. Schipper, 'Wewnętrzna organizacje Żydów w dawnej Rzeczypospolitej' (The Jews' inner organization in the Old Commonwealth), in *Żydzi w Polsce Odrodzonej* (Jews in reborn Poland) I, Warsaw, 1933, p. 93.
[98] H. Graetz, *Geschichte der Juden*, IX, 4th edn, Leipzig, 1907, pp. 430–1.
[99] Dubnow, 'Istoricheskie', p. 25.
[100] Schorr, *Żydzi w Przemyślu*, pp. 10, 60; idem, 'Organizacja', p. 486.
[101] Strzemski, 'Obraz Żydow', p. 564; see n. 36.
[102] I. Lewin, *The Jewish Community in Poland*, New York, 1985, p. 5.
[103] Bałaban, *Historia Żydów w Krakowie*, I, pp. 352–3.
[104] A. Gawurin, 'Dzieje Żydów w Tykocinie 1522–1795', (Jews in Tykocin 1522–1795), Master's dissertation, Warsaw, 1938, AŻIH, no. 37, p. 59. Another copy of this work is to be found in the archive of Warsaw University.
[105] S. Kutrzeba, *Historia ustroju w zarysie, Litwa* (Outline history of Polish State administration, Lithuania) II, 2nd edn, Warsaw/Lwów, 1921, pp. 150–1; idem, *Korona* (The Crown), I, 7th edn, Kraków, 1931, p. 257.
[106] See nn. 73–5; Leszczyński, 'Spór', pp. 85 ff.; see also *BŻIH* (129–30, 1984, pp. 135 ff.
[107] J. Tazbir, *Tradycje tolerancji religijnej w Polsce* (Traditions of religious toleration in Poland), Warsaw, 1980, p. 99.

'Jewish meetings – the so-called *vaad*',[108] without using any other names found in the sources. Generally speaking, it seems to me that this body, in addition, can and indeed should be referred to as the 'Diet of Polish Jews', 'Diet of Crown Jews', 'Diet of Lithuanian Jews', 'Tribunal' and 'Diet Court'.

---

[108] Z. Kaczmarczyk and B. Leśnodorski, *Historia Państwa i Prawa Polski* (A history of the state and law in Poland), 4th edn, II, from the fifteenth century to 1795, Warsaw, 1971, p. 73; J. Bardach, B. Leśnodorski and M. Pietrzak, *Historia Państwa i Prawa Polskiego* (A history of Polish State and law), 4th edn, Warsaw, 1985, p. 182.

11 · The Jewish Sejm: Its Origins and Functions

Jacob Goldberg

Jewish Diets (Sejmy), which lasted in the Polish Commonwealth from the second half of the sixteenth century until 1764, were an integral part of the state fiscal apparatus and, at the same time, a factor influencing the state's economy in general. The work of these Diets influenced, to an essential degree, the development of the well-established Jewish communities on Polish and Lithuanian territories and influenced the shape of mutual relations between Jews and Poles and other peoples of the Polish Crown Land and the Great Duchy of Lithuania. The Diets of the Polish, Lithuanian and Byelorussian Jews constituted a parliamentary representation *Sui generis* of the biggest and liveliest centre of world Jewry. The activities of the Jewish Diets in the Polish Commonwealth took place in a much wider area, and on a far bigger scale, than the Jewish self-government provincial organizations in other European countries. Yet interest in the history of Jewish central autonomous institutions has not – for the post-war generation of historians – led them to investigate this question in any organized way. A few contributions, popular articles and an edition of sources constitute the sum of historiographical efforts in this field in the past forty years. The fact that two volumes, comprising a new edition of known sources and first publication of hitherto unknown sources for the history of the Council of the Four Lands, have now been published does not seriously affect this judgement.

The role of the Jewish Diets has been recognized in Jewish historiography. Among Polish historians of law and the state it is Stanisław Kutrzeba who, above all, has stressed the importance of these institutions. Moses Schorr is the author of the only, albeit outdated, work devoted solely to this subject. His dissertation was published in the first issue of *Kwartalnik Historyczny* in 1899.[1] At

---

[1] M. Schorr, 'Organizacya Żydów w dawnej Polsce od najdawniejszych czasów az

the same time it appeared as a separate book.[2] A modified version was translated into German and appeared in 1917.[3] In the Polish version of his work, Schorr stated that

> the Jewish Diet was an institution of central autonomy which, with its activity and range of functions, covered not only single provinces but all the communities of the whole Polish Commonwealth and not only regulated the internal administration of these communities, but by its resolutions deeply affected social, ethical and pedagogical relations. As the highest organ, mediating constantly between all Polish Jews over a period of 200 years, it was . . . in essence the only phenomenon [of this type] in the history of European Jews.[4]

These Diets, he continued, were 'the highest form [of autonomy], a legislative body, and as such faced the state authorities, met regularly according to a stated procedure, and carried out useful work'.[5] Although true in general outline, this somewhat overblown view needs to be balanced and filled out after a lapse of many years, as well as to be checked against a wide range of sources.

Sejm Żydowski (Jewish Diet) is the best term for the highest Jewish autonomous body and accords with the Polish situation and parliamentary tradition, although such contemporary terms as Jewish Meeting, Jewish Conference or General Synagogue were used as well. The Hebrew name of the institution, Vaad Arba Aratsot means literally the Council (Diet) of the Four Lands: Great Poland, Little Poland, Wołyń and the Grand Duchy of Lithuania. In 1623, the communities of the Grand Duchy of Lithuania separated from the Crown, because of their different tax system and the creation of a separate Lithuanian court, which resulted in three proclamations of Lithuanian statutes establishing these legal differences. As a result, a new Jewish body, the Vaad Medinat Lita, that is the Diet of the State of Lithuania, was set up yet, despite this, the Jewish Diet of the Crown Lands retained its Hebrew name

do r. 1772' (The organization of Jews in Old Poland from the earliest years till 1772), *Kwartalnik Historyczny* 13, 1899, I.
[2] Lwów, 1899.
[3] M. Schorr, *Rechtsstellung und innere Verfassung der Juden in Polen. Ein geschichtlicher Rundblick*, Berlin/Vienna, 1917.
[4] Schorr, 'Organizacya', p. 52.
[5] Ibid.

Vaad Arba Aratsot, the Council of the Four Lands, until the very end of its existence.

Jewish Diets as well as the Jewish districts (*ziemstwa*) which elected representatives to the Diet, were well suited to the political system of pre-partition Poland, 'whose core comprised numerous meetings on various levels with different prerogatives'.[6] In any case, Jewish self-governing institutions, not only in the Polish Commonwealth but also, for example, in Silesia and in the Duchy of Ansbach, imitated already existing parliamentary institutions.[7] Some historians even insist that these adopted ideas and parallels are the most important question in the history of Jewish autonomy in that period.[8]

The sources for the history of the Council of the Four Lands are also an essential aspect of the history of Jewish and Polish culture. The need to establish them on a scholarly basis is connected with the need to fill the gap created when, probably in the eighteenth century, the minute books or records (*pinkas*) of the Council of the Four Lands were destroyed. The reconstruction, based on scattered copies and excerpts, of a large part of the destroyed minute books is a great tribute to the scholarly work of Israel Halperin, the historian of the Jews in the old Polish Commonwealth. The sources published by Halperin,[9] as well as the *pinkas* of the Jewish Diet of the State of Lithuania,[10] published by Simon Dubnow, form the groundwork for research on the history of these institutions.

Yet this does not eliminate the need for supplementing the no longer extant Hebrew sources of the lost records of the Council of the Four Lands with Polish records, especially as the wide functions of the Jewish Diets and the increasing intervention of the Crown Treasurers (*podskarbi*) and their assistants from the beginning of the eighteenth century became a factor leading to the creation of new sources. These include letters addressed to the royal treasurers and their appointed commissioners by the Marshal,

---

[6] J. Włodarczyk, 'Sejmiki jako szkoła wychowania obywatelskiego' (Dietines as a school of civil education), in J. Gierowski, ed., *Dzieje kultury politycznej w Polsce* (History of political culture in Poland), Warsaw, 1977, p. 69.

[7] D. Cohen, 'Ha´vaad ha´katan shel "Bney Medinat Ansbach"', in S. W. Baron, B. Dinur, S. Ettinger and I. Halperin, ed., *Yitschak F. Baer Jubilee Volume on the Occasion of his Seventieth Birthday*, Jerusalem, 1960, p. 356.

[8] Ibid.

[9] I. Halperin, ed., *Acta Congressus Generalis Judaeorum Regni Poloniae (1580–1764)*, Jerusalem, 1945 (Hebr.). Quoted further as *Acta*.

[10] S. Dubnow, ed., *Pinkas ha'medina o pinkas vaad ha'kehilot ha'rashiyot b'medinat Lita*, Berlin, 1925.

by secretaries of the Jewish Diets and by other Jewish leaders, along with documents, which were translated into Polish. Many of them, following normal procedure, were entered in the Town and Land Court Registers in order to have them authenticated. Thanks to this operation, much of the bureaucratic workings of the Council of the Four Lands has survived in a Polish-language version. Some of the translated texts were published by Halperin in his reconstruction of the *pinkas* of the Council of the Four Lands. On the basis of these documents, he tried to reconstruct the original Hebrew version of these texts. This is not always an easy task. My own research on the few surviving eighteenth-century manuscripts, which contain both the Hebrew original and its Polish translation, demonstrate that contemporary translations of Hebrew texts into Polish show marked differences from one to the other.[11] But the differences between the lost Hebrew documents and their Polish translations by no means diminish the research value of the latter. Documents originating in the offices of the Council of the Four Lands reached the Polish monarchs, treasurers, their assistants and others in Polish translation. The content of those translated documents varies and, beside matters connected with taxation, frequently refers to religious and practical problems which affected Jewish society.

As an example, one could cite the fact that in 1753 the Great Crown Treasurer, Karol Odrowąż Sedlnicki, requested Abraham ben Josef of Leszno, Marshal of the Council of the Four Lands, to send him a Polish translation of the full documentation of the *causae celebrae* in which Jakub Emden was accused of Sabbatarianism by Jonatan Eibenschutz. Sedlnicki learned about the case from his trusted steward Baruch Marek, who wanted his protector to use his influence to remove the *herem* (excommunication) placed upon Emden by the Lublin rabbi,[12] as Emden was his daughter's father-in-law. This was how information on internal relations and dissensions in the neighbouring, but culturally isolated, Jewish community reached Poles. Such far-reaching interference into the Jewish community's domestic life is worth attention as, on the one hand, it testifies to the range of contacts between the treasurer and the authorities of the Council of the Four Lands and, on the

---

[11] J. Goldberg, *Ha'mishar ha'kimoni ha'yehudi b'Polin ba mea ha'18*, forthcoming.
[12] J. Trunk, 'L'birur emdata shel Abraham ben Joske, parnas Vaad d'Aratzot b'makhloket beyn Jonatan Ejbeshits w'Yaakov Emden', *Tsion* 33:1–4, 1973, pp. 174–9.

other hand, it shows the sort of circumstances in which Polish translations of Jewish documents were made.

Yet when Schorr wrote his pioneering work on the *Organization of Jews in Poland*, the reconstruction of the later part of the *pinkas* of the Council of the Four Lands had not yet been prepared and he was not aware of the importance of Polish sources for historical research in the field of Jewish autonomy in Poland. Thus he took a pessimistic view, stating that 'unfortunately no sources have survived for the knowledge of the internal organization of the Jewish general meetings'.[13] This obstacle was overcome only in the inter-war period by Ignacy Schipper who found and published several Polish and Latin sources for the history of the Council of the Four Lands.[14] From this he determined the composition of the Jewish Diet in the Crown Lands,[15] and maintained that as far as the history of Jewish central autonomy in the Polish Commonwealth is concerned, 'a much more complete image is given by the Polish archival files than by the Hebrew sources'.[16]

The activity of the Council of the Four Lands reached beyond the Polish border. Published German sources inform us, for instance, that the Jewish districts and leadership interceded with the Silesian authorities and the Prussian king, Frederick II, on the question of permission for Jewish merchants' families to stay while attending the Breslau fair, as well as for Jews to have their prayer house and kosher restaurant.[17] Authorities testify to a wide range of problems dealt with by the Jewish Diets. However, this rich and varied, though irregular, collection of sources has hitherto been used on only a small scale by historians.

On the question of the origin of the Council of the Four Lands, Jewish historiography has reached two differing conclusions. Bałaban, Dubnow, Mahler, Schipper and Schorr link the origin of this institution with the lump system of Jewish poll tax assessment introduced around the year 1581, and with the Jewish administration's

---

[13] Schorr, 'Organizacya', p. 63.

[14] I. Schipper, 'Poylishe regesten tsu der geshikhte funem vaad arba aratsot', *Historishe Shriftn* I, 1929, pp. 85–113.

[15] Schipper, 'Der Tsuzamenshetel funem vaad arba aratsot', ibid. pp. 74–82.

[16] I. Schipper, *Komisja Warszawska: przyczynek do dziejów autonomii Żydów w dawnej Polsce* (Warsaw Commission: a contribution to the history of Jewish autonomy in Old Poland), Warsaw, 1931, p. 147.

[17] *Acta*, pp. xxiii–xxiv, xxvii–xxviii, xxx, xliv–xli, lviii–lxiii; B. Brilling, 'Friedrich der Grosse und der Vaad Arba Aratsot', 'Theokaratia' – *Jahrbuch des Institutum Judaicum Delitzschianum* I: 1967–1969 (1970), pp. 130–42.

handling its division among the various communities and districts. Other, especially earlier, historians maintained that the rabbinic court, which from the beginning of the sixteenth century used to meet during the Lublin fairs or markets, gave birth to the Jewish Diets in the Polish Commonwealth. Halperin, in his introduction to his partial reconstruction of the *pinkas*, remains sceptical and insists that this problem awaits further investigation. On the basis of the 1595 resolution of the Council of the Four Lands, he maintains that at first Jews entered only into short-term contracts with the Crown Treasurer to lease Jewish poll tax, and considers whether such transactions were profitable.[18]

Polish sources supply us with information on this subject. As the 1593 Diet constitution has it: 'Jews themselves in all royal Poland wanted to lease this poll tax',[19] and King Zygmunt III in the 1596 proclamation stated that 'for the Republic's swift rescue we leased out Jewish poll tax . . . to the Jews settled in royal Poland'.[20] The Crown Treasurer Jan Firlej also made an announcement in 1598 about Jews themselves wanting to lease this tax.[21] But in the 1601, 1603 and 1607 proclamations issued by him, we do not find the term 'lease' meaning a temporary situation; instead, the division and collection of Jewish poll tax is stated to have been transferred to the representation of Jews for 'some time',[22] which should be understood as a much longer period of time. The dividing of such a financial burden among the districts and communities needed nationwide representation, and the rabbinic courts, meeting periodically during markets, were not a permanently functioning body which could be expected to undertake such a duty.

Historians of Poland's finances have already shown that at the turn of the sixteenth century there was a growing tendency to introduce the lump system of tax assessment and collection. This was the effect of the developed fiscal apparatus of the Polish Commonwealth.[23] To put it simply, the primitive and inefficient fiscal

---

[18] Introduction to the *Acta* (Hebrew version).
[19] *Volumina Legum* II, p. 351.
[20] *Acta*, p. v.
[21] Ibid., p. iv.
[22] Ibid., pp. v–vii.
[23] M. Nycz, *Geneza reform skarbowych Sejmu Niemego. Studium z dziejów skarbowo-wojskowych z lat 1697–1717* (The origin of the fiscal reforms of the Silent Diet. A study of financial and military history 1697–1717), Poznań, 1938, p. 267: R. Rybarski, *Skarb i pieniądz za Jana Kazimierza, Michała Korybuta i Jana III* (The Treasury and currency in the time of Jan Kazimierz, Michał Korybut and Jan III), Warsaw, 1939, pp. 39–40.

administration was unable to raise tax, which resulted, *inter alia*, in a drop in Jewish poll tax revenues.[24] Roman Rybarski, an outstanding historian of Polish finance, wrote that 'farming-out of the poll tax by the Jewish elders was profitable for the treasury itself; it needed neither to maintain its own administrative apparatus, nor raise tax from too many taxpayers, who could not be considered as the best payers.'[25] In this statement – ignoring the sarcastic remark which Rybarski, as a National Party leader and a theoretician of the economic boycott of the Jews in the 1930s, could not resist – the essential motives for transferring this function to the Jewish self-governing institutions are explicitly stated. In any case, the treasurers themselves, as well as their appointed commissioners, were fully convinced that the Jewish institutions had far more effective means of raising tax from Jews than had the state fiscal apparatus. Kazimierz Granowski, Treasurer Sedlnicki's commissioner to the 1753 meeting of the Council of the Four Lands, wrote that the Jewish elders through control and use of 'excommunications, Jewish baptisms, and burial in the Jewish cemeteries' could force every Jew to pay his due.[26]

Meetings of a parliamentary nature were called together in the Polish Commonwealth by virtue of resolutions, and in the eighteenth century an analogous practice emerged with Jewish Diets, a sure sign of the influence of state officials. As the main point of the Jewish Diets' debates was the division of poll tax among the districts and communities and its collection, these proclamations were issued by the treasurers. It was these treasurers' proclamations, together with the Diet constitutions and the royal proclamations, announcing the prerogatives of the Jewish representatives with regard to Jewish poll tax distribution and collection, that legalized the functioning of the central institutions of Jewish autonomy in the field of finance. King Jan III's proclamation of 27 March 1694 states the following about the procedure of calling together Jewish Diets and their powers:

> Howbeit according to their tradition, Crown Jews hold their meetings every two years during the Jaroslaw fair, to which they have consented to send their elders with pre-stated orders, and

[24] Nycz, *Geneza*, p. 57.
[25] Rybarski, *Skarb i pieniądz*, p. 215.
[26] J. Goldberg and A. Wein eds, 'Ordynacja dla sejmu żydowskiego ziem koronnych z 1753 r.' (Regulations for the 1753 Crown Jews' Diet), *BŻIH* 52, 1964. Quoted further as 'Ordynacja'.

through them agree and decide the division of contributions imposed on them by the General Diets, many of which should be paid by Jews living in the districts.[27]

In the light of this proclamation, Schorr's opinion that the Council of the Four Lands was throughout the period of its existence a recognized legislative body needs fundamental revision.[28] After all, the Jewish Diets were created to divide the tax burden between districts and communities, not to fulfil legislative activity. One should rather take into account the view of Rybarski, who, despite the fact that he was not aware of the complicated structure of Jewish autonomy in the Polish Commonwealth, had a good conception of its functioning in the field of finance and the way this gave it further power. He argued that the introduction of the farming-out system of collecting Jewish poll tax 'had further consequences in the development of Jewish independent organization. *Kehillot* obtained power over co-religionists, tax organization became, as has often happened in the history of finance, the power base of a social organization furnished with self-governing laws.'[29] Rybarski did not even know of the existence of the three-tiered structure of Jewish autonomy: local community level (*kehilla*), regional district (*ziemstwa*) administration, and the central Council of the Four Lands and the Diet of the State of Lithuania, and thus mentions only *kehillot*. Likewise Michał Nycz, who, in his otherwise excellent book on the financial reforms of the Silent Diet of 1717 (Sejm Niemy), in which he devoted more space to the problem of Jewish poll tax than all other literature,[30] does not mention the existence in the old Republic of Jewish Diets under whose authority came matters of Jewish tax.

Although Jewish Diets were called officially to administer the division of tax levies among districts and communities, in practice their operations spread much further – to the fields of the economy, culture and religion. We base our explanation of this matter on Emanuel Rostworowski's observations of the dual nature of rural self-government in Little Poland.[31] His conclusions apply

---

[27] *Acta*, pp. xxxiii–xxxiv.
[28] Schorr, 'Organizacya', p. 55.
[29] Rybarski, *Skarb i pieniądz*, p. 214.
[30] Nycz, *Geneza*, pp. 57–63, 268–9.
[31] E. Rostworowski, 'Rola urzędu wiejskiego w walce klasowej wsi małopolskiej' (The role of the village office in the class struggle in Little Poland villages), in C. Bobińska, ed., *Studia z dziejów wsi małopolskiej w drugiej połowie XVIII wieku*

also to many other territorial, professional and religious self-governing organizations in pre-partition Poland. According to Rostworowski's division, one of their functions was to relieve the superior authority of some administrative burdens, the other was to defend the interests of the group it represented. For Jewish Diets, the first function – as one can easily guess – was the administration of Jewish poll tax. The work of the Jewish Diets in the financial sphere merged with their defence of the interests of the Jewish community, and it was through their efforts that Jewish tax rates were not raised. This called for intensive effort, intervention and manipulation as, according to contemporary tax assessments which took into account 'not only possessions and income, but also hierarchy and social . . . criteria',[32] it was peasants and Jews above all who bore the main tax burden. Increasing military expenditure and destruction in the seventeenth century, and economic decline in the second half of the century, ensured that no 'source which could simply be useful was omitted', as Rybarski expressed it.[33] But besides individual contributions and sudden impositions of summary poll surtax, the tax burden of the Jewish population essentially did not rise.[34] Any minor tax increases were usually the result of the fall in the value of money.[35]

The Council of the Four Lands, in its role as the central institution of Jewish autonomy, came up against certain limitations and obstacles to its work as a result of the decentralization of the fiscal system, which started in the mid seventeenth century. Rybarski has concisely characterized the Polish financial situation of the time, saying that there were 'as many financial systems as provinces'.[36] Some dietines (*sejmiki*) questioned the level of Jewish poll tax with which, according to the distribution list of the Council of the Four Lands, the Jewish population in various districts and provinces was burdened. In some cases it was inspired by the Jewish district and community authorities, which aimed at diminishing the sums imposed by the Jewish tax collectors and

(Studies in the history of the Little Poland village in the second half of the eighteenth century), Warsaw, 1957, pp. 370–2.

[32] A. Nowak, 'Podatki w procesie tworzenia i podziału dochodu w ustroju feudalnym' (Taxes in the process of creating and dividing income in the feudal system), *RDSG* 44, 1983, p. 40.
[33] Rybarski, *Skarb i pieniądz*, pp. 362, 359.
[34] Ibid., pp. 216, 220, 226–7, 230.
[35] Ibid., p. 218.
[36] Ibid.

transferring them to Jews in other regions. On the other hand, estate owners were interested in freeing their leaseholders from taxes, and thus restricted the operations of the Council of the Four Lands in the field of finance and hindered the carrying out of its resolutions.

The orders of payment, authorizing the execution of the *subsidium hibernale* from *arendors* in private estates, handed by Jewish authorities to army deputations, also led to noble objections. Kazimierz Granowski, Treasurer Sedlnicki's commissioner, said in 1753 that 'this is not without severe harm to the nobles' estates'.[37] The nobles might have felt offended at their estates being raided by army officials on the initiative of Jewish authorities. In reality their protests were not directed against this 'slur' on their honour, but at something completely different. Nobles wanted to prevent the overburdening of their leaseholders with taxes, being afraid that this would make it impossible for them to meet inn, brewery and alcohol distillery rents on time and thus result in the diminishing of the nobles' revenues from their taverns. Cases in which an *arendor* took advantage of his master's attitude and protection simply to stop paying his part of the poll tax, and only with a *herem* could be forced to comply, were not rare. Sometimes even the *herem* was not sufficient and in such cases Jewish authorities were forced to apply to the king's court in defence of its powers.

Such interventions made King Jan Kazimierz issue a proclamation which, based on an earlier Senate council's resolution reads,

> That some unbelieving Jews, shielding themselves with backing from various quarters, as *arendors* under various masters, as well as living under the nobles and clergy, are unwilling to pay the tax due to the Commonwealth, which is against the plain meaning of the constitution, where the elders of the unbelieving Jews are given the power to collect such taxes.[38]

King Jan III stated in the 1677 proclamation that some Jews '*rebelliter*' defend themselves, taking shelter with various masters, on whose estates they have *domicilia* on hold tenancies' and called on them to pay their due tax, at the same time appealing to the nobles to stop helping and supporting them.[39]

[37] 'Ordynacja'.
[38] AGAD, *Metryka Koronna* (The Registry of the Crown of Poland), no. 369, f. 179; no. 203, f. 532
[39] A. Leszczyński, ed., 'Uniwersał Jana III wydany 6. V. 1677 Żydom Korony w

It did in fact happen that owners appealed to the members of the Jewish leadership and asked for *arendors* from their towns and villages to be released from paying their share of tax. An instance can be seen in a letter from the year 1744 of Błeszyński, a well-informed nobleman, owner of the town Złoczew – who used the titles '*Sieradz* cup-bearer (*cześnik*), quart and hyberna writer of the Crown Treasury'. He wrote to the Marshal of the Council of the Four Lands thus: 'Master Abraham Józefowicz, orthodox Jew and the Crown Jews' Marshal . . . I hereby appeal on behalf of my Złoczew Jews, that they should not be caused distress but instead pay as follows: from the Jewish *arendor* in Nowa Wieś near Złoczew 100 złoty, from the Uników Jews 100 złoty and from the Gronów Jews 100 złoty.' He then asks for their release and, probably basing himself on information supplied by the Złoczew Jews, points to Jewish *arendors* from neighbouring villages belonging to other nobles, who were to pay taxes instead of the Jews under the protection of Błeszyński. He also makes it clear to Marshal Abraham Józefowicz: 'After all, you shall come to no loss and shall hold me under obligation . . . And I promise to help in all circumstances.'[40] Nobles who held fiscal office took pains to cultivate the leaders of the Council of the Four Lands.

Similar practices occurred where the second group of the Council's functions were concerned, namely representing and defending Jewish society. Schorr wrote that, in case of danger, 'the general meeting stood as the highest Jewish representation facing the state authorities'.[41] But Schorr did not go further into the matter and the question remains unanswered of how the state authorities reacted to such independently undertaken operations reaching beyond the sphere of fiscal matters. One can indeed see the reaction in the attitude of the treasurer's commissioners towards the 'internal aims' expenses of the Jewish community, which *inter alia* covered the costs incurred by the leadership of the Council of the Four Lands. Although these expenses were noted by Nycz, he failed to realize their real import. Despite thorough

sprawie placenia podatków i posłuszeństwa władzom kahalnym' (Jan III's proclamation of 6 May 1677 to the Crown Jews concerning tax collection and obedience to the *kehilla* authorities), *BŻIH* 113, 1980, pp. 85–86.

[40] 'Kopia listu jego mości pana Bleszyńskiego cześnika sieradzkiego do marszałka Żydów koronnych, pisanego dnia 2 Julii 1744' (A copy of the letter written on 2 July 1744 by the honourable Lord Bleszyński, Sieradz cup-bearer to the Marshal of the Crown Jews), AGAD, *Ks. Wieluńskie Grodskie Obl.* no. 8, f. 488.

[41] Schorr, 'Organizacya', p. 76.

investigation, he reckoned the full figure given in the Jewish fiscal sources, which remained after transfer to the State Treasury either as administrative expenses or, following an eighteenth century publication which in fact exaggerated the problem, as money embezzled by Jewish officials.

Crown Treasury Commissioner Działyński did indeed consider these expenses too high and gave an order for the 1739 meeting of the Council of the Four Lands 'that the trustees spend no more than 334 red złotys; in other words, 600 złotys for defence expenditure by the Diet and commissioners.'[42] But the very wording of the order allows for 'defence expenditure', which was none other than defence of the interests of the Jewish community. The emphasis is even greater in an order of the 1753 meeting of the Jewish Diet issued by treasury commissioner Kazimierz Granowski, which states that: 'The [Jewish] leadership cannot manage without legal as well as defence [and] other private expenses,'[43] especially in those cases 'where some rightful Jewish need absorbed money.'[44] He points, among other things, to the helping of the poor and other expenses connected with the needs of the Jewish community. The two orders quoted above are the only documents legalizing the Jewish leadership's economic activity beyond the bounds of taxation. They testify to an understanding of the financial needs of the Jewish community for its defence during a period when there was an increasing number of cases accusing Jews of ritual murder and host profanation.

The budget of the Council of the Four Lands reflects the wide range of this institution, with money set aside for charitable deeds, to send financial assistance, via Istanbul, to the Jews of the Holy Land, to back publishing ventures and to prevent the expulsion of the Jews from Mazovia.[45] We could add to the list those functions which were carried out by the members of the Jewish leadership but, since they did not need high expenditure, left no trace in the fiscal records. In some cases, they would underwrite contracts entered into by town authorities with Jewish communities which were unfavourable for the latter, providing compensation for loss. Such a role was played by Yuda Leib Marek, the 'Crown Jews' syndic', when he signed an agreement between the Międzyrzecz

---

[42] *Acta*, p. lvii.
[43] 'Ordynacja'.
[44] Ibid.
[45] *Acta*, p. 171.

Wielkopolski authorities and the Jews of that town, in which the Jews renounced the king's privilege allowing them to produce and trade cloth.[46]

Jewish Diets took their practice from the mechanisms of the general Diet of the Commonwealth but, at the same time, also evolved autonomously. In the first decades of its existence, the Council of the Four Lands comprised mainly deputies elected by the Jewish districts. But as time went by, smaller units emerged from the districts and larger communities gained prerogatives and laws for their representatives, identical in fact with those of districts. The Diet of the State of Lithuania had deputies from Jewish communities only,[47] but in the Diet of the Crown Jews, from the second half of the seventeenth century, there sat district deputies as well as community deputies from the following communities: Ciechanowiec, Kraków, Lublin, Międzyrzecz Podlaski, Poznań, Rzeszów, Tykocin and Węgrów. It appears that the composition of deputies to the Jewish Diets differed from the composition of the deputies' chamber of the Polish Sejm in which only district deputies sat and the role of Kraków and Danzig representatives was small. The factors which shaped the structure of the Jewish Diets were the urban nature of the Jewish community and the role played by the community (*kehilla*) as the basic unit of Jewish internal organization.

Disputes between deputies as to who held the place of honour in the Council of the Four Lands and the general Diet of the Republic display certain parallels. In a *komplanacja* ending a lengthy dispute between the Bełż-Chełm district and the district of the Zamoyski *Ordynacja* (entailed estate) it was agreed that from then on both districts should have a joint representation in the Council of the Four Lands, but the Bełż-Chełm deputies should sit in front of those from the *Ordynacja*.[48] Seating order was a matter of prestige for the groups and regions represented in both the Commonwealth's Sejm and in the Council of the Four Lands.

To put a stop to constant quarrels over this matter, the

---

[46] WAP, Poznań (Poznań State Archive), *Posn Castrensia*, rel. no. 166, ff. 88ᵛ–90ᵛ; see also A. Mączak, *Sukiennictwo wielkopolskie XIV–XVII w.* (Great Poland cloth industry from the fourteenth to the seventeenth centuries), Warsaw, 1955, p. 137.

[47] A. Gomer, *Beiträge zur Kultur und Sozialgeschichte des litauischen Judentums im 17 u. 18 Jahrhundert*, Bochum, 1930, pp. 17–21.

[48] WAP, Lublin (Lublin State Archive), *Castrensia Crasnostraviensia* RMO 55/19774, f. 381.

treasurer Sedlnicki's commissioner Kazimierz Granowski established a fixed seating order in the Council of the Four Lands for representatives of Jewish districts and communities, similar to the Republic's general Diet. The order was as follows: (1) the town of Kraków, (2) Kraków province, (3) the town of Poznań, (4) Poznań and Kalisz province, (5) the town of Lwów and province of Ruthenia, (6) the town of Lublin, (7) Lublin province, (8) Wołyń and Kiev province, (9) Bełż province with Bełż district and Zamoyski *Ordynacja*, (10) the town of Przemyśl, (11) Przemyśl district, (12) the town of Tykocin, (13) the town of Rzeszów.[49]

Informal ties linked the Diet of the Commonwealth to the Jewish Diets. Diets and elections to them were attended by, apart from the deputies themselves, numerous arbitrators and representatives of various organizations and lobbies;[50] these, in presenting their case, created further disturbance in what was in any case a problematic agenda.[51] And the deputies, being so used to their presence in the debating chamber, had no difficulty in tolerating the Jewish syndics who turned up in all the same places. They also appeared in the capital on other occasions,[52] as matters needing urgent intervention were frequent. In the Hebrew sources they are called the Warsaw commission (Vaad Varsha), but Schipper is wrong in maintaining that this term was used for a special separate unit of the Council of the Four Lands.[53] Their efforts showed clear results; for example, in 1720 they caused a group of deputies to request the primate and bishops to stop the persecution of Jews in towns owned by the clergy.[54]

Nevertheless, it would be an exaggeration to ascribe to the emissaries of the Council of the Four Lands – who did sometimes bribe poorer deputies to follow their own line – the power of breaking up a meeting of the Sejm, so as to prevent the proclamation of a resolution unfavourable to the Jews. Still, if Izaak Lewin wrote an article entitled 'Udział Żydów w wyborach

---

[49] 'Ordynacja'.
[50] J. Michalski, 'Sejm w czasach saskich' (The Diet in the Saxonian period), in idem, ed., *Historia sejmu polskiego* (A History of the Polish Diet) I, Warsaw, 1984, p. 312.
[51] W. Czapliński, 'Sejm w latach 1587–1696' (The Diet in the years 1587–1696), ibid. pp. 271–2.
[52] *Acta*, pp. 179, 218.
[53] Schipper, *Komisja Warszawska*.
[54] G. J. Podoski, *Teki* . . . (Portfolios . . .), .II, ed. K. Jarochowski, Poznań, 1855, pp. 42–7.

sejmowych w dawnej Polsce' (Jews' participation in Diet elections in old Poland,[55] then we can talk about 'Jewish participation in the general Diets of the old Commonwealth' with some conviction.

An important role was played by *serwitors*, who were members of the Jewish leadership and who lived at the royal court. One such was Fishel Lewkowicz, for many years a royal steward, who obtained a privilege of *serwitoriat* from King Jan III, later confirmed by King August II. In King August II's confirmation we read: 'having under our protection Fishel Lewkowicz, general scribe, chosen from among the Jews of the *Korona*, who . . . shall be allowed to live at our court and wherever our person shall be'.[56] The Council of the Four Lands' general scribe, with a right to live at the royal court, was in an excellent position to reach the king and the most influential people in the kingdom, and thus intervene where necessary. A different relationship with the royal court was enjoyed by Izaak Fortis, a personal physician of the Lubomirski and Potocki families, and a member of the Jewish leadership, whose son Mojżesz was a tenant of the king's Krzepice estate *ekonomia*.[57]

The Jewish leadership remained in direct and constant contact with the crown treasurer and his commissioners. Its envoys could be met in the meetings of the Diet and at the royal court, where they acquired a broader knowledge of the kingdom's politics, economy and social system than their kinsmen in the Commonwealth. They acquired their political education in the same way as any other deputy who had not been to college or university nor travelled abroad. The marshals, syndics, general scribes and other members of the Jewish leadership developed a fairly sound orientation in state matters and, by choosing the right methods of procedure, obtained considerable results. Almost all deputies to the Diet and diplomats were aware of the situation; so, too, were the French and Prussian envoys in Warsaw. In trying to break up the meeting of the Diet in the year 1750, they attempted to enlist the representatives of the Jewish leadership, by 'leaking' the news that

---

[55] I. Lewin, 'Udział Żydów w wyborach sejmowych w dawnej Polsce' (Jews' participation in Diet elections in Old Poland), in *Miesięcznik Żydowski*, 1932; reprinted in idem, *Z historii i tradycji. Szkice z dziejów kultury żydowskiej* (From history and tradition: sketches from the history of Jewish culture), Warsaw, 1983, pp. 35–63.
[56] *Acta*, p. xxiv.
[57] The manager of the Krzepice estate summoned Mojżesz Fortis to court in 1721 on the charge of ruining the land and oppressing the peasants, AGAD, *KS. Wieluńskie Grodzkie Obl.* no. 2, f. 23.

the Diet was preparing a resolution raising Jewish taxes.[58] We do not know the reaction of the Jewish representatives or whether they participated in this manoeuvre.[59] Certainly, they made use of bribery and managed to find the right people to do it, since they used the same Diet deputies earlier corrupted by the Prussian envoy.[60] Yet Kitowicz's statement that 'Ruthenian and Lithuanian deputies, raised among Jews, having no other fellow-citizens than Jews, supplied with their goods and all other needs of life by Jews, and even fed with Jewish cakes (*kukiałki*) and round cracknels, drunk on Jewish liquors . . . others caught with good payments (*kozubalce*) by Jews . . . raise loud voices in favour of the Jews'[61] is deceptive. It was not the round cracknels or even the payments, but mainly the knowledge and experience acquired by members of the Jewish leadership in the Commonwealth's Diets, as well as direct contact with the leading personalities of the state, which helped them obtain the desired results. Without doubt, a number of Jewish leaders adopted elements of contemporary Polish political culture.

The existence of Jewish Diets lasted only as long as the lump system of Jewish poll tax collection, introduced in the second half of the sixteenth century. Indeed, from the mid-seventeenth-century, voices criticizing the lump assessment of Jewish poll tax could be heard,[62] becoming yet louder and more frequent in the Commonwealth's Diet after the year 1717. Pressure on this point increased further in the 1730s and 1740s when the problem of raising money for the army had to be faced.[63] In practice, all attempts at finding a solution boiled down to increasing the financial burden of the Jewish population, and, as a consequence, the treasurers and their plenipotentiaries intervened more and more frequently in the operations of the Council of the Four Lands to find the financial resources which were supposedly at the disposal of the Jewish population.

Granowski's decrees of 1753 changed the division of functions within the Jewish leadership, and the organizational structure of the Council of the Four Lands. Although his decrees introduced a

---

[58] Z. Zielińska, '*Walka "familii" o reformę Rzeczypospolitej 1743–1752*', (The 'Family's' struggle for reform of the Republic, 1743–1752), Warsaw, 1983, p. 309.
[59] Michalski, *Historia sejmu*, p. 341.
[60] Ibid.; Zielińska, 'Walka', p. 129.
[61] J. Kitowicz, *Pamiętniki czyli Historia polska* (Memoirs i.e. the history of Poland), ed. P. Matuszewski and Z. Lewinówna, Warsaw, 1971, p. 42.
[62] Rybarski, *Skarb i pieniądz*, pp. 215–16.
[63] Nycz, *Geneza*, p. 58; Zielińska, 'Walka', pp. 253, 255.

certain order, they remained contrary to the leadership's tendency to maintain the secular character of their institution. As early as 1739, Jewish leaders addressed a petition to commissioner Działyński, requesting him to cut down rabbinic influence. They stated that

> great harm befalls the leadership also because the rabbis . . . interfere in economic matters . . . Themselves being the watchmen of our religion, they pay no taxes . . . They seek honours, which are due to us as secular masters who carry all burdens . . . So as to prevent this rivalry . . . we resolve and take precautions that no rabbi now, or in the future, hold office in any deputation, or administer the poll tax, or be a tax trustee [*symplarstwo* and *wiernikostwo*] upon penalty of losing rabbinic office.[64]

Despite this, Granowski wrote in his letter of appointment for the year 1753: 'On the strength of my commissioner's power, I appoint the Tarnopol rabbi, Lewek Szmulowicz, who with another is to [control] trustees.'[65] Yet even the appointment of a rabbi to the post of controller of trustees failed to increase the total revenue raised by Jewish officials.

The Treasury commissioner Działyński warned the Jewish leadership in 1739, that 'If, God forbid, similar, or even more serious attempts on the leadership occurred, as were heard of during last year's unfinished Warsaw Diet meeting, in order to prevent in good time the fall of the leadership, our trustees shall have the power to take wider powers.'[66] Not that the trustees were that strong but the reference to the 'attempts on the leadership' indicates the movement towards abolition of the lump system of tax assessment which would have had the dire consequences of ending Jewish central autonomy. However, proposals to abolish the lump system and institute certain modifications in the Polish tax system failed, because of the lack of an alternative apparatus to administer Jewish poll tax. Besides, the constant breaking up of the Polish Diets made it impossible to issue any law on this subject. During the 1744 Diet, various proposals were made to establish the necessary apparatus but again, for the same reasons, they never became binding law. The 1746, 1748 and

[64] *Acta*, pp. lv–lvi.
[65] Ibid., p. lxxi.
[66] Ibid., p. lvii.

1752 Diets' attempts to organize a fiscal commission also proved abortive. Thus central Jewish autonomy in the shape of the Jewish Diets and their leadership survived until the reforms of the Convocation Diet in 1764.

According to the Sejm minutes, 'A debate on the level of Jewish poll tax took place during the plenary assembly.' An inevitable consequence of the new updated tax system was the annulment of the system of lump assessment for Jewish poll tax.[67] As a result, a statement was entered into the constitution to the effect that 'all meetings [of the Jewish Council] . . . we forever cancel and forbid'.[68] On Prince Adam Czartoryski's motion, it was resolved that an annual census of the Jewish population be carried out whose figures would serve as the base for Jewish poll tax assessment.[69] In fact, this was never done.

Yet the Council of the Four Lands was in the Jewish community's eyes not only an arm of the fiscal system, but also the country's highest level of representation for a national group which, following its own traditions and aspirations, endeavoured to secure a degree of self-government. This is seen in the contemporary memoirs of Dov of Bolechów, who found the abolition of the Council of the Four Lands a tragic injustice and comparable with the first partition of Poland.[70] With the abolition of the Jewish Diets and districts, the whole operation of Jewish self-government was transferred from the general (that is central) and regional level to the local level, in other words to the communities (*kehillot*) headed by their elders. But the average community member, however active, could not hope to match the political experience of the now abolished central Jewish leadership. Also, the 1764 constitutional ban did not eliminate the traditional Jewish tendency for nationwide representation. Even though the institutions as such were suppressed, their former members remained, even if without prerogatives. They were clearly active over the next few years, despite the ban, holding several meetings of representatives of the Jewish Crown communities which, to a certain degree, continued the work of the non-existent Council of the Four Lands.[71] Deputies who attended a

[67] See M. Drozdowski, *Podstawy finansowe działalności państwowej w Polsce 1764–1793* (Financial foundations of state activity in Poland 1764–1793), Warsaw/Poznań, 1975, p. 19.
[68] *Volumina Legum*, VII, p. 44.
[69] AGAD, *Zbiór Popielów*, no. 20.
[70] Dov M'Bolechow, *Zikhronot*, ed. J. Wishnitzer, Berlin, 1922.
[71] *Acta* (Hebr. version); Czartoryski Library, Kraków, MS 80, 163.

meeting in 1767 addressed a supplication to King Stanisław August and signed it 'His Royal Gracious Majesty's faithful subjects, Jews living in the *Korona*'.[72] Indeed, the idea of meetings of the Jewish communities' representatives did not die out until the third partition of Poland. Yet the meetings of those representatives during the time of the Four Years' Diet were not a simple continuation of the Council of the Four Lands. The Four Years' Diet was based on the model of the general Polish Diet, while the Jewish representatives' meetings at that period resembled in character the meetings of town deputies, which took place at the same time.

---

[72] Ibid.

12 · Regional Aspects of the Autonomy of Polish Jews: The History of the Tykocin *Kehilla*, 1670–1782

Mordekhai Nadav

In this chapter, I shall concentrate on relations between the main Tykocin *kehilla* and its *przykachałeks* (subordinate *kehillot*) between 1670 and 1782. My conclusions are based mainly on the text of a *pinkas*, that is the register of records of the Tykocin *kehilla*. The original *pinkas* which was kept in the Tykocin *kehilla* was lost in the 1940s, during the Nazi occupation. Fortunately, we are in possession of a copy in Jerusalem, which was made in 1926–7 by Israel Halperin, at that time a sixteen- to seventeen-year-old boy from Białystok, later professor of Jewish History in Eastern Europe at the University of Jerusalem. Professor Halperin was my mentor and only recently have I taken up the task of preparing the text of this *pinkas* for publication. Allow me to pay tribute to this eminent historian who died in 1971. Thanks to him, we are in possession of the text of the Tykocin *pinkas*, such an important source for the history of Polish and Lithuanian Jewry.

As a result of the Lublin union of 1569, the Tykocin *kehilla* was incorporated into the Polish Kingdom (*Korona*) and into the Jewish Council of the Four Lands.[1] It was through this circumstance that

---

[1] Directly after the year 1569 the Tykocin *kehilla* did not become one of the Jewish Crown *kehillot*. In King Stefan Batory's privilege of 1576, confirming rights of the Lithuanian *kehillot*, we find the Tykocin *kehilla*, beside the Troki, Nowogródek, Grodno and Pińsk *kehillot*. Tykocin belonged among the Lithuanian *kehillot* at least till 1582. In another document of 1595 we find it together with the Węgrów *kehilla* and the Wołyń land, incorporated to the Crown Lands also in the year 1569, paying its taxes on behalf of the state through the Council of the Four Lands. On the basis of these documents, we can conclude that the Tykocin *kehilla* has accepted, at least partly, the authority of the Jewish Sejm in the years 1582–1595. Cf. *Regesty i nadpisy: svod materialov dla istorii Yevreyev w Rossii*, I, Petersburg 1899, p. 266,

conflicts arose between Tykocin, Grodno and the Tykocin *przykahałeks* in Zabłudów, Choroszcz and Gródek, which remained in Lithuania. Established opinion holds that in the period of Jewish settlement on Polish-Lithuanian soil, conflicts arose between founding communities and their branches and that, in the course of time, the branch *kehillot* sought their independence from the mother *kehilla*'s hegemony. Against this, the main *kehilla* tried with all its might to keep its authority over the branch *kehillot*. It is against this background that one should see the conflicts and strains between the main ruling *kehillot*, the other *kehillot*, and the communities subject to them. This hypothesis was first established with the publication by Shimon Dubnow in 1904 and 1912 of documents from the Tykocin *pinkas* dealing with a long-running quarrel between Tykocin and Grodno about their authority over branch *kehillot* in Zabłudów, Choroszcz and Gródek,[2] and with Majer Bałaban's account, a few years later, of the release of branch *kehillot* in Great Poland from the authority of Poznań at the beginning of the fifteenth century, and of Żółkiew from Lwów in the seventeenth century.[3]

Over the years, this theory has become commonplace, to be found also in the latest work of Dr-Anatol Leszczyński: 'Spór między kahałami Grodna i Tykocina o hegemonię nad skupiskami żydowskimi pogranicza Korony z Litwa' (The conflict of hegemony over Jewish colonies across the Crown Lands-Lithuanian border between the *kehillot* of Grodno and Tykocin) published in 1983, as well as in his important monograph *Żydzi ziemi bielskiej od połowy XVI wieku do 1795* (Jews of the Bielsko region from the mid

---

no. 577, and p. 290, no. 632; I. Halperin, 'Pinkas vaad arba aratsot' *Acta Congressus Generalis Judaeorum Regni Poloniae'* (1580–1764), Jerusalem, 1945, p. 10 (in Hebrew); further quoted as Halperin, PVAA. For information on the origins and history of the Tykocin *kehilla* consult I. Halperin, *Toledot ha-Yehudim be-Tiktin, Yehudim veyahadut Bemizrakh Evropa: mechkarim betoldoteyhem*, Jerusalem, 1968, pp. 139–51, (in Hebrew); Cf. also A. Leszczyński and A. Gawurin, as described in notes 5 and 9; also A. Leszczyński, *Żydzi ziemi bielskiej od połowy XVII w. do 1795 r. (Studium osadnicze, prawne i ekonomiczne)*, Wrocław, 1980, a broad and important monograph.

[2] S. Dubnow, 'Akty yevreyskogo koronnogo sieyma ili Vaada Chetyrokh Oblastiey, tykochinskaya kollektsiyja (1621–1699)', *Yevreskaya Starina* 4, 1912, pp. 70ff., 178ff., 453ff.

[3] M. Bałaban, *Tsentralnoye upravlenie polsko-litovskich Yevreyev, Istoria Yewreyskogo Naroda* XI, Moscow, 1914, p. 151; Cf. also M. Bałaban, *Historia i literatura żydowska* III, Lwów, 1925, pp. 215ff.

sixteenth century to 1795) published in 1980.[4] Dr Leszczyński has, in fact, developed this view further; according to him, 'The Tykocin *kehilla* authorities were extremely rapacious towards the Jewish centres administratively subordinate to them',[5] and used force to try to subject new Jewish settlements to their power.[6] In this, he agrees with the view expressed by Aron Gawurin in his unpublished Master's dissertation, also based on the Tykocin *pinkas*, which states that the Tykocin *kehilla* supposedly exercised dictatorial powers over its branches.[7]

Thus the question arises whether this really was the state of their relationship. Let me advance a contrary viewpoint: the accepted view should be revised, at least as far as Lithuania is concerned, since the relationship between Tykocin and the *kehillot* of its region was closer to the relations prevailing in Lithuania than in the Polish kingdom, even if in fact the *kehillot* were on Crown lands.

A comparison with what happened in the Pińsk region is revealing. For example, in the seventeenth and eighteenth centuries, the branch *kehillot* in northern Wołyń which, like Tykocin were on Crown lands,[8] were subject to the Lithuanian *kehilla* of Pińsk. These were the *kehillot* of Olewsk, Owrucz, Czarnobyl and Jezomierz, communities probably founded by Jews from Pińsk in the seventeenth century. But until 1719, there was no conflict of authority over them between Pińsk and the Wołyń *kehillot*, comparable to the long drawn-out struggle in the seventeenth century between Tykocin, Grodno and Zabłudów as to who should have authority over Zabłudów. The *kehillot* of northern Wołyń preferred to owe allegiance to their 'mother' *kehilla* in Pińsk in Lithuania; similarly, Zabłudów, Choroszcz and Gródek wanted to

---

[4] A. Leszczyński, 'Spór pomiędzy kahałami Grodna i Tykocina o hegemonię nad skupiskami żydowskimi pogranicza Korony z Litwą w XVII w. w świetle dokumentów', *BŻIH* 127–8, 1983, docs. 2, 3, pp. 85–95.
[5] Ibid., p. 88.
[6] A. Leszczyński, 'Organizactse un kehile struktur bey di yidn oyf der bielsker erd in 18-tn yorhundert', *Bleter far geshikhte* 13, 1985, pp. 59–86, (in Yiddish); on subjecting new colonies by force see p. 61.
[7] A. Gawurin, 'Dzieje Żydów Tykocina (1522–1795)', Archive of the Jewish Historical Institute (*AŻIH*) in Poland, no. 37. Only one chapter of this dissertation was published: 'Di Tiktiner kehile, ire batsiungen mit di kleyne prowints-kehiles, *Bleter far geshikhte* 13, 1960, pp. 60–102 (in Yiddish).
[8] S. A. Biershadskii, *Materialy dla istorii Yevreyev v yugozapadnoy Rossii, Yevreyskaya Biblioteka* VIII, 1880, pp. 1–32, appendix; M. Nadav, 'Toledot Kehilat Pińsk, 1506–1880', in W. Z. Rabinowitsch, ed., *Pinsk: Sefer edut vezykaron lekehilat Pinsk-Karlin*, historic section, I, 1, pp 50, 158–62; further quoted as Nadav, TKP, (in Hebrew).

come under the Grodno regional *kehilla*, although it was not their 'mother' *kehilla* since – as Dr Leszczyński correctly states[9] – conditions in Lithuania were more favourable for Jews than in the Polish kingdom. The will of the *kehillot* triumphed and this is why Tykocin lost its battle with Grodno for supremacy over these *kehillot*.

The Pińsk *kehilla*, up to its neck in debt,[10] found itself in the 1720s and 1750s at loggerheads with its branch communities. In the twenties it was the King of Poland who stopped the defection of the Wołyń branch *kehillot* from Pińsk; in the fifties, the disintegration of the Pińsk autonomous Jewish district proceeded headlong and the Pińsk *kehilla* was helpless to stop it, although it did not stop fighting for its rights in the courts and with the authorities.[11] The branch *kehillot* did not want to become Pińsk's partners in paying its enormous debts. Their interests now dictated a different approach and a different attitude towards the main *kehilla*.

Turning back to the Tykocin region, we must note that, at the turn of the seventeenth to eighteenth century, Tykocin was in conflict with yet another branch *kehilla*, namely Siemiatycze. This struggle lasted about fifty years until 1726.[12] Its origins are not very clear, but it is evident that the Tykocin *kehilla* was unable to coerce Siemiatycze into remaining its subject *kehilla*, even when an excommunication or anathema (*herem*) was cast on Siemiatycze. Possibly the ambitions of the Siemiatycze *kehilla* elders also played their part in gaining independence from Tykocin – besides not wanting to pay tax to Tykocin. Possibly, as Dr Leszczyński observed, they also had the backing of the owner of the town.[13] Although the Siemiatycze *kehilla* eventually cut loose from the Tykocin *kehilla*, it did not take with it those towns which had been its own subject *kehillot* when it was still Tykocin's branch *kehilla*.

I should explain that, according to the *kehilla* system of organization, several of the more important *kehillot* held sway over the small Jewish colonies and villages close to them in the Tykocin

---

[9] Leszczyński, *Żydzi ziemi bielskiej*, pp. 24–5.
[10] Nadav, TKP, pp. 167–72.
[11] Ibid. pp. 158–63.
[12] 'Pinkas of the Tykocin Kehilla, 1621–1795', I. Halperin's MS copy, 572 pp., pages, folio, microfilm, The Jewish National and University Library, Jerusalem, PHOT 406 (further quoted as PKT), documents 863, 777.1, 298.1, 866.
[13] We find a clear reference to it in the text of the oath taken by Siemiatycze elders in the Tykocin synagogue in 1686: 'And thus we are forbidden to free ourselves from the state taxes imposed on us in the past and in the future, with the help of our Lord by no means and combinations' (PKT, no. 863).

region, as well as in other regions. Orla, Boćki and Siemiatycze were examples of such *kehillot* in the Tykocin region.[14] I have already mentioned the conflict between Siemiatycze and Tykocin. On the other hand, the continuous co-operation between the Tykocin *kehilla* and its branch *kehillot* in Orla and Boćki should be stressed.

Why were there no conflicts between Tykocin and these two *kehillot*, and why were there no conflicts between Tykocin and the newly formed regional *przykahałeks* in the first half of the eighteenth century, such as those in Jasionówka, Mielnik, Rajgród, Zambrów and so on? There is no evidence of any rift between Knyszyn and Tykocin either. An explanation should be sought in the *kehilla* organization and, in particular, by examining the position of the Tykocin *kehilla*.

A number of documents from the Tykocin *kehilla* record book tell us of discussions between the main Tykocin community and deputies from the more important branch *kehillot* of the region, and of the agreements reached on tax levies (especially the poll tax) and contributions for the *kehillot*'s needs.[15] Nearly always, the branch *kehillot* would bargain with the Tykocin *kehilla*'s delegates to ease the burden of tax and to postpone overdue debt repayments. Usually the Tykocin *kehilla* representatives would give a little ground to reach a satisfactory settlement with the branch *kehillot*. The branch *kehillot* discussed the level of tax on the basis of the national Jewish poll tax assessment, following the most recent pronouncement of the Jewish Council of the Four Lands.

In the original sources, the discussions between the Tykocin *kehilla* and its branches are called *wspólnota okręzna* (*shutafut hagalil* or regional partnership). In its minuted records Tykocin never stresses its authority to rule as the main *kehilla*. Similarly, calculations between *kehillot* are always worked out on a regional partnership.[16]

It seems to me that the use of the term *wspólnota okręzna* is not accidental. In the light of talmudic law, this partnership (*wspólnota*) is characterized by the right of each partner to profit from his share in it while at the same time he takes upon himself the obligations as

---

[14] PKT, no. 394 and in many other documents; Cf. also Halperin, *Toldot ha-Yehudim be-Tiktin*, p. 147.
[15] For example PKT nos. 619, 648, 815, 869.
[16] For example PKT nos. 389, 394, 395, 679, 832, 955, 857.

other associates do. They mutually oblige one another to act for the prosperity of the partnership.[17]

Menachem Elon, an eminent authority on Jewish law, maintains that an analogy exists between partnership law and the statutes of the *kehilla*. Authorities on Jewish law had already laid down in the thirteenth century that a *kehilla* member's participation in general taxation of the *kehilla* is to be treated as a case of community association or partnership.[18] Clearly, a community could break up because of rifts between its members. The conflict could then be referred to the court for examination.

This view does not question the superior authority of the Tykocin *kehilla* over the branch *kehillot*. For example, in 1678 the delegates of the Siemiatycze *kehilla*, having been granted a tax reduction and allowed to pay their debts in instalments, promised a quick repayment of the community's debt, as they knew that, should they fail to do so, Tykocin would simply confiscate their goods on the roads and at fairs.[19]

The Tykocin rabbi was a member of the Tykocin delegation negotiating with the branch *kehillot* and doubtless helped them reach a settlement. Generally speaking, a consensus existed between the Tykocin *kehilla* and its branches in towns and villages that Tykocin was the main *kehilla*, and others would be subordinate to it within a general system.

Precise figures, annually recorded, of transactions between the Tykocin *kehilla* and its branches throw some light on the actual functioning of the administration and the financial mechanisms of the Tykocin region, and confirm my theory on the regional partnership. The region, as a community, not only distributed the burden of tax imposed by the Council of the Four Lands, but also helped *kehillot* meet various costs for which the whole community was responsible, sometimes within the *kehilla*, sometimes in the region. Thus the *wspólnota okręgu* helped the *kehilla* in a case where one of the latter's members was accused on false evidence; the *kehilla* supported the orphans of martyrs; it recompensed merchants whose goods had been seized without good cause at fairs; it

---

[17] Cf. A. Gulak, *Yesodey hamishpat haivri* II, Tel-Aviv, 1967, pp. 192–6 (in Hebrew).
[18] M. Elon, 'Taxation', *Encyclopaedia Judaica*, Jerusalem, 1972, XV, p. 844.
[19] PKT, no. 856.

supplied dowries for three women from two towns, and helped finance the building of a new prayer house.[20]

Thus it appears that the region helped finance those expenses which were too big for a single *kehilla*. However, the Council of Four Lands would have repaid the region for some of its expenses for such purposes, in its capacity as representative of all Polish Jews.[21] There is a strong element of common responsibility and mutual help in this system. Small *kehillot* were very much aware of the advantages of this system of regional organization, which is why they agreed to be under Tykocin's authority. It lay in their interest.

It seems to me that there was yet another reason for the co-operation by the majority of branch *kehillot* with Tykocin even in the eighteenth century prior to, and after, the liquidation of the Council of the Four Lands in 1764. The Tykocin *kehilla* was not heavily indebted to the monasteries and nobles, like most large communities in the Kingdom of Poland and Lithuania.[22] Thus, Tykocin escaped what would otherwise have been a deep financial crisis. Without the enormous debt burden, one could manage to meet normal payments and the increased taxation of the eighteenth century. In this situation the advantages of co-operating with Tykocin outweighed the disadvantages.

In conclusion, I should like to underline the paradoxical situation of Tykocin's relations with its branch *kehillot*. By the end of the 1760s and in the 1770s, after the liquidation of the Council of the Four Lands, those branch *kehillot* which had long been either independent of Tykocin or subject to the Grodno *kehilla*, returned to the fold of the Tykocin *kehilla*. Thus, in 1769, the Zabłudów *kehilla* took an oath to be subject again to the Tykocin *kehilla*.[23]

In 1771 the Tykocin *kehilla* transferred its authority over the towns and villages of the surrounding area, including Choroszcz and

---

[20] Ibid., nos. 389, 832, 855, 857.

[21] PKT, nos. 673, 790 from the years 1672–6; Cf. Halperin, PVAA, p. 179, no. 329; pp. 144–5, no. 342; p. 150, no. 353. Financial records were first published by Halperin, 'Heshbonot vaad arba aratsot be-Polin [mipinkas Tiktin]', *Tarbiz* 5, 1937, pp. 215–21.

[22] M. Bałaban, *Historia i literatura żydowska* III, pp. 328–32; I. Schipper, *Dzieje handlu żydowskiego na ziemiach polskich*, Warsaw, 1937, pp. 212ff. On the debts of the Lithuanian *kehillot* see S. Biershadskiy, *Litovskie Yevrei*, Petersburg, 1883, pp. 8ff; Cf. also Nadav, TKP, pp. 167–72.

[23] PKT, no. 953. Historians investigating the conflict between Tykocin and Grodno over the hegemony over Zabłudów have neither published nor mentioned this document.

Gródek which, together with Zabłudów, had in the seventeenth and eighteenth centuries been subject to Grodno, to the new Białystok *kehilla*. According to an agreement between the Tykocin and Białystok *kehillot*, all these branch *kehillot* were to come under Tykocin and not challenge its authority.[24] As late as 1782, the Stawiska *kehilla* approached Tykocin and became subject to it voluntarily.[25]

What happened to the relationship between Tykocin and its branches after the abolition of the Jewish Sejms of the Kingdom of Poland and Lithuania is not very clear. The affiliation system of branch and main *kehillot* disintegrated in Lithuania in the 1750s and 1760s. Should the sources be available, this development should be investigated. In my opinion, it was the fiscal interests that were responsible here, which is why the Tykocin branch *kehillot* took one attitude, while the Piński branches took another. We can observe that, even after the abolition of the Council of the Four Lands, there was still a desire to belong to the Tykocin *kehilla* and be subject to it until the partition of Poland in 1795.[26]

---

[24] PKT, no. 958; Cf. also Leszczyński, 'Spór', p. 95.
[25] PKT, no. 965.
[26] In this year Tykocin and its district were incorporated into Prussia, and here entries into the *kehilla* minute book end.

13 · The *Kehilla* and the Municipality in Private Towns at the End of the Early Modern Period

Gershon David Hundert

In contrast to recent historiography which has tended to revise the older notion that the inhabitants of private towns were something like urban serfs and, instead, to emphasize their relative freedom, Jewish historians of the past generation have stressed the dependence of the Jewish residents of such towns on the arbitrary whims of the town-owners.[1] At least in so far as Jews were concerned, these writers claimed, there was little to distinguish private towns from royal towns. Generally speaking, the judgements of Bałaban, Assaf, and others are based on colourful but unrepresentative anecdotes such as those to be found in the memoirs of Solomon Maimon, or of Ochocki, whose comments on Jews Bałaban himself published.[2] Indeed, it may be that the origin of this approach can be found in the anti-noble bias of the Warsaw

[1] Andrzej Wyrobisz, 'Polityka Firlejów wobec miast w XVI wieku i założenie Janowca nad Wisłą', *Przegląd Historyczny* 61, 1970, pp. 577–608; idem, 'Rola miast prywatnych w Polsce w XVI i XVII wieku', *Przegląd Historyczny* 65 1974, pp. 19–45; idem, 'Typy funkcjonalne miast polskich w XVI–XVIII w.', *Przegląd Historyczny* 72, 1981, pp. 25–41; Tomasz Opas, *Własność w miastach prywatnych w dawnej Polsce* (Rzeszów 1975); idem, 'Miasta prywatne a Rzeczpospolita', *Kwartalnik Historyczny* 78, 1971, pp. 28–47; idem, 'Sytuacja ludności żydowskiej w miastach szlacheckich województwa lubelskiego w XVIII wieku', *BŻIH* 67, 1968, 3–37. For the older views of Jewish historians see Simha Assaf, 'Le-korot ha-rabanut', in *Be-ohalei ya'akov*, Jerusalem, 1943, pp. 17–65; Shimon Dubnow, *Toledot ha-hasidut*, Tel Aviv, 1931, espy. pp. 9–12; Majer Bałaban 'Polskie Żydostwo w okresie Sejmu Wielkiego i Powstania Kościuszki', in *Księga pamiątkowa ku czci Berka Joselewicza*, Warsaw, 1934, esp. pp. 9–10.

[2] P. Lachover, ed., *Hayey Shlomo Maimon*, Tel Aviv, 1941, pp. 100–6; Majer Bałaban, 'Die polnischen Juden in den Memoiren des polnischen Adels', *Menorah* 5, 1927 pp. 383ff. 6, 1928, pp. 32ff. Cf. Israel Halperin, ed., *Beit Yisra'el be-Polin* II, Jerusalem, 1953, p. 278.

positivist historians as exemplified in the work of Władysław Smoleński: *Stan i sprawa Żydów polskich w XVIII w.* (The status and problem of Polish Jews in the eighteenth century).[3] That work also includes several anecdotes of arbitrary treatment of Jews by the *szlachta*. Be that as it may, the question of the situation of Jews living on private holdings is too important to be treated on the basis of anecdote alone. More than half, and perhaps three-quarters of the Jews in the Polish Commonwealth lived on private holdings; and Polish Jewry at that time constituted at least half of the world Jewish population. Thus the importance of the subject of the situation of the Jews living on private holdings can easily be seen.

In the private towns of the Polish Commonwealth, the *kehilla* and the Christian municipality were quite similar, most particularly in the subordination of their autonomy and their authority to that of the hereditary owner of the town. Nevertheless, there were some rather significant differences. Any comparison which seeks to identify these differences can focus on different aspects and some approaches will be, inevitably, more rewarding than others. In what follows, an attempt is made to identify a number of approaches to the comparison of the two corporate institutions as well as to suggest what some of the results of such comparisons might be. The presentation is based on the existing published literature, primary and secondary, as well as on my own archival research on the town of Opatów.

It has been maintained, and with justice, that in private towns, 'municipal self-government was a fiction'.[4] The first question to be taken up here is whether this was equally true of the municipality and of the *kehilla*. A good way to begin to seek an answer to this question is to examine the legal definitions of the relative autonomy of the administrative and juridical institutions of each and the ways in which office-holders were chosen.

Although it was not at all uncommon for the town-owner or his administrator to appoint the *burmistrz* and the *wójt*, or to choose them from a list of candidates submitted by the residents of the town, such practices were much rarer with regard to the *kehillot*.[5] The Jewish community almost always elected all of its adminis-

---

[3] Warsaw, 1876. See, A. F. Grabski, 'The Warsaw School of history', in *Acta Poloniae Historica* 26, 1972, pp. 153–70.
[4] Wyrobisz, 'Polityka', p. 605.
[5] In Opatów, like Rzeszów and other towns, there was no consistently applied policy. Municipal officials were sometimes elected and sometimes appointed. Marian

trative officers without interference.⁶ In terms of form, the relative independence of the municipal courts also seems to have been more limited than that of the *kehilla* courts. A 1763 instruction from Antoni Lubomirski, who owned Opatów, says the sessions of the courts of the *wójt* and the *burmistrz* must be presided over by the *gubernator*. Further, such courts were not to take up any matter which 'had not been allowed under the Saxon Key'.⁷

The juridical autonomy of the Jewish community, by contrast, was one of the most fundamental and universally applied principles of Jewish life in the Polish Commonwealth.⁸ That is to say, cases between Jews could be resolved in Jewish courts according to Jewish law or, at least, by Jewish judges. This sort of juridical autonomy was guaranteed in the earliest royal charters to Jews in Poland and it was seen as a privilege and as an incentive to attract settlers when offered to others. Mikołaj Firlej, himself a Calvinist, intended to persuade more Dutch and Flemish artisans to settle in his town by offering them not only freedom of worship, but that 'ut suo patrio iure utantur' (the law of their country would be followed).⁹ It might be added here, parenthetically, that if in the course of the eighteenth century some Jews began to abandon their own courts in favour of those of the hereditary owner of their towns, this was not so much because the town-owners sought such a change but because of the progressive disintegration of the Jewish institutions themselves.

Formally, in terms of the letter of the law, then, it would seem that the autonomy of the Jewish community was less a fiction than that of the Christian community in the private towns of the Commonwealth. Surely, though, this is not a complete picture of

Tadeusz Trojan, *Dzieje sądownictwa Wielkiego Opatowa*, Sandomierz, 1938, p. 24; A. Przybos, ed., *Akta radzieckie rzeszowskie 1591–1634*, Wrocław/Kraków, 1957, p. xxxviii; Bohdan Baranowski, *Życie codzienne małego miasteczka w XVII i XVIII wieku*, Warsaw, 1975, p. 27; and cf. Józef Mazurkiewicz, *Jurydyki Lubelskie*, Wrocław, 1956, pp. 70–1; A. Wyrobisz, 'Polityka', p. 592.

⁶ Jacob Goldberg, ed., *Jewish Privileges in the Polish Commonwealth*, Jerusalem, 1985, *passim*. See ibid., p. 142 for the exceptional case of Kutów where, according to the privilege, two of the four Jewish elders were appointed by the town-owner. And see Łucja Charewiczowa, *Dzieje miasta Złoczowa*, Warsaw, 1929, pp. 62–3 for a similar case. For the opinion that such practices were widespread see Benzion Dinur, *Be-mifneh ha-dorot*, Jerusalem, 1972, pp. 104–6.

⁷ AGAD, Archiwum Gospodarcze Wilanowskie: *Administracja Dóbr Opatowskich* (henceforth *ADO*), I/16.

⁸ Goldberg, *Jewish Privileges*, p. 25.

⁹ Zofia Rościszewska, *Lewartów (Lubartów) w latach 1543–1643* Lublin 1932, p. 31; Wyrobisz, 'Polityka', p. 581.

the situation and not of itself convincing. The reality was that the town-owners could and did intervene in the affairs of the *kehillot* whenever it suited their interests as they understood them, as will be seen below. There must then be other, more realistic, criteria for the evaluation of the differences between the Jewish and Christian corporate institutions of the private towns. Before suggesting what such criteria might be, it is necessary to discuss another approach to this problem.

We know of at least twelve towns where, during the seventeenth and eighteenth centuries, Jews participated in municipal elections.[10] It must be stressed, however, that this participation was usually collective, with representatives of the *kehilla* participating at some stage in the electoral process. These cases, therefore, represent neither the integration of a Jewish citizenry in the city, nor the enfranchisement of the Jewish residents of the town. Such participation in the choice of municipal leadership reflects merely the realization of the existence of certain common interests such as defence and hygiene in private towns where Jews comprised a substantial proportion of the population. It is true that there were cases of individual Jews being formally granted municipal rights, but such examples were relatively rare and their significance is difficult to evaluate.[11] In sum, the description of the prevalent situation as the 'exclusion of the Jews from municipal citizenship' is at least somewhat inappropriate and, perhaps, anachronistic.

Society was corporate in this period; and although disintegrative forces were clearly at work, neither the Jews themselves nor the town-owners aspired to achieve this kind of integration as a matter

---

[10] Brody: 'Żydzi bydż przytomnemi et ad actum electionis należeć; Końskowola; Kraśnik; Łask; Łęczna; Modliborzyce; Nowy Sącz; Opatów: 'że Żydzi usurpuią Sobie obieranie dwóch Burmistrzów'; Opole; Pińsk; Tarnopol; Żołkiew. Nathan Michael Gelber, *Brody, Arim ve-imahot be-yisra'el* 6, Jerusalem, 1955, pp. 25–6; idem, 'Toledot yehudey Tarnopol', in P. Korngruen, ed., *Tarnopol; Encyclopedia of the Jewish Diaspora*, Jerusalem, 1955, XXVIII; idem, 'Toledot yehudei Zhulkiev', 'Sefer Zhulkiev', in Y. Ben Shem and N. M. Gelber, eds, *Encyclopedia of the Jewish Diaspora*, Jerusalem, 1969, XLIII; Józef Mazurkiewicz, 'O niektórych problemach prawno-ustrojowych miast prywatnych w dawnej Polsce', in *Annales Universitatis Mariae Curie-Skłodowska [UMCS]* XI, section 6, 1969, pp. 110–11; Tomasz Opas, 'Sytuacja ludności żydowskiej w miastach szlacheckich województwa lubelskiego w XVIII w.', *BŻIH* 67, 1968, pp. 25–6; J. Goldberg, *Jewish Privileges*, pp. 27, 193; Raphael Mahler, 'Z dziejów Żydów w Nowym Sączu w XVII i XVIII w.', *BŻIH* 56, 1965, pp. 39–40; AP. Kraków (quoted as APK), Oddział na Wawelu, Archiwum X. Sanguszków w Sławucie [AS] 378; Trojan, *Dzieje sądownictwa*, p. 26.

[11] For examples see T. Opas, 'Sytuacja', p. 25; Goldberg, *Jewish Privileges*, pp. 26–8.

of consistent policy. This was certainly the rule though there may have been an occasional exception, particularly towards the end of the eighteenth century. For the Jews there were certain benefits to their distinctive situation, to their 'exclusion'. This was true of the hereditary owners of the towns as well. As Professor Wyrobisz has written, 'The magnates who owned towns generally were eager to take the Jews under their protection', and yet, 'The Jews were more oppressed by the lord than the other burghers'.[12] These are the two sides of the coin of incentive for both the Jews and the town-owners to preserve the corporate distinctiveness of the Jewish community. Thus, for example, in 1745, Paweł Karol Sanguszko declared to the Jews of Opatów:

> Because in a well-ordered state, the whole population depends on the Elders of the *Kehilla* . . . while the Elders are in their turn elected by the Commonality, therefore, we undertake that the Elders of the said Synagogue of Opatów should be freely elected every year according to the Jewish Laws and Customs without any interference from the Lordly power.[13]

Nevertheless, Sanguszko himself, and his successors, did not hesitate to interfere in various ways with the workings of the *kehilla*, and even, on at least two occasions, to annul the results of the *kehilla* elections themselves. In those latter cases the town-owners involved clearly believed that public order and peace, and thus their own interests, would be served by such interventions.[14] The point here is this: while the conception of the Jews as excluded from municipal citizenship is inappropriate, and while the Jews' legal autonomy may have been somewhat more extensive than that of their Christian neighbours, the degree of the difference in terms of the actual autonomy of the two corporate institutions should not be exaggerated.

When, in 1708, the Christian burghers of Opatów complained about various Jewish behaviours and privileges, the response was: 'The Jews, enjoying the rights and privileges of the town, as fellow

---

[12] A. Wyrobisz, 'Ludność żydowska w Tarłowie: Od połowy XVI do końca XVIII w.', *BŻIH* 89, 1974, pp. 11, 12.
[13] *ADO* I/121.
[14] *ADO* I/74; Trojan, *Dzieje sądownictwa*, pp. 28, 51; See also *ADO*, I/16, I/69, I/69a, I/76, I/79; Arch. Gosp. Wil. Anteriora, 102; APK, *Akty Sanguszków*, file 4, bundle 16, no. 1; Gershon David Hundert, *Bitahon u-talut: Yehudei ir peratit ahat be-mamlekhet Polin*, Spiegel Lectures in Jewish History, no. 5, Tel Aviv, 1983, pp. 9–10.

burghers, are entitled to equal treatment.'¹⁵ A few years later, the city's tax burden was reapportioned so that the Jews were to pay two-thirds and the Christians one-third. The *kehilla* protested and their petition listed a number of comparisons between the Jews and the Christians some of which are directly relevant here. Six points are made:

1. In the past when there were merchants here, 'who traded with Danzig, Breslau and Amsterdam' even then we paid but one-third. Now when several of the great merchants are bankrupt and the others carry on only very petty trade, our burden is doubled.
2. They [the Christians] have in their possession, outside the town, extensive fields, which they cultivate . . . we have only one street behind our quarter.
3. They undertake different types of trade: we are poor, have no agricultural holdings and only live from our miserable trade.
4. [We must pay taxes] to the treasury of the Crown.
5. [We have to pay] 'brokerage on noble and Church debts . . . the burghers have no debts.
6. There are several towns in the Kingdom (Korona) of Poland, where Jews live and carry on very active trade, and pay only one fifth or one sixth of the taxes.[16]

There are no complaints here about legal status nor are there demands for municipal citizenship. Such demands, except for certain relatively isolated Jewish reformers at the time of the Four Years' Sejm, were virtually unknown.

The last point on this list which contains, of course, a not so veiled threat, is significant. It reflects an important characteristic of relations between Jews and town-owners during this period. The threat of leaving for another town where conditions were better was not an idle one. And, as I have pointed out elsewhere, it was one of the factors which tended to enhance the relative security of the Jewish communities in the private towns.[17]

From what has been said thus far, one contradictory dimension of the private town with its Christian and Jewish institutions emerges clearly. On the one hand, there was a tendency at times for the hereditary owners to weaken, overrule, or even to eliminate

---

[15] APK, *AS*, 378.
[16] APK, *AS*, 9/9/15.
[17] Hundert, *Bitahon*, p. 12.

corporate structures such as guilds which stood between them and their subjects. On the other hand, the authority of those same corporate institutions, at other times, was buttressed and reinforced by the aristocratic hereditary owners of the towns. It has been suggested further that this latter tendency, to strengthen corporate institutions, when it served the owner's interests, may have been characteristic particularly of relations between the aristocrats and the *kehillot*. Józef Ossolinski demanded, for example, that a new arrival, wishing to settle in the town of Chrzanów, had to: 'be investigated by the Lordly authority to ensure that he was not a fugitive, not the subject of another or a suspicious person; a Jew, in addition had to produce a testimonial from the *kehilla*.'[18] The tendency here is to reinforce the authority of the *kehilla* which serves the interest of the town-owner. Thus, rather than speak of the exclusion of the Jews from municipal citizenship, it is more appropriate to evaluate the relative autonomy and independence of the Jewish and Christian corporate institutions in the private towns.

We might ask parenthetically about the relative standing of the Jewish and Christian residents of the towns as individuals. A systematic investigation of murder trials might well yield interesting results bearing on the significance of class divisions within the urban population as well as the question of Jewish status. In the absence of such a study, I merely call attention to two known cases in Zółkiew, one in 1649 and the other in 1746, in which Christians were executed for murdering Jews. In the second case, which occurred when the Radziwiłłs owned the town, the murderer, a miller, was caught, hanged and then decapitated. His head was placed on one of the gates of the town.[19] One hopes this subject will be investigated further, but for now the topic is restricted to the comparison of corporate institutions rather than the standing of individuals. The tension between the two categories, however, is indeed relevant to this inquiry.

As many scholars have pointed out, generally speaking, the Christian town-dweller of the early modern Polish Commonwealth formed his sense of himself, his identity, with reference to his occupation and his own particular town. There was no meaningful sense of belonging to a class extending beyond the individual's own

---

[18] Jan Pęckowski, *Chrzanów: Miasto Powiatowe w województwie krakowskiem*, Chrzanów, 1934, p. 20.
[19] Solomon Buber, *Kiryah nisgava: hi 'ir Zolkvo*, Kraków 1903, p. 3; Gelber, 'Toledot yehudei Zhulkiev', col. 34, 50.

town.[20] To an extent, this localized identity was characteristic of the Jews as well, but only to an extent. It was not only the involvement in commerce which necessitated the formation of links with merchants in other parts of the country and, indeed, in other countries. The Jewish tradition itself, of course, inculcated a sense of membership in the Jewish people. At times too, this larger body became quite tangible and visible. Thus, to take a less well-known example, in the midst of the difficult period of war and plague at the end of the first decade of the eighteenth century, the Jewish community at Opatów, together with a number of other Polish Jewish communities, received a donation from the Spanish and Portuguese Congregation of London. The latter intended this money 'for our poor brethren in Poland in view of their calamities'. This is revealed in the correspondence of the *Mahamad* of that congregation.[21] The most important manifestation of the trans-local, trans-national sense of membership characteristic of the Jews, for the present purpose, was the existence of these regional and national Jewish institutions in the Polish Commonwealth. Surely the existence of these regional and national institutions and the relations between them and the *kehillot* was one of the most significant distinctions between the Jewish corporate bodies and the municipalities. Indeed, some Jewish historians have emphasized that the political impotence of the cities which was a reflection of the failure of an articulate, self-conscious bourgeoisie to emerge in Poland before the end of the eighteenth century, was one of the main factors insuring the relative security of the Jews.[22] And I have myself stressed in an article, published several years ago, that not only Jews but other ethno-religious groups in Poland developed institutions of a scope larger than the individual town, most notably the Scots.[23] Here, however, I should like to frame the question somewhat differently.

[20] Maria Bogucka, 'Les Villes et le développement de la culture sur l'exemple de la Pologne au XVIe–XVIIIe siècles', in *La Pologne au XVe siècle: Congrès International des Sciences Historiques à Bucarest*, Wrocław, 1980, p. 161; I. Ihnatowicz *et al.*, *Społeczeństwo polskie od X do XX wieku* (Warsaw, 1979), p. 273.

[21] R. D. Barnett, 'The correspondence of the Mahamad of the Spanish and Portuguese Congregation of London during the seventeenth and eighteenth centuries', *Transactions of the Jewish Historical Society of England* 20, 1959–61, pp. 20–1.

[22] Benzion Dinur, 'Darka ha-historit shel yahadut Polin', *Moznayim* 11, 1940–1, p. 166.

[23] G. D. Hundert, 'On the Jewish community in Poland during the seventeenth century: some comparative perspectives', *Revue des études juives* 142, 1983, pp. 349–72.

Thus far, a certain contradiction has been detected in the treatment of corporate institutions and particularly of the *kehillot* by the town-owners. One way to resolve this contradiction which sees the town-owners on the one hand weakening the corporate mediators between themselves and the residents of their towns and, on the other hand, strengthening those same institutions has been suggested recently. According to this analysis, it is appropriate to see the *kehilla*, in its administrative and judicial functions, as it was seen by the aristocrat who owned the town. That is, the town-owners tried not so much to abolish the *kehillot* as to incorporate them within the administrative structure of their estates.[24] While this is correct, it is incomplete. To be sure, the aristocrats did not hesitate to instruct the *kehilla*, its officers and its judges as if these were his own appointees.[25] Yet, and this is the area I should like to look at, some of the kehillot's activities were unconnected to the administration of the *klucz* and indeed, some could have been seen as contrary to the interests of the magnate-aristocrat town-owners. An optimal prism through which to view this problem, as I have indicated, is the case of the relationship between Jewish communities in private towns and the inter-communal and national Jewish institutions.

Let us look at some examples first and then try to frame the theoretical problem. Earlier, the case of Chrzanów was mentioned, where new Jewish arrivals, the town-owner stipulated, had to be approved not only by the dwór but by the *kehilla* as well. If the *kehilla* is seen as an extension of the administrative apparatus of the town-owner, there is nothing contradictory in such a policy. A more complicated picture, however, is presented by Żółkiew where, in the first half of the seventeenth century, new Jewish settlers had to be acceptable not only to the elders of the local *kehilla* but also to the elders of the community of Lwów.[26] The right to sole control of the granting the right of residence, a sort of Jewish equivalent to the Saxon or Magdeburg law, had not yet been granted to Żółkiew which was thus still dependent on the metropolis of Lwów. This competing, external authority which

---

[24] M. J. Rosman, 'The Jews and the Polish magnates: Jews in the Sieniawski-Czartoryski latifundium, 1686–1731', PhD dissertation, Jewish Theological Seminary of America, New York, 1982, pp. 404–21.
[25] B. Baranowski *et al.* eds, *Instrukcje gospodarcze dla dóbr magnackich i szlacheckich z XVII–XIX wieku* Wrocław, 1958, 1963.
[26] Buber, *Kiryah*, pp. 81–2.

could, at least theoretically, determine which Jews might reside in his town, was accepted in this case by the town-owner.

A similar set of circumstances arose in certain towns in connection with the avenues of appeal against the decisions of the Jewish communal courts. It would seem that most such appeals in private towns were directed toward the town-owner. There were, however, some private towns in which the hereditary owners specifically permitted appeals of such decisions to be brought before 'district Jewish courts' (ziemstwa sądów żydowskich).[27] For example, the privilege granted the Jews of Solec on Wisła provided for appeals of the decisions of the Jewish courts to be brought before 'the elders of the Opatów district' (starszych ziemskich opatowskich).[28] In Opatów itself, on the other hand, and this as I said was more representative, appeals were brought before the owner of the town or his representative. In the latter case, he was to judge the case, 'according . . . to Jewish law and custom' (według . . . praw y zwyczaiów żydowskich); I quote from Sanguszko's 1737 instructions to a new *Gubernator* of Opatów.[29] This procedure seems clearly to be more in keeping with the interests of the town-owner than permitting judicial appeals to go beyond the territory and the jurisdiction of the aristocrat. Why, then, would the owners of Olesko, Solec, Swarzędz, Zamość, and other towns permit such appeals? Perhaps, before attempting to answer this question, it will be useful to look at one or two other variations on this same theme.

The Jews paid national taxes collectively in Poland from at least 1581 until the abolition of the Council of the Four Lands in 1764. The apportionment of the tax burden was carried out in stages, first at the national gathering, and later at regional assemblies of Jewish elders. In 1758, the owner of Opatów wrote to the *Starozakonny Marszałek Ziemski* demanding that the earlier agreement determining the proportion of the taxes of the district of Kraków-Sandomierz to be paid by the Jews of Opatów be strictly respected.[30] Earlier, probably around 1720, the Jewish community of Opatów had rejected Sanguszko's demand that no one hold office in the *kehilla* for more than one year out of four. One of the Jews' objections was that it was essential to have experienced people 'in

---

[27] Goldberg, *Jewish Privileges*, pp. 234–5; Opas, 'Sytuacja', p. 21.
[28] Wyrobisz, 'Ludność', p. 9.
[29] APK, *AS*, 530.
[30] AGAD, *ADO*, I/42.

our Jewish *sejmiki*' (w sejmikach naszych żydowskich).[31] We might ask why the town-owner tolerated the flowing of capital out of his town in the form of the taxes paid by the Jewish community of Opatów to the national Jewish Council.[32] The answer is that this was the law of the land. Jewish taxes constituted a significant proportion of national revenues. But this answer does not completely satisfy. It certainly does not address the other sorts of challenges to the town-owner's authority which have been mentioned.

In this particular connection, there is still another aspect which can be mentioned but not discussed in detail now. In 1687 (which incidentally was the same year in which the Opatów Jewish community gained control of the right of settlement as recognized by the Council of the Four Lands) Jan Sobieski took note of a petition from the same Council. The royal response cites the Jewish Council's claim that they could not meet the tax payments that year because: 'some Jews, living in towns, districts or noble estates . . . have avoided paying that part of their tax obligation because of the protection of their Lords.'[33] This question of individual Jews, but not, apparently, whole Jewish communities, utilizing the protection of the aristocrats to avoid or evade the payment of taxes cannot be taken up here. Our task is to try to understand the apparent willingness of the hereditary town-owners to tolerate the competition of an external authority. Let us take up one last case.

In 1745, Sanguszko addressed the *kehilla* of Opatów with a number of points, including the following:

> Since this is the custom that Synagogues in other important towns [Znacznych miastach] of the Polish Kingdom that, from their midst they choose responsible individuals for the General farming out of taxes [Dyspartyment Generalny], and that General Jewish Clerks are chosen by districts [Prowincyi] to moderate taxes, which otherwise would be too heavy for provinces or districts; therefore this custom should also be upheld by the Opatów synagogue and I permit them to send their Delegates chosen by the *kehilla* and commonality.[34]

[31] APK, *AS*, 9/9/15.
[32] Israel Halperin, ed., 'Pinkas vaad arba aratsot' in *Acta Congressus Generalis Judaeorum Poloniae (1580–1764)*, Jerusalem, 1945, no. 433, pp. 206–7.
[33] Ibid., no. 32, pp. xxix–xxx. Similar complaints can also be found earlier, for example, no. 253, p. 102; no. 256, p. 102; no. 297, p. 125.
[34] ADO, I/121.

If there was any doubt, the term *Dyspartyment Generalny* refers to the Council of the Four Lands. What seems to be at issue here is the question of changing the status of the community's relationship to the regional and national institutions. Until that year, Opatów had been one of the leading communities of the region of Kraków-Sandomierz and it was the region which sent representatives to the Council of the Four Lands. Now, certain *znacznych miastach* such as Kraków and Poznań were independent of their regions and sent representatives directly to the Council of the Four Lands. Sanguszko, either on his own initiative, or at the urging of certain Jews in Opatów, seems to be not only permitting them to seek such a change but advocating it. In fact, as nearly as can be determined from the frustratingly fragmentary records of the Council of the Four Lands, no such change occurred. Opatów continued to be a part of the 'Land' or region of Kraków-Sandomierz. But this is not the main concern here. The brief passage cited illustrates very well the ambiguities and contradictions which I have been trying to highlight here.

What emerges from these remarks is a depiction of a stage in the process in which Jewish autonomous institutions were moving, in stops and starts, toward disintegration. This process, which was characteristic, in its broadest outlines, of all of European Jewry, was subject to the particular conditions obtaining in the Polish Commonwealth. In some ways, it might be said that the town-owners resembled the absolutist rulers of Central Europe. The latter tended to eliminate corporate distinctions among their subjects, seeking allies regardless of their social class or religion. The consequence for Jews living in such states was their taking an uncertain and tentative step toward integration in the nascent nation-state. The conditions which resulted from the absolutist-like rule of the town-owners were, as we have seen, more ambivalent. Nevertheless, those conditions did tend to provide the Jews living in private towns with certain opportunities. Finally, though, these great estates were not states. The policies of their owners were predicated on their own self-interest, and were subject, in some measure at least, to the larger polity. Fundamental change in Jewish status would have to await broader political developments.

14 · Hasidism and the *Kehilla*

Chone Shmeruk

I

Hasidism is an innovative religious movement, seeking new ways and possibilities of serving God within the Jewish tradition – in particular in the principles of the late Cabbalistic mysticism. In the face of what appeared to be stagnation in the dominant Jewish religious tradition, Hasidic leaders sought to enlarge their intervention into the sphere of God's emanation both as individuals and as part of a religious community. The spiritual, theological and ethical assumptions of Hasidism in various shades and forms, though sometimes of a very diverse emphasis, constitute, without any doubt, the essential features of this religious movement. It is therefore understandable that initially the movement was, of necessity, exclusive and esoteric.

As time went by, in the second half of the eighteenth century, *tsaddikism* spread within Hasidism. This is a belief in the supernatural potentialities and forces of the *tsaddik*, the leader of the Hasidic community to whom is ascribed by his followers the ability to mediate between God and man. Gifted with such ability, the *tsaddik* is capable of intervening and working miracles even in worldly matters, helping the individual and the community. In other words, the *tsaddik* becomes the embodiment of God's omnipotence on earth.

The belief in the omnipotent *tsaddik*, latent in Hasidic thought from the very beginning, became concrete probably in the 1760s and was a fundamental element of the philosophy of the whole movement in the last quarter of that century. Because of the mass spread of Hasidism in Poland, the end of the eighteenth century and the beginning of the nineteenth century are significant in the history of Polish Jews, owing to the growing acceptance of the figure of the omnipotent *tsaddik*. In this period the number of Hasidic leaders' courts grew and new *tsaddik* dynasties came into being and established themselves, based on the belief that the *tsaddik*'s omnipotent powers were hereditary. In Polish cities and small towns where no *tsaddik* had settled, prayer houses – or *shtiblekh* – were created, assembling the followers of various Hasidic communities and testifying to the influence of a particular *tsaddik* in that town.

The *tsaddik*'s court, usually in a small town, became the centre for Hasidic communities and at least once a year, during the high holidays, the object of pilgrimage by his followers. Some Polish cities, small towns, even the most inconspicuous, as for example, Leżajsk, Kozienice, Opatów, Kock, Góra Kalwaria, Mszczonów, Łomazy and others, were transformed into famous centres of Hasidism because of their established *tsaddikim*. The influence of a Hasidic centre spread far beyond the town where the *tsaddik*, who ruled the spirits and the activities of his *Hasidim*, wherever they found themselves, had his court.

The spreading of the Hasidic movement over wide areas of Poland naturally changed the nature of the autonomy of Polish Jews. Hasidism, in reality *tsaddikim* and their communities, began to play a decisive role as a new religious and social factor in the various *kehillot*, the fundamental entity of Jewish autonomy in Poland. Hasidic communities, whose centre was often outside the main town, came to exercise control over many local matters.

In the early 1770s, interference by Hasidism in the operating of the *kehilla* raised strong objections from the established and traditional *kehilla* authorities. In the year 1772, the first-known *herem* or excommunication was proclaimed in Brody. Among other things, this anti-Hasidic *herem* forbade: (1) maintaining a separate Hasidic prayer house; (2) ritual slaughter (*shekhita*) by the Hasidic method with *ground knives*.

Where the prayer house was concerned, the *kehillot*'s objections, though superficially insignificant, were quite obvious. Hasidic prayer texts do not, in principle, differ much from the traditional. Even the *Sephardi* variety of prayer was recognized and authorized in Brody in the *kloys*, another prayer house of non- or pre-Hasidic Cabbalists. But the real objection was to the encroaching on the *kehillot*'s domain by a group not appointed to do so; moreover, without any previous agreement or permission from the *kehilla* authorities.

In this case, the *kehilla* was using the *herem* to defend itself against the newly emerging religious and social movement, which had demonstrably shown its independence since, as time went by, the prayer house, that is the Hasidic *shtibl*, became the basic cell of the Hasidic community in every town. The emergence of Hasidic *shtiblekh*, the number of people praying in them, and their rapid distribution and diffusion throughout vast regions of Poland at that time, were the gauge not only of the influence of individual *tsaddikim* but, above all, of the tremendous potential of the whole Hasidic movement.

Unfortunately we possess no sources to illustrate the dynamics of the Hasidic movement which would undoubtedly be demonstrated by complete documentation of the growth of Hasidic *shtiblekh* and their diffusion in various *kehillot*. It is true that the *Atlas of Jewish Dialects and Culture in Eastern Europe*, initiated by the late Uriel Weinreich and continued by Marvin Herzog in New York, covers the distribution of various *shtiblekh* in Poland before the Second World War. Yet despite their value, these documents can only to a small degree reflect the image of the historical development of Hasidism in the eighteenth and nineteenth centuries. Has any data concerning earlier *shtiblekh* survived in Polish archives? It would be worthwhile searching for them.

II

Less obvious and much more complicated than the *shtiblekh* problem was the problem of ritual slaughter by the Hasidic method which, as mentioned, raised objections from the *kehilla* of Brody which are repeated in other later anti-Hasidic *herems*. This is the matter to which this chapter is principally devoted.

As is well known, Jews consider meat as kosher only if it comes from 'clean' cattle and poultry and only if it is killed by ritual slaughter. Without going into detail, let us point out that the essential element of kosher slaughter lies in the quality of the slaughterer's blade – that is, its absolute smoothness and sharpness without a single notch or dent. Even the slightest imperfection makes meat *terefa*, prohibited for Jews. It is therefore accepted that every kosher butcher is obliged to present his knives to the local rabbi every week to have them carefully examined before use.

The quality of knives for ritual slaughter is determined by ancient rules of *halakha*, whilst their examination was ordered by resolutions issued by the institutions of Jewish self-government: in Poland from the Land Council through to the smallest *kehilla*. Despite these regulations, strict as they were, the *kashrut* or 'kosherness' of the ritual slaughter depended very largely on the orthodoxy, piety, and simple scrupulousness of the individual kosher butcher. After all, it was only the butcher who could assure the absolute *kashrut* of the slaughter. It was therefore a matter of religious ethics in the widest sense, going beyond the letter of any technical code or trade law. The kosher butcher was under twofold pressure. On the one hand, he did not want to sustain financial loss by admitting meat to be *terefa*; on the other hand, the maintaining of all the necessary regulations of *kashrut* depended on his absolute integrity.

The basis of religious and moral orthodoxy and the unblemished reputation of kosher butchers in eighteenth-century Poland was further confused by two additional factors:

1. Quite considerable groups of followers of the 'false Messiah' Shabtai Tsvi existed in Podole in the era of the dawn of Hasidism. They were later known as Frankists. Not without reason, it was suspected that, in accordance with the assumptions of their theological antinomy, and being kosher butchers at the same time, they made meat *terefa*, thus bringing whole Jewish communities into sin. A particular sensitiveness concerning such suspicions is very well documented in Hasidic sources.
2. In Hasidism, which was a movement with a mystical inclination, belief in reincarnation and the transmigration of souls, closely connected with ritual slaughter, gained great importance. If a Jewish soul – so that faith had it – was reincarnated into a 'clean' animal fit for kosher consumption, then the ritual slaughter and pious consumption, together with the necessary blessings and intentions, enabled that soul to be 'liberated' into another human embodiment. Making meat *terefa* was seen as the equivalent of another 'killing' of the soul, thus sentencing it to further non-human wandering.

Thus it can well be understood that the spread of this belief through Hasidism in eighteenth-century Poland caused far more scrupulous adherence to the rules of ritual slaughter, and corresponding suspiciousness of the morality and piety of kosher butchers. A macabre Jewish legend, which became very popular in Poland in the mid-eighteenth-century, strikingly illustrates how great the stress was which attached to the piety of the ritual slaughterer in folk beliefs. A kosher butcher famous for his piety 'kosherness' of the ritual slaughter depended very largely on the approached by a young man wishing to learn the art of ritual slaughter. To warn him of the possible sins and their consequence, the master called out and showed him a warning phantom. A figure with a ritual knife in his hand appeared on the roof and cut his own throat. Blood ran and ran. When the bleeding stopped the figure on the roof straightened up, then fell to the ground. A few moments later, the same phantom reappeared on the roof, and slaughtered himself once more. The scene was repeated a few times. The master explained to the young apprentice that the kosher butcher who had appeared on the roof had, during his lifetime, taken up a profession for which, owing to his sinfulness, he was unfit. This was his punishment.

There is a famous collection of hagiographic stories about the founder of the Hasidic movement, Israel Ba'al-Shem-Tov (1700–60), which, unsurprisingly, tell us not only how he personally inspected the tools of the kosher butcher's trade – even though this was done by the local rabbi in the usual way – but also about his ability to detect sinful kosher butchers and Frankists, who fed Jews with *terefa* meat. Israel Ba'al-Shem-Tov, according to the same stories, could also pick out pious kosher butchers. Early Hasidic hagiography commemorated almost every sign of preoccupation with kosher ritual slaughter within the movement.

Some time in the second half of the eighteenth century – we have no idea where and when but probably after the death of Israel Ba'al-Shem-Tov and before the year 1772, the date of the proclamation of the Brody *herem* – razor-like ground-steel knives appeared among Polish Jews. If the sharpening to perfection of an iron knife on a whetstone was a laborious task, absorbing both energy and time and therefore often not done to standard, then the new, tougher, ground-steel knives were not only suitable for ritual slaughter; they had the additional advantage of being labour-saving. By 1772 the Hasidim had not simply accepted the new-style ground-steel knives; they had, as we know from the Brody *herem*, deemed them the only permissible blade for ritual slaughter. The Hasidim had found for their communities an ideal solution to the tangled and distressing problem of kosher meat, which affected all Jews.

One should note in passing that although ground-steel knives could have raised doubts among traditional rabbis, yet some rabbinical authorities – widely respected, even among the anti-Hasidic – recognized ritual slaughter with such knives as kosher. Therefore, the real reason why the *kehilla* objected to Hasidic ritual slaughter was not the use of this 'new technology'.

At the same time as the weakening of Jewish autonomy in Poland, both through the suspension of the Council of the Four Lands in the year 1764 and through the failing powers of the *kehilla* in towns both big and small, the eighteenth century witnessed a dramatic drop in the range of indirect tax which could be collected from the Jewish population. As usual in such situations, the burden of consumer tax grew rapidly. Tax on kosher meat was known in Poland from at least the end of the sixteenth century but in the eighteenth century it reached exorbitant levels. In Wilno, for example, in the year 1785, the *kehilla*'s total income was 84,710 złoty, and 42 per cent of this sum came from various taxes connected with ritual slaughter. In Dubno in the year 1794, tax raised on ritual slaughter covered the budget of the *kehilla* – 53,000 złoty, part of that sum forming a sizeable income for the tax collectors. No wonder then that tax constituted 47.6 per cent of the price of kosher meat.

From these figures we can conclude that private unlicensed kosher ritual slaughter, as carried out by the Hasidim, caused painful losses to the eighteenth-century tax system. It is here that one should seek the true reason for the *kehilla*'s objections to independent Hasidic activities in this sphere.

In these circumstances, the *kehilla* under attack was backed by the kosher meat-tax collectors, butchers and non-Hasidic kosher butchers, who felt threatened by independent ritual slaughter. Yet, faced with the unyielding obstinacy of the Hasidim, their determination to keep ritual slaughter under their own control, the *kehilla* and its supporters had to seek compromise, and at least allow parallel Hasidic slaughter – properly taxed, of course. The above applies obviously to *kehillot* where the Hasidim did not form a majority, and thus were unable to control the institution of self-government.

Sources from Mińsk in Byelorussia, a town outside the sphere of strong Hasidic influence and well known for its *Mishne*, that is traditional and anti-Hasidic tendencies, well illustrate the gradual legalization of Hasidic ritual slaughter and concomitant imposition of tax. In the year 1794, the Mińsk *kehilla* decided to close the only *shtibl* in town. The Mińsk *herem* of 1795 prohibited ritual slaughter carried out with ground-steel knives or by an 'outside' kosher butcher. Either of these conditions meant that the meat was declared *terefa* and thus prohibited for pious Jews. In the year 1803, the Mińsk *kehilla* once more confirmed the *herem* and, moreover, forbade any steps to change or cancel it. Yet, probably the same year, slaughter of cattle for the Hasidim was permitted. This was caused by a painful tax deficit. Faced with the necessity of paying tax to the government and the Hasidic boycott of meat not slaughtered under their own control, the Mińsk *kehilla* had to back down. It was then decided that, after payment of tax, meat from Hasidic slaughter could be sold in Mińsk, in the courtyard of the *shtibl*. In the year 1805, the Minsk *kehilla* gave the Hasidim a shop in the market-place where, untroubled, they could sell their own ritually slaughtered meat.

All kosher butchers in Mińsk normally took an oath to carry out precisely the resolutions of the *kehilla*. Hasidic kosher butchers had an extra clause in their oath: that they would not slaughter in secret or outside the town, thus causing any loss to the *kehilla*. In the year 1817, there were already two kosher butchers in Mińsk, representing two different Hasidic communities of the two legal Hasidic *shtiblekh*.

If *Misnagdim* Mińsk saw the transition from the resolute and absolute *herem*, in twenty years, to the authorization of two Hasidic kosher butchers, then one can imagine how much faster and easier the process was in *kehillot* with a Hasidic majority. In the absence of detailed evidence on the situation in other *kehillot*, one must rely on a memorandum addressed in 1838 to the Austrian authorities by Józef Perl of Tarnopol. In it the author asserts:

> In Galicia it would be hard to find a kosher butcher who would not be a member of this sect [Hasidic], nor at least subordinate to it. Soon there will be not any [kosher butcher], who will not be totally affiliated to this sect. In general they are appointed only by the Hasidic leaders and not by the rabbi . . . Woe betide the community, its rabbi, or the collector of meat-taxes, who would dream of opposing such an appointment . . . And in general, one would not find a kosher butcher who would dare take on anywhere the post of kosher butcher against the will of a *tsaddik* . . . In this way, kosher butchers are completely under the domination of the *tsaddikim*, and even if with the rabbi insisting he wants to continue his duty, he [the rabbi] is asked for a formal confirmation of the appointment. Nevertheless, woe betide him, should he have the courage to refuse to confirm the appointment of such a Hasidic kosher butcher, or if [he dared] accept another kosher butcher. Only in Lwów and Brody, and

possibly in some other community could one find an exception from this rule. (pp. 88–9)

Whereas kosher butchers in the old days meant so little among Jews, now, since the Hasidim have prevailed in Galicia, they have become so important. Leaseholders, tradesmen, and, in general, the whole community are even now terrorized by these rascals. (p. 101)

Despite the undoubted bias of Perl – a very talented Hebrew and Yiddish writer, and an active supporter of the *Haskala*, who for a very long time fought desperately against Hasidim – his testimony appears quite reliable, at least where eastern Galicia is concerned. It is no exaggeration to assume that the state of affairs described by him was, in that period, quite common all over pre-partition Poland. It seems clear that, during the first half of the nineteenth century, the Hasidim took possession of the majority of Jewish self-government institutions, whether in *kehillot* or supervisory posts in synagogues in medium-sized towns in the Congress Kingdom, Galicia, Podole and Wołyń.

Even in many *kehillot* of the former north-eastern provinces of pre-partition Poland, that is in areas that were considered to be strongholds of the *Mishne*, the Hasidim gradually obtained authorization, largely due to the fact that the *kehilla* could not permit the loss of tax from Hasidic ritual slaughter. It is clear from the minute book of the Mińsk *kehilla* that Hasidic *shtiblekh* were authorized at the same time as Hasidic slaughter, even in those places where their existence had previously been questioned or prohibited on pain of excommunication.

III

Ritual slaughter by the Hasidic method and separate Hasidic prayer houses do not cover the full range of the Hasidic movement's involvement in Jewish self-government in Poland at that time. There were other functions with which the eighteenth-century *kehilla* could not or would not cope, and these were taken care of by the Hasidim. Let us mention just a few. An important one was the sanctioning of the *hazaka* (*hazuka* or *hazoka* depending on the Yiddish dialect) on certain properties leased by Jews, as well as ensuring that this *hazaka* (or legal title) was not encroached upon by competing claimants. This was an economic and juridical function of prime importance. The problem was to make the leaseholder secure, after the passage of three years, from the claims of his rivals, and thus enable him to receive permanent income. In the eighteenth century, the *kehilla* was not able to carry out this function properly, and rivalry among leaseholders often led them to bankruptcy. Sometime when several lease payments fell due together, they could not meet their commitments and landed up in gaol. Hasidic *tsaddikim* took over this function from the *kehilla*. With the force of their enormous authority and the fear of vengeance they inspired they sought not to let the *hazaka* of the multitude of leaseholders of inns, mills, alcohol distilleries and other properties be encroached upon. In a similar vein, Hasidic leaders carried out acts of 'ransoming tenants from prison', that is debtors jailed for failing to make due leasehold payments. The *kehilla* was unable or unwilling to fulfil this religious commandment, since it could not take over the burden of overdue tax payments. Hasidic leaders also organized money collections for Jews who settled in the Holy Land, probably because this charitable action had been neglected by autonomous Jewish institutions in the eighteenth century.

In the memorandum quoted earlier, Perl maintains that rabbis in Galicia were either appointed by Hasidic *tsaddikim*, or else rabbinical candidates had to obtain the *tsaddik*'s prior approval. He also refers to those rabbis who, as firm enemies of Hasidism, had to keep their opinions secret, either to remain in their posts or to obtain them. Despite his clear bias, there is much truth in his argument that rabbis' appointments were often controlled by Hasidic *tsaddikim*. It appears that the most important posts in each *kehilla* were filled by Hasidic communities, whose centres were often outside the towns and so beyond the jurisdiction of the town *kehilla*. The *tsaddik*'s court became the decisive factor in Poland, and it was an outside factor in relation to the local *kehilla*, sometimes directing a number of *kehillot*. This depended on the strength of a Hasidic community and the influence of its *tsaddik*.

Thus Hasidic intervention in the operations of the *kehilla* was made easier, and in fact possible in the first place, by the weakening of Jewish autonomy at the level of town *kehilla* in eighteenth-century Poland. This occurred especially after the year 1764, when the Council of the Four Lands officially ceased to exist. Let us then end this chapter with an important problem for future research. What was the connection between the decay of Jewish autonomy and the overall political, social and economic situation in Poland, at a time of confederations, disturbances, Cossack rebels and partitions, a situation that also indirectly influenced and favoured the development and spread of the Hasidic movement?

Part III

Legal Status

15 · The Kraków *Voivode*'s Jurisdiction over Jews: A Study of the Historical Records of the Kraków *Voivode*'s Administration of Justice to Jews

Stanisław Grodziski

Although it is not the aim of this chapter – in which I want to concentrate, above all, on the administration of justice by the Kraków *voivode* (governor), which extended over the Jews as well – I must begin with a fundamental question: Did the Jews in Poland constitute a separate estate?[1] This question, posed 120 years ago by an eminent lawyer and sociologist – Ludwik Gumplowicz,[2] has usually been answered with a qualified negative. As he put it, 'Jews

---

[1] When I was invited to take part in the proceedings of a conference held in Kraków in September 1986, I at first intended to write only about the *podwojewodziński* court. But in the course of my work, I decided to treat the subject far more broadly, as research devoted to the judicature over Jews had ceased with the works of Stanisław Kutrzeba and Majer Bałaban in the 1930s which are cited below. As a result of the Second World War, the possibilities for research and the number of scholars working on the subject has diminished so greatly that many topics have to be investigated anew. My aim is thus to survey the state of the sources that have survived. This is why the title of my paper suggests a connection with Stanisław Kutrzeba's work *Sądownictwo nad Żydami w województwie krakowskim* (The Jurisdiction over Jews in the Kraków province), Kraków, 1901, since I have followed in his footsteps in trying to clarify the field of research.

[2] Ludwik Gumplowicz (1838–1909), the descendant of a well-known Jewish family which had lived in Kraków for generations, failed to become a professor at the Jagiellonian University, and became instead a professor in Graz. He did not always use the term 'estate', yet asserted that: 'In Poland, Jews were a class within the nation, of which they were integral members, like the nobles, peasants, burghers ... Among those classes of the nation, Jews were by no means the lowest, as they stood equal with the burghers.' *Prawodawstwo polskie względem Żydów* (Polish judicature in regard to the Jews), Kraków, 1867, p. 109.

have for centuries with us constituted *corpus in corpore, status in statu*. Not admitted to any estate, having permission to use separate laws, they formed an independent body.'[3] Yet, if we define an estate as a closed group of feudal society, with an established social and juridical status, it is clear that this definition can apply to the Jews. Most works synthesizing Polish legal history, in discussing the 'estate' form of government with the privileges of nobles, clergy, burghers and peasants, distinguish also the situation of the Jews.[4] The fact that from the second half of the thirteenth century Jews had separate courts, in which (at least partly) they applied their own laws, is an important aspect of their special status.

It is to this jurisdiction that I want to confine myself, avoiding a discussion of the extremely broad problem of the Jews' legal situation and the nature of their self-government. Despite the prolific literature on Jewish history in Poland – and let us add that most works were published at the end of the nineteenth and beginning of the twentieth century – the juridical status of the Jewish people awaits a modern synthetic approach. An interesting starting point was suggested by Gumplowicz, when he remarked on the obvious fact that the three types of legislation which existed in pre-partition Poland, the monarch's immunities, synodal statutes and Diet resolutions, did not develop simultaneously, but often clashed with each other.[5]

Even when we limit our field of investigation to the administration of justice, we encounter complicated problems since, despite the excellent works of Stanisław Kutrzeba,[6] Moses Schorr and Majer Bałaban, the question of how the judicature evolved, how local

---

[3] As quoted in W. Smoleński, *Stan i sprawa Żydów polskich w XVIII wieku, w Pisma historyczne* (The estate and the problem of Polish Jews in the eighteenth century) in Historical Writings II, Kraków, 1901, p. 226.

[4] Jews are considered separately, or as a separate burghers' group, for instance, by Stanisław Kutrzeba in the various editions of his *Historia ustroju Polski* (The history of Poland's constitution), starting with the first edition in 1905. Zygmunt Wojciechowski took a similar view in *Państwo polskie w wiekach średnich* (The Polish State in the Middle Ages), Poznań, 1945, and stressed the separate status of both Jews and Armenians. Until Juliusz Bardach's *Historia państwa i prawa Polski* (A history of the Polish State and law), 2nd edn, Warsaw, 1964, no author has taken a firm position on the problem of whether we can consider Jews a separate estate.

[5] Gumplowicz, *Prawodawstwo*, pp. 1–2.

[6] S. Kutrzeba, *Historia źródeł dawnego prawa polskiego* (The history of the sources of Old Polish law) II, Lwów/Warsaw/Kraków, 1926, p. 305 and notes. See also the classification of norms for Jews in J. Goldberg, *Jewish Privileges in the Polish Commonwealth*, Jerusalem, 1985, p. 1 and notes.

differences developed and what principles of law applied in practice have not so far received thorough investigation. It is here that we come across difficulties because of the state of the sources. Those that have survived tell us more about how matters should have been handled, much less about how they really were. They include privileges, statutes, monarch's regulations, Diet resolutions. Much closer to everyday practice, however, were the *voivode*'s regulations. We must also remember that we are concerned with a society accustomed to the fact that, once a new piece of basic legislation had been passed, many people immediately sought ways of circumventing it, an attitude not unknown in Poland today. The theoretical situation found in the legal sources should be compared, therefore, with court practice, which is only possible for a few decades of the seventeenth and eighteenth centuries.

Stanisław Kutrzeba, when analysing the privileges issued by monarchs on behalf of the Jews, distinguished three groups:

1. General privileges, based on the fundamental privilege issued in the year 1264 by Prince Bolesław Pobożny (the Pious), extended by King Kazimierz Wielki (the Great), and modified by the rulers of the Jagiellonian dynasty, King Stefan Batory, and the subsequent elective kings. Although not always confirmed by the new king, they retained, in principle, their legal validity.[7]
2. Provincial privileges issued by the monarch on behalf of particular regions or provinces of Poland.
3. Local privileges, issued on behalf of communities in particular towns, usually based on several common rules formulated in the general and provincial privileges, although quite varied in character.

One should add that owners of private towns followed the monarch's example in their practice of enacting legislation affecting the Jews living on their estates.[8]

As a result of the intercession of the Jews of Great Poland, an important attempt to codify Jewish privileges took place on 5

[7] Limitations issued by the synodal statutes, and later by Diet constitutions, did not render void or cancel the monarch's privileges, but made use of inaccuracies and gaps in the existing laws to establish new norms in the law of the subject. This is an important problem which needs further comparative study.

[8] The constitution of the Kraków Diet of the year 1539 stated: 'Qui nobiles in oppidis aut in villis suis iudaeos habent, per Nos licet, ut soli ex eis fructus omnes et emolumenta percipient: *iusque illis arbitratu suo dicant*' (*Volumina Lequm* I, p. 550; my emphasis).

November 1669. It was undertaken by King Michał Korybut Wiśniowiecki, who put together – in a rather tentative way – all the general and provincial privileges issued in the period from the year 1264 until the mid seventeenth century. How far this codification agreed with the practice of those days still requires investigation. This code was, however, confirmed by successive monarchs; the last to do so, on 14 June 1765, was King Stanisław August Poniatowski.[9]

Even though this chapter is limited territorially to the old province of Kraków, we cannot base ourselves solely on local sources; analysis of the administration of justice relating to Jews must be considered within the general legislative framework. The provisions of the general privileges are the foundation, but they need to be supplemented with the rules established by local statutes and regulations over a long period. Only when there is a clash between theory and practice should we limit ourselves to the local regulations established in the Kraków province and to the court entries.

The origins of a distinct judicature for Jews is to be found in the privilege issued in the year 1264 by Prince Bolesław Pobożny.[10] King Kazimierz Wielki confirmed this privilege several times, in the years 1334, 1364 and 1367, extending it both in scope and territorially over the whole of Poland.[11] It was confirmed, albeit not without difficulty, by King Kazimierz Jagiellończyk.[12] Aleksander,

---

[9] M. Schorr, 'Krakovskii svod statutov i privilegii' (The Kraków collection of statutes and privileges), *Yevreyskaya Starina* 3, 1909. This codification awaits a monographic, modern approach.

[10] 'Item si Judaei inter se de facto discordiam moverint aut gueram iudex civitatis nostrae nullam iurisdictionem sibi vindicet in eosdem, sed Nos tantummodo aut noster palatinus vel eius iudex iudicium exercebit:' *Kodeks dyplomatyczny Wielkopolski* (Diplomatic code of Great Poland) I, Poznań, 1877, no. 605, p. 564.

[11] Accepting the privileges granted by Bolesław Pobożny (the Pious), Kazimierz Wielki (the Great) empowered the *starosta* as the official to administer justice to the Jews instead of the *voivode*. Gumplowicz has analysed these differences, *Prawodawstwo*, op.cit. p. 17 and notes, as has S. Kutrzeba, *Historia źródeł* II, pp. 299–300. The transfer of the prerogatives mentioned did not last long.

[12] He confirmed, with interpolations, Kazimierz Wielki's privileges of 1367 (see M. Bersohn, *Dyplomatariusz dotyczący Żydów w dawnej Polsce, na źródłach archiwalnych osnuty 1388–1782*, Documents concerning Jews in Old Poland, based on archival sources from the years 1388–1782, Warsaw, 1911, pp. 18–22). He also confirmed a second text from the same year, which has been claimed to be a very poor later falsification, as for instance, in R. Hube, *Przywilej żydowski Bolesława i jego potwierdzenia* (Bolesław's Jewish privilege and its later confirmations), Warsaw, 1880. Under pressure from the nobles, the king cancelled both these confirmations at Nieszawa in 1454; M. Bobrzyński, *O ustawodawstwie nieszawskim Kazimierza Jagiellończyka* (On Kazimierz Jagiellończyk's Nieszawa legal proceedings), Kraków,

after including the 1334 document in Łaski's Legal Statutes, incorporated it, with slight modifications, into the legal system where it remained over the next centuries.[13]

According to Prince Bolesław's privilege, with the changes made later by King Kazimierz Wielki,[14] the competent law court for cases between Jews themselves and between Jews and Christians was not the local municipal court, but the royal or monarch's court, the *voivode*'s court or the court nominated by the *voivode* judge.[15] King Kazimierz Jagiellończyk limited the competence of this last court, removing from it minor civil cases between Jews which were to be judged by the Jewish community's jurisdiction; in this way, he probably merely legalized actual practice.

Thus the *wojewodziński* court, that is the court appointed by the *voivode*, was not the only one. The court of the elders of the community, the *parnassim*, was fundamental in controversies between Jews.[16] Although confirmed in sources of the fifteenth century, it probably existed from the very start of Jewish community life in Poland, and surely functioned in Kraków. The royal or king's court stood at the top of the administration of justice for cases concerning Jews as well. It was both a court of appeal and a court of first and second instance. The judicial system as it affected Jews may, therefore, be presented in simplified, diagrammatic form (see Figure 15.1).

1873, pp. 96–7. Yet these charters were not taken away from the Jews, as they submitted them to later monarchs for confirmation.

[13] S. Kutrzeba, *Historia źródeł* II, pp. 302 and notes.

[14] Although more modern editions exist, such as B. Ploch, *Die General-Privileg in der Polnischen Judenschaft*, Poznań, 1892, this privilege is quoted according to the old, but valuable, edition of J. W. Bandtkie, *Ius Polonicum codicibus veteribus manuscriptis et editionibus quibusque collatis*, Warsaw, 1831, pp. 1–21, as this set out its evolution. Quoted further as *Ius Polonicum*.

[15] Jews had to defend themselves from attempts to have their cases tried by other courts according to the principle 'legis loci delicit'. See S. Kutrzeba, ed., *Zbiór aktów do historii ustroju prawa polskiego i kancelarii sądowych województwa krakowskiego z wieku XVI–XVIII* (A collection of acts for the history of the functioning of the courts of Polish law and of the offices of the Kraków voivodeship court in the sixteenth to eighteenth centuries) in *Archiwum Komisji Prawniczej* 8, part 2, Kraków, 1909, no. 111, p. 85, no. 112, pp. 85–7; no. 119, pp. 91–2; no. 141, p. 124; no. 169, pp. 138–9. The fundamental principle 'actor sequitur forum rei' affected Jews as well, although only to a limited degree; they could not be summoned before a Church court: 'Iudaeus non debet citari in ius spirituale . . . pro quaecunque re', *Ius Polonicum*, p. 13, XXX.

[16] *Ius Polonicum*, p. 7, X, XI. Included in the oath taken by the elders was the duty of 'administering justice' to Jews, *Zbiór aktów do historii ustroju*, no. 139, p. 106.

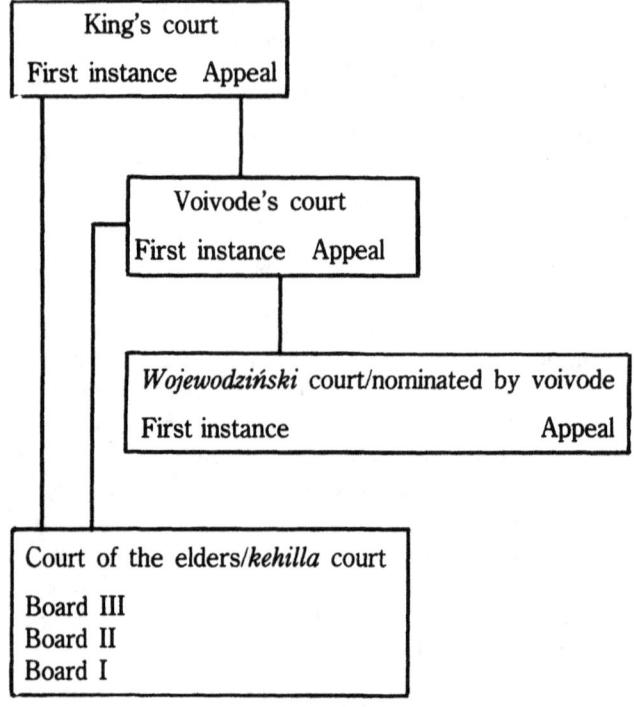

Figure 15.1 *The judicial system for Jews*

THE COURT OF THE ELDERS

Besides very general information on the privileges, we learn more about this court from the statute of the Kraków *kehilla* of 1595,[17] amended soon after, and from numerous regulations issued by *voivodes*.[18] In this court, three judicial boards can be distinguished.

---

[17] M. Bałaban, 'Die Krakauer Judengemeindeordnung aus dem Jahre 1595 und ihre Nachträge', *Jahrbuch der Jüdischen Literaturgesellschaft in Frankfurt a.Main* 10 (1913); 11 (1916); idem, *Historia żydów w Krakowie i na Kazimierzu 1304–1868* (History of Jews in Kraków and Kazimierz, 1304–1868; 2nd rev. edn of *Dzieje Żydow* (1912) – see ch. 18, n. 3), Kraków, 1931, pp. 327, 367 and notes. This is one of the sources badly in need of reprinting.

[18] The first of those that have survived till today was issued by the voivode Andrzej Tęczyński in the year 1527. Polish text in Bałaban, *Historia Żydów w Krakowie*, pp. 361–2; Latin text in *Zbiór aktów do historii*, no. 12, p. 14. It states that matters between Jews should be discussed by their elders. The Potocki regulation for Kraków Jews of the year 1659 stated in clause 6 that 'all matters

The first board, the lowest, tried the smallest civil cases – up to ten złoty value of the subject of disagreement, insults of honour, disputes between vendors. As a separate section within this board, the police court tried street disturbances, disruptions of others' business and the like. The middle board dealt with cases in which the value of the subject under dispute did not exceed 100 złoty, defamation and minor criminal offences. The highest board handled cases where the issue under dispute involved more than 100 złoty, as well as cases of defamation and similar matters, should litigants apply to it. Nevertheless this division of authority was not hard and fast. Jews could avail themselves of the privilege *prorogatio fori*, according to which litigants could transfer their cases to a different board from that dictated by the character of the case. Moreover, the practice was also followed of transferring cases to a court of conciliation, for instance headed by a well-known rabbi, and decisions thus obtained were respected.

As time went by, the competence of the Court of Elders grew. In King August's II privilege of 19 May 1702, the Court of Elders was to settle cases between Jews, with the possibility of appeal to the *wojewodziński* court; it could also settle mixed cases, that is between Jews and non-Jews, since a Christian had to summon a Jew to this court in a minor dispute.[19]

The judges of all boards of this court were elected annually, were not paid by the community, and court taxes and fines were to be used for synagogue purposes. But practice often differed.

At the beginning of the sixteenth century, an institution of Jewish self-government superior to the *kehilla* emerged, that is the general 'seigniors', with separate sections for Great and Little Poland;[20]

---

which take place between Jews, be discussed by the Jewish elders and their judges. Execution of all types in various matters of this character may be undertaken', *Zbiór aktów do historii*, no. 168, p. 137. Antoni Lubomirski's regulation from the year 1779, ibid., no. 272, p. 265, envisioned a rabbi and spiritual court in the *kehilla*; similarly Stanisław Dembiński's regulation from the year 1780, ibid., no. 273, p. 266.

[19] M. Bałaban, 'Ze studiów nad ustrojem prawnym Żydów w Polsce. Sędzia żydowski i jego kompetencje', in *Pamiętnik trzydziestolecia pracy naukowej prof. dr Przemysława Dąbkowskiego* (Studies of the Jews' legal status in Poland. The Jewish judge and his prerogatives, in 'A tribute to Professor Przemysław Dąbkowski on the thirtieth anniversary of his scholarly work'), Lwów, 1927, p. 268.

[20] Z. Kaczmarczyk and B. Leśnodorski, *Historia państwa i prawa Polski* (A history of the Polish State and law, II: from the mid fifteenth century to 1795), 2nd edn, Warsaw, 1966, p. 73.

the 'seigniors' also performed certain juridical functions.[21] Appointed by the king, the 'seigniors' were entitled 'doctors of the Law of Moses', that is, they were highly educated. They came into dispute with the community and appealed for an amicable judgement to a trusted and respected German rabbi, doubtless by analogy with the Magdeburg judgements. This practice was, however, prohibited by the monarch,[22] and the institution of general 'seigniors' thus soon disappeared. The subject has not yet been properly researched by scholars and needs further investigation.

THE WOJEWODZIŃSKI COURT[23]

In the province of Kraków, this court probably functioned from the year 1334, that is from the time when Prince Bolesław's privileges were confirmed by King Kazimierz Wielki. At this time, Mikołaj of Kamieniec, of the Pilawa coat of arms (died 1336) was the *voivode* of Kraków. It is not known whether he exercised his functions. Yet, although the 1264 privilege reserved jurisdiction over Jews for the prince himself, or the prince's *voivode*, and only in the third place mentioned a judge appointed by the *voivode* (the *wojewodziński* judge),[24] it was this officer who took up the main burden of these duties. This is why he was called 'the judge of the Jews', *iudex iudaeorum*. Despite the lack of specific instructions, the Kraków *voivode* always appointed an established noble with professional experience as a judge in Jewish cases.[25] By the

---

[21] M. Schorr, *Organizacya Żydów w dawnej Polsce od najdawniejszych czasów aż do roku 1772* (The organization of the Jews in Old Poland from earliest times till the year 1772), *Kwartalnik Historyczny* 13, Lwów, 1899, 1, p. 11 and notes.

[22] 'Ne ipsi deinceps ulliis extra Regnum appellationibus utantur, sed si quidem controversiae ob legem suam inter se habuerint, id ipsi Iudei in Regno nostro existentes recognioscant.' Acta Tomiciana III, no. 121. See also Bersohn, *Dyplomatariusz*, no. 37, p. 40: Mojżesz Fiszel's appointment as seignior, with the right to judge 'excessibus et delictis'.

[23] This name for the court is found in most Kraków sources. In the Lwów sources, investigated by Z. Pazdro, we more often come across the term 'podwojewodziński (*under-wojewodziński*) court'. See Z. Pazdro, *Organizacja i praktyka żydowskich sądów podwojewodzińskich w okresie 1740–1772, na podstawie lwowskich materiałów archiwalnych* (The organization and practice of the Jewish *podwojewodziński* courts in the period 1740–1772, on the basis of Lwów sources), Lwów, 1903. A similar terminology is found in Poznań sources.

[24] See n.-10 above. For more on the subject see Bałaban, 'Ze studiów nad ustrojem,' p. 246 and n.

[25] In the fifteenth century the following names are known from literature: Jerzy, *notarius SRM, iudex protunc iudaeorum Cracoviensium*, 1412; Pełka Bidliński, 1418;

seventeenth and eighteenth centuries, he was usually a lawyer who had practised in district (*ziemski*) or municipal (*grodzki*) court, and who treated the function of 'judge of the Jews' as a source of additional income.[26] Because of his function, he was also called *podwojewodzi* (*under-voivode*), although in Kraków these were two different functions.[27]

Jan Koczyński, *ad hoc specialiter deputatus*, 1436; Jan Chamiec from Dobranowice, 1459–69; Jan Goraj, 1469. In the sixteenth century only two names appear: Stanisław Górski, Kraków *podstarości*, from 1522; Jan Herburt from Fulsztyn, from 1544. From the seventeenth century Zygmunt Świerczowski from Świerczów, till 1621; Marcin Skoroszewski, Lelów frontier *komornik*, 1622–38; simultaneously Stanisław Stanisławski, *podwojewodzi*; Łukasz Kochański from Kochań, frontier *komornik*, 1624–48; Jan Ligęza from Bobrek, from 1649; Piotr Opocki from Opoka, from 1651; Michał Krzysztof Rupniewski, from 1658; Mikołaj Suliński from Sulanki, from 1661; Piotr Izdebski, from 1669; Ludwik Wąsowicz, *Łomża chorąży*, from 1672; Stefan Waźyński, from 1678. From the eighteenth century Michał Borzęcki, commissioner of the royal artillery, from 1702; Michał Szaszkowski, from 1706; Jan Stroński, *Czernichów łowczy*, from 1718; Stanisław Oraczewski, from 1721; Stanisław Łętowski, Biecz municipal judge and Kraków *chorąży*, from 1726; Franciszek Miklaszewski, 1728; Krzysztof Rudnicki and Piotr Gordon, 1745 (see Bałaban, 'Ze studiów nad ustrojem', p. 275, for their dispute over this post); Jan Skiwski, from 1747; Ignacy Kurdwanowski, from 1762.

[26] This was not a good practice, as during a 1633 Diet it was demanded that *podwojewodzi* should not take on any additional municipal posts (*Volumina Legum* III, p. 808). Thus the same applied to the Kraków *voivode*.

[27] See Bałaban, 'Ze studów nad ustrojem', p. 259, on the division of functions between the Kraków *podwojewodziński* and the *wojewodziński* judge. The 1631 Diet resolution 'on *podwojewodzi*' stated:

> Much relies on the *podwojewodzi* being sworn in, thus *authoritate conventus praesentis* we decide that *podwojewodzi* must take an oath on their function, *in hanc iuramenti rotam*, that: I judge justly and with respect to all matters and in all I shall fulfil the functions of my office in accordance with the written law, having no concern either for a friend or foe or passer-by, nor for presents, which would be contrary to the just decision. (*Volumina Legum* III, p. 697)

The decision to take an oath was repeated in a strict form by the 1633 constitution, ibid., p. 808, which reads:

> We grant to those *podwojewodzi*, and judges and established nobles set over the Jews, justice according to laws and privileges . . . fulfilling it for people of all conditions, trying minor cases *post definitivam sententiam* in this court, and in some matters letting appeal be made to their *voivodes*, with this added, that Jews be not summoned to any other courts *in civilibus causis*, but only the *voivode*'s and that their appeals which *centum florenos non excederent* should not circulate between the voivodes and the royal court. (ibid., p. 809)

In the fifteenth century and maybe in the sixteenth as well, we find a post of *podsędek* in the *wojewodziński* court. Modelled on an office of the land court, it later disappeared. S. Kutrzeba, 'Studia do historii sądownictwa w Polsce, VIII: Sądownictwo nad Żydami w województwie krakowskim' (Studies on the history of Polish judiciary, VIII: Jurisdiction over Jews in the Kraków *voivodeship*), *Przegląd Prawa i Administracji* 26, 1901, pp. 931–932.

Analysis of the *wojewodziński* court staff is absolutely essential, as it demonstrates what law was applied by this court in actual practice. The surviving court registers prove that this was principally the law of the land. Next to the judge, a scribe sat in court, usually also a noble, or an experienced lawyer with noble status. His functions were to keep records, hand out rulings and prepare documents; we can assume that he also took part on the passing of sentence.[28] Assessors appointed from among the elders of the community also participated in the work of the *wojewodziński* court. Even though it is not possible to determine their number – which probably varied – the presence of at least one Jewish assessor was obligatory.[29] This was of fundamental significance in assuring the overall fairness of the court's sentences.

A specific function was fulfilled by the *szkolnik*. Being a synagogue servant, in the administration of justice he played the role of an usher. His job was to state claims – the trial proceedings began by the court ascertaining whether the claim has been delivered in time – to keep order during the course of the trial and to perform various services during the hearing of evidence.[30]

Court sessions were usually held in a synagogue in Kraków, in

---

[28] Although we have no legal sources from the period, this post is already mentioned in the fifteenth century. According to the King Stefan Batory privilege of 1578, the *voivode* was to consult the elders of the *kehilla* about the appointment of the scribe ('Notarius iudicii alio non eligatur aut deponatur, nisi ita prius seniori Iudaeorum visum fuerit, cuius electionem calculo suo approbet'). See Bałaban, *Historia Żydów w Krakowie* I, p. 376.

We know of the following seventeenth-century scribes in Kraków: Seweryn Janowski, from 1620; Jan Rorajski, from 1623; Hieronim Władysław Proszyński, from Proszno, from 1631; Jan Chrząstowicz, from 1642, who also fulfilled the function of scribe in the *podkomorski* court. From the 18th c. Florian Pawłowski, 1702-7; Wojciech Szeligowski, from 1728; Kępski, 1740; Kazimierz Olearski, from 1740; Franciszek T. Miklaszewski, 1746. Jan Zamoliński – instigator of the Jewish court – is mentioned under the year 1725.

[29] Andrzej Tęczyński's regulation for Kraków Jews of 9 April 1527 stated that the judge (called *vicegerens*) should decide with the participation of the community's elders (*Zbiór aktów*, no. 12, pp. 1, 14). According to King Zygmunt August's regulation of 19 March 1554, 'numquam per solum iudicem iudicentur, sed adhibitis senioribus, under the restriction of the validity of the sentence' (Bałaban, 'Ze studiów nad ustrojem', p. 362). Janusz Wiśniowiecki's regulation of 18 December 1717 read that 'not wanting to be *contrarius* in the smallest element of Jewish law and their ancient customs . . . [I decide] that one of Jewish elders be always present at court.' (*Zbiór aktów*, p. 185, no. 208). Jan Klemens Branicki's regulation of 2 November 1747 made a similar ruling (ibid., no. 248: 9, p. 225). A few names of such elders and *szkolniks*, and the functions fulfilled by them in court are discussed for the seventeenth century by Stanisław Kutrzeba (ibid., index, p. 377).

[30] The *szkolnik (scolny, ministerialis iudaicus)* besides exercising functions analogous to those of an usher, had duties similar to those of an 'expulser' in the country court:

the Old Synagogue near Szeroka street in Kazimierz, where there were prison cells for criminals as well.[31] Yet some judges broke this tradition and conducted trials at Wawel Castle, where the municipal (*grodzki*) court functioned.

Dates of court hearings were not definitely fixed. Saturdays, Sundays and other holidays of both religions were of course excluded. Thus Monday and Thursday became the generally accepted days for court sessions.[32] In the first half of the eighteenth century, the *voivode* Janusz Wiśniowiecki reduced the number of sessions to two a year but this reform met with opposition.[33]

Judge, scribe and *szkolnik* were paid for their functions. We have data for their highest rates of pay only for the first half of the eighteenth century.[34] Essentially, court functions were performed *gratis*, according to the old principle: 'nullus palatinus aut capitaneus debet aliquos redditus alias poplathky seu contributiones alias dany

'relating to all offences that took place . . . to all quarrels if the Jews started fighting, to all matters of theft, stealing, he is to report at once to the judge' (ibid., no. 151, p. 123 – from the oath). We also have detailed 'Statutes for *szkolniks*' from the year 1632. They were published by F. H. Wettstein, 'Divre hefets. Dokumenta hebrajskie z pinaksów [*sic*] gminnych w Krakowie' (Hebrew documents from the *pinkasim* of the Kraków community), *Hameasef*, 1902, quoted in M. Schorr, *Kwartalnik Historyczny* 27, 1903, pp. 487–90.

[31] Stanisław Potocki's regulation of 28 May 1659 ordered: 'All types of Jewish courts are to be held in a certain place in Kraków or Kazimierz according to old customs and privileges, and not in Wawel Castle' *Zbiór aktów*, no. 168, 1, p. 137.

[32] A *kehilla* statute of 1595 stated: 'Seigniors should endeavour to see that the judge fulfils his duties in his house on no other days but Mondays and Thursdays. Exceptionally, he may appoint a different time in the case of an important person or an outsider' (M. Bałaban, 'Ze studiów nad ustrojem', p. 378). The custom of the court sitting on Mondays and Thursdays was confirmed by Stanisław Potocki's regulation of 28 May 1659 (*Zbiór aktów*, no. 168: 2, p. 137: 'those courts that are held only on Monday and Thursday, always according to the privileges, in the morning, not in the afternoon').

[33] Regulation of 14 May 1725, sect. 2: 'That court sessions be held twice a year, first after St Michael's day, and second after St Adalbert's day, which should function not longer than two Sundays (that is, two weeks – translator's note) *exceptio* fair days, and holidays, Catholic and Jewish' (ibid. no. 220, p. 197); this rule was already abandoned by 16 October 1725 (ibid. no. 222, p. 199). Jan Klemens Branicki tried to restore it (it was probably very convenient for the *voivode*) in his regulation of 2 November 1747 (ibid. no. 248, p. 226). See M. Bałaban, 'Ze studiów nad ustrojem', p. 269.

[34] 'A few years back, by my authority and under pressure from me, the Kraków synagogue . . . decided that the judge of my *wojewodziński* court should be paid, namely, one and a half thousand złoty annually, *hac conditione*, that *aggravati* in court should not be given sentences of fines and should give nothing more to the judge.' (Janusz Wiśniowiecki's regulation of 14 May 1725, *Zbiór aktów*, no. 220: 1, p. 197.

judeos excipere', except for what they themselves were willing to pay, or what was due to the king's court.[35]

In general, it seems clear that the Kraków *wojewodziński* court not only maintained its position during the crisis period of the seventeenth century but strengthened itself. From the time of Kazimierz Wielki, it was the main court, both for mixed Jewish-Christian cases and for appeals from the elders of the *kehilla*. Although we need more detailed research into the operations of the court, what does emerge from the investigation so far undertaken, is the efficiency of its procedure, including the execution. Its verdicts had a high reputation, and Jews sought the protection of this court whenever attempts were made to put them under municipal jurisdiction.[36]

THE VOIVODE'S COURT

Despite the fact that the *voivode* appointed a Jewish judge, and set up the whole apparatus of the *wojewodziński* court, he did not, in fact, divest himself of all his judicial powers. In particular he reserved for himself two domains, namely: (a) supervision over all jurisdiction in Jewish matters;[37] (b) his personal jurisdiction in cases of the first and second instance.

The first of these was treated very seriously by *voivodes*, as is confirmed by regulations which survive to this day, dealing with a number of fundamental questions in accordance with the general privileges. Table 15.2 gives a list of the essential features of ten acts of this kind.

The second of the domains of the *voivode* – jurisdiction in the first or second instance – was exercised by him personally but

---

[35] *Ius Polonicum*, p. 7.

[36] Jews never succeeded in defending themselves against these accusations of kidnapping Christian children or of stealing the Host for their rituals. Such matters often ended with the execution of the accused; see Bałaban, *Historia Żydów*, p. 62 and notes 100, 126-7 (case of Weiglowa), pp. 156, 180-1. For similar accusations and trials albeit not always ending in the death sentence, see the detailed S. Grodziski and I. Dwornicka, eds. *Chronografia albo Dziejopis żywiecki* (Chronography or history of 'Żywiec), Żywiec, 1986, under index of names: 'Żydzi'.

[37] Within the scope of this rule, *voivodes* protected Jews from being summoned before other courts, thus preserving their own prerogatives.

[38] Published in Bałaban, 'Ze studiów nad ustrojem', p. 362, without the opening and closing formulae. Probably King Zygmunt August issued this act with cooperation of the voivode Stanisław Tęczyński, as there is no doubt that such an act affected the competence of the voivode. In my opinion, it is identical to the later confirmation by Jan Kazimierz of the voivode Stanisław Potocki's regulation of 1659 (text of the confirmation in Bersohn, *Dyplomatariusz*, no. 270, pp. 151-3).

Table 15.2
Essential features of the *voivode*'s privileges in supervising Jewish jurisdiction

1	2	3	4	5	6	7	8	9	10	11	12
Voivode date of regulation	Type of the court	Place/time	Statement of claim	Non-appearance	Means of appeal	Execution of sentence	Court fees	Limit to fines	Taxes	Securities	Election of Elders
Andrej Tęczyński 9.4.1527	+	–	+	–	–	–	–	–	–	–	–
Court statute of King Zygmunt August 19.3.1554[38]	–	+	+	+	+	+	–	–	–	+	–
Jan Tęczyński 1.12.1620	–	–	–	–	–	–	–	–	–	+	–
Stanisław Lubomirski 28.2.1640	+	+	–	–	–	–	–	–	–	–	+
Stanisław Potocki 28.5.1659	–	–	–	–	+	–	–	–	–	+	–
Janusz Wiśniowiecki 18.12.1717	–	+	–	+	–	+	–	+	–	–	+
Janusz Wiśniowiecki 14.5.1725	–	–	–	–	–	+	–	–	–	–	+
Jan Klemens Branicki 2.11.1747	–	+	–	+	–	+	+	+	+	+	–
Antoni Lubomirski 15.8.1779	–	–	+	–	+	–	–	+	–	+	–
Stanisław Dembiński 29.1.1780	–	–	+	–	+	–	–	+	–	+	–

[38] See note on page 200.

irregularly, during his stay in Kraków and probably in his own residence (*in curia palatini*) or at the Wawel Castle. Of course, this *iudicium palatinale* took place in the presence of a judge, a scribe and, possibly, the elders of the community, but the *voivode* himself passed sentence. We cannot say more about these activities, as only a small excerpt from the judicial decisions of the *voivode* Stanisław Lubomirski has survived.[39] As head of an appeal court, the *voivode* decided on appeal from the decision of the court of elders, but only in more important cases.[40] This was by no means a simple undertaking, as the sentences of the court of the elders were based on talmudic law, while the *voivode*, on receiving a case on appeal, examined it according to the principles of Polish law of the land (polskie prawo ziemskie).[41] This also formed the basis in cases of appeal from sentence passed by the *wojewodziński* court, in other words, by his own appointee. We have no doubt that even before appeal became a feature of the law of the land – as happened in the year 1523 in the codification *Formula processus* – the *voivode* decided in cases where a complaint was made against a Jewish judge. Appeal in Jewish proceedings became established after this codification, and is already known in the year 1527.[42]

The answer to the question of whether the *voivode* played the role of protector of the Jews on behalf of the monarch should be sought in Jewish sources. We should differentiate here between the role of the institution itself, which, in principle acted for the benefit of the Jews, and the actions of the *voivodes*, especially when they treated it as an important source of income.

---

[39] See Archiwum Miasta i Wojewodztwa Krakowskiego, Oddział na Wawelu (Kraków Town and Provincial Archive, Wawel Division), *Acta palatinalia iudaica Cracoviensia, Varia 12*, pp. 1675–1766: *Decreta iudicii palatinalis 1642–1647*, (see below, n. 55).

[40] The commentary on Stanisław Potocki's regulation (Bałaban, 'Ze studiów nad ustrojem', p. 372), quotes it according to a no longer extant volume, *Akta Izraelskiej Gminy Wyznaniowej* (Files of Israelite religious community). Dating from 1659, this states 'despite warranting by his privilege that appeals *in causis* between them *privatis* and in all matters be submitted to his Enlightened Honourable Prince, yet, so that there be no doubt, it is hereby declared that, in those matters in which taxation does not exceed 100 złoty, the decision is to be *sine appellatione*.'

[41] This was observed by Bałaban, 'Ze studiów nad ustrojem', p. 385. Yet probably the *voivode* sought rules which would reconcile and not be at odds with the two law systems. He could also, if he wished, become acquainted with the principles of Talmudic law, through reading one of the many editions with commentary, which were printed in Kraków or in Lwów (see *Bibliografia Estreichera* XXXI, Kraków, 1936, pp. 19–20).

[42] See Andrzej Tęczyński's regulation of that year, sect. 2: 'Et quicumque eorundem iudaeorum a domino vicesgerente meo seu de iudicio eorum ad me appelare voluerit, ut sibi admitteretur libere causam coram me prosequi et attentare' (*Zbiór aktów*, no. 12, p. 14).

THE KING'S COURT

The monarch's jurisdiction over Jews can be divided into first instance decisions and appeal decisions. Decisions in the first instance were executed according to an old, but still-observed, principle of the 1264 privilege, that 'si Iudei inter se . . . discordiam moverint aut guerram Nos tantummodo aut noster palatinus vel eius iudex iudicium exercebit.'[43] The very fact that King Zygmunt III confirmed, in the year 1617, that the royal court could receive complaints directly from Jews, despite the precedent of King Zygmunt I's refusal in 1518 to grant justice to peasants accusing nobles, confirms the legal validity of this privilege.[44] Moreover, it sometimes happened that the monarch granted a privilege to an individual Jew, giving him the right to be summoned only to the king's court.[45]

In particular, in cases of Jews accused of ritual murder or of stealing the host, which recurred down the centuries, King Zygmunt August decided that these were to be heard before the Diet court.[46] This was modified by King Władysław IV in the year 1633, when he laid down that if a Jew was accused of a capital crime ('crimen seu maleficium capitale'), theft of the host, or the shedding of Christian blood, the local municipal authorities should imprison the accused, and hand him over to the *starosta* (mayor); the latter, in turn, was to bring him before a special commissioner's court, composed of the municipal (*grodzki*) court and a special royal commissioner.[47] The aim was to ensure that these specific charges, born in an atmosphere of xenophobia, intolerance and rivalry, would not lead to judicial murder, but that the evidence would be fully examined without recourse to confessions extracted through torture. This could not always be carried out in practice.

In its capacity as a court of appeal, the king's court examined appeals made directly against sentences passed by the court of the

---

[43] See n. 10 above.
[44] Kutrzeba, 'Studia do historii, VIII' (see above, n. 27), p. 940.
[45] Ibid., and Bałaban, 'Ze studiów nad ustrojem', p. 385.
[46] Kutrzeba, 'Studia do historii, VIII', pp. 940–1.
[47] Ibid., p. 941. This procedure was not, in principle, applied to Jews living in villages or small private towns, as they were subject to the local lord's court. This seldom used the death penalty as it was too expensive, because of the cost of bringing the executioner from a big town. Yet it often used primitive torture as its main means of extracting evidence.

elders, and, above all, against the *voivode*'s judgements. It was thus a court of second, or even third, instance. The assessor's court decided in such cases as the court of highest municipal instance, presided over by the chancellor.

On the basis of the general, provincial, and local privileges, augmented by such valuable sources as the *voivode*'s regulations, we can reconstruct a general picture of the organization of the judicial system in Jewish matters, and even try to establish some principles of juridical proceedings.[48] Yet how it functioned, in reality, can only be made clear through investigation of court entries. Few of these have survived, and even they have not yet received a thorough examination.

It is known that, at least from the sixteenth century, some *kehillot* kept minutes referred to in Hebrew as *pinkasim*,[49] where resolutions of Jewish Diets (*vaadim*) were recorded together with activities undertaken by the *kehilla* and also – unfortunately rarely – decisions of the court of the elders. These, written in Hebrew, were also minuted as municipal records.[50] *Pinkas* books can be useful – albeit on a small scale – in reconstructing the activities of the court of the elders of the community, which were based on Jewish common law and talmudic law. The Kraków *pinkas* were destroyed with the whole *kehilla*'s archives in a fire that broke out during the Swedish invasion of 1655. Later entries, investigated only to a small degree and published only in short excerpts, have survived in a vestigial form from the catastrophic damage of the First and Second World Wars. The problem of whether relevant municipal law influenced local Jewish common law remains so far unresolved.

---

[48] This applies mainly to the form of statements of claim and, to a lesser degree, to the trial itself. As far as the hearing of evidence is concerned, we know most about the oath, applied *secundum morem*, that is according to Jewish custom, in two forms: in minor matters, in front of the synagogue gate, in more serious cases *super rodale*, on the Torah. The text of the oath also contained a curse. More might be said about proceedings in disputes over loans and securities. We have information about fines and court taxes, but not much about the execution of sentences.

[49] In older literature (especially M. Bałaban) the name *Pinaks* predominates. Probably this is not solely a printing mistake. Today *pinkas* is widely used.

[50] See F. H. Wettstein, *Quellenschriften zur Geschichte der Juden in Polen, insbesondere in Krakau*, Kraków 1894 (a work criticized by M. Bałaban, 'Die Krakauer Judengemeindeordnung,' p. 562 and n.); idem, 'Divrey hefets', (see above, no. 30); M. Bałaban, *Zabytki historyczne Żydów w Polsce* (Jewish historical monuments in Poland), Warsaw, p. 36. Maybe the phrase 'I shall not support inscriptions in non-customary books' from the *szkolniks*' oath applied to the *pinkas* (*Zbiór aktów*, no. 151, p. 123).

A slightly better – though still far from good – state of affairs surrounds the problem of the records of the operations of the *wojewodziński* court. We cannot say when *voivode* records first appeared. It may have been as early as the fifteenth century, since we find a scribe as a member of the *wojewodziński* court then.[51] There is no doubt that records existed by the beginning of the sixteenth century as Andrzej Tęczyński's regulation of 1527 mentions the need to enter laws in 'registers'.[52] This was confirmed by a 1538 Diet constitution.[53]

Until the Second World War, six extensive manuscripts called Acta vicepalatinalia were kept in Lwów in the Land and Town Files' (Acta Grodzkie i Ziemskie) Archives. They contained entries of matters undertaken by the *wojewodziński* court, files not in litigation, and some other sources concerning Jews from the years 1740–75. Fortunately, these records have been examined by Zbigniew Pazdro, and now that the files are not easily accessible we can make use of his precise and solid monograph.[54]

A less valuable collection has also survived to our times in Kraków. Called Acta palatinalia iudaica Cracoviensia, it consists of three manuscript, analogous to those from Lwów, containing sources from the years 1620–49, and thus a century older.[55] These manuscripts have still to find a historian as searching and scrupulous as Zbigniew Pazdro. They were looked through and copied by Stanisław Kutrzeba;[56] few researchers have since consulted them, which is equally true for the author of this paper.

---

[51] See n. 28 above.
[52] *Zbiór aktów*, no. 12, p. 14.
[53] It ordered Jews '... pignora ... inscribere in libros', which would testify to regular entries being made (*Volumina Legum* I, p. 525).
[54] Pazdro, *Organizacja i praktyka*.
[55] Archiwum Miasta i Wojewodztwa Krakowskiego, Oddział na Wawelu, *Acta palatinalia iudaica Cracoviensia*: Varia 10 is a 2816-page manuscript, filled, with slight exceptions, to the 2811th page, containing Decreta officii palatinalis (pp. 1–1655); Decreta iudicii palatinalis (pp. 1657–766); *Acta inscriptionum, pignorum et relationum* (pp. 1775–2243); *Acta inscriptionum, quietationum et protestationum* (pp. 2245–648); *Acta pignorum* (pp. 2649–724); *Acta plenipotentiarum* (pp. 2749–811), from the years 1620-6. Varia 11: 1842-page manuscript containing *Acta inscriptionum, quietationum et protestationum* (pp. 1–1842) from the years 1631–41. Varia 12: 2116-page manuscript filled, with slight exceptions, to p. 2109, containing *Acta inscriptionum, quietationum et protestationum* (pp. 1–1670), Decreta iudicii palatinalis (pp. 1675–766) from the years 1642–7, in very good condition, with metal closures.
[56] See *Zbiór aktów*, no. 138, pp. 105–6; no. 139, pp. 106–7; no. 149, pp. 121–2; no. 150, p. 122; no. 151, pp. 122–3; no. 153, pp. 124–5.

It is unfortunately only a small fragment of a rich collection. How big it once was is testified by the authorities. One of them is a royal mandate of King Zygmunt August of 31 August 1570, ordering the release of the *wojewodziński* court registers from private hands;[57] we do not know whether it was carried out. The second is the 'Register (Regestr) of Jewish books, which the Honourable Mikołaj Suliński of Sulanki received from the Honourable Lady Chrząstowiczowa' dating from the year 1662, and listing 25 manuscripts.[58]

The surviving part of the collection dates from the years when the Kraków voivodeship was held by Jan Tęczyński of the Topór coat of arms (died 1638) and Stanisław Lubomirski of the Śreniawa coat of arms (died 1649).[59] In these sources we find Zygmunt Świerczowski from Świerczów, Marcin Skoroszewski and Łukasz Kochański from Kochań – known as old hands in the judiciary. As scribes we come across: Seweryn Janowski, Jan Rorajski, Władysław Proszyński from Proszna and Jan Chrząstowicz. These were people of the Roman Catholic faith, nobles or given noble status, acquainted with the law of the land. Without doubt, this was the law they applied when it affected the Jewish population.

Looking more closely at the Kraków *iudaica*, we must note that they were very carefully prepared and kept as fair copies. The basic language of these entries is Latin, yet one comes across insertions or whole entries in Polish. Thus we can conclude that the hearings were in Polish and minuted as such. Unfortunately the originals are lost; only later were they formulated in Latin and rewritten as fair copies.

Most entries concern litigation. Kraków Jews were summoned to the *wojewodziński* court by local burghers and quite often by the neighbouring nobles. They were only seldom summoned by clergy,

---

[57] Ibid., no. 58, pp. 42–3: mandate addressed to Mikołaj Dłuski, who [has till today kept to himself] 'files or registers of Jewish matters or cases in Kraków after the late Honourable Stanisław Myszkowski from Mirów, Kraków *voivode* and *starosta*, owing to which keeping injustice is being done to some of our people, as minutes from those Jewish books are accessible, and handed out.' It seems therefore that there were at least a few registers at that time.

[58] Ibid., no. 171, pp. 140–1. Regina Chrząstowiczowa was the widow of Jan Chrząstowicz, a court scribe (see n. 28 above, and *Varia 12*, p. 178). It appears that court registers were kept in the scribe's home.

[59] It is clearly not by chance that the Kraków Judaica survived till the year 1649, that is, till the death of the *voivode* Stanisław Lubomirski. Perhaps they were kept in his palace whilst the newer ones started by the new *voivode* (Władysław Zasławski) were destroyed in a fire in Kazimierz in the year 1655.

and only exceptionally by peasants.[60] Few cases of litigation between Jews were recorded, as these came before the court of the elders of the community. In addition, 'varia' were entered into books.[61]

Most of the entries deal with civil law,[62] though not all areas are equally represented; primarily it is the law of obligations, that is litigation over securities, loans, receipts and so on, followed by property law. The almost complete lack of entries concerning inheritance and matrimonial law proves these to be – by agreement of the parties – within the competence of the court of the elders, which followed talmudic law. The same applies to common criminal cases, which are only rarely to be found on the pages of these books.[63]

These sources are not unknown. Stanisław Kutrzeba has selected and published that part of the entries which he found more important. Majer Bałaban made considerable use of them. Archivists have made use of them in detailed research and scholars have investigated them to bring them into the light of day. Yet what has been done so far appears not to answer the needs of today's research. As the questions we ask have grown in number, the importance of these sources has increased enormously. The *wojewodziński* registers, the last fragment of a once vast collection of entries concerning a society that, owing to the tragic happenings of our epoch, has ceased to exist, should be published in full – along with other records relating to the Jews.

If we were able to publish not only those court entries that found their way into the surviving *pinkasim*, but also – to obtain a full

---

[60] As mentioned earlier, I have abstained from preparing a detailed analysis of the entries' statistics (on the lines of the work done by Z. Pazdro for the Lwów registers).

[61] As in Lwów, we come across the courts' activities as a court (*judicium*) and as an office (*officium*), making various entries in records. Beside some entries published by S. Kutrzeba (see above n. 56), an entry of a regulation on laws for Jewish butchers in Kazimierz is worthy of attention (*Varia 10*, pp. 1657–60). It ended a disagreement between the town, represented by the town authorities, and the Jewish community.

[62] Entries connected with the organization of the community, as well as the administration of justice may also be found. They were partly published by S. Kutrzeba (see above n. 56). Criminal cases, see for example *Varia 12*, pp. 1675, 1786 and elsewhere.

[63] As they took place in the court of the elders, their traces, in the form of entries, should be looked for in the *pinkas*. But such entries had to be paid for, (according to an old institution of *memoriale*), and entering cases in the records was not always to the advantage of the parties to the conflict.

picture – the entries relating to Jews scattered in municipal and assessors' registers, we could end up with an extensive series of acts which would enable scholars to investigate jurisdiction over Jews from the lowest to the highest court.[64] We might even come across a case which, following a trial by the court of the elders according to Talmudic law, passed on to the *wojewodziński* or the voivode's court, where it was tried according to the law of the land, and finally ended in the assessors' royal court – the highest court in municipal cases – where municipal law often applied. Such a publication could recreate the complex character of the culture of Jewish society, with its mixture of conflicting legal codes, and thereby give a more accurate picture of its historical position in Polish society.

---

[64] As I see it, the successive stages of this work, which would need a well prepared scholarly team, with a good knowledge of law, history and the Polish, Latin and Hebrew languages, as well as palaeography, should proceed as follows:

(a) A thorough search for surviving *pinkasim* in their original form or copies; extracting from them all entries connected with the administration of justice.
(b) A search in municipal, town and assessors' registers (partly published already) for entries concerning Jews, and also in other collections of sources (for instance magnates' archives) where one comes across *wojewodziński* manuscripts.
(c) Copying the *wojewodziński* court entries, that is the three Kraków Judaica.
(d) Arranging the entries according to chronology and the type of court, so that, independently of the source they came from, whole sequences can be formed.
(e) Preparing a scientific apparatus (text and subject notes, and so on).
(f) Preparing indexes according to place, name and subject.
(g) Publishing the series.

16 · The Individual versus the Community in Jewish Law in pre-Eighteenth-Century Poland

Shmuel Shilo

Before we begin to discuss the specific topic of the individual versus the community in Jewish Law in pre-eighteenth-century Poland, I think that it is appropriate to outline the history and nature of Jewish Law.[1] Just as the Jewish people are unique in that they are the only people on earth today who have kept their own identity for such a lengthy period, way back into the pre-Christian era, so has Jewish law been a living law, for as long as the Jewish people have existed. Jewish law encompasses not only the relationship between man and his Maker, but also his relationship to his fellow-man and to the society as a whole in which he lives. For jurists who are engaged in the legal discipline of Jewish law, our emphasis is placed on those questions and institutions which are of interest to the jurist in any given legal system.

The scattering of the Jews after the destruction of the Temple – and even before the destruction – did not bring in its wake the abrogation of autonomy. The Jews remained as autonomous communities in the lands where they lived throughout the Middle Ages even though they had lost political independence, and there was now no physical bond with their natural environment, the land of Israel.

The judicial and religious autonomy which was part of the Diaspora life, allowed the Jewish courts to impose sanctions on the members of the Jewish community. In this setting judicial autonomy could prosper since the judgements of the courts could be enforced. Sanctions included flogging, attachment of property and imprison-

---

[1] In general, see M. Elon, *Hamishpat haivri*, Jerusalem, 1973; idem; ed., *The Principles of Jewish Law*, Jerusalem, 1975, pp. 5–46.

ment, just to mention a few. At times, even the death penalty was sanctioned. This extreme penalty was meted out almost solely to informers who would endanger the entire Jewish community by their treachery. Probably the most potent of all sanctions was the threat of excommunication (*herem*). To be divorced from the Jewish community was a type of social death which was especially effective in the closed society of medieval times.

The scope of the Jewish community's autonomy was different from place to place and generation to generation. For example, wide autonomy was given to the Jews of Spain for many years. This judicial autonomy led to the further development of the criminal law, as well as public administrative law. Besides the external force which helped keep the Jewish people and Jewish law together – that is, the central government's granting of limited self-rule to the Jewish communities – an internal cause had an even more profound effect. This was the stringent prohibition against litigating in Gentile courts. This prohibition dates from Mishnaic times and was codified in all the subsequent codes. According to Maimonides, basing himself on the Mishna: 'Whoever litigates according to Gentile law and in their courts, although their laws are the same as the laws of Israel, is an evil-doer and he is deemed to have reviled and blasphemed and rebelled against the Torah of Moses our teacher.'[2]

To sum up, we can say that there were two basic factors for the survival of Jewish Law. First, the internal discipline of the traditional Jewish society and, second, the political circumstances of the corporate medieval state. Justice Agranat, former President of Israel's Supreme Court, had the following to say in one of his leading judgements, *Skornik* v. *Skornik*, concerning the nature of Jewish law:

> The very moment that we admit – as we are obliged to admit – the continued existence of the Jews in all generations and in all lands of their dispersion as a separate people, we must test the nature of Jewish law by the historical relationship of the Jewish people to this law. We shall then conclude that the Jewish people indeed treated Jewish law, throughout their existence and their dispersion, as their special property, as part of the treasure of their culture. It follows that this law served in the past as the

---

[2] Maimonides, *M.T.*, Sanhedrin, 16, 7.

national law of the Jews, and even today possesses this national character in respect of Jews wherever they may be.³

When a dispute arises between a community and an individual,⁴ the usual rules of law are referred to; there are, however, some basic legal rules which are specific to the community as a public body. The latter serve as a basis for what is classified in other legal systems as public law. The following are four examples of special rules regarding the community, and of the specific application of these rules in the *halakhic* scholars of the historical period under discussion.

The first of these rules, which was specifically cited in the standard code of law – the *Shulkhan Arukh* – by Rabbi Moses Isserles,⁵ in his glosses which are an integral part of the code, and amplified upon by one of the foremost commentators on the code, R. Joshua Falk⁶ – concerned *kinyan*, that is a technical legal form of acquisition of objects or of validating agreements. Generally a transaction is not valid if there is no such formal act of acquisition accompanying the transaction or agreement.⁷ The need for *kinyan* is waived when one of the parties is a public body.⁸

Rabbi Joshua Falk goes so far as to say that when the community agrees to something and it turns out that the agreement was based on a mistake of law, both Rabbi Moses Isserles (Rema)⁹ and he himself¹⁰ are of the opinion that the community cannot avoid the agreement. This latter point is also specifically noted in one of Rema's responses.¹¹ Precedent for this view is taken from the writings of Mordekhai Hakohen of thirteenth-century Germany.

One of the accepted rules of procedure concerning community – individual disputes in the Jewish legal system is that of transposing the usual presumption that the defendant is in possession of the

---

³ *Skornik* v. *Skornik*, C.A. 191/51 8 *P.D.*, 141 at p. 177.
⁴ As to individual v. community disputes in Poland see, in general, J. Katz, *Masoret Umashber*, Jerusalem, 1958, pp. 96, 117–19. This book appeared in an English translation as *Tradition and Crisis*, New York, 1961. Since the English translation omits the copious notes, I will be referring to the Hebrew text.
⁵ 1525 or 1530–72, Kraków.
⁶ c. 1555–1614, Lublin.
⁷ See I. Herzog, *The Main Institutions of Jewish Law* I (2nd edn), London, 1965, pp. 137–200; Elon, *Principles*, 205–10.
⁸ Elon, *Principles*, pp. 647–8.
⁹ *Sh. Ar. H.M.* 22, 1.
¹⁰ Rema, gloss to ibid., subsect. 12.
¹¹ Resp. *Rema*, no. 50.

amount or item about which there is a dispute. According to Jewish public law, the community is defined in law as the possessor, and in fact the defendant must pay or give the community what it demands, and only afterwards the suit between individual and community is heard. In other words, although in the great majority of cases the community demands something – usually taxes – from the individual, and in law the community should be the plaintiff and the individual the defendant, rules of public law turn the tables on the two parties to the suit, forcing the individual to become the plaintiff as against the community which is now in possession of the disputed sum. Here we have a clear public policy decision in favour of the community as a whole. The rule is, of course, only a procedural one and if the individual proves the validity of his claim, he will be reimbursed but, as all lawyers know, even if possession is not nine parts of the law, it certainly is of value to a litigant. This general principle was enacted before the period under discussion:[12] let us now see how this rule was put into practice by the rabbis of sixteenth- and early seventeenth-century Poland.

Rema surveyed the *halakhic* literature on this topic in his commentary *Darkey Moshe*,[13] including a view that this rule is relied upon only in matters of taxation. In other matters, according to this view, the regular rules concerning plaintiff and defendant are to be applied. In his glosses on the *Shulkhan Arukh*,[14] Rema brings in the rule, stating that the individual must give the community a pledge equal to the worth of the claim, and then adjudicate with the community. The view that this is the case only concerning disputes about taxes is not mentioned in his glosses; on the other hand, he states that where the argument of the individual is that he is a Talmudic scholar and therefore exempt from taxes, the rule about paying first and arguing later is not applied. Rabbi Moses Isserles' brother-in-law, Rabbi Joseph Katz,[15] was of the same general view, as can be observed in one of his responses concerning the Kraków Jewish community,[16] as was Rabbi Yehuda Lev Ash of Ludmir[17] and Rema's disciple Rabbi Mordekhai Yaffe.[18]

This principle was referred to by Rabbi Menachem Mendel

---

[12] See Elon, *Principles*, pp. 691–2 and the sources cited therein.
[13] Rema, *Darkey Moshe H.M.* 4.
[14] Rema's glosses to *Sh. Ar. H.M.* 4.
[15] c. 1510–1591, Kraków.
[16] Resp. *She'erit Yosef*, no. 38.
[17] 17th c., Ludmir. Resp. *Hinukh Bet Yehuda*, no. 102.
[18] 1530–1612, Lublin. *Levush Ir Shushan H.M.*, sect. 4.

Krochmal[19] the most prominent early seventeenth-century rabbi in Moravia, whose birth, education and early rabbinical positions were in Poland proper. The circumstances of the case brought before Rabbi Krochmal concerned the Moravian Jewish community of Prostejov. The king's army passed through Prostejov and the soldiers had to be quartered in the town. It was customary to billet them in different homes but the Jews of the community were fearful of such an arrangement which included full board and lodging for the first three days' stay; after these initial three days, their food was paid for by the army but they demanded of the townspeople 'board, water, salt, drink and similar small things'. The community feared that these soldiers might steal from the Jews' homes, that they would lose business since people would prefer to stay away from homes harbouring the soldiers and there was concern about being able to keep the dietary laws (*kashrut*), since these soldiers would most likely mix foods which it was forbidden to mix, such as meat and milk. Therefore the community was about to come to an agreement with the soldiers' commanding officer. The proposed agreement stated that the community would pay a lump sum to the army in lieu of physically harbouring the soldiers. But there was a hitch to the imminent agreement. The wealthy Jews of the community would consent to such an agreement only on the basis of having each household pay an equal amount. The community as a whole was of the opinion that payment should be made in accordance with one's wealth and means – the wealthier one was, the more one would be made to pay. Without going into details as to what Rabbi Krochmal's view as to the substantive law was in this case, for our present purposes what is significant is that, as a preliminary order, the rabbi ordered the individual wealthy members of the community to follow the community's decision. Then, afterwards, they could sue the community for the reimbursement of what they thought was an illegal levy placed on them. This decision is based on the principle we have been discussing, that is that the community is to be paid first and only afterwards can the individual sue the community for a refund. From the circumstances of the case as described in the *responsum*, it also appears that time was pressing and there was no room for prolonged litigation before making the proposed agreement between the community and the commanding officer. The respondent clearly states that especially in such a case, where there would be evident

[19] *c*. 1600–61, Poland, Moravia.

damage to the public if such an agreement were not ratified, the individual concerned must first and foremost join the community's efforts to allay the clear and present danger and then adjudicate with the community.[20]

In a gloss to one of the major commentaries to the *Shulkhan Arukh*, a further development of the above-mentioned principle was enunciated. According to this gloss, where the community is deemed to be the possessor, and there is a difference of legal opinion as to what the law is in a particular instance, judgement should be given in favour of the possessor-defendant, that is, in favour of the community.[21] Here we can clearly see that this seemingly procedural rule of law concerning possession can have very clear substantial consequences.

As an offshoot of the above-mentioned rule of placing the community in the position of possessor, another rule developed. According to this new rule, a community is allowed to seize the disputed object, or sum, from the individual, without prior legal proceedings. This general right of self-help on the part of the community is not fettered by other rules of law which sometimes restrain individuals who attempt to gain physical possession of an object under dispute in order to better their legal position.[22] This new rule seems to apply only if the individual is a member of the community with whom he is litigating.[23]

From these legal rules, which were accepted by the Polish rabbis and further defined by them, we can observe that on the one hand the law is stringent towards the community and a community's undertaking or agreement is valid even if flawed by technicalities of private law, which would invalidate the same transaction between private individuals. The basic premise is that the community must always keep its word. On the other hand, the exigencies of life were such that it was imperative for survival to pay one's tax first and argue afterwards. Therefore the law was changed to favour the community. This constant friction between individual and community did not lead to any rigid principle of favouring one as against the other; the rabbis who developed the law took a more pragmatic approach, trying to find the middle path which would both preserve

---

[20] Resp. *Zvemah Tsedek*, no. 18.
[21] Gloss to *Rema, Sh. Ar. H.M.* 163, 3.
[22] Resp. *Rema*, no. 52.
[23] See *Sh. Ar. H.M.*, r. Cp. *Rema H.M.*, ibid.

the rights of the individual and also take the larger needs of the community into account.[24]

In legal systems in general, as well as in the Jewish legal system, there are different approaches towards the interpretation of legislation. One of the major questions is whether the law is to be interpreted literally, or whether the purpose behind the legislation, that is the purposive intent of the legislator, should be taken into account.[25] These two opposing views of interpretation are found in *halakhic* literature concerning the interpretation of communal enactments.[26] They are also found in the *responsa* of Polish rabbis when dealing with legislation concerning the individual member of the community, as opposed to the community itself.

Rabbi Joseph Katz had to deliver a verdict concerning a dispute between the community and certain hard-up slaughterers of animals. The question which interests us is more of a procedural than a substantive nature. The slaughterers demanded that the competent lay court, which usually decided such cases, should be composed of members of another Jewish community; members of the community involved might be prejudiced since the community itself was a party to the proceedings.[27] What interests us, though, concerns one specific point which was raised about the interpretation of communal legislation.

The case concerned tax-farming rights which the community had leased. The community was making a profit from their taxing of the slaughterers. One of the community's arguments against the change of venue was based on a communal enactment which stated that disputes concerning taxes should be adjudicated before the community's judges. Rejecting this argument, Rabbi Katz gave the enactment a very strict interpretation. He decreed that the enactment refers only to regular tax matters and does not cover the situation in the case involved, since the claim is based on a

---

[24] See Katz, *Masoret*; H. H. Ben-Sasson, *Hagot Vehanaga*, Jerusalem, 1959 (Hebrew), pp. 147–8, 237.

[25] In the English legal system, for example, the basis for the literal interpretation are the two cases known as the *Sussex Peerage Case* (1844), 11 Cl. and F 85, 8 E. R. 1034 and *Grey v. Pearson* (1857), 6 H.L.c. 61, 10 E. R. 1216. The leading case which declares the purpose of the legislation rule is known as *Heydon's Case* (1854), 3 Co. Rep. 7a, 76 E. R. 637. There are many learned works on the interpretation of statutes. For a comparatively recent one, which discusses these questions in detail and in depth, see E. A. Driedger, *Construction of Statutes* (2nd edn), Toronto, 1983.

[26] See Elon, *Principles*, pp. 71–2, 695–6, and the sources cited there.

[27] Ibid., pp. 693–4, and the sources cited there.

tax-farming transaction, and not regular taxation.[28] It seems to me that this interpretation is a strained one, and demonstrates the sympathy of Rabbi Katz toward the hard-up slaughterers and his feeling that they would not get a fair trial if the case was to be heard by the community's own appointed judges.

Another example of strict interpretation of communal legislation is found in a *responsum* of Rabbi Menachem Mendel Krochmal.[29] Here the respondent is well aware of the two different manners of interpretation and even brings precedent for both of the opposing views: the one, that the intent of the legislator is paramount in the interpretation of communal legislation; and the other, that enactments must be interpreted narrowly and literally.

The dispute was between the Jewish community of Vienna and one particular individual; this individual was extremely wealthy and for many years had contributed his share of the community tax based upon an agreement reached by him with the community's leaders. The present leaders of the Vienna community claimed that during the years that the defendant paid taxes as agreed upon, he was in fact much wealthier and should have paid even higher taxes. They wanted him to pay back-taxes retroactively, according to an estimate of his wealth which had recently been made by the community tax assessors.[30] One of the questions debated by the parties was the following:

The community's argument was that the agreement signed between the community leaders and the defendant was *ultra vires* and therefore void. According to communal legislation, any transaction whereby the community paid out 300 gold Reichsthaler, had to be approved by a select panel of ten of the community's members. Since the community claimed that the agreement reached involved a waiver by the community of an amount which was in excess of 300 gold Reichsthaler, the agreement was null and void.

Rabbi Menachem Mendel Krochmal rejected this argument. He decided that the plain meaning of the enactment was that the communal leaders could not make an outlay of over 300 gold Reichsthaler, but the compromise involved was not an outlay of

---

[28] Resp. *She'erit Yosef*, no. 11. Cf. Ben-Sasson, *Hagot Vehanaga*, p. 231 concerning this *responsum*.
[29] Resp. *Zemah Zedek*, no. 37.
[30] There were various means of assessing taxes in the Jewish communities. See Elon, *Principles*, pp. 685–90. Cf. the circumstances of this case with that appearing in the *responsum* of Rabbi Yair Haim Bachrach (1638–1701, Worms), *Havat Yair*, no. 57 and the respondents' decisions in both cases.

funds. The dispute concerned the possible *income* of the community, which was not yet even in the hands of the community, not the outlay of funds about which the enactment speaks. The respondent quoted the great thirteenth-century Spanish scholar Rabbi Salomon ibn Aderet, who wrote that any unclear wording in a communal enactment cannot be interpreted by what appears to be the circumstance surrounding the enactment, but according to the wording of the enactment. Rabbi Menachem Mendel Krochmal adds that even according to the view of Rabbi David HaKohen (sixteenth-century, Ottoman Empire) who wrote that in the interpretation of enactments one should prefer the legislator's intent. Here too, the final judgement was in favour of the individual, and not the community. Of course, the poor slaughterers in the case previously discussed are certainly different types of individuals from the Viennese defendant, but rich or poor, if the law according to the rabbi's understanding of the law is against the community's claim, so will judgement be given.

A third and final example from this period in Poland exemplifies judgement based on the canon of interpretation which was rejected by Rabbi Joseph Katz and Rabbi Menachem Mendel Krochmal: here Rabbi Yehuda Lev Ash of Ludmir followed the lead of those *halakhic* scholars who preferred the intention of the legislator as against the language of the enactment.

A certain community enacted that any member of the community who buys an animal must pay a sales tax. The defendant claimed that he was an agent for a Gentile who did the buying and selling, he was not the real owner of the animals bought and sold, he received a salary from the Gentile owner based on the number of cattle he bought or sold, and he therefore wanted to be exempt from payment of the tax. The community claimed the tax from him, basing themselves on the afore-mentioned legislation. They argued that it was immaterial whether the defendant bought or sold on his own account, especially since he was profiting by acting as middleman. The respondent rejected the defendant's arguments. He explained that there was a general principle concerning disputes between individuals and communities, namely, that the burden of proof is on the individual where he claims that he is exempt from complying with an enactment. As to the interpretation of the enactment, Rabbi Ash's view was that from the wording of the enactment, it is clear that the legislators attempted to snare one and all in the tax net and tried to tighten loopholes which tax-avoiders might seek. Rabbi Ash sided with the community, basing his view both on purely legal arguments and also on policy motives. As to our topic, Rabbi Ash specifically cited as precedent the same judgement of Rabbi David HaKohen which Rabbi Menachem Mendel Krochmal rejected, as well as *responsa* of other rabbis, contemporaries of Rabbi HaKohen. Rabbi Ash wrote that since the enactment did not specifically refer to a case such as ours, one should follow Rabbi HaKohen's reasoning, which is that one must attempt to surmise what was in the minds of the legislators even if the conclusion leads one to reject the clear meaning of the enactment, and even if this leads us to extending the enactment by adding the missing clauses.

In other words, even though the more logical interpretation of a statute which refers to A and B, if it seems that the legislator would have included C in the statute but for some reason did not include him, C should be regarded as having been included. Here, by giving a very wide interpretation to the enactment, the respondent judged in favour of the community as against the individual.[31]

Two points should be emphasized. First, this was not the only basis for the judgement and it appears from the *responsum* that policy motives were also important in deciding, such as a fear of further attempts to evade paying this tax if the decision were in favour of the defendant.[32] Second, the reliance on the legislator's intention as against the simple meaning of the enactment does not go so far as to reject entirely the clear wording of an enactment; it only states that one can *add* to the enactment a clause which is missing.

There are numerous examples of questions which arose concerning the proper manner of dividing the tax burden between individual members of the community. These problems arose both in regard to the general tax burden and to specific taxes on property and the like. As everywhere, and in all generations, individuals would claim, sometimes rightly, that they were being overtaxed or illegally taxed. Many of these cases came before *halakhic* scholars in Poland during the period under discussion. All strata of Jewish society were involved, the poor usually complaining about their dire straits and the burden of taxation, and the rich also claiming that they

---

[31] Resp. *Hinukh bet Yehuda*, no. 102.
[32] As to public policy in favour of the community in Jewish law in Poland see for example Ben-Sasson, *Hagot Vehanaga*, p. 237 concerning communal legislation in favour of the community.

were bearing too much of the brunt of taxation. Just to illustrate one aspect of this problem, I have chosen to discuss two *responsa* of Rabbi Menachem Mendel Krochmal concerning similar questions which arose in different communities. In both cases the adversaries of the general public were wealthy individuals.

Both of these cases concerned a claim for back-taxes. The communities claimed that in both instances the taxpayer was very wealthy and did not pay anything like what he should have paid. A pertinent difference between the cases was that in the first case the community's claim was lodged against the individual's heirs, since the taxpayer had died; in the latter case the taxpayer was alive at the time of the adjudication. In both cases, the individual concerned was not only undeniably wealthy and a most respected member of his community, but he also was a talmudic scholar.

A certain Rabbi Jacob Fisk was reported to be a very wealthy individual, and gossip had it that he had been paying only about a third of what he should have been paying in taxes. After his death, an inventory of his assets was made and the suspicions about him were confirmed: he had indeed only been paying about a third of what he should have paid over the years. The community sued his heirs for back-taxes.

Rabbi Menachem Mendel Krochmal decided in favour of the deceased, basing his judgement on two arguments. First, if the communal leaders were in fact aware of the amount of his wealth, and did not tax him more for some reason or another, they waived their claim. If one wants to argue that they did not want to tax him to the maximum, out of respect and fear of him, this line of reasoning is faulty. The community was not one which would knuckle under to any one individual, whoever he might be. Furthermore, if there was any suspicion of fear of adjudication within the community, the law allowed adjudication in another community. It would seem, the respondent continues, that since he was both a respected leader of the community and a talmudic scholar, and most of his time was devoted to communal work and the study of Torah, without remuneration, it was highly probable that the community leaders decided to tax him less.

Even if his true wealth was not known to the tax-assessors, the community's claim against the estate could not be accepted since it might well be that a good part of the wealth was accumulated *after* the last tax assessment. In other words, the amount of wealth now in his estate could not prove what his wealth in fact was over the years.[33]

From reading this *responsum* in detail, one is left with the impression that Rabbi Menachem Mendel Krochmal was most sympathetic to the individual who was described in glowing terms. The second *responsum* was written in 1645.[34] This dispute concerned a certain Rabbi Isaac who was the son-in-law of the head of the Rabbinical Academy and chief judge of the Jewish Court in Vienna. Rabbi Krochmal was asked to be chairman of a court of arbitration to settle the dispute between the Vienna community and the said Rabbi Isaac.

The community claimed back-taxes for the past eight years that Rabbi Isaac had been living in the community. He had paid a comparatively small sum over those years, and now the community decided to sue for what it felt was the proper amount of money he should have paid over the years. Rabbi Isaac was about to leave the community and the leaders of the community also demanded from him his share in the payment of special debts the community owed together with the Kraków community, as well as taxes for two additional years – as was decreed in the communal legislation of the Vienna community. Rabbi Isaac's reply to the claim was that he should never have been regarded as a member of the community but was living temporarily in Vienna to be with his father-in-law, who was selected to be a teacher and head of the Talmudic Academy in Vienna. Therefore, he claimed, he was not taxed like other members of the community, and had already come to an agreement with the community leaders that he would be leaving Vienna shortly. Therefore, he asked that judgement be given against all the claims of the community. Rabbi Isaac also produced a waiver in writing dated August 1644 from the community leaders, exempting him from all the afore-mentioned taxes. The community leaders who signed the waiver were subpoenaed and gave verbal evidence concerning the waiver.

In a lengthy judgement, the details of which we cannot go into, Rabbi Menachem Mendel Krochmal concluded as follows. The defendant was not to be regarded as a regular member of the community, but as a temporary resident who had come to the city as a refugee from the wars, probably referring to the Thirty Years

[33] Resp. *Zemah Tsedek*, no. 24.
[34] Ibid., no. 37.

War. The waiver was valid for what was written in it, but not for the time after the date of the waiver. Rabbi Isaac was to be looked upon as a war refugee, temporarily resident in Vienna, but in the class of other refugees, who did not have to pay the regular taxes of the community. However, special levies placed on the community had to be paid by all residents – whether permanent or temporary. The respondent mentioned that at the moment a special levy of 16,000 gold coins had been placed on the community. Hence, in the *responsum*, the outcome seems to have been a compromise judgement. The decision recognized Rabbi Isaac's special status, which was conferred upon him by the former community leaders, but anything above and beyond the waiver he received was not recognized. His status was no better or worse than that of other refugees. It would seem that, all in all, the judgement was more favourable to the defendant than to the community. In spite of his lengthy stay in the community, he was still regarded as a temporary resident bearing the lesser obligations of a temporary resident.[35]

During the period we are discussing, attempts were made to disenfranchise poorer members of the community. In two standard codes of law, it was stated that communal decisions which concern expenditure are to be decided upon by the majority of wealth and not by the majority of voters.[36] In fact, most major communal decisions did concern financial matters and there was constant tension between rich and poor members of the community. On the one hand there was fear of oligarchy and, on the other, fear of unbridled democracy and rule of the commoners.

There was good precedent for the rule that a majority of better-off citizens be considered a legal majority for decision-making; Rabbi Asher ben Yehiel, a great thirteenth-fourteenth century *halakhic* authority, decided so in the clearest terms. However, the exigencies of life brought about a novel interpretation of Rabbi Asher's words as well as those of the great sixteenth-century authority Rabbi Moses Isserles. According to this interpretation, Rabbi Asher and Rabbi Moses Isserles never meant to say that financial majority has precedence over the numerical majority of voters; what they meant, it was explained, was that neither one of these majorities could by itself force the other majority to comply

---

[35] On problems discussed in this *responsum*, such as the status of refugees who fled to another community, the duty to pay certain levies before being allowed to leave a community, and the like, see Katz, *Masoret*, pp. 130, 132, 146–7.

[36] Rema's glosses to *Sh. Ar. H.M.* 163, 3; *Levush Ir Shushan H.M.*, 163, 3.

with their decision. They had to arrive at some compromise between them. This line of reasoning, first enunciated by Rabbi Joshua Falk in Poland,[37] was followed by Rabbi Menachem Mendel Krochmal in two of his *responsa*. In both of these *responsa* we can clearly see the statute of this prominent rabbi and his awareness of the social dimensions of a rabbi's legal decision.

Close to the time of his arrival in Kremzir (1636) to function as the community's rabbi, Rabbi Krochmal was asked to decide a case which pitted the majority of the community, which numbered fifty families in all, against a minority of the community consisting of one individual and his two sons and two sons-in-law. These five individuals paid 60 per cent of the community's taxes.

The community wanted to hire someone to fulfil a certain position but the five did not agree to the candidate. It seems that this was just a symptom of a general problem in that the communal laws stated that decisions should be made by the majority of the people as well as by the majority of wealth. The members of the community complained that the enactment gave veto power to these five family members and the community could not be effectively run in such a manner.

In principle, Rabbi Krochmal followed the view of Rabbi Joshua Falk, adding that it is equitable and proper that neither the wealthy nor a majority of the poor should compel the other. However, through a novel, ingenious interpretation of the communal enactment, he came to an operative decision.

Rabbi Krochmal explained that in the case before him there was, in fact, this twofold majority. There was a majority of members of the community, since all forty-five wanted to hire this specific individual. But there was also a majority of wealth in favour of the hiring, said Rabbi Krochmal. How so? He explained that the custom of the community was to pay such employees of the community in the following manner: half his salary based on the wealth of the members of the community, and half on the number of community members. If then, for example, Rabbi Krochmal explained, the employee's salary was 50 gold coins, half, that is, 25, were divided among the families – that is, each of the fifty families in the community was to pay half a gold coin, in total 25 gold coins. The other 25 gold coins were paid according to wealth. Therefore, the five who comprised 60 per cent of the community's wealth should

---

[37] *Rema* to *Sh. Ar. H.M.*, 163, 3, n. 18.

pay him three-fifths of 25, which is 15 gold coins. Their total then came to 15 plus two and a half (five times half a gold coin, based on per capita payment) which meant that the oligarchic five paid only 17.5 gold pieces, while the popular majority of the community (45 members) paid 22.5 gold coins (half a gold coin per capita) and another two-fifths (40 per cent of the wealth) of 25 gold coins, that is, 10 gold coins. Together, the majority paid 32.5 gold coins. Hence the community had both a numerical and monetary majority, and their decision to hire the specific employee could stand. Rabbi Krochmal's novel interpretation was also affirmed by the general leadership of Moravian Jewry.[38]

In another *responsum*, Rabbi Krochmal was faced with the question of whether poor taxpayers could be disenfranchised, the argument being that it is unfair to run the community on the principle of one man one vote, giving the same voting power to the poor and uneducated members of the community as to the rich leading taxpayers. Rabbi Krochmal, in a most eloquent defence of the poor, upheld their rights of equal voting power, asserting that a small tax burden on the poor is at least equal to, if not more than, a heavy one on the rich. He delved into classical biblical sources in order to prove that both rich and poor stand equally before God, and so the rule should remain in the community. In addition, the arguments against the poor and uneducated were disposed of by reasoning showing a keen understanding of human nature. If these seemingly lesser individuals were disenfranchised, they would become very resentful and in the end could secede from the community and cause bitter strife between the social strata. Rabbi Krochmal brings Talmudic precedent to show that for the sake of peace, even the law has sometimes to bend.[39]

In both the above-mentioned *responsa*, Rabbi Krochmal clearly takes the side of the weaker party; his social outlook is clear. Although Rabbi Krochmal, like other rabbis of his time, was appointed by the Jewish communities and received his salary from them, this did not in any way seem to influence his anti-establishment decisions, both in the cases just mentioned and in other situations, throughout his varied lifetime.

The questions we have discussed almost always referred to conflicts between individuals and communities, concerning taxation.

[38] Resp. *Zemah Tsedek*, no. 1.
[39] Ibid., no. 2. A detailed discussion of this *responsum* is found in Ben-Sasson, *Hagot Vehanaga*, pp. 158, 229–31.

Although not very many sources were referred to, these legal decisions give an accurate picture of the major area of friction between the individual and the community. No other topic pitted person against public as did that of taxation. The examples cited are representative of the ongoing conflicts within the Jewish communities in general, and the Polish autonomous communities in particular. The rabbinic authorities did not adopt rigid positions favouring either the private litigant or the general community, but tried to adjudicate each case on its merits. One is struck by the rabbis' legal acumen, the striving for justice as it is understood and interpreted in the Jewish legal system, and the first-hand knowledge and deep understanding of the political circumstances of the Jewish community, all of which, together with the respondent's personal psychological make-up, went into the decision-making process. If, in cases of disputes between private individuals, I am in the company of those who feel that extra-*halakhic* circumstances play a relatively minor role in the *halakhic* decision-making process,[40] I tend to agree with those who emphasize non-legal phenomena as a strong influence on the arbiters of the law, when the problems concern the individual versus the community.

---

[40] According to Salo Baron, 'No systematic, comprehensive, up-to-date analysis of the entire structure and administration of pre-partition Poland and Lithuania is yet available. The material is admittedly widely scattered, incomplete, and very difficult to access. Not surprisingly the part played by Polish and Lithuanian Jews as taxpayers in the local commonwealth and its political subdivisions, or in their own communities, is even less known.' Salo W. Baron, *Social and Religious History of the Jews* 16 (1973), p. 450, n. 84.

17 · The Condition of the Jewish Population of Wschowa in the Mid Eighteenth Century

Jacek Sobczak

A number of measures undertaken in the mid eighteenth century in the Polish Commonwealth sought to ameliorate the state into which the towns had fallen. They were initiated with the resolutions of the 1764 Convocation Sejm (Diet) as a result of which the *Ubezpieczenie miast* (town security) charter cancelled most *jurydyki* (noble-controlled areas in the towns) and made municipal tax payable by nobles who held real estate within town limits, thus putting a stop to the practice of transferring town estates to the clergy.[1] Also, by making the *starostas* now responsible for controlling the royal towns' accounts, taxation and payments were put into order. The next move was the establishment of the Good order (Boni Ordinis) Commission for Warsaw, as was done by the monarch in 1765.[2] The findings of this commission must have been well received, as in 1768 the Sejm decided to establish Good Order Commissions (Komisja Dobrego Porządku – abbr. KDP) for all major royal towns setting out the reasons for their foundation and range of activities in the charter *Warunek miast i miasteczek naszych królewskich w Koronie i w W.X. Litewskim* (The condition of our royal towns and small towns in the Kingdom of Poland and in the Grand Duchy of

---

[1] *Volumina Legum* (further quoted as *VL*) VII, p. 82. In 1764, during the session of the Sejm, the national Jewish representation of the Council of the Four Lands was abolished and only the *kehilla* authorities were left. Rabbis were obliged to supervise the Jewish population together with *Kwartalnys* and *szkolniks* and a representative of the *szlachta* (a Catholic): *VL* VII, pp. 26–9.

[2] W. Smoleński, *Komisja Boni Ordinis warszawska (1765–1789)* (The Warsaw Boni Ordinis Commission, 1765–1789), Warsaw, 1914; idem, *Mieszczaństwo warszawskie w końcu wieku XVIII* (Warsaw Burghers at the end of the eighteenth century), Warsaw, 1976, p. 99 and notes.

Lithuania). The commissions' powers were set out again in the royal decrees establishing every single commission. The content of these decrees was, in principle, in line with the *Warunek miast* charter, though not in every case.

The *Warunek miast* charter devoted much attention to the Jewish population. Emphasis was laid on the fact that Jewish inhabitants could and should enter into special contracts or accords with the authorities, specifying and regulating the range of their duties towards those authorities and the limits of their privileges, especially in those towns where Jewish privileges had not been confirmed by the Sejm. Not that the charter spelt out in detail how the accords should be applied, merely stating in a general manner that those already in existence should be taken as models. Any conflicts which might arise between the authorities and Jewish population in the preparation and drafting of these accords were to be resolved by the KDP commissions after hearing from both sides. The commissions were also charged with the completion of the accords, that is, getting them signed, or even – as we can assume from their contents – drafting them themselves. At the same time, it was decided that Jews from towns without signed and agreed accords had no right to trade, engage in crafts or run inns.[3]

It is a matter of debate whether Wschowa had its own, separate KDP commission, or whether it fell under the Poznań KDP. Deresiewicz and Rolbiecki are convinced that a separate commission was established for Wschowa.[4] This view has been questioned by the author of this chapter, who maintains that no special commission was formed in Wschowa, but that the members of the Poznań KDP worked there.[5] It is worth looking at the position of the Jewish population of Wschowa, bearing in mind that it was a town of unusual character, lying of the western edge of the Polish

---

[3] *VL* VII, p. 352.

[4] J. Deresiewicz, 'Wielkopolskie Komisje Dobrego Porządku' (Great Poland's Good Order Commissions), *Czasopismo Prawno-historyczne* (Legal-Historical Journal) 18:2, 1966, pp. 155–213; G. J. Rolbiecki, 'Prawo przemysłowe Wschowy w XVIII w.' (Wschowa industrial law in the eighteenth century), in *Badania z dziejów społecznych i gospodarczych* (Studies in Social and Economic History) 38, Poznań, 1951. B. Tyszkiewicz, who examined the Poznań commission in her work *Działalność poznańskiej Komisji Dobrego Porządku 1779–1784* (The Work of the Poznań Good Order Commission), Poznań 1965, does not touch on this problem.

[5] J. Sobczak, 'Działalność Komisji Dobrego Porządku we Wschowie' (The work of the Good Order commission in Wschowa), in *Rocznik Leszczyński* (Leszno Annual) VII, Lęszno, 1983, pp. 113–53.

Commonwealth and inhabited largely by Protestants of German background. But they were closely linked to the Polish Commonwealth, as is attested by their demand, put forward at the end of the eighteenth century, that Polish be used as the language of instruction in school.[6]

In the mid eighteenth century, Wschowa ranked as one of the Kingdom's major towns. The 1775 hearth-tax collection list named Wschowa, together with Kraków and Poznań, as one of the three biggest towns in the Kingdom after Warsaw.[7] The special treatment given to Wschowa is not easy to understand, as the town was outstripped in Great Poland not only by Leszno, albeit a private town, with its 7,000 inhabitants,[8] but also by Lublin whose population in 1787, according to W. Ćwik, was 8,550 (4,320 Christians and 4,230 Jews).[9] It appears that Wschowa owed its high ranking, in relation to its size, to its wealth and to politics. It was here that, in the Saxon period, the monarch met senators and foreign envoys and ambassadors came. Wschowa was a major political centre of the time. Sporadically named as Fraustadt in deeds, registers and documents written in German, Wschowa, during the period of the KDP's activity, had three centres. The biggest was Stara (Old) Wschowa, often referred to simply as Wschowa. Next to it stood Nowa (New) Wschowa (Neustadt), which had its own town authorities and a *jurydyka* subject to the Wschowa parish priest. Finally, there were two villages, Przyczyna Górna and Przyczyna Dolna (Upper and Lower Przyczyna),

---

[6] AP, Zielona Góra, kept in Stary Kisielin (further quoted as APZ), Records of the town of Wschowa, 153, pp. 33–5; see also J. Sobczak, 'Wschowski sąd apelacyjny wydziałowy' (Wschowa Regional Appeal Court), in *Rocznik Leszczyński* VI, Leszno, 1982, p. 321; idem, 'Szkolnictwo wschowskie w dobie Komisji Edukacji Narodowej' (Education in Wschowa in the period of the National Education Commission), ibid., p. 140.

[7] VL VII, p. 881, see also T. Korzon, *Wewnętrzne dzieje Polski za Stanisława Augusta* (Poland's internal history in the time of Stanisław August), Warsaw, 1897–8, p. 213.

[8] B. Baranowski, *Życie codzienne małego miasteczka w XVII i XVIII w.* (Everyday life in a small town in the seventeenth and eighteenth centuries), Warsaw, 1975, pp. 7–8. A somewhat different listing of the population of the towns of Great Poland from B. Baranowski's is given by Z. Kulejewska-Topolska, 'Nowe lokacje miejskie w Wielkopolsce od XVI do końca XVIII wieku, Studium historyczno-prawne' (New town incorporations in Great Poland from the sixteenth to the end of the eighteenth century, a historico-legal study), *Proceedings of the Law Faculty of the Adam Mickiewicz University in Poznań* 11, 1964, pp. 52–3.

[9] W. Ćwik, *Miasta królewskie Lubelszczyzny w drugiej połowie XVIII w.* (Royal towns in the Lublin region in the second half of the eighteenth century), Lublin, 1968, p. 18.

belonging to Wschowa. The KDP's commissioners consistently treated Nowa Wschowa as a separate municipal unit. Later on, the Sejm settled a dispute which started on 10 August 1791 within the Commission, by stating that Nowa Wschowa was not a separate town, but merely a *jurydyka*.[10]

In 1783, when the KDP was at work, Stara Wschowa numbered 3,479 inhabitants, Nowa Wschowa 742 persons and its parish priest's *jurydyka* 501, while 858 people lived in the two villages. Altogether we arrive at 5,530 people living in the three parts. Only in the parish priest's *jurydyka* were Catholics predominant; elsewhere Protestants formed the majority. According to official censuses, Jews lived only in Nowa Wschowa, yet the KDP's assessment showed them living – illegally – in Stara Wschowa as well. The few Wschowa Jews were said by the KDP to number 301 persons. This would mean that Jews constituted only 5.36 per cent of the total population of all three parts of Wschowa. But other KDP calculations show that their numbers were greater. The age and sex of the Jewish population cannot be determined nor can their professional structure be assessed but we can assume that they were mostly tailors and workers in various crafts connected with hide and leather manufacture and, of course, merchants. That there were Jewish butchers is certain. We have no data for Jewish guilds in Wschowa – perhaps Jewish craftsmen belonged to the guilds of Poznań and Leszno. We can only regret that the inventory of the Wschowa Jewish population drawn up in 1764 by order of the Convocation Sejm has not survived. All we know about it is that it was presented, along with other documents, to the KDP by the Jewish population. From the Jewish poll tax assessment that has survived, it appears that 214 Jews lived in Wschowa in 1775.[11] The KDP noted an increase in the number of Jews living there, giving the new figure as 301.[12] It is impossible to determine whether this was due to natural population increase or other factors.

The tasks of the KDP in Wschowa are described in a royal belonging to Wschowa. The KDP's commissioners consistently

---

[10] AP, Poznań (further quoted as APP), Laws of the town of Poznań, I 213, pp. 243–62; *VL* IX, pp. 379–80.

[11] APP, Wschowa, *Wschowa Municipal Records (Księgi Grodzkie – KG)*, 223, fo. 178.

[12] According to the inventory, which is borne out by a KDP summary, stating that the Jews of Wschowa paid 602 złoty in poll tax. According to the 1764 charter, Jews had to pay 2 złoty a head including children). Thus it appears that 301 Jews lived in Nowa Wschowa. See *VL* VII, pp. 26–9; *Stan Miasta J.M. Mci. Wschowy* (The state of H. R. M. town of Wschowa), Leszno, 1783, p. 83.

collect all the town's privileges and prepare a map and inventory of municipal territory. With regard to the Jewish population, the KDP was to see whether Jewish privileges would stand in the way of the town's development. The commission's recommendations were to be presented to the assessors' office in a separate, sealed document.[13] It is hard to explain why the KDP's recommendation had to be kept secret. Perhaps it was intended to prevent any maltreatment of the commissioners by the town authorities or by the Jews. But it is more likely that the central authorities did not want to treat the KDP's views as binding, and wished to be free to take their own decisions. In looking into the state of the Jewish population, the KDP also acquainted itself with the conflicts between Jews and Christians.

The KDP received the collection of privileges granted to Stara and Nowa Wschowa from the representatives of these towns. The Jewish population brought in their privileges as well. The commission arranged all these documents for both Jews and the rest of the citizens in chronological order, summarized them and made an inventory of their contents. The commission expressed no doubts about the completeness of the documents and privileges regulating Jewish status which were presented to it. This fact is worth noting, as the KDP was not satisfied that it had been given all the municipal authorities' documents and urged further search, which in fact proved fruitful.[14]

The Jews presented the commission with fourteen privileges granted to them between 8 January 1642 and 12 January 1769. Doubts may arise whether this is the full number of privileges issued to them by the central authorities, which regulated their legal position in the town. The answer is no. Although the present condition of sources for Wschowa is deplorable and most of the documents which existed before the Second World War have not survived, we do know of many more acts regulating the legal status of the Jewish population.[15] What the Jews gave to the KDP was

[13] APP, *Wschowa KG*, 230, fo. 252, *Poznań KG*, 1152, fo. 91 and n.
[14] *Stan miasta*, pp. 7, 72. This volume has survived in a few copies and the KDP's work forms its contents. The manuscript of the book is in Kórnik Library, and a printed copy with ring seals of the members of the KDP is kept in the University of Poznań Library.
[15] J. G. Rolbiecki, *Prawo przemysłowe*, pp. 557–8 notes King Jan Kazimierz's edict of 29 August 1659, in which are described the attitude of the *starosta* towards the Jewish population; the decisions of the royal commission of 10 May 1732 on Jewish status; King Stanisław August's edict of 26 April 1766; the assessor's court decision

mainly those documents which granted them rights and privileges and not any later limitations or qualifications.

We do not learn from these documents when the Jewish community was founded in Wschowa but from other sources we know that Jews settled in Wschowa at the latest by the end of the sixteenth century.[16] As appears from their documents, Wschowa Jews owned meadows and grazing land in 1642. Later decrees supply us with information on municipal property owned by Jews. Apparently, Jews had their own cemetery within Nowa Wschowa, despite strong church opposition. The ban on a new cemetery was set aside only with the decree of a Poznań official, Józef Pawłowski, on 27 June 1759.[17] The information on the Jewish cemetery in Wschowa is very interesting as it was not listed by the KDP in its inventory of municipal territory. Final permission (*consens*) to open this cemetery was issued by the *starosta* Franciszek Antoni Kwilecki on 10 July 1759, and the decision was confirmed on 27 April 1765 by King Stanisław August Poniatowski. Before having their own cemetery, the Wschowa Jews had to bury their dead in the Leszno cemetery. On the leased property – five

---

of 20 March 1777 expelling Jews from the town, and the affidavits issued by the Jews and the town authorities in the case examined by the assessor's court over the clash of 3 January 1780. See also M. Horn, ed., *Regesty dokumentów i ekscerpty z Metryki Koronnej do historii Żydów w Polsce 1697–1795* II, *Rządy Stanisława Augusta (1764–1795)* (The rule of Stanislaw August), part 1, Wrocław, 1984, summaries 77, 198, 312, 388.

[16] S. F. Lauterbach, *Kleine Fraustadliche Pest–Chronica*, Leipzig, 1710, p. 72; A. W. Braune, *Geschichte der Stadt Fraustadt*, Fraustadt, 1889; F. Moritz, 'Die älteste judische Niederlassung in Fraustadt', *Historische Monatsblätter für die Provinz Posen* 2:12, 1901, pp. 179–84; G. Brandt, 'Die Pest der Jahre 1707–1713 in der heutigen Provinz Posen', *Zeitschrift der historischen Gesellschaft für die Provinz Posen* 17, pp. 301–28; J. Kothe, 'Zur Geschichte Fraustadts im XVIII Jhdrt', *Historische Monatsblätter für die Provinz Posen* 20 pp. 76–7; A. Heppner, I. Herzberg, *Aus der Vergangenheit und Gegenwart der Juden und die judische Gemeinden in der Provinz Posen*, Koźmin-Bydgoszcz, 14, 1909; J. Joneman, 'Dzieje ziemi wschowskiej i stołecznego jej miasta Wschowy', (History of the Wschowa region and its capital Wschowa), Warsaw University Library, MS 226, also Raczyński Library MS 59. It is known that the Wschowa citizens obtained the privilege *de non tolerandis Judaeis* in 1592, which also prohibited Jews from living in the suburbs and *jurydykas*. It is not clear whether the privilege was valid for the Nowa Wschowa area as well. See J. Morgensztern, 'Regesty z Metryki Koronnej do historii Żydów w Polsce (1588–1632), (Summaries from the Crown Registers for the history of Jews in Poland), *BŻIH* 51, 1964, p. 61, para. 9.

[17] *Stan miasta*, 'Summarium documentorum per infideles judaeos Neustadiens commonstratorum et comportatorum', p. 83.

perches long and five perches wide – they had to pay an annual rent of 600 złoty.[18]

We do not learn from the commission's assessment what properties were employed by the Jewish population in Nowa Wschowa nor the appearance of their houses. Like all the buildings there, they were probably made of wood, usually with a single storey.[19] The fact that the community had its own synagogue should be noted, though we have no specific information about it.

As is clearly apparent from the documents presented by the Jews to the KDP, the Jewish population, for all the prohibitions and fines imposed by the town authorities, made repeated attempts to settle in Stara Wschowa. The reason is hard to make out but in the final analysis it must have been profitable for both sides, the Christians who rented out the houses and the Jews. There were earlier clashes over Jewish ritual slaughter in the municipal slaughterhouse. This problem was settled by a verdict of the assessor's court of 3 January 1716, which was presented to the KDP, and which granted Jews the right to practise their method of slaughter in return for regular payments to the town.[20]

Arguments between the town authorities and the Jewish community did arise on occasion, but mainly on economic, not doctrinal or religious grounds. We can glean no information from them of any persecution of the local Jews. But King Władysław IV intervened to defend the Wschowa Jews on two occasions – on 31 March 1643 and on 20 August 1644, when he instructed the town authorities not to obstruct Jews from trading. It is quite clear from the documents of the Metryka Koronna (Registry of the Crown) that Jews did in fact settle in Wschowa despite the privilege *de non tolerandis Judaeis*, as is evidenced by the fact that on 17 October 1659 King Jan Kazimierz obliged the Wschowa *starosta* to drive the Jewish population out of town.[21] There were frequent quarrels between Jews and burghers. A safe-conduct issued to the Wschowa Jews by King Stanisław August on 3 February 1766, to protect them from the persecutions by the town authorities is, doubtless,

---

[18] AGAD, *Księgi Kanclerskie* (Chancellors' Records – *KK*) 27, pp. 112–14. See also Horn, *Regesty*, p. 55.
[19] J. Sobczak, *Działalność Komisji*, pp. 143–4.
[20] *Stan miasta*, Summarium, p. 82.
[21] J. Morgensztern, 'Regesty z Metryki Koronnej do historii Żydów w Polsce (1633–1660)' (Summaries from the Crown Registers for the history of Jews in Poland), in *BŻIH* 58, 1966, p. 118, paras. 59, 60.

connected with one of those cases.²² While the KDP was in operation, further misunderstandings occurred between the town authorities and some Jews over economic matters. The fact that the commission transferred the case to the assessor's court for trial while, according to its own remit, it could have handled the matter itself, is significant. The reasons for this procedure cannot be determined. Again, we cannot discover the cause of the quarrel nor the positions taken by parties to it. It is only known that both town authorities and Jews made sworn statements (*inkwizycje*) on 3 January 1780. The assessor's verdict on the case has not been found.

The KDP looked into a complaint from the elders of the shoemakers' guild that foreign Jews (probably from Silesia and Prussia) arrived in town, took rented accommodation in Stara Wschowa and bought up raw hides and wool for export outside the Polish Commonwealth's borders. The KDP therefore forbade all inhabitants of Stara Wschowa to rent premises to Jews, especially those from abroad. Discovering that hide and wool were vital raw materials for Wschowa manufacturers, the KDP banned their purchase and export by foreign Jews under pain of confiscation, as well as prohibiting them from transacting any other business.²³ We should point here to the conflict of interest in economic terms within Wschowa and other towns, which probably explains the frequent breaching of the prohibitions against the Jews, and the acts limiting their privileges. It would seem that some people had a profitable interest in Jewish settlement in towns.

Before the KDP began its operations, the legal status of the Wschowa Jews was controlled by Antoni Mycielski's edict of 14 February 1721 (entered into municipal records in 1726). Some of its regulations were changed during later reviews by the Wschowa *starosta* on 20 June 1758 and in 1765.²⁴ These were the documents presented, with additional material, to the KDP by the Jews of the town.

Attempts to reconstruct a detailed picture of the organization of the Jewish community in Wschowa have not been successful. We know only that Gershel Pinkus and Jan Samuel held the position of the elders of the *kehilla* and Abraham Isak was treasurer. We

---

²² AGAD, *Sigillata* 30, p. 96ᵛ.
²³ *Stan miasta*, pp. 286–7.
²⁴ APP, Wschowa, *KG 42* and *KG 225*, pp. 311–24.

cannot say who held the remaining offices.[25] But we can assume that the organization of the Wschowa community was not very different from that of other Jewish communities in the Polish Commonwealth. Nevertheless the question of contacts between this community and the *kehillot* of other Great Poland towns, especially Leszno, requires an explanation. That there were such contacts seems to be borne out by the problem, already mentioned, of the cemetery. Perhaps the Wschowa Jewish craftsmen were members of the Poznań and Gniezno guilds. A rabbi lived within the community boundaries but took no part in the operations of the KDP.

As appears from the KDP's records, the commissioners prepared a text for the Accords, that is, regulations concerning mutual relations between Jews and Christians in that area, based on the collected documents, in fulfilment of their obligations under the 1768 charter *Warunek miast* to get a contract agreed between the town authorities and the Jews. It is impossible to judge how much influence the town authorities and the Jews had over the contents of this document. The KDP filed the draft forms with their documents after they were signed by both parties and accepted by the *starosta*.[26]

The final Accords go far beyond the limits of the *Warunek miast* charter, as regulations on details of the Jewish community's internal organisation and its courts are to be found in all twenty-seven of those Accords – matters which were no concern of the KDP.[27] The Accords stipulated that the community was to be governed by a rabbi and elders, whose elections were to be confirmed annually

---

[25] *Stan miasta*, 'Summarium', pp. 83–4.

[26] *Pakta między sławetnym magistratem i porządkami miasta J K Mci Nowej Wschowy z jednej a niewiernymi Żydami w tymże Nowym Mieście mieszkalnemi z drugiej strony* (Accords between the distinguished Town Council and supervisors of HRM town of Nowa Wschowa on the one side and the Infidel Jews of the same new town on the other side), Leszno, 1783. The printed edition is usually bound together with *Stan miasta*.

[27] On the organization of the Jewish communities in Poland, see M. Balaban, 'Ustrój kahalny w Polsce XVI–XVIII w.' (*Kehilla* organization in Poland in the sixteenth to eighteenth centuries), *Kwartalnik poświecony badaniom przeszłości Żydów w Polsce* (Quarterly for studies of the Jewish past in Poland) 1:1, 1912; M. Schorr, 'Organizacya Żydów w Polsce' (Organization of the Jews in Poland), *Kwartalnik Historyczny* 13, 1899, p. 735 and n., also J. Sobczak 'zadłużenie kahałów żydowskich w końcu XVIII w. w świetle obliczeń sądu ziemiańskiego w Kaliszu' (Debts of the Jewish *kehilla* at the end of the eighteenth century as illustrated by the Kalisz Land Court's Assessments), *Rocznik Kaliski* (Kalisz Annual) 11, 1978, pp. 107–23.

by the Wschowa *starosta*. But the fragment about the *starosta*'s power to confirm the leaders of the Jewish community is not clear, even though it is written in Polish. It could also be understood to mean that the rabbi was to be confirmed every year. Also the Accords do not go into detail on the election of elders. They say nothing about other officials and methods for their appointment. The rabbi, with the elders of the community, was to judge in all cases, both civil and criminal. It is also laid down that sentence must be passed in all cases within ten days of a summons being made or a charge brought to court. Yet no place of session is given nor its working days and times. One could appeal from a verdict passed by this court to the assessor's court headed by the *wójt*. An appeal from the assessor's court could be made to the *starosta*'s court, but only in cases involving a minimum value of 60,000 złoty.[28] It is striking that there is no mention of any appeal to the *podwojewodziński* court.

Every year, the community elders had to disclose their financial accounts to the *starosta* and a list of the inhabitants of the community. They were also subject to a penalty of a hundred grzywnas to be used for road-surfacing or building repairs, if they failed to stop Jews from other towns moving into the area of the town. They were responsible for the punctual collection of poll tax. The Accords also forbade the rabbi to perform weddings for Jews without a steady job and who were not paying tax. Jews who did get married had to pay two złoty towards repair and restoration of the castle. This last regulation was in line with similar customs from other towns. The rabbi was also forbidden to excommunicate his co-religionists without prior consent from the town authorities or *starosta*. However, Jews were guaranteed the right of further use of the cemetery.[29]

Most of the provisions of the Accords dealt with economic concerns. In the first place, Jews were banned from buying houses from Christians, although when a Jew wished to sell his property, the other citizens could claim right of pre-emption. But Jews could, with the *starosta*'s consent, buy empty plots and live in the houses they built on them, on payment of rent to the *starosta*. These provisions were based not so much on a policy of discrimination as on the town's economic plight. Because of the numerous wars and

---

[28] The KDP made changes to the Wschowa town authorities and courts. See J. Sobczak, *Działalność Komisji*, pp. 147–50.
[29] *Pakta miedzy sławetnym magistratem*, pp. 1–3.

plagues which affected it in 1709 and 1711, many of its building sites lay empty. But Jews were still permitted to settle only in the area of Nowa Wschowa, and were expressly excluded from Stara Wschowa, the parish priest's *jurydyka* and the two villages close to town. It was made clear that if Jews moved to the villages, the town's economy would be ruined, thus creating a loss to the Crown treasury. Anyone moving into one of the nearby villages would incur a prison sentence and the sequestration of his property. Any rent agreement between a Jew and the Christian owner of a building was to be put into writing by the municipal scribe and signed by both parties. The Accords also allowed for two Jewish butchers to operate in Nowa Wschowa, and an agreement with the authorities of Stara Wschowa was confirmed, by which Jews could work as butchers in Stara Wschowa. This last regulation seems to prove the presence of Jews in Stara Wschowa who were not listed in the Jewish population censuses.

Under the Accords, the Jewish population, like the rest of the townsfolk, had to pay for the maintenance of municipal buildings and road-surfacing. They were also in charge of fire-fighting equipment. Jews had to take their slops out to the *starosta*'s ploughland at their own expense, and to work at hay-raking and haymaking but no number is specified for the workdays they each had to perform.

On fair days, Jews were allowed to purchase merchandise only after 9 a.m. (in Stara Wschowa only after 10 a.m.). The reason for this regulation is not clear but the likely motive was fear of prices being forced up if the Jews came in earlier to buy. The Accords clearly aimed at preventing Jews from outside Wschowa participation in the town's Jewish trade, on the grounds that it constituted a danger to the town's economy. The rabbi was supposed to excommunicate any such person and refuse him access to kosher meat. At the same time, Jews were instructed to try to export Wschowa's produce and were forbidden to import goods which were manufactured locally, especially wool and linen textiles and candles. They were subject to a high fine if they traded on Sundays and Christian holidays.

The Accords stated that Jews could only engage in those crafts which Christians did not fill. Finally, both the Jewish and the Christian population were duty-bound to give mutual aid.[30]

---

[30] *VL* IX, pp. 402–3: *Zalecenie sądom ziemiańskim względem długów kahałów żydowskich* (Recommendation to the Land Court on the debts of the Jewish *kehillot*); see also J. Sobczak, 'Zadłużenie kahałów żydowskich', pp. 107–23.

Although the limitations imposed on the Jewish population by the Accords were far-reaching, in reality they were not too severe. They did not exceed existing customs and legal limitations. It is hard to say to what extent the Accords actually prevented disputes and tensions in the town. It is a fact that they did not stop them totally, and it is doubtful if they could ever have done so.

Neither the Accords nor the KDP in its early stages dealt with the community's financial basis, the state of its debts, or the burden of tax imposed upon it. These were problems for the land court to handle later on.

A detailed discussion of the Wschowa community's liabilities is beyond the scope of this chapter. But I should like to mention that its creditors were mainly priests and monasteries, sometimes at quite a distance from the town. From the land court's settlements one cannot deduce the use to which the community put this money. Doubtless, part of it went to pay overdue taxes and bribe officials. Seeing the amount of the borrowing and its lack of time limit or, if one was given, its long-term duration, for a dozen or so years, one can assume that the clergy and nobility treated the Jewish community as a quasi-banking institution.

The question of *kehilla* debts cannot be examined only from the point of view of the Jewish community, as has been done so far. It has to be looked at in conjunction with the nobles' affairs, as the latter were concerned with the profit they got from their interest, not with questioning the details of the financial operations.

It would be extremely interesting to know what happened to the money once it came into the possession of the community but this problem will probably remain unsolved. On the other hand, it is doubtful if the community itself used the borrowed money. We should assume rather that its richest members, who were probably part of its leadership, made use of it.

What stands out from the KDP's assessments? Probably this, that the limitations imposed on the Jewish population originated in economic, not ideological concerns. Also, thanks to the KDP's activities, we can discover, at least in general terms, the urban distribution of the Jewish quarters. A certain division of social functions between German, Polish and Jewish citizens is also apparent. A final interesting fact, which has already been mentioned, is that the KDP actually tolerated Jewish disregard for the law in transgressing the settlement limitations.

Part IV

The Economy

18 · The Chronology and Distribution of Jewish Craft Guilds in Old Poland, 1613–1795

Maurycy Horn

LITERATURE AND SOURCES

The origin and development of Jewish guilds have generally been overlooked in our historiography. Economic historians have, in most cases, passed over the very existence of Jewish craft fraternities, or at best have treated them as an oddity. A different approach was taken by those historians of Polish Jews at the end of the nineteenth century who, in discussing the state of Jewish crafts in Poland in the seventeenth and the eighteenth centuries, did notice the function and role of Jewish corporations. Even if we omit T. H. Wettstein, who in 1892 published (though not critically) the original text of the *pinkas* (minute book) of the Jewish tailors' guild of Kraków in 1613,[1] and Wolf Feilchenfeld, who in 1895 published a German summary of a 1737 Poznań *kehilla* resolution on the establishment of Jewish craft guilds in Poznań,[2] we must, nevertheless, acknowledge Moses Schorr, later on a member of the Polish Academy of Sciences and Letters, as a pioneer in their field. In 1898, he published in *Kwartalnik Historyczny* a wide-ranging analysis of the organization of Jews in Poland before 1772,[3] a large section of which was devoted to Jewish guilds. This section, based mainly on the Przemyśl town and municipal files, though with some

---

[1] F. H. Wettstein, 'Kadmoniyot mi'pinkasot yeshanim', *Hameasef*, 1892, no. 8.
[2] W. Feilchenfeld, 'Eine Innungsordnung für die judischen Handwerker zu Posen', *'Zeitschrift der historischen Gesellschaft für die Provinz Posen'* 10, 1895, pp. 310–16.
[3] M. Schorr, 'Organizacya Żydów w Polsce od najdawniejszych czasów aź do 1772 r.' (Organization of the Jews in Poland from earliest times to 1772), *Kwartalnik Historyczny* 13, 1899, I, pp. 482–520, 734–75.

support from the Lwów *podwojewodziński* records, includes information on the organization of Jewish guilds in Przemyśl and Lwów. He also described in detail the history of Przemyśl's Jewish guilds in a monograph devoted to the history of Jewish population in that town before the third partition of Poland. This work included excerpts from rabbinical court records and seventeen documents from the Przemyśl tailors' guild *pinkas* from 1689 to 1790.[4] This was the start of academic publication of original sources for the history of Jewish guilds in Poland.

In the same year as Moses Schorr, Zbigniew Pazdro reconstructed the organization of the Jewish guilds of Lwów, which came under the *podwojewodziński* administration in the province of Ruthenia. Like Schorr, he added source appendices to his work, illustrating various aspects of their work in eighteenth-century Lwów.[5]

A year later, Louis Lewin, in his history of the Jewish community in Leszno, not only furnished data on several Jewish guilds, but also published the *pinkas* of the Leszno furriers' guild.[6] In 1906, Majer Bałaban's history of the Jews of Lwów at the turn of the sixteenth to seventeenth century appeared,[7] in which the author turned some attention to the Jewish tailors' guild in Lwów. Five years later the author published an article in a Petersburg periodical, *Yevreyskaya Starina*, on Jewish craft guilds in Kraków in the seventeenth and eighteenth centuries.[8] This article, enriched with data from new literature and sources, was reprinted in the first volume of the author's history of the Jews of Krakow.[9] Some time earlier – in 1919 – the same author furnished some details of the

---

[4] M. Schorr, *Żydzi w Przemyślu do końca XVIII wieku* (Jews in Przemyśl up to the end of the eighteenth century), Lwów 1903.

[5] Z. Pazdro, *Organizacja i praktyka żydowskich sądow podwojewodzińskich* (The organization and practice of the Jewish *podwojewodziński* courts in the period 1740–1772, on the basis of Lwów sources), Lwów, 1903.

[6] L. Lewin, *Geschichte der Juden in Lissa*, Pniewy, 1904.

[7] M. Bałaban, *Żydzi lwowscy na przełomie XVI i XVII wieku* (Lwów Jews at the turn of the sixteenth and seventeenth centuries), Lwów, 1906.

[8] M. Bałaban, 'Riemieslennie tsekhi v Krakovie v XVI–XVIII v.' (Craft guilds in Kraków in the sixteenth to eighteenth centuries), *Yevreyskaya* Starina 4:3, 1911, pp. 464–83.

[9] M. Bałaban, *Historia Żydów w Krakowie i na Kazimierzu 1304–1868*, (History of Jews in Kraków and Kazimierz 1304–1868), I: 1304–1656, Kraków, 1931, pp. 298–319. The author insists, for instance, that in the first half of the seventeenth century there was a Jewish haberdashers' guild in Kraków, quoting town and municipal sources from 1614 to 1669, none of which mention this guild, but talk about a struggle between Jewish specialists in this area and the town guild (pp. 311–13).

Lublin tailors' guild in a book on Lublin Jews.[10] These works are very useful in determining the chronology of Jewish craft corporations. Occasionally, Bałaban's conclusions are not fully supported by his sources, which makes it difficult to fix the date of first reference for some guilds.

Before the First World War, several works on Jewish craft fraternities were published in Petersburg, including the publication in Hebrew[11] in 1902 of the *pinkas* of a number of Jewish guilds – unfortunately in an uncritical and non-academic way – and in 1911 the Russian edition of sources for the brewers' fraternity in Sokołów.[12] Mark Wischnitzer, the leading specialist in this field, published his first work on the Jewish guilds in Old Poland in Petersburg in 1914.[13] In the 1920s, Wischnitzer produced several articles on the constitutions of the tailors', furriers' and haberdashers' guilds in Kiejdany,[14] on the structure of Jewish guilds in Poland and Lithuania in the seventeenth and eighteenth centuries,[15] and also on the history of Jewish guilds in the same area in the same period on the basis of the most recent literature and sources.[16] Unlike so many other historians, a very precise methodology characterizes this author's work. We can only regret that, in naming several craft *pinkas*, which he himself made no use of and which are kept in the archives in Leningrad and elsewhere, he did not state the date of their foundation.

Lack of space prevents me from more detailed discussion of the contribution by Polish and foreign historians to the history of Jewish

---

[10] M. Bałaban, *Die Judenstadt von Lublin*, Berlin, 1919, pp. 63–7.

[11] *Pinkas* of the Łuck tailors' guild, published 1902 by J. Kraszyński (*Measef*, 2 (1902), doc. 1, pp. 286–90), and the trimmers' guild statute in Kraków in 1758 published F. H. Wettstein in a collection 'Divrey hefets', Petersburg, 1902, doc. 21 (see ch. 14 n. 30).

[12] N.N., 'Iz istori yevreyev gorodov Vengrova i Sokolova' (On the history of the Jewish towns of Węgrów and Sokołów), *Yevreyskaya Starina*, 4:3, 1911, pp. 286–98.

[13] M. Wischnitzer, 'Yevrey-riemieslenniki i tsekhovaya organizatsia ikh' (Jewish craftsmen and their guild organization in history of the Jewish nation), in *Istoria Yevreyskogo Naroda* XI, Moscow, 1914, pp. 286–99.

[14] M. Wischnitzer, *Die Statuten der judischen Handwerkzunft in Keidan*, *Blätter für Demographie, Statistik und Wirtschaftskunde der Juden* 3, 1925, pp. 72–7.

[15] M. Wischnitzer, 'Di struktur fun yidishe tsekhn in Poyln, Lite un Vejsrusland inem 17-tn un 18-tn jorhunderts', *Tsaytshrift far yidishe geshikte, demografie, sprakhvisnshaft un etnografie* (further quoted as *Tsaytshrift*) 2–3 (1928), pp. 72–87.

[16] M. Wischnitzer, 'Die judische Zunftverfassung in Polen und Litauen im 17. und 18. Jahrhundert', *Vierteljahrschrift für Sozial und Wirtschaftsqeschichte* 20:3–4, 1928, pp. 433–51.

guilds in Poland. For further information, one can refer to my paper on the origin and spread of Jewish guilds in the old Polish Commonwealth, published in the *Biuletyn Żydowskiego Instytutu Historycznego*.[17]

In post-war Poland, research on the history of Jewish crafts and guilds has been inspired mainly by the Jewish Historical Institute. In 1954 a wide-ranging dissertation on Jewish crafts in the Nobles' Commonwealth was published by its director, Professor Bernard Mark.[18] A large part of his work concentrated on the factors responsible for the formation of Jewish craft fraternities, their economic activity, and their struggle against the *kehilla* oligarchy. He also put forward a hypothesis about the common pronouncements of Jewish craftsmen and Christian 'burghers'. The main weakness of this otherwise valuable work is the inaccurate and sometimes misleading methodology, as the author occasionally adduces previously unknown facts without indicating the sources from which they are derived.

Of other works on the origin and functions of Jewish guilds in old Poland, one can mention: Franciszek (Efraim) Kupfer's article on the attitude of the *kehilla* authorities towards Jewish craftsmen and commoners in the Nobles' Commonwealth,[19] the edition of the *pinkas* of the Jewish tailors', furriers' and haberdashers' guild in the town of Nasielsk (with an introduction and commentaries by Adam Wein),[20] and Maurycy Horn's study on Jewish craftsmen in Red Ruthenia at the turn of the sixteenth to seventeenth century.[21] Many new hypotheses on the origin and functioning of Jewish guilds in the province of Białystok in the eighteenth century can be found

---

[17] M. Horn, 'Powstanie i rozwój terytorialny żydowskich cechów rzemieślniczych w dawnej Polsce 1613–1795' (Birth and geographical spread of Jewish craft guilds in Old Poland 1613–1795), part 1: to 1648, *BŻIH* 242–2, 1987, pp. 3–17.
[18] B. Mark, 'Rzemieślnicy żydowscy w Polsce feudalnej' (Jewish craftsmen in feudal Poland), *BŻIH* 9–10, 1954, pp. 5–89.
[19] F. Kupfer, 'A tsushtayer tsu der frage fun der batsiung fun kahal tsum yidishen ba'al melokhe, meshures armshaft in amoliken Pozln', *Bleter far Geshikhte* (Yidd.) 1:1–4, 1949, pp. 207–22.
[20] A. Wein, 'Księga cechu krawców, kuśnierzy i szmuklerzy żydowskich miasta Nasielska' (The Book of the Nasielsk Jewish Tailors', Furriers' and Haberdashers' Guild), *BŻIH* 42, 1962, pp. 128–30; J. Goldberg, A. Wein, 'Der pinkas fun khevre shnayder in Nasielsk', *Bleter far Geshikte* 15 (1963), pp. 155–67.
[21] M. Horn, 'Rzemieślnicy żydowscy na Rusi Czerwonej na przełomie XVI i XVII w.' (Jewish craftsmen in Red Ruthenia at the turn of the sixteenth and seventeenth centuries), *BŻIH* 34, 1960, pp. 3–27.

in a book by Dr Anatol Leszczyński on Jews in the Białystok region 1651–1795, and in his account on Jewish crafts in this region.[22]

Apart from the works and sources listed above, this paper is based on town files from the Lwów and Lublin archives, the records of the Registry of the Crown of Poland (*Metryka Koronna*), documents on inspections of royal towns, the municipal records of Lwów and several other towns in Red Ruthenia, and other sources.

DEVELOPMENT OF JEWISH GUILDS IN THE POLISH COMMONWEALTH FROM 1613 TO 1795

Older historical works took the end of the sixteenth century, and then the turn of the sixteenth to seventeenth century, as the starting point for the first Jewish craft fraternities.[23] In modern literature, general opinion takes the year 1613, that is the date of a document establishing a furriers' guild in Kraków, as the start of the history of Jewish guilds in Poland. The development of Jewish guilds in the Polish-Lithuanian state depended primarily on the overall economic and political situation in the state, but also on the stage of development reached by Jewish crafts. Thus I have divided the history of the Jewish craft fraternities in the years 1613 to 1795 into three periods; 1613–48; 1649–1763, and 1764–95.

1613–48

In the first period, covering barely thirty-six years, the position of the town guilds, despite signs of the economic crisis of the Nobles' Commonwealth, was one of considerable power, and their struggle against the ever-growing strength of Jewish crafts was typically stubborn. This is evidenced by numerous guild acts prohibiting Jews from carrying out trades handled by various Christian guilds, and

---

[22] A. Leszczyński, 'Rzemiosło żydowskie ziemi bielskiej od połowy XVII w. do 1795 r.' (Jewish crafts in the province of Bielsko from the mid seventeenth century to 1975), *BŻIH* 101:1, 1977, pp. 17–19; idem, *Żydzi ziemi bielskiej od połowy XVII w. do 1795 r. – studium osadnicze, prawne i ekonomiczne* (Jews of the Bielsko region from the mid seventeenth century to 1795 – an economic, legal and colonial study), Wrocław, 1980, pp. 130–3.

[23] Schorr, *Żydzi w Przemyślu*, p. 63; I. Schipper, 'Dzieje gospodarcze Żydów Korony i Litwy w czasach przedrozbiorowych' (Economic history of the Crown and Lithuanian Jews in Pre-Partition Poland), in I. Schipper, A. Tartakower and A. Hafftka, eds, *Żydzi w Polsce Odrodzonej* (Jews in Reborn Poland) I, Warsaw, 1932, p. 157.

also by laws promulgated by both kings and *starostas* prohibiting Jews from rendering services to Christians.

On the whole, Jewish craftsmen paid scant heed to guild and town laws issued against them where they threatened their own means of livelihood. The period under discussion witnesses the first, unsuccessful, attempts of Jewish masters to obtain the status of a member with full rights of municipal craft corporations. As a result, Jews were forced to enter into contracts with the town guilds. At this time, such contracts were entered into by, among others, the butchers of Buśko (1624) and Tarnopol (1642), the Lwów furriers (1629, 1637, and 1643),[24] and the Grodzisk Wielkopolski tailors (1634).[25] In several towns, such as in Tarnów and Biała Cerkiew, Jews became members of Christian guilds; but in this period such membership was limited to paying a specified sum to the municipal guild for the right to practise one's profession.

Sometimes the matter of legal status of Jewish craftsmen was dealt with by the authorities of the Jewish communities, which contracted on their behalf with the town authorities. In this period the Jaworów[26] and Przemyśl *kehillot*,[27] among others, negotiated with the town authorities for contracts which governed the conditions under which Jews could proceed with their trades.

The legal status of Jewish craftsmen in the royal towns of the Grand Duchy of Lithuania was regulated by King Zygmunt III's privilege of 26 March 1629, according to which 'any Jewish craftsman of whatever trade is to be allowed to practise it without major obstacles [but] they must not be members of guilds'. This privilege was confirmed by King Władysław IV on 15 February 1633.[28] Thirteen years later King Władysław IV, in a privilege issued on 1 December 1646, allowed Jews of the 'upper towns of the Grand Duchy of Lithuania' to settle in them and freely carry on their professions.[29] On the strength of these privileges, Jewish

---

[24] Horn, 'Rzemieślnicy żydowscy', pp. 34, 44, 50–2; idem, *Żydzi na Rusi Czerwonej w XVI i pierwszej połowie XVII w. Działalność gospodarcza na tle rozwoju demograficznego* (Jews in Red Ruthenia in the sixteenth and the first half of the seventeenth centuries; economic activity against the background of their demographic development), Warsaw, 1975, p. 114.

[25] A. Heppner, I. Herzberg, *Aus der Vergangenheit und Gegenwart der Juden und judischen Gemeinden in der Provinz Posen*, Koźmin-Bydgoszcz 1904–14, p. 420.

[26] See Horn, *Żydzi na Rusi Czerwonej*, pp. 90–1.

[27] See Schorr, *Żydzi w przemyślu*, pp. 67–8; doc. 74, pp. 147–52.

[28] *Akty izdavayemye Vilenskuyu Arkheograficheskuju Komisyeyu dla rozbora drievnikh aktov*, V, Wilno, 1871, p. 301.

[29] Ibid. pp. 292–3.

craftsmen protested against harassment from the guilds and town authorities, and fought against being forced to pay for the right to work. In 1632, King Zygmunt III ordered the Wilno municipal council to see that the town guilds did not prevent the local Jewish craftsmen from carrying out their work. A year later, King Władysław IV permitted them to take up what were then called non-guild crafts, that is, haberdashery, furriery and glaziery.[30] But the Wilno and Grodno town guilds,[31] invoking different privileges, did not heed the pro-Jewish royal resolutions, and stopped their harassment only on condition that Jewish masters paid 'voluntary' contributions to the Christian craft guilds. The level of payment was negotiated between the parties every few years.

These negotiations undoubtedly quickened the process of creating independent Jewish craft fraternities. The first Jewish guild in Poland, whose establishment is confirmed by a document from the year 1613, in our possession, as already mentioned, was the furriers' fraternity in Kraków.[32] Probably a Jewish butchers' guild was already established in Lwów. By virtue of a royal edict of 1613, the owners of eight butcher's stalls in the centre of Lwów were allowed to engage in the slaughter of animals and selling of meat. The owner of each stall could employ one Jewish master butcher and three journeymen ('lanio magister Judaeus et tres coadiutores artem lanificum exercere possint').[33] The remark about Jewish master butchers and their assistants does suggest that a Jewish butchers' guild existed in Lwów in 1613, whose members were engaged in cutting and selling meat. At the beginning of the seventeenth century, a trimmers' guild was organized in Kraków, its members engaged in the trimming of meat (clearing away membranes and sinews) according to Jewish law. This guild, so Bałaban maintains, owned a 'guild letter' confirmed by the Kraków (Kazimierz) *kehilla*, which regulated, among other things, the appointment and employment of assistants. A new statute, adopted

---

[30] J. Morzy, 'Geneza i rozwój cechów wileńskich do końca XVII w.' (The origin and development of Wilno guilds to the end of the seventeenth century) in *Zeszyty Naukowe Uniwersytetu im. Adama Mickiewicza w Poznaniu, Historia* 4, 1959, p. 86.
[31] *AWAK* V, pp. 280–2.
[32] Bałaban, *Historia Żydów w Krakowie*, I, pp. 304–5; Wettstein, 'Kadmoniyot', no. 8.
[33] Central State Historical Archive of the Ukrainian Soviet S.R. in Lwów, collection: *Sąd Grodzki Lwowski* (further quoted as *SGL*), vol. 371, p. 1235.

in 1674, changed several points in the old guild law.[34] According to Bałaban, at the beginning of the seventeenth century, a guild of Jewish pedlars (*torbiarzy*, literally 'baggers') was established. Their constitution was signed by the community's secretary, Moses Schorr Liberls, a scribe in Kazimierz around the year 1620.[35]

In the 1620s at least two more Jewish craft corporations existed in Poland, those of the Lwów tailors and Kazimierz butchers. Our knowledge of the former is due to a 1627 complaint from the suburban tailors, who came under the *starosta's* jurisdiction and were organized in a separate guild from the municipal tailors in Lwów. The complaint against the Jewish tailors' guild (Judaicorum sartoricum contubernium) was caused by the fact that Jews were to employ Christian assistants in their workshops.[36] A 1629 order of the Kazimierz *kehilla*, regulating the powers of Jewish butchers, has survived. The execution of this order, according to the communal authorities, was to be supervised by the leading Jewish butchers,[37] which suggests the existence, even then, of a separate trimmers' and butchers' guild in that town.

Our first information about a Jewish furriers' guild in Lwów comes from the year 1637.[38] In 1640 a constitution was drawn up for the Jewish barber-surgeons' guild in Kazimierz.[39] Three years later, the Kazimierz goldsmiths' fraternity offered 400 Polish złoty to have the 'Kupa' synagogue in Kazimierz finished, obtaining two seats facing the altar in return.[40]

Altogether, according to the incomplete data we have, at least nine Jewish guilds were started in Poland between 1613 and 1648, in Kazimierz near Kraków and in Lwów. Two corporations were created by furriers and butchers in Kraków and Lwów, and one each by tailors, goldsmiths, barber-surgeons, trimmers and pedlars.

---

[34] Bałaban, *Historia Żydów w Krakowie* I, pp. 310–11; Wettstein, 'Divrey hefets', part 1, no. 21, pp. 22–4.
[35] Bałaban, *Historia Żydów w Krakowie* I, pp. 306–7.
[36] Bałaban, *Żydzi lwowscy*, part 2: *Materiały* (Sources), doc. 75, p. 99.
[37] Bałaban, *Historia Żydów w Krakowie* I, p. 308.
[38] *SGL*, vol. 388, p. 177, year 1637.
[39] Wettstein, 'Divrey hefets', part 1, no. 25, pp. 28–9.
[40] Bałaban, *Historia Żydów w Krakowie* I, p. 316.

1649–1763

Bohdan Chmielnicki's revolt in 1648 and the wars in the second half of the seventeenth century intensified the crisis in the Polish Commonwealth. In the domain of economics it brought about a sharp regress in agriculture and a very clear decline in the cities. Cultural regression followed. Extreme conservatism and clericalism started to dominate in the Commonwealth. Despite a noticeable improvement in culture and economics in the mid-eighteenth century, the end of the reign of King August III (the early 1760s) is generally accepted as the end of the great crisis of the Nobles' Commonwealth.

The Jewish population felt the effects of the crisis no differently from burghers and peasants. The first signs of the fall experienced by the Jewish economy in Poland were already apparent in the 1620s,[41] but a clear break was brought about by Bohdan Chmielnicki's revolt, as a result of which the Jewish population was decimated, and the majority (including craftsmen) found itself without any means of subsistence. Wars against Russia, Sweden, Turkey and the Tartars, which lasted almost without interruption until 1721, did the rest. The decline of Jewish crafts was deepened by the extreme poverty of the peasants and the reversion of towns to countryside which, by reducing the Jewish craftsmen's customers, forced many of them to emigrate to Germany, the Netherlands, Italy and Turkey.

Nevertheless, Jewish crafts did not break down completely. This situation was encouraged not only by the Jewish craftsman's ability to accommodate to dire working conditions combined with minimal earnings, but also by the protective policy of the Polish kings, notably Jan Kazimierz, Michał Korybut and Jan III Sobieski. By granting privileges to various Jewish communities, which enabled them to proceed freely with trade and crafts, these monarchs worked for the speedy regeneration of the towns which had been ruined by the Crown's enemies.[42] Also many leading noble families, linking their plans for the renewal of municipal life with the Jewish population, backed the development of Jewish crafts and trade, sometimes by promoting the birth of Jewish guilds

---

[41] Schipper, 'Dzieje gospodarcze', pp. 158–61.
[42] M. Horn, 'Król Jan III a Żydzi polscy' (King Jan III and Polish Jews), *BŻIH* 128:4 1983, pp. 5–9.

independently of the municipal guilds. Despite that, in many towns, especially the larger royal ones, anti-Jewish guild laws were in force, so that Jewish masters had to compromise and come to an agreement with the town guilds.[43] Some of those agreements or contracts had additional clauses stipulating the possibility of Jewish craftsmen's membership in Christian guilds. In this period mixed Christian–Jewish guilds appear in Nowy Sącz, Gniezno, Tarnogród, Jarosław, Rzeszów, Lubartów and other towns in the Polish Commonwealth.[44]

Despite continuous wars, the Jewish craftsmen, backed by Polish kings and magnates, and now working additionally for the needs of war, not only did not stop production in their traditional trades, but started working in new specialities as well. At the same time, they reduced their bespoke services and turned to mass production for a mass market. In the periods of relative peace, the number of Jewish craftsmen grew successively, which was conducive to the formation of Jewish craft corporations.

Taking advantage of the backing of *kehillot*, *voivodes*, *podwojewodes* and *starostas* in the royal towns, and of the leading nobles in the private towns, Jewish craftsmen from 1649 to 1763 formed at least forty-two guilds, among them one comprehensive fraternity of all craftsmen in that particular town (Lubartów), thirty-four separate guilds, that is, for a single profession, and seven mixed guilds, where masters of two or three crafts were represented.

Of these forty-two Jewish guilds (among them two fraternities of petty tradesmen), sixteen were established in royal towns, and twenty-six in towns that were nobles' property, principally magnates'.[45] There is no surviving material from which to infer the existence of any Jewish guild during this period on clergy estates.

1764–95

Although King Stanisław August reigned during a period of political decline and the partition of the Polish Commonwealth, at the same time this was a period of economic growth and of a renaissance in national culture. King Stanisław's reign saw changes in the social and economic domain and, even though Poland in these years of the

---

[43] See Horn, 'Powstanie i rozwój', part 2: years 1649–1795, *BŻIH* 143:3, 1987, p. 7.
[44] Ibid., p. 11.
[45] Ibid., p. 12.

Enlightenment was still largely feudal, some elements of capitalism started to emerge. Manufacturing started under royal, noble and burghers' and municipal auspices. Jewish merchants and financiers also played their part in the development of these relatively modern processes.

Taken on a nationwide scale, the number of Jewish workers in the new workshops at that time was minimal. Jews were still principally engaged in trade and financial operations, but the role of the Jewish craftsman grew, both absolutely and relatively. The most intensive development was in Great Poland, with somewhat less in the towns of the eastern provinces of the Commonwealth.

The monarch's policy towards Jewish industry did not basically change during this period. On the one hand, King Stanisław August confirmed most of the privileges granted by his predecessors, among them the privileges granting Jews the right to develop their crafts in some of the Crown's towns and in all towns of the Grand Duchy of Lithuania; on the other hand, he confirmed the town and guild privileges which prohibited, or drastically limited, Jewish rights to carry on their work.

We see a similar inconsistency in the Diet resolutions and in proposals for new laws put forward during various Diets. Indeed, a 1766 proposal for municipal reform included a condition that no burgher be refused guild membership, especially on the basis of religious difference,[46] *did not apply to Jewish craftsmen.* A 1768 Diet resolution treated Jews as a foreign element, harmful to the towns' and burghers' business. 'Because Jewry is intolerable for towns and its members do harm and take away their means of survival,' so runs the text of the Diet resolution, '[therefore] in all Our towns and elsewhere, Jews are allowed no other trades except what has been specifically agreed by accords with the towns.' Under this constitution, Jews were allowed 'neither to trade, nor run taverns, nor engage in crafts' without permission from the municipal authorities, under pain of a 500 grzywnas fine.[47]

Once this constitution was put into effect, the authorities of the bigger royal towns and town guilds began a frontal attack against Jewish crafts. In smaller royal towns and in most private towns, the situation of Jewish craftsmen was far more favourable. Jewish

---

[46] J. Michalski, 'Zagadnienie polityki antycechowej w czasach Stanisława Augusta' (The question of anti-guild activity in Stanisław August's time), *Przegląd Historyczny* 45, 1954, p. 63.
[47] *Volumina Legum*, VII, Petersburg, 1860, p. 352.

Table 18.1
Jewish craft guilds in the Polish Commonwealth 1613–1795

No.	Date of first mention	Name of guild	Type of guild			Town	Property		Province
			single trade	multiple trades	general (comprehensive)		Royal	Noble Magnate	
1	2	3	4	5	6	7	8	9	10
1	1613	Furriers	X	–	–	Kazimierz	X	–	Little Poland
2	1613	Butchers	X	–	–	Lwów	X	–	Red Ruthenia
3	about 1620	Trimmers	X	–	–	Kazimierz	X	–	Little Poland
4	about 1620	Peddlers	X	–	–	Kazimierz	X	–	Little Poland
5	1627	Tailors	X	–	–	Lwów	X	–	Red Ruthenia
6	1629	Butchers	X	–	–	Kazimierz	X	–	Little Poland
7	1637	Furriers	X	–	–	Lwów	X	–	Red Ruthenia
8	1640	Barber-surgeons	X	–	–	Kazimierz	X	–	Little Poland
9	1643	Goldsmiths	X	–	–	Kazimierz	X	–	Little Poland
10	1651	Butchers	X	–	–	Poznań	X	–	Great Poland
11	1652	Tailors	X	–	–	Grodno	X	–	G. Duchy of Lithuania
12	1654	Furriers	X	–	–	Przemyśl	X	–	Red Ruthenia
13	1662	Musicians	X	–	–	Leszno	–	X	Great Poland
14	1665	Brewers	X	–	–	Sokołów	–	X	Podlasie
15	1668–76	Haberdashers–loopmakers	–	X	–	Kazimierz	X	–	Little Poland
16	1669	Butchers	X	–	–	Przemyśl	X	–	Red Ruthenia
17	1676	Brewers–maltsters	–	X	–	Kazimierz	X	–	Little Poland
18	1678	Tailors	X	–	–	Lwów	X	–	Red Ruthenia

19	1686	Furriers	x	–	–	x	Rzeszów	–	x	Red Ruthenia
20	1689	Tailors	x	–	–	Przemyśl	x	–	Red Ruthenia
21	1700	Musicians	x	–	–	Kępno	–	x	Great Poland
22	1721	Tailors	x	–	–	Łuck	x	–	Wołyń
23	1722	Tailors	x	–	–	Czortków	–	x	Red Ruthania
24	1727	Tinsmiths–glaziers	–	x	–	Lwów	x	–	Red Ruthenia
25	1727	Tailors	x	–	–	Kazimierz	x	–	Little Poland
26	1730	Butchers	x	–	–	Międzybóż	–	x	Podole
27	1732	Tailors	x	–	–	Berdyczów	–	x	Ukraine
28	1734–50	General	–	–	x	Lurartów	–	x	Little Poland
29	1735	Butchers	x	–	–	Orla	–	x	Podlasie
30	1737	Haberdashers	x	–	–	Brody	–	x	Red Ruthenia
31	1737	Tailors	x	–	–	Poznań	x	–	Great Poland
32	1740	Tailors	x	–	–	Tarnów	–	x	Little Poland
33	1741	Goldsmiths	x	–	–	Leszno	–	x	Great Poland
34	1742	Tailors	x	–	–	Śrem	x	–	Great Poland
35	1743	Tailors	x	–	–	Tykocin	–	x	Podlasie
36	1750	Tailors–furriers	–	–	–				
37	1750	Tailors–furriers–haberdashers	–	x	–	Sudyłków	–	x	Ukraine
38	1754	Tailors	–	x	–	Nasielsk	–	x	Great Poland
39	1754	Pedlars	x	–	–	Kórnik	–	x	Great Poland
40	1756	Tailors	x	–	–	Lwów	x	–	Red Ruthenia
41	1757	Tailors	x	–	–	Sokołów	–	x	Podlasie
42	1757	Tailors	x	–	–	Brody	–	x	Red Ruthenia
43	1757	Furriers	x	–	–	Zabłudów	–	x	Podlasie
						Zabłudów	–	x	Podlasie

Table 18.1 continued
Jewish craft guilds in the Polish Commonwealth 1613–1795

No.	Date of first mention	Name of guild	Type of guild			Town	Property		Province
			single trade	multiple trades	general (comprehensive)		Royal	Noble Magnate	
1	2	3	4	5	6	7	8	9	10
44	1757	Tailors–furriers	–	X	–	Wieledniki	–	X	Ukraine
45	before 1760	Tailors–furriers	–	X	–	Biłgoraj	–	X	Little Poland
46	after 1760	Tailors	X	–	–	Biłgoraj	–	X	Little Poland
47	1761	Tailors	X	–	–	Stawiska	–	X	Podlasie
48	1762	Tailors	X	–	–	Jedwabne	–	X	Podlasie
49	1762	Bakers	X	–	–	Szkłów	–	X	G. Duchy of Lithuania
50	1762	Butchers	X	–	–	Szkłów	–	X	G. Duchy of Lithuania
51	1763	Tailors	X	–	–	Śniadowo	–	X	Podlasie
52	1764	Furriers	X	–	–	Leszno	–	X	Great Poland
53	1765	Butchers	X	–	–	Dubno	–	X	Wołyń
54	1765	Bakers	X	–	–	Dubno	–	X	Wołyń
55	1765	Goldsmiths	X	–	–	Lwów	X	–	Wołyń
56	1765	Goldsmiths	X	–	–	Lwów	X	–	Red Ruthenia
57	1766	Armourers	X	–	–	Lwów	X	–	Red Ruthenia
58	1767	Tailors–furriers	–	X	–	Ostróg	–	X	Wołyń
59	1767	Butchers	X	–	–	Ostróg	–	X	Wołyń
60	1769	Tailors	X	–	–	Sokal	X	–	Red Ruthenia
61	1770	Butchers	X	–	–	Brody	–	X	Red Ruthenia
62	1772	Bakers	X	–	–	Tykocin	–	X	Podlasie

MAURYCY HORN

#	Year	Trade				Town	Region
63	1772	Capmakers	X	–	–	X	Tykocin	Podlasie
64	1772	Haberdashers	X	–	–	X	Tykocin	Podlasie
65	1772	Hosiery workers	X	–	–	X	Tykocin	Podlasie
66	1772	Tailors	X	–	–	X	Leszno	Great Poland
67	1772	Butchers	X	–	–	X	Leszno	Great Poland
68	1773	Shoemakers–tanners	–	X	–	X		
69	1773	Tailors	X	–	–	X	Pawołocz	Ukraine
70	1777	Tailors	X	–	–	X	Pawołocz	Ukraine
71	1777	Furriers	X	–	–	X	Białystok	Podlasie
72	1777	Bakers	X	–	–	X	Białystok	Podlasie
73	1777	Barber-surgeons	X	–	–	X	Białystok	Podlasie
74	1779	Tailors	X	–	–	–	Gniezno	Great Poland
75	1779	Tailors	X	–	–	–	Kleczew	Great Poland
76	1780	Tailors–furriers	–	X	–	–	Latyczów	Podole
77	1781	Tailors	X	–	–	X	Lublin	Great Poland
78	1783	Tailors	X	–	–	X	Czerniejewo	Great Poland
79	1783	General	–	–	X	–	Wieledniki	Ukraine
80	1789	Tailors	X	–	–	X	Płock	Mazowsze
81	1789	Tailors	X	–	–	–	Kobylin	Great Poland
82	1790	Tailors–furriers	–	X	–	X	Międzyrzecz Podlaski	Podlasie
83	before 1792	Tailors	X	–	–	X	Skoki	Great Poland
84	before 1792	Tailors	X	–	–	X	Witkowo	Great Poland
85	before 1792	Tailors	X	–	–	X	Września	Great Poland
86	before 1792	Butchers–furriers	–	X	–	X	Września	Great Poland

Table 18.1 continued
Jewish craft guilds in the Polish Commonwealth 1613–1795

No.	Date of first mention	Name of guild	Type of guild			Town	Property		Province
			single trade	multiple trades	general (comprehensive)		Royal	Noble Magnate	
1	2	3	4	5	6	7	8	9	10
87	1792	Furriers	X	–	–	Lubraniec	–	X	Great Poland
88	1792	Furriers	X	–	–	Lubraniec	–	X	Great Poland
89	1792	Butchers	X	–	–	Lubraniec	–	X	Great Poland
90	1792	Haberdashers	X	–	–	Poznań	X	–	Great Poland
91	1792	Damask producers	X	–	–	Poznań	X	–	Great Poland
92	1792	Silk fabric producers	X	–	–	Poznań	X	–	Great Poland
93	1792	Tailors	X	–	–	Kutno	–	X	Mazowsze
94	1792	Furriers	X	–	–	Kutno	–	X	Mazowsze
95	1792	Haberdashers	X	–	–	Kutno	–	X	Mazowsze
96	1792	Capmakers	X	–	–	Kutno	–	X	Mazowsze
97	1792	Furriers	X	–	–	Płock	X	–	Mazowsze
98	1792	Tailors	X	–	–	Sochaczew	X	–	Mazowsze
99	1792	Furriers	X	–	–	Kobylin	–	X	Great Poland
100	1793	General	–	–	X	Kępno	–	X	Great Poland
101	1795	Tanners	X	–	–	Leszno	–	X	Great Poland
102	1795	Locksmiths	X	–	–	Leszno	–	X	Great Poland
103	1795	Haberdashers	X	–	–	Leszno	–	X	Great Poland
104	1794	Embroiderers	X	–	–	Leszno	–	X	Great Poland
105	1795	Tailors	X	–	–	Jarocin	X	–	Great Poland

craftsmen found good conditions, especially in towns belonging to magnates who, seeking ways of enlarging profits from their estates, issued licences for the establishment of separate Jewish guilds.

Altogether during the reign of King Stanisław August, at least fifty-four guilds came into being,[48] twenty-two of them in royal, and thirty-two in nobles' towns. Moreover, as appears from data from a Prussian poll of 1793/4, scores of other Jewish craft fraternities sprang up then in Great Poland.[49] These last have not been included in Table 18.1, a list of Jewish guilds constituted between 1613 and 1795.

As appears from Table 18.1, most guilds in Old Poland covered one profession only. There were only twelve guilds combining two or three professions, approximately 11 per cent of the total number, excluding the two fraternities of petty tradesmen in Lwów and Kazimierz near Kraków. We have even less information about comprehensive or general guilds, combining all independent craftsmen in a particular town. Only three such guilds were formed between 1734 and 1793. Of the single-profession guilds, the tailors were the most numerous and guilds were formed in thirty-four towns and one village. Next came the guilds of the haberdashers (five towns), bakers (four towns) and goldsmiths (three towns). There were two bodies for capmakers, barber-surgeons and musicians. Trimmers, brewers, armourers, weavers, tanners, locksmiths, embroiderers and hosiery workers who produced both damask and silk goods formed just one guild each.

Multi-profession guilds were found mostly in the garment industry. Six guilds covered tailors and furriers, one combined tailors with furriers and haberdashers, one combined haberdashers with loop-makers (*pętlarze*), shoemakers with tanners, brewers with maltsters, and tinsmiths with glaziers.

Until 1654, Jewish guilds were founded only in royal towns, only later were they formed in the magnates' towns as well. But from 1732, Jewish fraternities developed much faster in the magnates' estates than in the royal towns, so that finally, out of a total of 105 Jewish guilds established between 1613 and 1795, 68 (or 64.8 per cent) were in private towns and only 37 (or 35.2 per cent) in royal towns.

Of the number of guilds established in each town, most were to be found in Kazimierz and Leszno (9 in each). Lwów with 8 guilds

---

[48] See Horn, 'Powstanie i rozwój', part 2, p. 15.
[49] Ibid., p. 17.

was in third place, followed by Poznań and Tykocin with 5 each. The tailors' guild in Tykocin controlled 4 branch fraternities from the main guild. Until the mid seventeenth century, most Jewish guilds were instituted in Little Poland and Red Ruthenia; and in the second half of the eighteenth century, most comments on newly established Jewish guilds relate to towns in Great Poland and Mazowsze. (The information comes mainly from *Opis miast polskich* [Description of Polish towns] in 1793/4.) Most Jewish guilds were founded between 1613 and 1795: 32 in all in Great Poland; and 18 in Podlasie, 16 in Red Ruthenia, 15 in Little Poland, 7 in Mazowsze, 6 in Ukraine, 6 in Wołyń, 3 in the Great Duchy of Lithuania and 2 in Podole.

19 · Jewish Trade at the End of the Sixteenth Century and in the First Half of the Seventeenth Century

Jan M. Małecki

Trade, at least from the sixteenth century, was the Polish Jews' main occupation. It has aroused the interest of historians investigating Jewish history, and thus is relatively well known. Above all, we have the monumental work of Ignacy Schipper,[1] which – although published over half a century ago – is today the basic source of information, thanks to its collection of facts which includes a wide coverage of the Kraków Jews' trading activity.[2] Majer Bałaban's classic work on Kraków Jews also devotes a fair amount of space to the problem, among other detailed topics.[3] Post-war literature on Jewish trade in Old Poland, however, is very scanty,[4]

---

[1] Ignacy Schipper, *Dzieje handlu żydowskiego na ziemiach polskich* (History of Jewish trade on Polish territory), Warsaw, 1937.
[2] The term 'Kraków Jews' may appear inaccurate, as from the end of the fifteenth century Jews lived only in Kazimierz – formally and legally a separate township. Yet the 'Jewish town' was only a part of Kazimierz which, together with Kraków, Kleparz and suburbs evidently formed one economic unit. This is why we can talk about Kraków Jews, as is done in the scholarly literature and in the sources. In the Kraków customs registers, which are the basis of this chapter, the term 'Jew of Kraków' is constantly used.
[3] Majer Bałaban, *Dzieje Żydów w Krakowie i na Kazimierzu 1304–1868* (History of Jews in Kraków and Kazimierz), I: 1304–1655, 1st edn, Kraków, 1912 (reprinted: Kraków, 1986); 2nd edn, enlarged and revised, Kraków, 1931, under the title *Historia Żydów w Krakowie i na Kazimierzu 1304–1868*.
[4] Maurycy Horn, *Żydzi na Rusi Czerwonej w XVI w. i pierwszej połowie XVII w. Działalność gospodarcza na tle rozwoju demograficznego* (Jews in Red Ruthenia in the sixteenth and the first half of the seventeenth centuries: Economic activity against the background of their demographic development), Warsaw, 1975 (ch. 4); Daniel Tollet, 'Entreprise commerciale et structures urbaines en Pologne au XVIe et au XVIIe siècles (1588–1668). L'Example des Juifs de Poznań', in *Studia Historiae Oeconomicae*, 16, 1981, pp. 117–47; Anatol Leszczyński, 'Handel Żydów ziemi bielskiej od XVI w. do 1795' (Jewish trade in the Bielsko district from the 16th c. to

although interesting items of information on Jewish trade do find their way into numerous works on commercial exchange.[5] This, however, does not alter the fact that the topic under discussion has been neglected in the last few decades and needs to be re-examined.

The period on which I would like to concentrate here (the end of the sixteenth century and the first half of the seventeenth century) is included in the period covered by Schipper, namely, 1573–1648.[6] According to him, the advance in Jewish trade in Poland is already visible at the beginning of the sixteenth century – at first in foreign trade (with foreign countries and between bigger towns in the Polish-Lithuanian State), and later also in domestic trade (on the scale of regional and local markets). The year 1580 was to witness the peak of this trade. A certain instability was to appear later, mainly due to a crisis in credit which was reflected in the numerous bankruptcies of Jewish merchants, especially in the years 1610–30.[7] As a result of his research, Schipper arrived at the conclusion that by the first half of the sixteenth century, Jewish merchants already predominated over Poles in foreign trade, especially with the east.[8] As far as Kraków Jews are concerned, they took part in trade with Poznań, Lwów, Brześć Litewski and Wilno, whereas their participation in the Lublin fairs was small.[9]

The research of Schipper and other pre-war scholars was based on rich archival collections: municipal files, files of the Jewish communities, customs records from the treasury files, as well as contemporary polemical literature.[10] Most of these sources do not

1795), *BŻIH*, 2 (1981), pp. 33–51; Wiktor Ojrzyński, 'Żydzi z Przedborza w handlu mazowieckim w świetle akt komór celnych z lat 1764–1766' (Przedbórz Jews in the Mazowsze trade in the light of the customs-house files 1764–1766), *BŻIH*, 1: 2 (1982), pp. 71–6.

[5] See e.g. Jan M. Małecki, *Związki handlowe miast polskich z Gdańskiem w XVI i pierwszej połowie XVII wieku* (Trade relations of Polish towns with Gdańsk in the 16th c. and first half of the 17th c.), Wrocław, 1968, pp. 52–4; Joseph Reinhold, *Polen/Litauen auf den Leipziger Messen des 18. Jahrhunderts*, Weimar 1971, *passim*; Andrzej Wyrobisz, 'Materiały do dziejów handlu w miasteczkach polskich na początku XVIII wieku' (Sources for the history of trade in small Polish towns at the beginning of the 18th c.), *Przegląd Historyczny*, 63 (1971), pp. 703–16.

[6] Schipper, *Dzieje handlu*, pp. 71–93.
[7] Ibid., pp. 123–33.
[8] Ibid., pp. 30–52.
[9] Ibid., p. 53.
[10] Especially an anti-Jewish work by Sebastian Miczyński, *Zwierciadło Korony Polskiej urazy ciężkie i utrapienia wielkie, które ponosi od Żydów wyrażające* (The mirror of the Crown of Poland, which expresses all the strong resentments and

exist today. This is true not only of the Jewish archives destroyed during the Nazi occupation, but also of the priceless customs registers from pre-partition Poland burned in Warsaw in 1944. Almost no trace has remained of the records after the seventeenth and eighteenth centuries. That the sixteenth-century records are known to us is due entirely to the works of Roman Rybarski who, in the second volume of his pioneering work on Polish sixteenth-century trade,[11] published data from them in the form of tables. Thus we have no possibility of verifying Rybarski's data or of checking details. Tables permit a great variety in interpretation, an example of which may be the estimates of the amount of Jewish trade in sixteenth-century Poland made by Rybarski himself and by Schipper. It was clearly reasons of a non-scholarly character which led Rybarski to diminish the role of the Jews,[12] while Schipper exaggerated it. When the former wrote about the weakness of Jewish trade in sixteenth-century Poland,[13] the latter, on the basis of the same tables, compiled by Rybarski, wrote of the domination of Jews in Polish trade.[14]

Thus, the subject of Jewish trade in Poland needs new research based on hitherto unused authorities.[15] We are in possession of a very valuable source material, containing detailed information, capable of statistical analysis, which has not so far been used by historians of Jewish trade. These are the customs registers (*regestra thelonei*) kept in the State Archive (formerly the Municipal Archive) in Kraków.[16] As a reward for its contribution in 1587 to defence against Archduke Maximilian's army, Kraków was granted the right in 1589 to collect customs dues. Thus the royal custom house in Kraków ceased to function. The customs registers were

great troubles, which it suffers from the Jews), Kraków, 1618, includes many invaluable details of information about Jewish trade.

[11] Roman Rybarski, *Handel i polityka handlowa Polski w XVI stuleciu. I: Rozwój handlu i polityki handlowej, II: Tablice i materiały statystyczne* (Polish trade and trade policy in the sixteenth century development of trade and trade policy; II: Tables and statistical material), Poznań, 1928–9 (republished Warsaw, 1958).
[12] Roman Rybarski, a distinguished economist and economic historian (killed in the Auschwitz concentration camp in 1942) was active in the *Narodowa Demokracja* known for its anti-Jewish attitudes, propaganda and activity.
[13] Rybarski, *Handel i polityka* I, pp. 223–7.
[14] Schipper, *Dzieje handlu*, pp. 35–6.
[15] It is possible to do further research on the basis of traditionally used sources, such as the municipal records, as has been confirmed by Daniel Tollet's works on Poznań Jews in the Vasa era.
[16] AP. Kraków (APK), MS Kat. Gł. 2115–273.

kept in the town archives and this is why they have survived to our day, with the exception of a few years' entries. We have Kraków customs registers from the years 1589–1772 (excepting the years 1689/1700 and 1713/1736) and for the year 1792.[17] They consist of routine entries in Polish, usually including the merchant's name (sometimes the wagoner's as well), his place of origin, number of horses and wagons in the convoy, plus the goods carried: description, quantity and value, especially in regard to foreign trade.[18]

In fact, not all goods conveyed in and out of Kraków were entered at customs. A certain, fairly small, proportion was carried duty-free on horseback. Water-borne or smuggled goods escaped registration. Thus the data obtained from the customs registers should be treated as a base line. But in general they give a fairly accurate picture of Kraków's domestic and foreign trade, within which we can isolate Jewish trade.[19] In this way the Kraków customs registers appear as a highly valuable source not only for our knowledge of trade carried out by Kraków Jews but also for the history of Kraków's trade with Jews outside the town, against the general background of trade in the town.

Customs entries are an ideal data base for statistical analysis. But long and laborious research is needed to complete this work. This paper is just an attempt to analyse, on a limited scale, entries from two years separated by almost half a century, 1593 and 1636.

The year 1593 is the first in which we have a complete annual customs register.[20] The 1636 register, coming at the peak of Kraków's trade, is one of the most extensive.[21] Therefore both these registers, on analysis, give a relatively full picture of commercial activity, and the interval between them allows us to

---

[17] Altogether 136 volumes called *Regestra Thelonei civitatis Cracoviensis*, 20 volumes of 'new' tax (*Regestra novi thelonei*) covering 1659–79, 3 volumes of 'bridge' tax (*Regestra pontalium Cracoviensium*), covering 1615–28.

[18] Jan. M. Małecki, 'Księgi celne krakowskie i ich znaczenie jako źródła do historii handlu', (Kraków customs registers and their importance as sources for the history of trade), *Sprawozdanie z posiedzeń Oddziału PAN w Krakowie*, January–June 1960, Kraków, 1961, pp. 47–9; idem, 'Krakowskie księgi celne i problem ich wydania' (Kraków Customs Registers and the Problem of Publication), in *Kwartalnik Historii Kultury Materialnej*, 9:2, 1961, pp. 252–73.

[19] The person recording customs due usually made a note next to the name of the merchant or wagoner indicating that he was a Jew. Very occasionally, one comes across entries without this marginal note when the name recorded clearly indicates a Jew.

[20] APK, MS Kat. Gł. 2117.

[21] Ibid., MS 2146.

capture the development of certain tendencies. It should be noted, however, that in presenting these data, a very primitive statistical method (albeit the only possible one at this stage of research) was used: a simple listing of entries for Jewish merchants, without any differentiation of the quantity and quality of convoys. Although such a selective and simplified analysis can hardly be considered satisfactory, it gives us an approximate view of the situation, and with its pointers to possible further lines of investigation, can still be useful.

Firstly, we can study the territorial range of Jewish trade in Kraków. The area covered by Jewish merchants is close to that of Christian merchants, but with some characteristic features (see Table 19.1).

Table 19.1
Territorial range of Jewish foreign trade, by number of entries in the Kraków customs registers

Country	Town	1593	1636
(abroad)	(unspecified)	16	65
Bohemia	Prague	33	2
Moravia	(unspecified)	39	4
	Kromieryź	–	5
	Lipnik		
	Morawski	2	2
	Nikolsburg (Mikulov)	–	3
	Olomuniec	1	–
	Prościejów (Prostejov)	2	6
Silesia	(unspecified)	6	7
	Bielsko	1	–
	Brzeg	1	–
	Cieszyn	1	3
	Franksztyn (Ząbkowice Śląskie)	2	–
	Jelenia Góra	–	1
	Nysa	8	11
	Breslau	8	9
Hungary	(unspecified)	1	10
	Bardiów	–	1
Spisz	Lewocza	1	–
Austria	Vienna	2	1
Italy	Venice	1	–
?	Nerbark (?)	2	–
	TOTAL:	126	130

Source: AP, Kraków, MS Kat. Gl. 2117, 2146.

Table 19.2
Territorial range of Jewish domestic trade, by number of entries in the Kraków customs registers

Province (*wojewodztwo*)	Town	1593	1636
Kraków	Będzin	8	–
	Bochnia	4	–
	Lelów	21	22
	Miechów	–	1
	Myślenice	–	1
	Nowy Sącz	–	1
	Olkusz	33	23
	Oświęcim	3	2
	Pilica	1	4
	Wiśnicz	–	–
	Wodzisław	1	9
	Zator	1	–
	Żarnowiec	–	2
	Żmigród	–	1
Sandomierz	Chęciny	23	19
	Nowe Miasto Korczyn	7	9
	Opatów	9	3
	Opoczno	1	–
	Osiek	1	–
	Pacanów	13	–
	Pińczów	14	14
	Połaniec	2	1
	Przedbórz	7	2
	Radoszyce	–	2
	Sandomierz	5	–
	Secemin	–	2
	Stopnica	3	–
	Szydłów	23	2
	Tarnów	–	2
	Wiślica	1	–
Ruthenia	Jarosław	17	33
	Kańczuga	–	2
	Mościska	–	2
	Lesko	2	2
	Lwów	10	28
	Przemyśl	2	16
	Rzeszów	5	3
Lublin	Kurów	1	–
	Lublin	70	119
	Łuków	1	2
Mazowsze	Radzymin	1	–
	Warsaw	8	–

Table 19.2 continued

Province (wojewodztwo)	Town	1593	1636
Rawa	Łowicz	–	1
Sieradz	Koniecpol	–	3
	Piotrków	1	8
	Wieluń	–	1
Łęczyca	Łęczyca	2	5
Kalisz	Gniezno	9	3
	Kalisz	1	2
	Krotoszyn	–	1
Poznań	Poznań	–	1
	Wschowa	–	6
Brześć Kujawski	Brześć Kujawski	1	1
Chełmno	Toruń	4	10
Prussia	(unspecified)	–	3
Mińsk	Mińsk Litewski	–	1
?	Karbowa (?)	–	1
?	Wodzimin (?)	–	1
	TOTAL:	315	379

Source: AP, Kraków, MS Kat. Gł. 2117, 2146.

Where foreign trade is concerned, the closest contacts in 1593 were maintained with Prague, which is understandable when we recall the numerous Prague Jews who settled in the 'Jewish town' of Kazimierz. Yet it was mainly Prague merchants who came to Kraków, far less frequently Kraków citizens who travelled to Prague. The second region with strong commercial ties with Kraków – Moravia – was the Kraków merchants' exclusive domain. Kraków Jews travelled with goods to such Moravian towns as Lipnik, Olomuniec, Prostejov, Kromieryż and Nikolsburg (Mikulov). Fairly strong commercial activity also went on with Silesian towns; Breslau, Nysa, Ząbkowice, Brzeg, Bielsko and others. Hungary, the towns of Spisz, Austria (Vienna) and Venice appear only sporadically on the trade routes of Kraków Jews.

In 1636 the picture changes. Prague disappears almost completely from Kraków's commercial partners (two entries against 33 in 1593) and trade with Moravia drops (20 entries against 44 in 1593). Possibly the Thirty Years War influenced the situation. Instead, trade with Hungary and Silesia, with Nysa taking the lead, and Cieszyn and Jelenia Góra appearing, grows visibly.

In Jewish domestic trade (see Table 19.2), Kraków above all maintained strong ties with towns known for their well-attended fairs and markets: Lublin, Jarosław and, on a smaller scale, Gniezno. Goods were also exchanged with most of the Commonwealth's bigger towns: primarily Lwów, then Przemyśl, Warsaw, Sandomierz, Toruń and others. But the liveliest trade relations were maintained with the smaller towns of Little Poland – especially those in whose vicinity Jewish communities were relatively strong. These included Chęciny, Szydłów, Lelów, Olkusz, Pińczów, Pacanów, Opatów, Nowe Miasto, Korczyn, Przedbórz, Będzin and Wodzisław among many others.

In 1636 the pattern of domestic trade changes, and trade with main centres, especially in the east, grows: with Tarnów, Rzeszów, Przemyśl, Lwów. Very occasionally, towns further away appear, such as Łowicz, Poznań, Lithuanian Mińsk or Prussian towns. At the same time, Kraków Jews took a greater share in their town's commerce, compared to Kraków's traders from abroad. In general, Kraków merchants carried on business with major commercial centres, while Kraków's relations with the smaller towns of Little Poland were maintained mainly by Jews from those towns. However, in purely local trade, that is between Kraków and its immediate surroundings, which took place at the weekly market, Jewish participation was insignificant. This impression may, however, be simply the effect of the character of the sources upon which our information is based, as the customs officers took very little notice of goods aimed at the local market (mainly cattle brought to town for slaughter).

Another subject for closer investigation is the type of goods dealt with in Jewish trade (mainly foreign trade). On the whole, we can say that the same situation obtained as in Christian trade, but for the occurrence of certain characteristic items in Jewish transactions.

In 1593 the main imports to Kraków by Jewish merchants, both from the bigger centres and the small towns of Little Poland, were hides, wax and honey. Also many oriental goods, that is of Turkish or Tartar origin, such as oriental fabrics (*czamlet, muchajer*), Turkish carpets, and so on, were imported. These goods, especially hides and wax, were destined for re-export. Jewish merchants exported locally produced goods, for example velvet caps, Jewish books and even 'pharmaceutical products'. The pattern of trade in 1636 was similar: wax, honey, hides and furs came to Kraków and were then exported as principal items of trade. There were goods which up till then had been exclusively handled by Christian merchants: lead and lead oxide from the Olkusz mines, dried plums and apples, salt herring and other fish, as well as wool from Great Poland. Cinnamon, ginger and sugar were imported – not from the east, but from the north, from Toruń, at what was effectively the trade crossroads. Also, smaller quantities of feathers, pots, even firewood on rare occasions, were imported by Jews – as well as droves of oxen. A completely new item of merchandise appeared in Jewish exports and in vast quantities – vodka, referred to as Russian alcohol in the customs registers. Moreover Jews exported beef cattle (oxen), feathers, some lead and litharge to Hungary, sulphur and groceries. They did not, other than on a few occasions, trade in salt. Specifically Jewish exports in 1636 were grey squirrel caps, 'Jewish birettas' and Hebrew books.

From abroad Jewish merchants imported many different wares. In 1593 these included: Silesian linen and woollen cloth, silk fabrics, Moravian wines, saffron, haberdashery, such as laces, thread and mirrors. These goods, often known as market-stall wares, were then distributed to all the towns of Little Poland, big and small alike. In 1636, besides those already mentioned, the following goods appear as imports to Kraków: paper, steel products (especially scythes), Italian wines and citrus fruits. These goods were then sold by Jews in Little Poland and further afield.

How big was this trade? Together with entries, which do not specify the origins of goods imported by Kraków Jews, the 1593 register lists about 450 Jewish convoys, and the 1636 one over 600. It was a considerable growth – by almost one-third (see Table 19.3). At the same time, the total number of entries (that is, foreign plus domestic) in the Kraków customs house dropped by

Table 19.3
Jewish trade, by number of entries in the Kraków customs registers

Trade	1593	1636
Domestic	315	379
Foreign	126	130
unspecified[a]	26	105
TOTAL:	467	614
Growth dynamics	100	131

[a] Entries of goods brought to Kraków by Jewish merchants from unspecified towns. (One entry in 1593 and one in 1636 refers to goods sent from Kraków to places not specified further.)
Source: AP, Kraków, MS Kat. Gł. 2117, 2146.

almost 30 per cent. Reconciling these figures leads us to the conclusion that Jewish trade in 1593 constituted about 5 per cent of Kraków's total business, growing to about 9–10 per cent by 1636. This would have been far less – at least as far as Kraków trade is concerned – than was assumed by Schipper. On the other hand, it does testify to the fast growth of Jewish business representation in Kraków's total trade at that time.

In any case, these calculations need careful consideration, as convoys differed in size and value. As the total picture is difficult to obtain, let us make use of specific instances. The following are some examples of foreign trade in 1593:

11 January: Marek, a Prague Jew, brought velvet and woollen cloth valued by the customs officers at 125 grzywnas.[22]

26 January: Izaak, a Prague Jew, exported weasel hides, wolf furs etc., valued at 86 grzywnas.

26 February: a Kraków Jew, Jeleń, sent to Wien (Vienna) 3,100 squirrel furs and 2,500 other hides by means of 18 horses.

2 March: a Kraków Jew, Marek Aleksander, sent to Olomuniec fur coats, chamois leather, oriental fabrics etc. to the total value of 160 grzywnas.

5 March: a Kraków Jew, Aron son of Abraham, sent to Breslau 1340 Russian hides. (He was exempted from dues on the testimony of Marek, an elder of the Jewish community.)

15 March: a wagoner, Janusz Rożanka, carried merchandise of a Kraków Jew, Abraham, to Moravia (hides, oriental fabrics, clothing) valued at 127 grzywnas, and the 'old and new' books of Dr Marek, Jew of Kraków.

16 March: a Kraków Jew, Abraham, Marek's son-in-law, sent 3,900 grey squirrel furs, ox hides and other skins, valued in total at 167 grzywnas.

19 March: a Kraków Jew, Izaak the printer (probably Izaak Prostic, the son of Aron) sent Jewish books to Moravia, doubtless from his printing house.

---

[22] One grzywna equalled 48 groszys. According to Zbigniew Żabiński's estimations for one grosz, at the end of the sixteenth century one could buy a little less goods than for one *trofa*. *Trofa* is a biological ratio (co-efficient) equal to the cost of one day's norm of food of a working man: Z. Żabiński, *Systemy pieniężne na ziemiach polskich* (Monetary systems on Polish territory), Wrocław, 1981, p. 102.

> **14 July**: a Kraków Jew, Markuse's son Abram, reported two big convoys containing 10,000 grey squirrel and other furs, valued at 550 grzywnas.
> **5 August**: the Kraków Jew Jeleń sent to Moravia various hides (raw ox, calf, Russian leather, grey squirrel), ribbons, Jewish books, to a total value of 327 grzywnas.
> **17 September**: a Kraków Jew, Józef Długi, sent to Nysa oriental fabrics and Jewish books, all valued at 72 grzywnas.
> **21 October**: a Kraków Jew, Franczek Szczebrzeszyński, sent 40 sables valued at 90 grzywnas, and next day another sable convoy valued at 7 grzywnas, to Breslau.[23]

Many more such examples may be cited.

Big convoys were seldom used in domestic trade. Their contents are harder to pin down, as they were taxed not by value but by the number of horses in the team. Thus there was no need to spell out in detail the goods carried. Yet even on the basis of the data we have, we can estimate some of the convoys registered at the customs house to have been of considerable size. For example:

> **12 May**: a Lesko Jew, Icyk, carried goods home with 4 carts drawn by 12 horses. On the same day, another Lesko Jew, Samuel, carried goods with 10 horses.
> **21 May**: hides for the Kraków Jew Jeleń were carried with 12 horses from Lwów.
> **4 June**: a Kraków Jew, Jakub, Abram's son-in-law, sent cloth to Lublin with 11 horses.
> **12 July**: goods were brought with 12 horses from Lublin for the Kraków Jews Mojżesz, Aron and Abram.[24]

The 1,636 customs registers record even higher numbers of big convoys to Jewish merchants, who occasionally exported large quantities of hides and furs. For example:

> **4 January**: a Kraków Jew, Jeleń Toszka, sent abroad 1,500 grey squirrel furs and 4 otters valued at 122 grzywnas.[25]
> **28 January**: a Kraków Jew, Jakub Pinkus, sent 550 grey

---

[23] APK, MS Kat. G. 2117, ff. 20, 61, 139, 150, 153, 178, 180, 280, 354, 376, 418, 482, 484.
[24] Ibid., ff. 264, 284, 309, 350.
[25] In the 1630s one grosz equalled about 1/3 *trofa* (see note 22): Z. Żabiński, *Systemy*, p. 128.

squirrel furs, 18 Morocco leathers and 2 rabbit furs, valued in total at 537½ grzywnas.

8 April: a Kraków Jew, Szymon Wolf, sent 450 Russian leathers and 2,000 grey squirrel furs valued at 600 grzywnas.

23 September: the same Szymon Wolf's fur and hide convoy (600 Russian leathers and 9,000 grey squirrel furs) was valued at 675 grzywnas.

26 November: a Nikolsburg Jew, Lewek, exported 50 horse and cattle hides.[26]

Also large consignments of groceries and such like were sent from Kraków, mainly to Hungary, for example:

9 April: a Kraków Jew, Salomon Lewkowicz, paid duty on a consignment to Hungary of 4 stone of sugar,[27] 9 pounds of mace,[28] 490 pounds of woollen yarn and 50 bolts of dyed linen, to a total value of 495 grzywnas.

31 July: a Kraków Jew, Wolf Jakubowicz, exported via Oświęcim 12 stone of pepper valued at 135 grzywnas.

18 September: two Jews, a small trader Marek from Kraków and Izaak from Prościejów, together sent 98 stone of sugar valued at 1,260 grzywnas.

15 December: the above-mentioned Salomon Lewkowicz sent a convoy to Hungary valued at 303 grzywnas, consisting of spices (pepper, ginger, cloves, bay leaves), oriental fabrics (*muchajer, perpetuana*), hosiery and other 'knick-knacks'.[29]

On a smaller scale, Jews exported oxen, but here also there were occasional large consignments, for example on 14 July, a herd of 300 oxen was driven across the border by a Lwów Jew, Zelman Mojżeszowicz.[30] Jewish merchants of Kraków exported large consignments of alcohol as well, for example on 8 January, Abram Izraelowicz – 100 gallons;[31] on 10 November, Salomon Lewkowicz – 125 gallons; on 17 September, Wolf Hesterczyk – 120 gallons; on 24 December, Jakub Szczęsny – 100 gallons.[32]

---

[26] APK, MS Kat. Gł. 2146, ff. 9, 38, 97, 243, 310.
[027] One stone was equal to about 12 kg.
[028] One pound was equal to about 0.4 kg.
[029] APK, MS Kat. Gł. 2146, ff. 97, 196, 239, 326.
[030] Ibid., f. 180.
[031] Gallon = about 4 litres.
[032] APK, MS Kat. Gł. 2146, ff. 13, 292, 298, 336.

Large convoys from abroad arrived less often. Among them were: on 28 February, 525 warps[33] of Moravian cloth belonging to Izaak Jakubowicz of Kraków (jointly with a Christian merchant Franciszek Cyrus); on 19 November, Szymon Wolf's convoy of Italian wine and citrus fruits on 12 carts drawn by 53 horses (!); on 24 November, a convoy of 5 carts belonging to Salomon Lewkowicz of Kraków with groceries – pepper, olive oil, rice, raisins, etc.[34]

In domestic trade, single large convoys did take place – usually of oxen for Kraków butchers (on 8 July, the Kraków Jew Józef – 80 head; on 31 October, the Kraków Jew Jezko – 100 head), but also of other articles. (On 8 October, the Kraków Jew Marek took 50 stone of saltpetre, valued at 187 grzywnas, to Prussia; the Chęciny Jew Izaak brought to Kraków, on 26 May, 150 stone of wax).[35]

Naturally, medium-sized convoys predominate in the customs register, but, alongside them, small-scale commercial operations by Jewish merchants or pedlars, especially in domestic trade, can be traced. These were principally tradesmen from small towns, who brought goats, hides, honey, wax, and so on to Kraków, and usually left with 'pedlar's wares' in small quantities. Typical are the following, chosen from among many others:

15 January: a Przedbórz Jew, Mojżesz, took home pedlar's goods with one horse.
9 February: the Kraków Jew Marek, brought in goats, using two horses, from Pinczów.
8 March: a Lelów Jew, David, brought in honey and took back plums (dried, of course) with a two-horse cart.
12 May: a Wiślica Jew, Aron, brought in hides on one horse.
11 September: a Pacanów Jew, Jakub, brought in 'some wax' on one horse.[36]

Similar entries may be found in the 1,636 registers:

9 January: a Wodzisław Jew, Wiktor, took home a barrel of herring.

---

[33] Warp-length measures varied depending on the type of cloth and was equal to about 17–32 metres.
[34] APK, MS Kat. Gł 2146, ff. 66, 302, 309.
[35] Ibid., ff. 176, 284, 260, 138.
[36] Ibid., ff. 31, 90, 161, 260, 510.

280   THE ECONOMY

> **22 January**: a Kraków Jew, Jonas Złotnik, sent a firkin of dried plums to Olkusz.
> **4 March**: a Jew, Marcin, brought in firewood on a cart.
> **11 March**: an Olkusz Jew, Jakub, brought in a barrel of honey.
> **14 March**: a Kraków Jew, Lewek Daniel, brought in a cartload of pots.
> **26 March**: a Kraków Jew, Wolf Będziński, sent a one-horse cart with goods to Opatów.
> **4 June**: a Lelów Jew, Marek, took home one cart of scythes.[37]

Because the entries include the name of the duty-payer, the customs registers give us an overall view of Jewish merchants both in Kraków and outside. Often we come across merchants known elsewhere in literature, such as the Jeleń family, Lewek Świetlik, Wolf Esterczyk, Józef Włoch, Marek Bocian and others. But we also come across hitherto unknown persons, who carried on a high level of trade. Szymon Wolf may serve as an example of a large-scale businessman who is not mentioned at all in Schipper's work, and only once – and then not as a merchant – by Majer Bałaban.[38] In the light of the customs registers, he appears as one of the biggest Jewish merchants in Kraków in the first half of the seventeenth century. In the 1,636 registers, 109 convoys were recorded as sent in his name, that is 17 per cent of all entries for Jewish trade. Possibly there were even more convoys, as entries under the name 'Kraków Jew Szymon', which could apply to him, were not taken into consideration in our calculations.

Trade operations conducted by Szymon Wolf had a wide range, centring on Lublin at fairs and market time, and covering Lwów, Jarosław, Przemyśl and places abroad. Principal merchandise of that time included hides, furs, wax, scythes, groceries and pedlar's wares. Convoys sent by Szymon Wolf were not only numerous but also large (some of them mentioned above), although there were also some smaller ones.[39] The fact that Wolf sent and received convoys sometimes several times a day testifies to the scale of his

---

[37] Ibid., ff. 15, 31, 71, 79, 82, 138, 148.
[38] M. Bałaban, *Historia Żydów*, 1st edn, p. 172 (mentioned as Simon Wolff under the year 1648); 2nd edn, p. 355 (mentioned as Kraków judge under the year 1644 – Simon Wolff son of Abraham).
[39] On 25 April 1636 he received from Lublin a variety of merchandise on one cart drawn by one horse – APK, MS Kat. Gł. 2146, f. 112.

operations. For example, on 1 July 1636, he sent two convoys of scythes to Lublin and received from there a big convoy of Russian hides (4 carts with 13 horses); on 28 November, he exported 700 Russian hides on 3 carts drawn by 18 horses, and a second convoy of 23 quintals of wax,[40] receiving from Lublin 2 wagons with 8 horses, which brought in various goods.[41]

Customs registers may also, to a certain degree, enable us to investigate trade privileges of Jews living in Kraków and outside, in their practical application rather than legal theory. But this would require further analysis. For now, even a rough observation shows that these privileges were big. In particular, the dispensation from paying dues was comparable to the position of Christian merchants. In small towns, however, these dispensations differed. We can also use the registers to trace signs of co-operation between Jewish and Christian merchants, possibly indicating the existence of trade partnerships.

The above observations, though far from being a complete analysis of the subject, enable us to formulate several conclusions and propose further lines of research. Despite the enormous damage caused by the war, sources still exist for the history of Jewish trade in Poland which have not so far been used. These include the Kraków customs registers with their rich store of information. They not only broaden our knowledge of various subjects, but confirm or even correct some of our current hypotheses. But they need basic research and statistical analysis. Publication of these sources – best in full, which might be difficult due to technical reasons (the sheer size of the project), or in a selection of certain chronological sections – is highly desirable. Such an edition would serve not only economic historians but also researchers in the history of Polish trade at home and abroad.

---

[40] A quintal was equal to 5 stones, i.e. about 60 kg.
[41] APK, MS Kat. Gł 2146, ff. 171–2, 313–14.

20 · Jewish Trade in the Century of Kraków's Decline

Janina Bieniarzówna

The mid seventeenth century marks the beginning of a century of decline for Kraków. The starting point of this period is easily dated. The great plague – probably black smallpox – of 1651–2 which decimated the town's population, and the Swedish invasion of 1655, followed by two years of occupation, mark a distinct turning point in the history of Kraków. A once populous town, humming with activity, now declined rapidly, unable to rebuild its industry and struggling with tax payments. There was a drop in trade, both foreign and domestic, handled by Kraków businessmen, including Jews, which went hand in hand with the general deterioration of the economic situation.

The return of the plague, which affected the town worst in the years 1677–80 and 1707–10, brought about a rapid drop of population in every age group. The Jewish quarter felt its effects to a far higher degree than Kraków proper, owing to its bad housing conditions. The politically turbulent Saxon period, and especially the second Swedish invasion, sharpened the crisis and only the second half of the eighteenth century brought about a gradual improvement, whose movements can be followed in trade figures.

I should like to examine the situation in Jewish trade as shown by the Kraków customs registers from the years 1661, 1681, 1701 and 1751.[1] A fairly large gap of fifty years in the eighteenth century is due to the absence of records between 1713 and 1744. Of older works dealing with this topic, the monographs of Ignacy Schipper and Majer Bałaban remain indispensable; among more recent ones, Mariusz Kulczykowski's work on Kraków as a trading centre in the

---

[1] Wojewódzkie Archiwum Państwowe w Krakowie (WAPKr), *Reg. Thel.*, nos. 2177, 2196, 2203, 2217, 2219.

second half of the eighteenth century should be mentioned.[2]

Two groups of issues show up from the Kraków customs registers: exclusively economic and socio-economic problems. In the first case, one must look at the development of Jewish trade, noting its range and influence and its categories of goods, all of which can be specified with a fair degree of precision. Where social questions are concerned one can point to the main individual merchants and relations between Jewish and Christian trade, including the money trade, although this goes beyond our research. While the purpose of this chapter does not permit deeper analysis, the lines of further research may be indicated.

I should like to begin with the statistics based on the number of entries for Jewish trade. We have 200 of these in 1661 (including Jews in Christian merchants' groups), 80 entries for 1681, 75 for 1701, and 321 for 1751. Thus, never in the period of Kraków's decline were the pre-mid-seventeenth-century figures reached, as, according to Jan Małecki's research, the number of entries in 1593 was 467, and in 1636 was 614.[3] Thus taking the year 1593 as a base, the index would be 131 for the year 1636, 42.8 for 1661, 17.1 for 1681, 16 for 1701, and finally 68.7 for the year 1751. From the nadir at the beginning of the eighteenth century (please note that MS 2209 covering the post-plague years 1710–11 has been omitted in this chapter) a gradual improvement took place. The 321 entries for Jewish trade in 1751 constitute 40 per cent of all that year's entries.

FOREIGN TRADE

The year 1661, with its 39 entries, is well documented in foreign trade. Trade with Silesia appears to be fairly lively (Breslau 10 entries, Nysa 1, Silesia, with no town specified, 2). The town of Krems on the Danube comes next with 10 entries. Jews took 9 transports 'extra Regnum'. Trade with Moravia, Leipzig and Lubowla shows up in one entry each.

---

[2] Ignacy Schipper, *Dzieje handlu żydowskiego na ziemiach polskich* (History of Jewish trade on Polish territory), Warsaw, 1937; Majer Bałaban, *Historia Żydów w Krakowie i na Kazimierzu 1304–1868* (History of Jews in Kraków and Kazimierz), 2nd edn, Kraków, 1936; Mariusz Kulczykowski, *Kraków jako ośrodek towarowy Małopolski zachodniej w drugiej połowie XVIII wieku* (Kraków as the trading centre of western Little Poland in the second half of the eighteenth century), Warsaw, 1963.

[3] See Jan M. Małecki, this volume, ch. 19.

In their trade with Krems, Jews were interested mainly in the import of iron goods, buying – like the biggest Kraków merchants – Styrian scythes, but we also find chests of silks in some Jewish transports and young Austrian wine. They exported ox hides, feathers, raw linen, brass and bronze, litharge (lead oxide) and lead. Ten carts full of these metals were exported by the able Abraham Wiedeńczyk, who had almost a monopoly on this trade with Austria.

A huge variety of goods was imported from Breslau by mainly Christian merchants, but in 1681 we observe the growth of Jewish business. Breslau with its 18 transports, in which Jewish merchants participated, replaced Krems as the leading trade partner of Kraków. In 1701, Breslau with its 9 transports represented Jewish foreign trade, and the whole consignment consisted of three sacks of feathers. Imports remained mainly in the hands of Christian merchants, who travelled in groups. Jewish participation was limited to a few units or packs.

The situation became even worse in 1751, when goods from Silesia were delivered only through Breslau merchants or reached Jews indirectly, via Wolbrom and Wodzisław. It seems that the enactment of new Prussian laws were having some effect.

The settling in Silesia of the former Kraków rabbi Jozue Janas Fränkl in 1744 may probably be viewed as an attempt to get round these restrictions. Fränkl opened an export house in Breslau where he dealt in linen, wool and silk textiles with Poland, Lithuania, Russia and Moldavia. 'A group of emigrants from Kraków, who functioned as links between the trading companies in Silesia and Jewish merchants in Kraków gathered around Fränkl and his rich family.'[4]

We have no direct information from our sources about Leipzig and the participation of Kraków Jews in its famous fairs. A single remark in the 1661 customs register does not help much.[5] Other than that, we know that 632 Jews travelled to Leipzig from Poland between 1681 and 1699, but only 40 of them came from Kraków. Far more Jews came from Poznań (249), Leszno (149) and Kalisz (105).[6] In the next century, especially in the 1760s, we come across numerous Kraków Jews at the Leipzig fairs, whose lodgings were maintained by their co-religionists.

[4] Bałaban *Historia Żydów* II, p. 411.
[5] WAPKr, *Reg. Thel.*, 2177, p. 23.
[6] Schipper, *Dzieje handlu*, pp. 183–4.

DOMESTIC TRADE

Trade between the Jews of Kraków and Danzig was not impressive. In 1661 various merchandise in 7 transports was recorded, especially spices, and in 1681 we have just 2 transports. Trade stopped in 1701, and fifty years later Danzig goods did go directly to Kraków but via Pilica and Żarki.

When Jewish trade is concerned, Toruń and Warsaw are mentioned four times each in the customs registers and Lublin eight times. But Lublin is first to disappear from the later registers, while Warsaw is mentioned seven times for 1681. To search for those big trading centres in the 1751 registers is fruitless. Domestic trade is shown in Table 20.1.

In 1661, trade covered nineteen Polish towns. Kraków province was represented by Olkusz (4 entries), and Wodzisław (2); Sandomierz province by Pińczów (18), Przedbórz (16) and Stopnica (1); the province of Ruthenia by 7 towns with Jarosław (10 entries) in the lead. Lublin, Warsaw, Piotrków, Łęczyca, Łowicz, Toruń and Danzig constituted the rest.

Twenty years later we have trade with Będzin (3 entries) and Wodzisław (9) in Kraków province; Pińczów (18) and Przedbórz (4) in Sandomierz province as Stopnica disappears. Trade in Ruthenia grows where, besides Jarosław (12 entries), the following appear: Kańczuga (1), Mościska (3), Lwów (3), Przemyśl (2), Rymanów (1), Rzeszów (2), Sokal (1) and Sambor (1). The remaining centres drop by a few transports and Jewish trade grows only with Warsaw (7 entries).

The year 1701 witnesses unfavourable changes, especially in Ruthenian trade. Only contacts with Jarosław, Lwów and Rzeszów are maintained. Warsaw is mentioned in only one entry, Danzig in none. Altogether, only eight centres are named.

In 1751, the number of towns named in the registers grows to 53, if we omit the Kraków complex, that is Kazimierz and the Royal Gardens (Ogród Królewski). The absence of Jaroslaw is striking, as is that of Lublin and Warsaw. The area covered moves east along the line of Dubno, Tarnopol and Buczacz. The following towns are named in the registers at least six times, that is, at least once every two months: (in alphabetical order) Buczacz (7), Gorlice (6), Pińczów (44), Tarnogród (14), Wiśnicz (9), Wodzisław (8), Wolbrom (14), Żmigród (13).

Table 20.1
The geographical range of Jewish domestic trade in second half of the seventeenth century, as shown by the number of entries in the customs registers denoting the place of origin of merchandise

Province	Town	Year		
		1661	1681	1701
Kraków	Będzin	–	3	–
	Gorlice	–	–	1
	Olkusz	4	–	–
	Wiśnicz	–	–	5
	Wodzisław	2	9	1
Sandomierz	Chmielnik	1	–	–
	Pińczów	18	9	8
	Przedbórz	16	4	6
	Stopnica	1	–	–
Ruthenia	Jarosław	10	12	3
	Kańczuga	7	1	–
	Mościska	8	3	–
	Lwów	1	3	–
	Przemyś	6	2	–
	Rymanów	–	1	–
	Rzeszow	6	–	–
	Sambor	–	1	–
	Sokal	–	1	–
	Tyczyn	4	–	–
Lublin	Lublin	8	–	–
Mazowsze	Warsaw	4	7	1
Rawa	łowicz	4	2	–
Sieradz	Piotrków	1	1	–
Łęczyca	Łęczyca	2	–	–
Chełmno	Toruń	4	2	4
–	Gdańsk	7	2	–
TOTAL		114	63	29

Podolian tobacco from Buczacz was traded for scythes, groceries and textiles (linen, camlet – mixed fibres, woollen cloth) while Hungarian tobacco was imported from Gorlice. Untreated honey was the main item – 184 barrels in 1751 – in transports from Tarnogród. Wiśnicz Jews were dealers in Hungarian and Podolian tobacco and in honey, as were Żmigród Jews. A more detailed study of the role of Wodzisław and Wolbrom would be valuable, as other merchandise arrived there from extremely varied sources: Turkey, Breslau, Silesia generally, even Brandenburg.

Honey was the main article imported from Pińczów. In 1751, 155 barrels were transported on 39 carts altogether, making an average of one cart every ten days. The agent was undoubtedly the major trader Salomon (Slama) Majer, importing saltpetre, furs, Russian leathers, Podolian tobacco, Turkish goods and, of course, honey into Kraków. He exported a variety of goods, especially ironware.

RANGE OF MERCHANDISE

The outstanding feature of Jewish trade was its enormous variety, starting with foodstuffs and working through haberdashery, hides, textiles and raw wool to ironware. The retail scythe trade, for instance, was very much in Jewish hands. In the seventeenth century we find the majority of comments referring to otherwise unspecified 'Jewish merchandise'. Some items were practically a Jewish monopoly, others figure only in certain periods.

Aniseed

Trade in aniseed stands out in the 1661 registers. Aniseed – *anisum* – the seed of the anise plant, with its sweet piquant taste and characteristic aroma can be used as medicine or as flavouring for alcoholic beverages or as a spice for bread and gingerbread. Out of 200 entries for Jewish trade in 1661, 25 – exactly 12.5 per cent – refer to the trade in aniseed, which was then imported mainly from Pińczów, 1.5 tons arriving in one year. Later on, this import appears only sporadically and finally comes to a stop.

Tobacco

A second item worth noticing is tobacco. This first appears in the customs registers in the seventeenth century, but is a major factor in Jewish trade in 1701. Of a total 71 entries, 20 or 28 per cent refer to tobacco imported into Kraków, a third of which came from Pińczów.

The use of tobacco, particularly as snuff, spread in the eighteenth century. The most popular was the Hungarian type, of which 3,367.5 stones (1 stone = 36 pounds) were imported in 1750, constituting 85.6 per cent of total imports. Podolian tobacco, of which 472.5 stones reached Kraków, took second place with 12 per cent, then Turkish tobacco with 92.5 stones or 2.4 per cent.[7] Jewish participation in the tobacco trade was very high (54.2 per cent) in the mid eighteenth century, dropping to 17.3 per cent in 1763. This is an exception to trade in other goods, in which the Jewish share grew. But after the first partition of Poland, the Austrians introduced a tobacco monopoly administered by two Jews, König and Schrenk, and the merchants' and peasants' trade crashed to a halt.

Table 20.2
Imports of tobacco to Kraków in the mid eighteenth century by different trading groups[8]

Year	1750		1755		1760	
	stones	%	stones	%	stones	%
TOTAL	3992.5	100	3619.5	100	4600	100
Jewish merchants	2131.5	54.2	1825	50.4	707.5	17.3
Lubowla merchants	825	20.9	1109	30.6	1612.5	51.9
Other merchants	975	24.9	685.5	19.0	1358.5	28.9

Source: M. Kulczykowski, *Kraków jako ośrodek towarowy Małopolski zachodniej w drugiej połowie XVIII wieku* (Warsaw, 1963) p. 51.

Honey

Sugar in the seventeenth and eighteenth centuries was an imported expensive luxury item, so the consumption of honey stayed high. In 1661, the main deliveries of honey to Kazimierz took place on Fridays and Saturdays, but we have not been able to trace their source. Altogether 32 entries from that year – 15 per cent of the total number – refer to honey.

In the mid eighteenth century, honey imports to Kraków reached an impressive amount (see Table 20.3).[9] The major exporters to Kraków in 1750 were: Tarnogród 230 barrels (17 per cent), Lubowla in Spisz (47.5 barrels), Biłgoraj (33 barrels) and Koniecpol (30.5 barrels). The following year, Tarnogród remained the main exporter with 169 barrels, then came Pińczów (155 barrels) and Żmigród (63 barrels) apart from the smaller deliverers.

[7] Kulczykowski, *Kraków jako osrodek*, p. 50.
[8] Ibid., p. 51.
[9] Ibid., p. 52.

In 1760, Brody (52.5 barrels), Jarosław (85.5), Lubaczów (63), Oleśno (101.5) and Wiśnicz (39.5) joined the exporters. Abraham Jakubowicz from Ogród Królewski, an estate belonging to the governor of Kraków, was the main honey trader. In 1750 his business made up 11 per cent of all the honey trade and in 1755 it was 14.3 per cent.[10]

Woollen cloth

Woollen cloth was the most important local industry. Kraków had close ties with the Austrian textile producers of Silesia. Cloth made in Little Poland was often sent to Silesia for finishing, which included calendering (a form of pressing), cutting and dyeing. A special niche in the cloth trade was filled by the Kazimierz Jews, who dealt in a locally produced coarse fabric known as 'paklak'. They bought this cheaply in Biała, Kęty, Staszów, Radomsko and other small centres, and brought it 'on themselves' to the town. In this way they brought 142 'statues' of 'paklak' to Kraków in 1751. Jews are also known to have exported considerable quantities of cloth to Jarosław and Brody.[11]

Linen

Little Poland in the eighteenth century had a flourishing linen industry, centred mainly along the Podgórze (the foothills). The main producers west of Kraków were: Biała, Andrychów, Wadowice, and Myślenice. To the east, the manufacturing villages were Gorlice, Dębowiec, Łańcut, Przeworsk and Sanok. Textiles from the western area were handled mainly by Christian merchants, those from the east by Jews, who took over complete control as financiers, buyers and trade managers, as far as Danzig.[12]

Iron products

In iron wares, a flourishing scythe trade stands out. In the second

---

[10] Ibid., p. 57.
[11] Ibid., pp. 87–9.
[12] Ibid., pp. 97–8.

half of the seventeenth century, the trade was dominated by the Krauz family, burghers of Kraków, and in the next century by Laśkiewicz. In the eighteenth century, the big wholesalers dealt mainly with Jews. Thus, according to Mariusz Kulczykowski in 1750 Jewish merchants exported 20,650 scythes from Kraków. In 1763 the number rose to 43,005, about 46 per cent of the whole scythe trade, later falling to about 29.5 per cent. Almost 90 per cent of the traders buying scythes from the Jarosław warehouses were Jews. Of every 26 debtors at the warehouse of Kraków burgher, Samuel Mittman, 22 were Jews, and another merchant, Stanisław Fachinetti, was in a similar position.[13]

A customs entry in 1751 clearly indicates an active Jewish presence in other lines of trade. On 17 August, '*Infidus* Izrael Bunisiewicz from Buczacz *signavit* out of town various merchandise bought from the Honourable Sir Józef Haller, namely 1 barrel of sugar, 1 sack of pepper, 1 pack of white paper [and] woollen cloth, 1 pack of czamlet, *in summa* 4 pieces.'[14]

THE MERCHANTS

It must be stated that, compared with the Christians, Jewish trade was carried on by a far larger number of persons. We can put names to major figures among the Polish merchants, turning up at the customs again and again. For example, in 1668 Krzysztof Krauz, a merchant and member of the town council in Kraków, is named in the registers 96 times and Tomasz Rebel, of Scottish origin, 57 times, and there are others. We also get a clear picture of the merchants of Italian origin. But when it comes to Jewish businessmen, we have no such clues. We have problems in identifying the leading figures in the customs entries. Sometimes Jewish merchants are entered in their own name, more often in their own and their father's name, sometimes also by their family name. Often we come across family businesses but to disentangle family relationships is extremely difficult.

---

[13] Ibid., pp. 108, 112.
[14] WAPKr, *Reg. Thel.*, 2217, p. 158.

Among the more interesting personalities of the second half of the seventeenth century is Jakub Melles from Kraków, who was registered twenty-two times for customs in 1681. He is known to have often visited Rzeszów, Jarosław, Przemyśl, Lwów and Kańczuga, and his name was known in Pińczów and Wodzisław. In 1681 King Jan III Sobieski granted a debt moratorium in his favour, together with his partners Noach Mordys and Joachim Fiszer, after they were robbed during the Rzeszów fair on 3 October 1678, and lost the rest of their goods in fires in Jarosław and Wodzisław. The moratorium was soon repeated, when the same merchants' shops were looted during an anti-Jewish riot in Kraków in March 1682.[15]

Abraham Jakubowicz, the great honey wholesaler of the mid eighteenth century, who was entered in the Kraków customs twenty-six times in 1751, had a fairly wild youth. As Majer Bałaban writes, the son of the far-seeing Jakub Abrahamowicz 'was an excellent pupil who learned from the nobles how to spend his father's money. Once, when his mother took him with her to Warsaw, to make a lease payment of 11,750 złoty to the Treasury, Abraham took the money, and, moreover, misappropriated a deposit of 280 ducats put down against stock, then ran away to Riga, where he spent this and more within 18 months.'[16] Yet, according to the recorded entries, his entrepreneurial instincts must have gained the upper hand; as time went by, he became the busiest Jewish dealer in Kraków, employing a whole group of pedlars.

BANKING

The customs registers yield very little information about banking. Since silver is seldom mentioned, we can say very little about King Jan Kazimierz's agent, Tsodek Izaakowicz, a *kehilla* elder, who traded in silver on a large scale. Tsodek was even reprimanded by the mint supervisor, Tomasz Tymf, who accused him of taking silver and gold coins out of the country.[17] Joachim Pacanowski,

---

[15] Bałaban, *Historia Żydów*, II, pp. 62, 105.
[16] Ibid., p. 156.
[17] Janina Bieniarzówna and Jan M. Małecki, *Dzieje Krakowa. Kraków w wiekach XVI–XVIII* (History of Kraków: Kraków in the sixteenth to the eighteenth centuries), Kraków, 1984, p. 439.

who had wide banking interests, was officially recognized as a royal agent in 1675, but has few mentions in the customs registers.[18]

In finance, one should note that relations between Polish and Jewish traders did not confirm the often-held view that money-lending was a Jewish trade. In fact, the reverse was more often the case. Kraków merchant and councillor Krzysztof Krauz junior conducted business not only with individual Jews, as is testified by his frequent joint transports with Jewish partners going east, but also with the Kraków *kehilla*, for which he charged high rates of interest. For example in 1675 he took as surety the *kehilla*'s income, including the so-called 'meat tax' (*krupka mięsna*). After lending the large sum of 21,000 złoty, Krauz gave instructions that all income from kosher slaughter should be put into his funds, and that not a single head of cattle should be slaughtered without his consent. The Jewish community elders disliked this, so the case was sent to a *vehm gericht* (special tribunal), and the Jews sought protection with Bishop Trzebicki.[19]

Robert Forbes, a Kraków trader of Scottish origin, was deeply involved in the *kehilla*'s activities. In 1692 he was appointed royal secretary *in conquirendis elegantioribus apud remotas gentes mercibus et in subministranda pro artilleria Regni ammunitione*. Forbes took up trade and banking. He instructed his commissioners to purchase goods for various other merchants and pay against bills bearing his signature in all Polish towns, especially during fairs. In 1692 the Kraków *kehilla* pledged with him *skrzynkowe* (box payments) worth 21,000 złoty, *krupka mięsna* worth 14,000 złoty, liquor sale tax to bring in a weekly income of 260 złoty (13,520 annually), all to be collected by Forbes' officials. He lent money to the *kehilla*, himself becoming the nobles' and clergy's debtor. He also had individual Jews as debtors, such as Zelig Tsodek, Joachim Pacanowski and Jakub Melles, whom we have already come across. When Forbes's debts reached the enormous sum of 133,621 złoty, his firm went bankrupt. The report of a special commission established in 1699 by the monarch, and currently constituting a separate 478-page volume in the Kraków Municipal Files, reveals 187 Jews among Forbes's debtors. The commission put Forbes's creditors and debtors into direct touch with each other. The result was that the Kazimierz Jewish community ended up with a large

---

[18] Ibid.
[19] Bałaban, *Historia Żydów*, II, p. 145.

Table 20.3
Imports of honey to Kraków in the mid eighteenth century by different groups

Year	1750		1755		1760	
	barrels	%	barrels	%	barrels	%
TOTAL	1340	100	1152	100	1476	100
Jews	908.5	67.8	702	60.9	1120	75.9
Burghers	190.5	14.3	227	19.8	317	21.5
Nobles	185	13.8	183	15.9	15	1.0
Clergy	22	1.6	–	–	–	–
Peasants	34	2.5	40	3.4	24	1.6

Source: Kulczykowski *Kraków jako ośrodek towarowy Małopolski zachodniej* ..., p. 52.

number of creditors instead of just one from whom repayment could more easily have been obtained.[20]

This incident shows us – and here I follow Schipper's view – that money-lending to Jews at high rates of interest by the nobles and the clergy was a means of capital investment. The *kehilla*'s funds were also placed with community members at interest.[21]

Trade and finance went hand in hand during this period. In 1661 joint expeditions to purchase goods made up to 23 per cent of the records concerning Jews. This comes out clearly in foreign trade, with Krems and Breslau taking pride of place, followed by the Polish towns of Warsaw, Danzig and Jarosław which, through their regular fairs, attracted Christian and Jewish merchants alike. Practically the same number of Jews are recorded in 1701, although the total number of entries fell about 2.5 times.

In 1681 Jews appear together with other Kraków merchants, but only in partnership with Polish and Scottish merchants dealing in iron products. There were joint expeditions by Armenian and Jewish traders, but apparently none between Jewish and Italian merchants.

---

[20] Bieniarzówna and Małecki, *Dzieje Krakowa*, p. 438.
[21] According to I. Schipper, the *kehillot* turned into banks, in which the nobles and the clergy kept their money at a high rate of interest. The community's land and property, plus that of the individual members of the community, was used as security. The nobles and clergy, having an interest in the *kehilla*'s ability to repay, became their protectors in the economic sphere, removing all possible obstacles. Schipper, *Dzieje handlu*, pp. 212–13.

THE DECLINE OF JEWISH TRADE

The year 1751 sees a distinct separation between Polish and Jewish trade. The worsening of mutual relations is evidenced by the common use of the term *infidus* (infidel). Only Breslau merchants coming to Kraków took the occasional Jewish pack alongside merchandise for Christian traders.

Another feature of the 1751 registers (MSS 2217, 2219) is the complete disappearance of the earlier term 'Kraków Jew', although we do find Jews mentioned from the Ogród Królewski and Kazimierz. The latter are mentioned in only 45 out of 321 entries for Jewish trade, making barely 15 per cent. We also often find Kazimierz Jews registered as carrying their goods 'on themselves', implying small quantities. For example, 142 'statues' (*postawy*) of coarse cloth were carried out of Kazimierz by traders 'on themselves'. Locally produced caps, exported to Łowicz, are mentioned only once, Turkish goods three times, Danzig goods once and Breslau goods four times. For such a big Jewish centre these trade figures are so tiny as to raise doubts over the reliability of our source.

There is also the fact that Abraham Jakubowicz, the honey wholesaler who imported 35 carts of honey and 11 carts of other goods to Kraków, is registered only once, and that as an exporter of scythes to Ruthenia (4 carts drawn by 8 horses). It is hard to believe that he sent his carts back empty. Again, if we assume that the 'infidus' Abraham Jakubowicz from Wolbrom bringing goods to Kraków is the same Abraham who is registered as from Ogród Królewski, we cannot be certain of any other name. In other words, it is impossible to determine whether the place name entered in the customs registers denotes the merchants' or the goods' provenance or both. Generally, however, different names are linked to different locations, which seems to prove that Jews from small towns played a considerable part in eighteenth-century trade.

This chapter, based on previously unexamined sources, aims to broaden our knowledge of Jewish trade in the second half of the seventeenth and first half of the eighteenth centuries, but it is not meant to exhaust the subject. Methodologically speaking, three-year averages should have been used instead of yearly data, to eliminate accidental conclusions. For instance, a town could drop out of trade in any one year because of purely local factors. In this regard, one might look at the effect of disease, whether human or agricultural, on Jewish participation in Polish economic life. Let us hope that this volume on Jews in the Polish-Lithuanian Commonwealth will encourage scholars to undertake further research on this important question.

Part V

Population

21 · Jews and the Village in the Polish Commonwealth

Antoni Podraza

If one tried to work out where Jews lived in Poland on the basis of Polish works of literature, the conclusion might well be that they lived mainly in the countryside. All the best-known Jewish characters in literature are people who lived in villages. One need only mention Jankiel from *Pan Tadeusz*, Rachela from *Wesele*, or the characteristic Jewish figures in *Chłopi* and *Noce i dnie*. The reality was different. The majority of Jews in Poland lived in large and small towns, not in the countryside. All statistical research into the Jewish population in Old Poland points to this. And we shall look at this further later on in this chapter. However, despite the fact that most Jews lived in towns, there were extensive mutual relations between Jews and the rural population, and these played an important role in the life of both communities. The notion of 'both communities' is not, however, a very accurate one. There were certainly two 'communities' if we divide society on religious lines, but in the estate society that existed in the Polish Commonwealth dividing the population simply on the basis of religion would not show the wide range of differences within that society.

The country was inhabited by peasants as well as by the *szlachta*. These two very different groups also showed a completely different attitude towards the Jews. Yet both were closely linked with the Jews, with those living in villages, as well as those in the towns. Jews from the towns in any case also largely made a living from their economic activities in the villages (rents, usury, trade in farm produce, and so on).

With such extensive contacts between the nobles, peasants and Jews, it may appear surprising that there are hardly any studies which examine this problem of mutual relations, which is a vital one for our understanding of the economy of the time. Why have these problems been neglected by previous historians? The state of archival material is certainly one reason. Knowledge of Hebrew is essential to make use of Jewish sources, and such knowledge is very rare among the Polish historians. An important partner in the Jews' relations with the village, the peasants, have not left sources on a scale that could help us because of their general illiteracy. It would be wrong to say that they produced no sources, since at least some indirect ones exist, for example such sources as rural court records – very rich for the province of Little Poland – and peasants' petitions. The latter are especially worth investigating. Also of interest are ancient songs, poetry and folk tales. Oscar Kolberg's well-known collection contains a number of such works, which throw some light on peasant attitudes towards the Jews. The old folk proverbs should also be mentioned. Josef Sommerfeldt tried to collect this type of material, but only from one side.[1]

The third partner, the *szlachta*, has left the most sources. This is especially true of economic sources, which, if properly investigated, can reveal a lot about the role of Jews in the functioning of the economy of the great landed estates in pre-partition Poland. Bills, contracts, receipts, inventories, economic correspondence, and so on, still await thorough investigation. Pamphlets and diaries may also provide an excellent source for establishing the attitude of the nobles towards the Jews.

The sources for the research on the topic 'Jews and the village in the Polish Commonwealth' have numerous gaps, which we shall never be able to fill. This is partly because of the state of the surviving records, but even more because of their character. A whole group of subjects was never covered in the written sources, and rough written notes were simply lost. This applies above all to the sphere of economic relations between Jews and peasants, as no written records in fact were kept about them. Economic matters are much easier to follow in the contacts between Jews and the large estates, especially the latifundia ones. Very rich archives have often survived for this type of estate, unlike for the properties of the middle and poor *szlachta*.

Without going into details, it seems to me that the sources for the present topic are not as poor as might appear at first sight. However, the extent they have been used in previous research is minimal. Thus it is vital to examine carefully this source material, and to obtain the maximum information from what has survived.

Interest in economic history, unlike in political history, is of very

---

[1] Josef Sommerfeldt, 'Die Juden in den polnischen Sprichwörtern und sprichwörtlichen Redensarten', *Die Burg* 3 (1942) pp. 313–54.

recent date. In Polish historiography the first valuable works on economic history, including village history, only appeared at the end of the nineteenth century. A large part was played in this by Professor Franciszek Bujak, who was educated at the Jagiellonian University. Soon after Professor Jan Rutkowski joined him in research in this field. These two scholars grouped round them a number of other historians, and the inter-war period saw the emergence of two large research centres for economic history. One of them, headed by Professor Bujak, was in Lwów, and the other under Professor Rutkowski in Poznań. At both centres economic history was understood in a very wide sense, but rural topics predominated. Despite the undoubted achievements of Polish historiography on the subject of the village before the First World War and in the inter-war period, the essential problem of the role of the Jews in the rural economy in pre-partition Poland did not find a historian. We not only lack a synthesis on the subject, but also monographs devoted to various regions and topics (for example credits, trade, leases, and so on).

After the Second World War there was an upsurge of interest in the history of the Polish village. It would be difficult to find an historian in the first decade after the war who had not made at least a few contributions to this problem. I do not want to discuss here this common and short-lived interest in rural history, but I believe it was caused by a misunderstanding of Marxism in Polish historiography. Whatever the cause of this phenomenon, the fact is that there was certainly a growth in interest in the history of the village and one would have expected this to have included the topic of 'The Jews and the village'. But this was not the case. Here are two examples of how this subject of the Jews was omitted in research on the rural history of the 'Golden Age'.

The first is in works devoted to the investigation of rural subjects undertaken by the Zespół badań agrarnych (Committee on Agrarian Studies) headed by Professor Celina Bobińska in Kraków.[2] I have participated in the activities of this body. We tried to investigate, as thoroughly as possible, the history of the village in Little Poland during the Enlightenment period. We were

---

[2] My article 'Z krakowskich doświadczeń w zakresie zespołowych prac badawczych w dziedzinie historii' (The Kraków experiences in collective historical research in history), in *Struktury, ruchy, ideologie XVIII–XX wieku* (Structures, movements, ideologies from the eighteenth to the twentieth centuries), Kraków, 1986, provides information about the work of this group.

interested in relations between the peasants and the *szlachta*, various types of rural social conflict, relations between various rural groups, relations between the population and the parish, the functioning of rural self-government and so on. Yet the vital question of the Jews' role in the life of the rural community, and relations between them and the villagers, were ignored.

The second example of ignoring Jews in research on rural history is J. Burszta's work on the role of inns in the life of feudal villages.[3] It would appear impossible to leave out such a characteristic figure as the Jewish innkeeper in this kind of research topic. None the less we find almost nothing in Burszta's work about the role of the Jewish population in the *arenda* (leases) and the court alcohol monopoly, or about Jewish innkeepers and their contacts with the peasants.

The Jewish issue is almost completely missing in existing research on the history of the pre-partition Polish village. This means that the history of the Jews in Poland is incomplete without their role in rural life having been investigated. Similarly our knowledge of rural life itself is also incomplete because it lacks the Jewish element.

This chapter is in no way intended to fill this important gap: its aim is more modest. As research on the topic is so undeveloped, this chapter also cannot synthesize the results achieved so far. What I should like to do instead is to suggest a programme for further research and to encourage other Polish and Jewish historians to investigate it thoroughly. I believe it might be a very interesting study for Kraków's historical community, which already has a rich tradition of research in the rural history of pre-partition Poland. It seems worthwhile to begin doing so with the province of Little Poland, which traditionally has been our field of interest, and to build further studies on our work from the 1950s and 1960s as well as on the rich source collection.[4] I hope that this book will help us to speed up work on this subject.

---

[3] Józef Burszta, *Wieś i karczma. Rola karczmy w życiu wsi pańszczyźnianej* (The village and the inn. The role of the inn in the life of the villein village), Warsaw, 1950.

[4] I have in mind a rich collection of transcripts made from sources in various archives, relating to the village in Little Poland in the second half of the eighteenth century, kept in the Institute of History at the Jagiellonian University. This collection is the result of many years' work by the group for agrarian studies headed by Professor C. Bobińska.

JEWISH POPULATION DISTRIBUTION

The first question I should like to examine is the size and distribution of the Jewish population. A number of historians have studied this (especially R. Mahler),[5] yet it is far from exhausted.

The fundamental source used by historians to try to calculate the size of the Jewish population in the pre-partition Commonwealth was the 1764 census of the Jews. This census has been criticized several times, and it is certain that the figures provided by it for the number of Jews in Poland are much too low, even if one ignores the fact that babies less than one year old were not even included.

According to this census the Jewish population in Poland was 587,658; of these 430,009 lived in the Kingdom of Poland and 157,649 in Lithuania. R. Mahler tried to correct these figures by adding babies (6.35 per cent) and by assuming that about 20 per cent of Jews were not included in the census. He estimated that the real number of Jews was about 750,000; of these 549,000 in the kingdom and 201,000 in Lithuania.[6] I believe these figures are probably correct. However, I am more interested in the proportions of Jews in the various provinces of the Polish Commonwealth rather than precise numbers. The results of the 1764 census, published by J. Kleczyński and R. Mahler, show the differences were enormous, as can be seen in Table 21.1.

In this table I have grouped various provinces differently from R. Mahler. The first five provinces in my table (Royal Prussia, Kujawy, Great Poland, Province of Sieradz-Łęczyca and Mazowsze) constituted one group for Mahler which he calls 'Eastern Poland', while Podlasie, treated as a separate unit by me, was treated by R. Mahler as part of Little Poland. Other divisions are identical. I believe that the division proposed in my table, sensible given Poland's historical

---

[5] R. Mahler, 'Żydzi w dawnej Polsce w świetle liczb. Struktura demograficzna i społeczno-ekonomiczna Żydów w Koronie w XVIII wieku' (Jews in Old Poland in the light of their numbers. The demographic and socio-economic structure of the Jews in the kingdom in the eighteenth century), in *Przeszłość demograficzna Polski. Materiały i studia* (Poland's demographic past. Sources and studies), Warsaw, 1967, is essential.

[6] Ibid., pp. 154–5; for data from the same census in Archiwum Kom. Hist. PAU, 8, also see J. Kleczyński and F. Kluczycki, eds, *Liczba głów żydowskich w Koronie z taryf 1765* (Number of Jewish heads in the Kingdom according to 1765 lists), Kraków, 1898, pp. 388–407; A. Czuczyński, ed., *Spis Żydów wojew. krakowskiego z 1765 r.* (Jewish census from the year 1765), Kraków, 1898.

Table 21.1
Jews in Poland according to the 1764 census, by province

	Province	No. Jews[a]	Regional Total
Royal Prussia	Pomorze	2731	
	Malbork	87	
	Chełmno	577	3395
Kujawy	Inowrocław	1422	
	Brześć-Kujawy	1267	
	Dobrzyń	1,082	3771
Great Poland	Poznań	19,913	
	Kalisz	12,995	32,908
Sieradz-łęczyca	Sieradz	5002	
	Wieluń Land	2988	
	Łęczyca	2903	10,893
Mazowsze	Płock	3960	
	Mazowsze	10,662	
	Rawa	5332	19,954
Little Poland	Kraków	18,677	
	Sandomierz	42,972	
	Lublin	20,191	81,840
Podlasie	Podlasie	19,043	19,043
Ruthenia	Bełz	16,442	
	Ruthenia	100,111	
	Chełm Region	9787	
	Wołyń	50,792	
	Podole	38,384	
	Bracław	20,337	
	Kijów	22,352	258,205
TOTAL on Crown Lands			430,009
Western Lithuania	Brześć	21,994	
	Troki	23,738	
	Wilno	26,977	
	Żmudź	15,759	
	Nowogródek	21,500	119,968
Eastern Lithuania	Mińsk	13,422	
	Mścisław	2615	
	Połock	6689	
	Witebsk	11,959	
	Inflanty (Livonia)	2996	37,681
TOTAL in Lithuania			157,649
TOTAL IN POLISH COMMONWEALTH			587,658

Note: [a] Population figures exclude those under one year old.
Source: R. Mahler, 'Żydzi w dawnej Polsce' (see note 5), p. 159.

division, illustrates more clearly the considerable differences in the number of Jews inhabiting the various provinces, especially those provinces which were ethnically Polish. Unfortunately there was no simultaneous census of the whole population in 1764, so we cannot calculate the percentage of Jews compared with the whole population in various provinces. Censuses of population and households were only carried out in the Commonwealth in the 1780s and early 1790s, and then within the new borders created by the first partition and thus without the territories annexed by Russia, Prussia and Austria. We therefore have to abandon any attempt to calculate the percentage of the Jewish population in relation to the whole population. However, even without this important calculation, the figures in the 1764 census shown in Table 21.1 allow us to make several interesting observations.

First of all, the data enable us to establish the regional differences in the Polish Commonwealth according to the number of Jews living there. Consequently we can suggest that future research on this topic should take into account these regional differences. Mutual relations, the economic role of the Jewish population and mutual cultural influences must have been different when the Jewish population constituted a considerable part of the whole population from when they only formed a fraction of the community, as for example in the north-western territories of the Polish Commonwealth (Royal Prussia, Kujawy).

One should also remember that the regional differences which were expressed in the different sizes of the Jewish population had their historical character and were subject to various fundamental changes from diverse factors. This may also be observed in Table 21.1. For example Great Poland itself, that is, Poznań and Kalisz province, was inhabited in the last years of Polish independence by a relatively high number of Jews. More Jews lived there than in the neighbouring Łęczyca and Sieradz provinces or in Mazowsze. This was only to change fundamentally in the nineteenth century.[7]

---

[7] To illustrate the relatively large number of Jews in Great Poland in comparison with Mazowsze and Sieradz-Łęczyca region, I have made the following calculations: on the one hand I have added up the Jews in these three regions to arrive at the figures (according to the 1764 census) 63,755 in Great Poland, being 51.62 per cent of it, in Mazowsze 31.30 per cent and in the Sieradz-Łęczyca region 17.08 per cent. Next, on the basis of the 1789 census, published in *Dziennik Handlowy* and republished by J. Gieysztorowa in her work *Wstęp do demografii staropolskiej* (Introduction to Old Poland's demography), p. 114, I have calculated the total number of the population for the three regions, obtaining a figure 1,439,174. Of them

Table 21.2
Jewish population of towns and villages in selected provinces, according to the 1764 census

Province	Total nos.	In towns		In countryside	
		no.	%	no.	%
Inowrocław	1422	1290	90.72	132	9.28
Gniezno[a]	6530	6427	98.42	103	1.58
Kalisz[a]	6465	6387	98.79	78	1.21
Sieradz	5002	3878	77.53	1124	22.47
Wielun	2988	2161	72.32	827	27.68
Łęczyca	2903	1926	66.35	977	33.65
Mazowsze	10,379	4092	39.43	6287	60.57
Kraków	18,677	12,911	69.13	5766	30.87
Lublin	20,191	13,871	68.70	6320	31.30

Note: [a] In Table 21.1 these appear together as one province, Kalisz

The 1764 census shows that the Jewish population of pre-partition Poland lived above all in the ethnically non-Polish territories, where the majority was Ukrainian, Byelorussian or Lithuanian. In investigating our subject of the 'Jews and the village', it is very important to remember that the majority of the Jewish population in the Polish Commonwealth lived side by side not with Polish, but Ukrainian, Byelorussian or Lithuanian peasants. As for the relations between the Jews and the *szlachta*, the situation was different, as most nobles were either Polish or had become Polonized. According to the 1764 census 171, 804 Jews, that is 29.24 per cent of all Jews, lived in the territories which were ethnically Polish, while 415,854 Jews, that is 70.76 per cent, inhabited the non-Polish territories.[8]

Let us now concentrate on another very important issue: namely, how many Jews lived in the towns and how many in the countryside. Before considering the region of Little Poland in detail, I intend to calculate the proportions for several regions of Poland, using the

---

38.42 per cent lived in Great Poland, 36.04 per cent in Mazowsze and 25.54 per cent in the Sieradz-Łęczyca region. Therefore, after the first partition, Great Poland had 38.42 per cent of the population of Poland's northern territories, and 51.62 per cent of all Jews living in those territories. These proportions were to change drastically in the nineteenth century.

[8] Cf also Mahler, *Żydzi w dawnej Polsce*, p. 161.

figures presented in R. Mahler's work.[9] The results of this are in Table 21.2. Unfortunately I only had the figures for nine ethnically Polish provinces. I had none for the eastern territories of the Commonwealth, where the situation might have been different. But even these figures for the nine provinces show wide variations. Three groups can be clearly distinguished.

The first is made up of Inowrocław, Gniezno, and Kalisz provinces, where the percentage of the Jewish population living in the villages was very small. In Inowrocław it was almost 10 per cent (9.28), and in the other two it was below 2 per cent – 1.58 in Gniezno and 1.21 in Kalisz. The situation was completely different in Mazowsze, where the majority of the Jewish population lived in the countryside (60.57 per cent). This was the only example of this concentration of Jews in the countryside, although it is hard to say if this was so for the whole of the Polish Commonwealth. Finally the third group, which seems typical of Poland, was made up of provinces and districts from the Sieradz-Łęczyca and Little Poland regions. The percentage of the Jewish population living in the countryside in these regions varied between 20 per cent and 35 per cent.

Thus, on the basis of these figures, it does seem valid to assert that the majority of the Jewish population in the pre-partition Polish Commonwealth lived in towns. However, at the same time we must stress that there were regions where the majority of the Jewish population lived in rural areas, Mazowsze for example. When the whole Polish territory is considered, the percentage of Jews living in the countryside was relatively high, about a third of all Jews. But in the north-western territories (Great Poland, Kujawy) Jews lived almost entirely in towns.

We shall now try to analyse how Jews were distributed on the territories of historical Little Poland. This analysis will not be based on the 1764 census but on the 1787 Kraków diocese census published by J. Kleczyński.[10] Much has been said and written about

---

[9] Ibid., Tables 5 and 6. They are attempts to divide the Jewish population according to sex and civil status, but as they provide separate figures for the towns and countryside, they can be used to evaluate the ratio of the two groups – town and countryside.

[10] Józej Kleczyński, ed., *Spis ludności diecezji krakowskiej z r.1787* (1787 census of the population of the Kraków diocese; Archiwum Komisji Historycznej PAU, 7), Kraków, 1894, pp. 269–478.

the value of this census, beginning with J. Kleczyński himself. The eighteenth-century censuses as a whole have been criticized by Karol Buczek, in my opinion unjustly. I have already used this census and expressed my views on it.[11] I believe that its value lies in that it was not prepared for fiscal needs, and therefore there was no need to hide or falsify information. The census was carried out on the orders of the Polish primate Michał Jerzy Poniatowski, by the parish priests in all the parishes of the diocese of Kraków, and a uniform questionnaire was used. It is important that the census not only lists the total number of people in all the administrative units (towns and villages), but also lists the number of people in three groups: Catholics, dissidents and Jews. Towns and villages were grouped into parishes and the latter into decanates. The administrative areas (province, district or region) they were attached to were also noted. Thus the 1787 census gives detailed information about the number of Jews in each town or village, and also allows us to calculate the percentage of the Jewish population compared with other groups. Unfortunately the census was only carried out in the diocese of Kraków, which was just a small part of the old Commonwealth, and its administrative borders after the first partition of 1772 also did not include the southern parts of Kraków and Sandomierz provinces.[12]

At the time the census was taken the Kraków diocese covered the northern part of Kraków province, with the districts of Kraków, Proszowice, Książ and Lelów, the Sandomierz district of Sandomierz province (except for several villages on the right bank of the River Vistula, which already belonged to Austria), the eastern part of Chęciny district, the Wiślica district (except for a few villages on the right bank of the River Vistula), the Radom district and the Stężyca region. The western part of the Chęciny district and the whole Opoczno district were not included in the census, as they were not part of the diocese of Kraków. On the other hand it did cover the whole Lublin province (Lublin, the Urzędowo district and Łuków region), and also the Duchy of Siewiersk, which belonged to the bishops of Kraków. Although part of Silesia, which

[11] H. Madurowicz and A. Podraza, *Regiony gospodarcze Małopolski zachodniej w drugiej połowie XVIII w.* (Economic regions of western Little Poland in the second half of the eighteenth century), Wrocław, 1958.
[12] Data concerning the counting of the population in these regions exist from various censuses carried out by the Austrian authorities in the 1770s and 1780s. For those parts of the Kraków and Sandomierz provinces which in 1772 were incorporated into Austria, see Table 21.3.

Table 21.3
Religion of the population of southern parts of Kraków and Sandomierz provinces which were annexed by Austria in 1772, according to a military census of 1773

Administrative unit	Population	Christians	Jews	% Jews
Oświęcim-Zator	102,613	101,892	721	0.7
Szczyrzyc	116,985	112,425	4560	3.8
Sącz-Czchów	16,0241	156,917	3324	2.0
Biecz	100,190	96,962	3228	3.2
TOTAL for Kraków Province	480,029	468,196	11,833	2.5
Pilzno	178,377	168,581	9796	5.4
Wiślica	22,603	21,008	995	4.0
Sandomierz	68,226	64,295	3931	5.7
TOTAL for Sandomierz Province	266,106	254,484	11,622	4.5

belonged to Prussia, was part of the diocese of Kraków, it was not included in the census. Several villages of Mazowsze province (Głowaczów parish) and Brześć Litewski province (part of Parczów parish) which were included in the census will not be considered here.

Using the figures provided by the census it is possible to make a number of observations on the distribution of the Jewish population of Little Poland, which will be understood here as being the three south-western provinces of the Polish Commonwealth, that is, Kraków, Sandomierz and Lublin provinces and the Duchy of Siewiersk, which belonged to the bishopric of Kraków.

Table 21.4 shows the religious distribution of the population of the territory under investigation. It is clear from the figures there, that the number of Jews in relation to the total population increases as one moves east. This is apparent even on the evidence of what was merely a fraction of the Polish Commonwealth. The River Vistula provides a district boundary separating territories with differing densities of Jewish inhabitants. In Lublin province, wholly on the east bank of the Vistula the percentage of Jews is much higher (10.84 per cent), than in Kraków (4.35 per cent) or Sandomierz provinces (7.54 per cent) on the west bank of the river. Stężyca region, which was part of Sandomierz province but

Table 21.4
Religion of the population of the Kraków diocese, on the basis of the 1787 census

Admin Unit	Population (nos)				Population (percentages)		
	Catholics	Dissidents	Jews	Total	Catholics	Dissidents	Jews
Town of Kraków	19,827	111	3653	23,591	84.05	0.47	15.48
Kraków dist.	84,208	18	2207	86,433	97.43	0.02	2.55
Proszowice dist.	54,415	9	1345	55,769	97.57	0.02	2.41
Lelów dist.	61,917	54	2913	64,884	95.43	0.08	4.49
Książ dist.	47,179	34	2054	49,267	95.76	0.07	4.17
TOTAL Kraków Province	267,546	266	12,172	279,944	95.57	0.08	4.35
Duchy of Siewiersk	18,553	1	10	18,564	99.94	–	0.06
Sandomierz dist.	95,932	137	7233	103,302	92.87	0.13	7.00
Wiślica dist.	84,865	111	6993	91,969	92.28	0.12	7.60
Radom dist.	77,486	100	6382	83,968	92.28	0.12	7.60
Chęciny dist.	25,958	25	490	26,473	98.05	0.10	1.85
Stężyca region	30,912	33	4660	35,605	86.82	0.09	13.09
TOTAL Sand. Province	315,153	406	25,758	341,317	92.34	0.12	7.54
Lublin dist.	90,941	257	13,308	104,506	87.02	0.24	12.74
Urzędów dist.	68,606	49	6949	75,604	90.75	0.06	9.19
Łuków region	39,187	55	3963	43,205	90.70	0.13	9.17
TOTAL Lublin Province	198,734	361	24,220	223,315	89.00	0.16	10.84
Fragments of Mazowsze and Brześć Litewski Provinces	1063	–	69	1,132	93.90	–	6.10
TOTAL Kraków Diocese	801,049	944	62,229	864,272	92.69	0.11	7.20

Source: J. Kleczyński (ed.), Spis ludności 1787 (see no. 10), Table IV.

on the east bank of the Vistula, is very interesting. The percentage of Jews there was very different from other regions of Sandomierz province, although this region was part of the latter. It was similar to, or even higher than, the adjoining regions of Lublin province.

We shall now examine the proportions of Jews living in the countryside and the towns. This is illustrated in Table 21.5. As was

Table 21.5
Jews living in towns and rural areas in Little Poland on the basis of the 1787 Kraków diocese census

Administrative unit[a]	Total no. Jews	Living in town		Living in the country	
		no	%	no	%
Kraków province	12,172	7617	62.58	4,555	37.42
Sandomierz prov.	25,758	14,937	57.99	10,821	42.01
Lublin province	24,220	15,602	64.42	8,618	35.58
TOTAL	62,150	38,156	61.39	23,994	38.62

Note: [a] Fragments of the Mazowsze and Brześć Litewski provinces, as well as the Duchy of Siewiersk, where there were only 10 Jews, have been omitted, even though they were part of the diocese.

Table 21.6
Number of Jews in relation to the population of towns and villages in Little Poland, on the basis of the 1787 census

Administrative unit	Total pop. of towns	Jews among them		Total pop. of villages	Jews among them	
		no.	%		no.	%
Kraków prov.	50,986	7617	14.94	228,958	4555	1.99
Sandomierz prov.	63,998	14,937	23.34	277,319	10,821	3.90
Lublin prov.	47,791	15,602	32.64	175,524	8618	4.91
Duchy of Siewiersk	3324	–	–	15,240	10	0.07
TOTAL	166,099	38,156	22.97	697,041	24,004	3.44

discovered in the 1764 census, and confirmed by the figures in Table 21.5, the majority of Jews lived in the towns, but the number living in villages was also relatively high, as much as 40 per cent of the total Jewish population. The percentage of Jews living in the towns and the rural areas is shown in Table 21.6. From these figures it can be clearly seen that the Jews made up an important part of the population of the towns. Throughout Little Poland the Poles amounted to 22.97 per cent of the town population, with the percentage of Jews increasing as we move eastwards. It began at 14.64 per cent in Kraków province, 23.34 per cent in Sandomierz province and then reached 32.64 per cent in Lublin province. In the villages Jews were only a small part of the population, from 2 per cent in Kraków province up to less than 5 per cent in Lublin province.

Taking advantage of the fact that the 1787 census provides detailed information about the number of the general population and the number of Jews in each settlement, I have examined in detail the figures for over 4,000 villages in the census. This was to determine how many villages had no Jewish inhabitants, as well as those with Jews. I have divided the latter into several categories, depending on the number of Jews living there, as follows: 1–5 Jews, 6–10, 11–20, 21–50, and over 50. The results for various provinces are presented in Tables 21.7–21.9, and in Table 21.10 for all Little Poland.

Analysing these tables leads to interesting conclusions. For example it shows that at the end of the eighteenth century there were no Jews in many villages in Little Poland. The stereotype Jewish innkeeper as an indispensable element of the Polish village is not true for the territories of Little Poland. In the majority of villages of Kraków province there were no Jews at all (53.19 per cent). Of the villages inhabited by Jews (46.81 per cent), the most common were those where there were no more than five of them, presumably one family. These villages account for 20.17 per cent. Of the villages, 17.28 per cent had 6–10 Jews, or 1–2 families living there. The rest, which amount to less than 10 per cent, were the villages with more than 10 Jews. Those villages with more than 20 Jews were exceptional.

In Sandomierz province only about 30 per cent of the villages had no Jews, while the most common were those with 6–10 Jews (30.16 per cent), and those with fewer than 5 Jews (25.91 per cent). The number of villages with 11–20 Jewish inhabitants (11.24 per cent), and those above 20 Jews (over 3 per cent), was much higher than for the corresponding groups in Kraków province. Two administrative units in this province differ from the rest of the province in the percentage of those with no Jewish inhabitants, and those where some had settled. These were the Stężyca region on the right bank of the River Vistula, where only 13.13 per cent had no Jews, and the Chęciny district, where villages of this kind were as much as 61.87 per cent. These differences are easy to explain. The Stężyca region is very similar to the neighbouring districts of Lublin province, while in the case of the Chęciny district only a small part of it was investigated, as the rest was not part of the

Table 21.7
Jewish population in the villages of Little Poland on the basis of the 1787 census

Province	Admin. unit	No. of villages	Villages without Jews		Villages grouped according to numbers of Jews living in them									
					1-5		6-10		11-20		21-50		over 50	
			no.	%	no.	%	no.	%	no.	%	no.	%	no.	%
Kraków	Kraków dist.	295	192	65.08	40	13.56	37	12.54	20	6.78	5	1.69	1	0.35
	Proszowice dist.	300	148	49.33	74	24.67	55	18.33	18	6.00	5	1.67	–	–
	Książ dist.	287	132	45.99	64	22.30	63	21.95	26	9.06	2	0.70	–	–
	Lelów dist.	293	153	52.22	59	20.14	48	16.38	23	7.85	8	2.73	2	0.68
TOTAL		1175	625	53.19	237	20.17	203	17.28	87	7.40	20	1.70	3	0.26

Table 21.8
Jewish population in villages, on the basis of the 1787 census

Province	Admin. unit	No. of villages	Villages without Jews		Villages grouped according to numbers of Jews living in them									
					1-5		6-10		11-20		21-50		over 50	
			no.	%	no.	%	no.	%	no.	%	no.	%	no.	%
Sandomierz	Chęciny dist.	118	73	61.87	22	18.64	22	18.64	1	0.85	–	–	–	–
	Wiślica dist.	447	121	27.07	136	30.42	126	28.19	51	11.41	13	2.91	–	–
	Sandomierz dist.	681	192	28.20	184	27.02	244	35.83	59	8.66	2	0.29	–	–
	Radom dist.	486	160	32.92	131	26.95	129	26.54	53	10.91	12	2.47	1	0.21
	Stężyca region	198	26	13.13	27	13.64	61	30.81	53	26.76	29	14.65	2	1.01
TOTAL		1930	572	29.64	500	25.91	582	30.16	217	11.24	56	2.90	3	0.15

Table 21.9
Jewish population in villages, on the basis of the 1787 census

Province	Admin. unit	No. of villages	Villages without Jews		Villages grouped according to numbers of Jews living in them									
					1-5		6-10		11-20		21-50		over 50	
		no.	no.	%	no.	%	no.	%	no.	%	no.	%	no.	%
Lublin	Lublin dist.	368	56	15.22	66	17.93	115	31.25	86	23.37	43	11.69	2	0.54
	Urzędów dist.	236	68	28.81	35	14.83	61	25.85	46	19.49	19	8.05	7	2.97
	Łuków region	252	26	10.32	57	22.62	84	33.33	61	24.21	22	8.73	2	0.79
TOTAL		856	150	17.52	158	18.46	260	30.37	193	22.55	84	9.81	11	1.29

Table 21.10
Jewish population in the villages of Little Poland on the basis of the 1787 census

Administration unit	No. of villages		Villages without Jews		Villages grouped according to numbers of Jews living in them									
					1-5		6-10		11-20		21-50		over 50	
	no.		no.	%	no.	%	no.	%	no.	%	no.	%	no.	%
Kraków	625		237	53.19	203	20.17	87	17.28	20	7.40	3	1.70	3	0.26
Sandomierz	572		500	29.64	582	25.91	217	30.16	56	11.24	3	2.90	3	0.15
Lublin province	150		158	17.52	260	18.46	193	30.37	84	22.55	11	9.81	11	1.29
Duchy of Siewierz	73		2	97.33	–	2.67	–	–	–	–	–	–	–	–
TOTAL	1420		897	35.18	1045	22.23	497	25.90	160	12.31	17	3.96	17	0.42

Kraków diocese and was therefore not included in the census. On the other hand, the part that was covered by the census included several villages belonging to the bishops of Kraków and Jews were not allowed to settle there.

Lublin province had only 17.52 per cent of its villages with no Jews living there. It should be noted that in the Łuków region part of the province this percentage falls to 10.32 per cent. The most common villages were those inhabited by 6–10 Jews (30.37 per cent), and 11–20 Jews (22.55 per cent). In other 10 per cent of the villages there were over 20 Jews.

When analysing the figures for the whole of Little Poland, once again the same phenomenon can be seen of the number of Jews increasing as one moves eastwards.

THE JEWISH ROLE IN THE ECONOMY

After having considered the size and distribution of Jews in prepartition Poland, we shall now examine their professions and occupations, and their role in the economy. We shall concentrate on their activities in the villages.

The village Jews, who were a considerable percentage of the Jewish population, farmed only on a small scale. They engaged in various activities which we would now call service industries. Also those Jews who lived in towns had considerable relations with the countryside. This applies mainly to Jews living in private towns, which were often the main economic centres of magnates' latifundia.

To understand the role fulfilled by the Jewish population in the last years of the Polish Commonwealth, one has to go back to the mid seventeenth century when, as is well known, a great strain was put on the Polish economy by the lengthy conflicts on Polish territory. Beginning with the Cossack rebellion in spring 1648, which brought great misery to the Jewish population of the Ukraine, the Polish Commonwealth was to know no peace over the next thirty years. The crisis of wars with foreign enemies (Russia, Sweden, Transylvania, Turkey, Crimean Khanate) was made worse by domestic conflicts. The experience Poland went through in the mid seventeenth century resembled the earlier Russian catastrophe of the 'Time of Troubles' or that in Germany during the Thirty Years War. The consequences were also similar. There was a sharp decline in the population, and economic collapse. Thanks to the research of J. Rutkowski during the First World War,[13] and later research in the 1950s,[14] we know a lot about the scale of this crisis in Poland in the second half of the seventeenth century. It is also worth remembering that even before the military catastrophe, there were several problems in the workings of the Polish feudal economy. The catastrophe therefore hit an economy which was already showing several symptoms of crisis.[15]

The last years of the seventeenth century were much more peaceful for the Polish Commonwealth. Wars occurred outside Polish territory, and the Polish economy started to recover from the decline produced by the events of the mid century. Yet the pace of recovery was rather slow, because the problems of the feudal system still retarded economic development.

The beginning of the eighteenth century saw another blow to the Polish economy in the shape of a further Swedish invasion. The lengthy struggle, which took place throughout Polish territories, worsened the crisis, which had not yet been resolved, and also increased the related political decline of the state. It took a long time for the Polish economy to recover from the decline. It only reached pre-crisis levels by the end of the eighteenth century. To explain the causes of the Polish economic crisis merely by military defeats and the destruction of wars would be to oversimplify the problem. As I have said, the workings of the feudal system were one of the reasons for the backwardness of the Polish economy, reaching back to before the seventeenth-century catastrophe. The inefficiency of villein service and the consequent need to keep

---

[13] J. Rutkowski, 'Przebudowa wsi w Polsce po wojnach z połowy XVII w.' (Reconstruction of the Polish village after the wars of the mid seventeenth century), *Kwartalnik Historyczny* 30, 1916.

[14] Many studies on the destruction caused by the Swedish war (1655–60) in various Polish provinces have been published in a collection *Polska w czasie drugiej wojny północnej* (Poland during the second northern war), Warsaw, 1957, vol. II. Several articles on the topic have been published since as well. E. Trzyna's paper 'Kwestia zniszczeń wojennych i wojskowych oraz zahamowanie rozwoju gospodarczego królewszczyzn województwa krakowskiego w drugiej połowie XVII w.' (The question of war and military destruction and the stagnation in the economic development of royal estates in Kraków province in the second half of the seventeenth century), in *Małopolskie Studia Historyczne* 8:, 1965 is worth noting on the region we are interested in.

[15] S. Śreniowski, 'Oznaki regresu ekonomicznego w ustroju folwarczno-pań szczyźnianym w Polsce u schyłku XVI w.' (Signs of the economic decline of the folwark-villein system in Poland at the end of the sixteenth century), *Kwartalnik Historyczny* 61, 1954.

increasing it, which caused the peasants almost to abandon their own economic activities because they were weighed down with labour services, their isolation from the market, the decline of the towns, and the unproductive three-field system are among the fundamental reasons for the Polish economic crisis. This was made worse by wars and the destruction brought by them.

The list of causes of the long crisis of the Polish economy would not be complete without mentioning the changes in the European grain trade which began in the mid seventeenth century.[16] The Polish economy, geared to producing and exporting agricultural products, experienced an unfavourable and very painful change in the economic situation. There was a sharp decline in the level of grain exports from Poland to Western Europe. In the first half of the seventeenth century grain exports through Danzig (excluding Elbląg) and the Prussian ports, reached 100,000 *lasts* a year, with a peak of 129,000 *lasts* in 1618. The war years led to a general decline in grain export, which is shown by the following figures: in 1651 – 55,000 *lasts* of grain exported; in 1653 – 34,000 *lasts*; in 1656 – 11,000 *lasts*; and in 1659 – 54,000 *lasts*. It was not till after 1661 that there was a rise. This at first came to about 30,000 *lasts* a year, reaching 60,000 in the last quarter of the century.[17] The beginning of the eighteenth century once again saw a decline to 20,000 a year because of the Swedish invasion. There was then an increase to 30,000, reaching over 50,000 in the 1760s. Prussian policy after the first partition led to a further decline to 23,000 *lasts* a year, and only in the last years of independence (1793–5) did exports rise to 28,000 *lasts* a year.[18]

It is hard to determine whether these variations in grain exports were caused by a fall in production or by the European economic situation. Both factors certainly played an important part. The decline in the price of grain and the decreased demand for exports made the producers of grain, that is mainly the *szlachta* and the magnates, look for other ways of making money from grain. They found this above all in producing alcohol from grain (mainly vodka, but beer as well), and selling it to their subject in their own inns. Peasants were prohibited from purchasing alcohol produced on

---

[16] W. Abel, *Agrarkrisen und Agrarkonjunktur in Mittleuropa vom 13 bis 19. Jahrhunderten*, Berlin, 1935.
[17] J. Rutkowski, *Historia gospodarcza Polski (do 1864 r.)*, (Economic history of Poland up to the year 1864), Warsaw, 1953, p. 118.
[18] Ibid., p. 252

other estates or sold in other inns. They were also forbidden to produce it themselves, and forced by their lords to buy a certain quantity of vodka from them. All this is quite well known from existing historical literature and there is no need to discuss it here further.

What is important for us is the magnate and noble grain producers turning from exporting grain to processing and selling it in the form of alcohol as a way of raising revenues from the feudal economy. This change provided opportunities for the Jewish population which grew in number in the Polish Commonwealth at that time. Jews started to play an important role in this new development in the noble economy. This phenomenon was apparent mainly in those regions which had a grain surplus and were far from the rivers flowing towards the Baltic and therefore had less opportunity to export the grain by sea to Western Europe. These regions were largely in the south-east of the Polish Commonwealth, that is the Ukraine, Wołyń, Podole and, to some extent, Red Ruthenia. Here the new ways of raising revenue from alcohol production became most common, and here the Jewish role in the economy of these territories became exceptionally important.

During the bloody Cossack rebellions, especially the Chmielnicki revolt, part of the Jewish population of these territories was murdered by the Cossacks and local peasants, and part fled the Ukraine through fear of looting and murder. When the situation became more settled in the eighteenth century, and the feudal economy was again intensively developed in the south-eastern borderlands of the Commonwealth, there was an increasing influx of Jews and a growth of their role in the working of the *szlachta* economy. Even the new wave of social unrest in the 1750s and 1760s, including the famous *Koliwszczyzna*, did not frighten them away, even though they suffered considerably, and the Ukraine proved no exception. The role of the Jews in the noble economy also grew in the second half of the seventeenth and in the eighteenth centuries in the other territories of the Commonwealth, even though it probably never matched its importance in the south-eastern territories. Further detailed research should enable us to be clearer about how different regions were affected.

The growing role of the Jewish population in village economic life during the years of crisis will now be discussed. Its importance here clearly grew because of the nobles' new way of raising revenue through distilling alcohol and the increasing part this played in the income of the estate owners. Several works by Polish historians on the problem of the incomes of large estates show this phenomenon of the steady growth of the role of revenue from alcohol in their total income.[19] In the region which is of particular interest to us, Little Poland, a very interesting analysis of the changes in incomes of the royal estates of Sandomierz and Kraków provinces from the sixteenth to the eighteenth century has been presented by two young historians from the Jagiellonian University, Andrzej Burzyński and Krzysztof Zamorski.[20]

It appears from the figures in Burzyński's work that, even in the territories which were better placed for exporting grain, the revenue from the industrial and processing economy, mainly from the alcohol industry and mills, amounted to the following: in 1565–5.4 per cent, in 1629–9 per cent, in 1664–6.7 per cent and in 1789–39.3 per cent of total income.

Alcohol production in the eighteenth century was largely dominated by Jews. This also applies to its sale, which was carried out by innkeepers. The inn as an institution in Poland, as in most of Europe, has a tradition dating back to the Middle Ages. Its evolution has largely been a reflection of more general changes in the agrarian economy and the structure of rural relations. This is quite well known, partly thanks to Burszta's research.[21]

In the eighteenth century inns were almost exclusively the

[19] Even before the Second World War J. Rutkowski was interested in the income patterns of the great estates. In 1938 he published an introductory volume devoted to this subject: *Badania nad podziałem dochodów w Polsce w czasach nowożytnych*, I: *Rozważania teoretyczne – Klasyfikacja dochodów wielkich właścicieli ziemskich* (Research on the distribution of incomes in Poland in the early modern times, I: Theoretical considerations – Classification of incomes of the great landowners), Kraków, 1938. Unfortunately, further volumes were destroyed during the war. In the post-war years many historians (J. Leskiewiczowa, L. Żytkowicz, J. Chlebowczyk, A. Falniowska-Gradowska, H. Madurowicz-Urbańska, A. Podraza, M. Różycka-Glassowa, I. Rychlikowa, W. Serczyk, E. Trzyna, A. Wyczański and others) have worked on these problems, devoting special studies and monographs to them.

[20] A. Burzyński, 'Struktura dochodów wielkiej własności ziemskiej XVI–XVIII wieku (Próba analizy województwa sandomierskiego)' (Income patterns of the great estates from the sixteenth to eighteenth centuries (An attempt at analysis of Sandomierz province)), *Roczniki Dziejów Społecznych i Gospodarczych* 34, 1973; K. Zamorski, 'Struktura dochodów wielkiej własności ziemskiej XVI–XVIII wieku. Próba analizy na przykładzie dóbr królewskich woj. krakowskiego' (Income patterns of the great estates from the sixteenth to eighteenth centuries. An attempt at analysis on the basis of the royal estates of Kraków province), *Roczniki Dziejów Społecznych i Gospodarczych* 39, 1978.

[21] Burszta, *Wieś i karczma*.

property of the landowners, and the revenues engendered by them were a relatively large part of the owners' total income. To fulfil such a role it had to be run by a canny person, who knew about trade and had some general education (that is, literate and numerate). Jews were better able to fulfil such functions than the local peasants. Moreover, Jews often did not drink alcohol themselves, which would probably not have been the case if innkeepers had been chosen from the local peasants. Drinkers were hardly the right people to run inns which were to provide their own incomes and also provide the greatest possible profit for the owner of the village. Thus Jews were much more in demand than peasants as innkeepers. It is hardly surprising therefore that at the end of the eighteenth century a large percentage of innkeepers in the Polish Commonwealth were Jews. This does not, however, mean that it was the case everywhere, as especially in the western part of the Commonwealth the number of Jewish innkeepers was very small. In the western part, in the territory of Great Poland, revenues from alcohol were still a relatively minor part of the estate owners' income. Western Little Poland came somewhere in the middle, as over 50 per cent of all the villages in Kraków province did not have even one Jew and therefore did not have Jewish innkeepers. Further to the east the number of these villages diminished, and the percentage of revenues from alcohol played a greater part in total incomes. Innkeepers, usually Jews, were generally called *arendors*. This was because innkeepers obtained their inns through a lease or *arenda*. But the term *arenda* did not apply only to inn leases. Various leases, which were all called *arenda*, were purchased by Jews from the landlords to allow them to collect various revenues. There were cases of the lease of whole estates to Jewish *arendors* in the east, but the most common lease or *arenda* was that of part of a landlord's revenues, such as the peasants' dues, income from sawmills, bleaching works and other industrial enterprises, including distilleries and breweries. Jewish *arendors* also played a considerable role in the exploitation of woods. The Jews in the villages managed to acquire a large part of what trade there was in them. This was true for the trade of the large estates as well as for that of the peasants. Jews often acted as agents in the sale of the estate crops and other products of the feudal economy.[22] Trade in peasants' crops as well as the import

[22] Cf. L. Rychlikowa, *Studia nad towarową produkcją wielkiej własności w*

of craft work and industrial goods needed by the village was also largely concentrated in the hands of Jewish village innkeepers and Jewish town merchants. Finally Jews played an increasingly important role in the countryside's credit relations, both of peasants and landowners.

Thanks to R. Rybarski's research we have a good idea of the credit relations in the villages belonging to the great royal complex, the Samborsk Economy, in the eighteenth century.[23] This research shows that while the Jews were not the dominant creditors, their part in lending money to peasants was relatively important, amounting to about 20 per cent. In credit relations with the large estate owners it was the *kehilla* banks that played an important role. Both the lay nobility and the clergy invested their money in these banks at an interest rate of 7 to 10 per cent. Part of the money invested went to finance Jewish trade and loans to nobles and burghers.[24]

Jewish economic activity was diverse, and only a brief account of it has been given in this chapter. Further research will allow us to present a more complete and adequate assessment of the role of Jews in the economic life of the village in pre-partition Poland. Another interesting research topic would be how this role was viewed by contemporaries.

Małopolsce w latach 1764–1805 (Studies on the production of goods in the great estates in Little Poland in 1764–1805), part 1, Wrocław, 1966.

[23] R. Rybarski, *Kredyt i lichwa w ekonomii samborskiej w XVIII w.*, (Credit and usury in the Sambor Economy in the eighteenth century), Lwów, 1936.

[24] Rutkowski, *Historia gospodarcza*, p. 261.

22 · The Jewish Population in the Towns on the West Bank of the Vistula in Sandomierz Province from the Sixteenth to the Eighteenth Centuries

Zenon Guldon and Karol Krzystanek

Modern research on the population within Poland's borders during the Nobles' Republic was begun in the years 1882–3 with the pioneer works of Tadeusz Korzon and Adolf Pawiński.[1] This research was based primarily on such indirect sources as registers of land tax (*Łanowe*), hearth-tax (*podymne*) and poll tax (*pogłówne*) assessments from the sixteenth to eighteenth centuries, and on the examination of state and church statistics from the second half of the eighteenth century. Closer research into this source material has suggested that its varying degrees of accuracy and incompatible statistical methods have resulted in a lack of consistency, not only in absolute numbers, but also in analysing demographic trends from the sixteenth to the eighteenth centuries.[2] Thus the view is often expressed that demographic research on this period can go no further, given the disappointing and controversial results so far achieved,[3] and also that future research should be based, above all, on public registers, which could verify results obtained from

---

[1] See Z. Sułowski, 'Stulecie polskiej demografii historycznej 1882–1982' (A century of Polish historical demography 1882–1982), in *Przeszłość Demograficzna Polski* (henceforth *PDP*) 15 1984, pp. 9–35.

[2] Z. Guldon, 'Zaludnienie Kujaw w końcu XVIII w.' (The population of Kujawy at the end of the eighteenth century), *PDP* 14, 1983, pp. 137–44.

[3] L. Gieysztorowa, 'Wytyczne prac nad rewizją i korektą statystyki demograficznej ziem polskich XIX w. – Uwagi wstępne' (Guidelines for works on the revision and correction of demographic statistics in Polish territories in the nineteenth century – preliminary notes), *PDP* 12, 1980, p. 191.

fiscal authorities. This possibility does not, however, exist with regard to the Jewish population.

Our knowledge of the size of the Jewish population from the sixteenth to the eighteenth centuries is due to the research of Ignacy Schipper,[4] whose results, with some slight modifications, have been recently accepted by Salo Baron[5] and Maurycy Horn.[6] In Zygmunt Sułowski's work, however, we find a somewhat different approach to, and view of, the mechanics of Jewish demographic expansion.[7] For the mid eighteenth century, Raphael Mahler's results are of great value.[8] Among the works concentrating on selected periods and regions, one can also mention Professor Horn's monograph on the Jewish population of Red Ruthenia in the second half of the sixteenth and first half of the seventeenth century,[9] and Anatol Leszczyński's monograph devoted to the Jewish population of Bielsko district in the period from the mid seventeenth to the end of the eighteenth century.[10] One of the authors of this chapter, Zenon Guldon, has attempted to estimate the Jewish population in towns of Sandomierz province in the second half of the seventeenth century.[11] As some of the research on Jewish population lacks a close analysis of original sources, Guldon tried elsewhere to determine the usefulness of the various

---

[4] I. Schipper, 'Rozwój ludności żydowskiej na ziemiach dawnej Rzeczypospolitej' (The Development of Jewish Population on the Territory of the Old Commonwealth) in *Żydzi w Polsce Odrodzonej* (Jews in reborn Poland) I, Warsaw, 1933, pp. 29–35.

[5] S. W. Baron, *A Social and Religious History of the Jews*, XVI: *Poland-Lithuania 1500–1650*, New York/Philadelphia, 1976.

[6] M. Horn, 'Ludność żydowska w Polsce do końca XVIIIw.' (Jewish population in Poland to the end of the eighteenth century) in M. Fuks, Z. Hoffman, M. Horn and J. Tomaszewski, eds, *Żydzi Polscy. Dzieje i kultura* (Polish Jews, history and culture), Warsaw, 1982.

[7] Z. Sułowski, 'Mechanizmy ekspansji demograficznej Żydów w miastach polskich XVI–XIX wieku' (The mechanics of Jewish demographic expansion in Polish towns from the sixteenth to the nineteenth centuries), *Zeszyty Naukowe Katolickiego Uniwersytetu Lubelskiego* 17:3, 1974, pp. 93–110; also in French as 'Les Mechanismes de l'expansion démographique des Juifs dans les villes de Pologne aux XVIe–XIXe siècle's *Zeszyty Naukowe KUL* 21, special edn, 1978, pp. 89–100.

[8] R. Mahler, *[Jews in Old Poland in the Light of Figures]* (in Yiddish), Warsaw 1958. Fragments of this work were published in *PDP* 1, 1967, pp. 131–80.

[9] M. Horn, *Żydzi na Rusi Czerwonej w XVI i pierwszej połowie XVII w.*, (Jews in Red Ruthenia in the sixteenth and first half of the seventeenth centuries), Warsaw, 1975, pp. 42–82.

[10] A. Leszczyński, *Żydzi ziemi bielskiej od połowy XVII w. do 1795 r.* (Jews of Biała Podlaska Region from the mid seventeenth century to 1795), Wrocław 1980, ch. I.

[11] Z. Guldon, 'Ludność żydowska w miastach województwa sandomierskiego w II połowie XVII (Jewish population in towns of Sandomierz province in the second half of the seventeenth century), *BŻIH* 3–4, 1982, pp. 17–29.

types of source material and the nature of the methods applied to the assessment of Jewish population in the kingdom of Poland during the Nobles' Commonwealth.[12] This was a much-needed piece of research as this problem had not yet really been faced in research devoted to the sources of Old Poland's demography.[13]

In the first half of the sixteenth century, tax was levied only on Jewish families (1538),[14] or on Jews *qui proprio foco utuntur* (1552).[15] In the first case, the *patres familias* were to pay. There is no justification for assuming that the 1549 Diet instituted a regular Jewish poll tax.[16] Only once in that year did the king – not the Diet – impose a tribute on Jews living in royal towns and, under penalty of the deprivation of their privileges and liberties, 'encourage' them to pay it by also levying the tax on the Jews living in private towns. The tribute was imposed in *singula capita Iudaeorum omnis aetatis et sexus utriusque*.[17] A regular Jewish poll tax was introduced by a 1563 tax edict.[18] Tax was to be paid at the rate of one złoty 'per head'.[19] All were subject to the poll tax – 'nobody of either sex, big or small, to be exempted',[20] apart from impoverished Jews, specified in the edict as 'living on alms'. In 1569, total tax collected in the kingdom slightly exceeded 6,000 Polish złoty,[21] and if we treat the data literally, we should conclude that the Jews numbered 6,000.

Schipper has assumed, without giving a reason, that the poll tax was assessed on households. Therefore, taking between 6 and 11 persons to one złoty of poll tax, he reaches an estimate of about

---

[12] Z. Guldon, 'Źródła i metody szacunków liczebnosci ludnosci żydowskiej w Polsce w XVI–XVIII wieku', (Sources and methods of estimating the numbers of Jewish population in Poland from the sixteenth to the eighteenth centuries), *Kwartalnik Historii Kultury Materialnej* (henceforth *KHKM*) 34:2, 1986, pp. 249–63.
[13] Z. Guldon and K. Wajda, *Źródła statystyczne do dziejów Pomorza wschodniego i Kujaw od XVI do poczatków XX w.* (Statistical sources for the history of eastern Pomorze and Kujawy, 16th to early 20th centuries), Toruń, 1970; I. Gieysztorowa, *Wstęp do demografii staropolskiej* (Introduction to the demography of Old Poland), Warsaw, 1976.
[14] AGAD, *Metryka Koronna* 54, p. 395v.
[15] *Volumina Legum* II, Petersburg, 1859, p. 10.
[16] See Baron, *History*, p. 19.
[17] AGAD, *Metryka Koronna* 77, pp. 214v–15v.
[18] W. Pałucki ed., 'Uniwersały poborowe z 1563 r.' (Tax collector's edicts from 1563), *KHKM* 14:3, 1966, p. 527.
[19] *Volumina Legum* II, p. 40.
[20] Ibid., pp. 407–8.
[21] Z. Guldon and N. Krikun, 'Przyczynek do krytyki spisów żydowskich z końca XVIII wieku, '(Contribution to a critical approach to Jewish censuses from the end of the eighteenth century), *Studia Źródłoznawcze* 23, 1978, Table 1.

100,000 Jews living in Poland in the second half of the sixteenth century.[22] Horn accepted the poll character of the tax and is convinced that a large part of the Jewish population evaded payment. Thus he estimates 3.3 persons per 1 złoty of poll tax.[23] Recently, Sułowski, following Horn's research, proposed tripling Schipper's figures, and thus argued that by the end of the sixteenth century, Polish territory was inhabited by about 300,000 Jews.[24] He failed to realize that, if one follows Horn's results, one should reduce Schipper's figure by at least half, certainly not raise it by 300 per cent. In conclusion, we can say that the size of the Jewish population within the borders of the Nobles' Commonwealth in the second half of the sixteenth century was between 100,000 and 300,000 persons, but that no figure is fully confirmed by the poll tax registers, since this tax was paid by only a few thousand people.

The situation is no better for the seventeenth century. The numbers estimated by Schipper for the first half of this century,[25] are – as Weinryb has pointed out[26] – completely hypothetical. According to his estimates, in the first half of the seventeenth century about 180,000 Jews died or left Poland.[27] Demographic research for the second half of the seventeenth century is based primarily on the registers of general poll tax from 1662 to 1676. Schipper used the 1676 registers. He enlarged his findings by adding in children under twelve, who did not pay tax, on the assumption that they formed 24 per cent of the whole population. He therefore arrived at about 180,000 Jews living in Poland in those days.[28] It is certainly true that in 1676 the number of poll-tax payers declined to 49 per cent of those in 1662.[29] But this,

---

[22] Schipper, 'Rozwój ludności', pp. 29–30.
[23] Horn, Żydzi na Rusi Czerwonej, p. 62.
[24] Sułowski, 'Mechanizmy', Table 1.
[25] Schipper, 'Rozwój ludności', p. 31.
[26] B. D. Weinryb, The Jews of Poland: A Social and Economic History of the Jewish Community in Poland from 1100 to 1800, Philadelphia, 1973, p. 397, n. 34.
[27] Schipper, 'Rozwój ludności', p. 32. A smaller loss is assumed by S. W. Baron, History, p. 207 and M. Horn, 'Ludność żydowska', p. 16.
[28] Schipper, 'Rozwój ludności', p. 32.
[29] R. Rybarski, Skarb i pieniądz za Jana Kazimierza, Michała Korybuta i Jana III (The Treasury and money in the time of Jan Kazimierz, Michał Korybut and Jan III), Warsaw, 1939, pp. 190–1.

according to Dobrowolski,[30] was 'the effect of falsification, not a real decline in the number of people'.[31] In any case, we can assume that Schipper's estimate for the second half of the seventeenth century is too low and Baron's figure of 350,000 is much closer to the truth.[32]

For the second half of the eighteenth century, the registers of Jewish poll tax from 1765 to 1790 are the major source. There has already been much discussion of the accuracy of those registers.[33] To this we can add that the 1787 Jewish census in the districts of Radom and Sandomierz shows only 58 per cent of the Jews included in the Kraków diocese's census from the same year.[34] A recent account of the latter has concluded that in it 'barely half of them are registered, to the extent that where ten Jews are to be found, there barely five are listed'.[35] In the town of Lubar in Wołyń in 1790, only 70 people were registered 'and more were hard to find (although this town could number more than over 1000 Jewish heads), as they had escaped earlier to the woods and across the River Słucz'.[36]

In the light of poll-tax registers from 1765 to 1776, the number of Jews in the comparable area of Poland after the first partition went down from 258,000 to 162,000, increasing later to 219,000 in 1787.[37] It is known from elsewhere that the first partition left about a quarter of a million Jews outside Poland, about 225,000 of these in Galicia.[38] The Austrian authorities forced indigent Jews to leave Galicia, as is confirmed by a report of the customs administrator of the province of Ruthenia, who wrote in 1783:

> We are to undergo a new mean of expelling over the border the ever-multiplying tramps, rascals and those of no use to the state.

---

[30] K. Dobrowolski, 'Dzieje wsi Niedźwiedzia w powiecie limanowskim na schyłku dawnej Rzeczypospolitej' (The history of the village of Niedźwiedź in the district of Limanowa at the decline of the Commonwealth), in *Studia z historii społecznej i gospdoarczej poświęcone prof. dr. Fr. Bujakowi*, Lwów, 1931, p. 518.

[31] Gieysztorowa, *Wstęp*, p. 196.

[32] Baron, *History*, p. 207.

[33] See Guldon, 'Źródła i metody', pp. 257–61.

[34] Ibid., Table 5.

[35] J. Kracik, *'Wokół spisu ludności diecezji krakowskiej z roku 1787'* (On the 1787 census of Kraków Diocese), *Studia Historyczne* 1 1985, pp. 35–6.

[36] Guldon and Krikun, 'Przyczynek', p. 156.

[37] Z. Guldon and L. Stępkowski, 'Spis ludności żydowskiej z 1790 roku' (1790 Jewish population census), *BŻIH* 3–4 1986, Table 1.

[38] Schipper, 'Rozwój ludności', p. 35.

Jews from across the border with no means of livelihood or ability to pay taxes, together with gypsies and other tramps convicted of theft and other crimes, are driven in large numbers to our side of the border by military force. Recently, at the beginning of May, Jews of towns across the border supplied the commissioner of the Zaleszczyki *kreis* [district], Hayszechger, and its secretary Pokorny who collects taxes, with a list of their poor kinsmen who are unable to meet payments. They were given an order from headquarters to drive them across the border. Thus one party of those from Czortków, Jezierzany and other towns were driven by hussars through Zbrucz and then across the border to the Polish side. Our guard standing there tried as best he could to stem their movement but being expelled by force from the toll-gate, he had to give way to the military. Similarly in Husiatyń, the guard, seeing a crowd of Jews approaching, closed the toll-bar, pushed them away and made them turn back. Some time later, a captain, the commanding officer of Husiatyń, Haagsen, forced open the toll-gate and forcibly drove the aforementioned Jews across to our side.[39]

This policy on the part of the Austrian authorities was maintained until a Statute of Toleration was passed in 1789.[40]

In the historical literature, it is assumed that the number of Jews grew in the years 1765 to 1790, from 750,000 within the pre-partitioned Poland of 1765[41] to 900,000 in 1790,[42] within the new borders after the first partition. This increase is due, to at least some degree, to the different methods used for the estimates of 1765 and 1790.

Results of research so far on the size of Jewish population in the Nobles' Commonwealth in the sixteenth to eighteenth centuries are shown in Table 22.1. According to Baron's research, it appears that in the period between the mid sixteenth and mid seventeenth centuries, the ratio of Jews to the whole population of Poland grew from 2 to 6.6 per cent.[43] In the mid seventeenth century, Poland

---

[39] AGAD, *Archiwum Królestwa Polskiego* (Archives of the Polish Kingdom) 37, p. 670.
[40] J. Karniel, 'Das Toleranzpatent Kaiser Joseph II für die Juden Galiziens und Lodomeriens', *Jahrbuch des Institut für Deutsche Geschichte* 11, 1982, pp. 55–89.
[41] R. Mahler, 'Żydzi w dawnej Polsce', *PDP* 1, 1967, p. 161.
[42] T. Czacki, *Rozprawa a Żydach i Karaitach* (Dissertation on Jews and Karaites), Kraków, 1860, p. 117.
[43] Baron, *History*, p. 207.

Table 22.1
Enumeration of Jews on the territory of the Polish Commonwealth in the sixteenth–eighteenth centuries

Year	Number of Jews in the Commonwealth				Population of Greater Poland, Little Poland and Mazowsze	
	Schipper and Czacki est.[a]		Baron est.[b]		Gieysztorowa est.[c]	
	pop. 000s	chain co-eff[d]	pop. 000's	chain co-eff.	pop. millions	chain co-eff.
1578	100	100	150	100	3.1	100
c.1650	450	450	450	300	3.8	122.6
1662–76	180	40	350	77.8	2.9	76.3
1765	–	–	750	214.3	–	–
1790	900	500	–	–	4.0	137.9

Notes: [a] I. Schipper, 'Rozwój ludności' (see no. 4); T. Czacki, *Rozprawa* (see no. 42).
[b] S. W. Baron, *History of the Jews* (see n. 5).
[c] I. Gieysztorowa, *Wstęp* (see n. 13).
[d] The chain co-efficient represents, in percentage terms, the relationship of each figure in the 'population' column to its preceding figure.

was inhabited by 30 per cent of world Jewry, and at the turn of the eighteenth century this percentage grew to almost 45.[44] According to Schipper's research, the number of Jews in Poland between 1662 and 1676, and from then until 1790, increased five times. The whole population of Great Poland, Little Poland and Mazowsze in that period increased by only 38 per cent, as has been demonstrated by Gieysztorowa.[45] These figures require further investigation, using modern demographic methods.

Let us now try to analyse the change in the numbers of Jews in towns situated on the western bank of the River Vistula in the province of Sandomierz. Besides fiscal documents such as tax registers, catalogues and lists, this chapter is based on such sources as municipal records, church sources and the surprisingly rich series of charters. These last need critical appraisal, because of the recent discovery of the activities of the man who was probably the biggest Jewish forger of documents in old Poland, Abraham

---

[44] Z. Sułowski, 'Liczebność Żydów na ziemiach polskich' (The number of Jews on Polish territory), in *Naród – Kościół – Kultura. Szkice z historii Polski* (Nation – Church – Culture. Studies in Polish History), Lublin, 1986, p. 239.
[45] I. Gieysztorowa, 'Ludność' (Population), in *Encyklopedia historii gospodarczej Polski do 1945 roku* I, Warsaw, 1981, p. 431.

Moskowicz from Ryczywół, who, *inter alia*, produced privileges for Jews from Żelechów and Gniewoszów. The mere fact of his turning up in Ożarów was enough to induce the owner of the town to appeal in both synagogue and school for the return of the documents forged by him.[46]

In scholarly theses, especially those on the subject of regional history, it is still taken for granted that the issuing of the proclamation *de non tolerandis Judaeis*,[47] or an order moving Jews out of town, are proof that the town was closed to Jews. But very often such orders were not carried out. Radom, which had its privilege *de non tolerandis Judaeis* granted in 1724, and orders proclaimed in 1743 and 1746 for the expulsion of Jews, is a good example. Only in 1769 did the town agree to the temporary settlement of Mendel Zelik's family in homesteads at the foot of the castle.[48] Yet in 1765 we have confirmation of a fairly large Jewish community in Radom. The 1790 census showed 125 Jews living in town,[49] and three years earlier, in 1787, Jews owned nineteen houses and rented two more from Christians. Jews should have been expelled from Sandomierz according to proclamations in 1656 and 1712.[50] This last order was repeated in 1757, but because

---

[46] Z. Guldon, 'Abraham Moskowicz z Ryczywołu – fałszerz dokumentów z końca XVIII wieku' (Abraham Moskowicz of Ryczywół – falsifier of documents from the end of the eighteenth century), *Studia Kieleckie* 4, 1985, pp. 107–9.

[47] J. Goldberg, 'De non tolerandis Iudaeis,' in *Studies in Jewish History Presented to Professor Raphael Mahler*, Merhavia, 1974, pp. 39–52.

[48] J. Gacki, 'Radom i fara nowo-radomska do roku 1800', *Pamiętnik Religijno-Moralny* (Radom and the new Radom parish church before 1800; religious and moral memoir), ser. 2, 5 1860, p. 143; J. Luboński, *Monografia historyczna miasta Radomia* (Historical Monograph of the Town of Radom), Radom, 1907, p. 30.

[49] J. Kleczyński and F. Kluczycki eds, 'Liczba głów żydowskich w Koronie z taryf roku 1765' (The number of Jewish heads in the Crown according to the 1765 records), *Archiwum Komisji Historycznej* (Archive of the Historical Commission), VIII, Kraków, 1898, p. 394; Guldon and Stępkowski, 'Spis ludności żydowskiej', Table 2; Pracownia Słownika Historyczno-Geograficznego Ziem Polskich w Średniowieczu Instytutu Historii PAN w Krakowie, kartoteka materiałów do słownika województwa sandomierskiego w dobie Sejmu Czteroletniego (Workshop of the Historical and Geographical Dictionary of Polish Medieval Territories of the Polish Academy of Sciences in Kraków, file of sources on Sandomierz province during the Four Year Diet): entry – Radom.

[50] M. Bałaban, *Historia Żydów w Krakowie i na Kazimierzu 1304–1868* (History of Jews in Kraków and Kazimierz 1304–1868) II, Kraków, 1936, p. 11, writes that in 1656 King Jan Kazimierz prohibited Jews from living in the town of Sandomierz and its surroundings. Yet by 1658, the king had allowed Jews to rebuild their houses in Sandomierz; M. Horn, ed., *Regesty dokumentów i ekscerpty z Metryki Koronnej do historii Żydów w Polsce 1697–1795* (Summaries and excerpts from the Crown

Jews were useful in offering their services to institutions of the Catholic Church, the proclamation remained on paper only.[51] Again, in 1715, Opoczno Jews were ordered by King August II to destroy their synagogue and leave the town, yet the order had to wait 100 years before being executed in 1815.[52] No more effective was the Abbot of Tyniec's injunction of 1540 prohibiting Jewish settlement in monastically owned Opatowiec – in 1576, six Opatowiec Jews paid poll tax.[53] On the other hand, after a court case in 1610 on a charge of ritual murder, Jews were expelled from Staszów.[54]

In the fourteenth to sixteenth centuries, Jewish population was registered only in Sandomierz[55] and Szydłów.[56] By the second half of the sixteenth century, we find Jews in eighteen out of eighty towns. Taking them all together, Jews paid only 270 Polish złoty in poll tax.[57] Owing to the variety of statistical methods applied, it is hard to estimate the size of the Jewish population, but it is worth recalling that Jewish communities existed already in five royal towns (Sandomierz, Szydłów, Korczyn, Wiślica, Zwoleń) and two

---

Registers for the history of the Jews in Poland 1697–1795) I, Wrocław, 1984, reg. 34. After the charge of ritual murder, King August II ordered the expulsion of Jews from the town and the conversion of the synagogue to a catholic Church in 1712; M. Bersohn, ed., *Dyplomariusz dotyczący Żydów w dawnej Polsce na źródłach archiwalnych osnuty* (Charters regarding Jews in Old Poland taken from the archives), Warsaw, 1910, nos. 298, 377. The sentence was not carried out as in 1721 we have confirmation that Jews lived in the town; A. Getter, *Dzieje Żydów w Sandomierzu do I połowy XVIII w.*,' Archiwum Żydowskiego Instytutu Historycznego (History of Jews in Sandomierz before the first half of the eighteenth century), Master's dissertation, no. 52, p. 31.

[51] J. Wiśniewski, *Katalog prałatów i kanoników sandomierskich 1186–1926 tudzież sesje kapituły sandomierskiej od 1581 r. do 1866 r.* (A catalogue of the Sandomierz prelates and canons 1186–1926, including Sandomierz 'Chapter Sessions' 1581–1866), Radom, 1926, p. 169; W. Wójcik, 'Miasto i Kościół w Sandomierzu w XVI-XVIII w. (Town and church in Sandomierz from the sixteenth to the eighteenth centuries *Czasopismo Prawno–Historyczne*, 14:2, 1962, p. 103.

[52] Archiwum Państwowe w Radomiu, Rząd Gubernialny Radomski (Radom State Archive, Radom Provincial Government), MS 2130a, f. 238.

[53] Archiwum Państwowe w Kielcach, Rząd Gubernialny Radomski, (Kielce State Archive, Radom Provincial Government), MS 2528.

[54] W. Siek, *Opis historyczny miasta i parafii w Szydłowie* (Historical description of town and parish in Szydłów), Sandomierz, 1937, p. 23.

[55] F. Kiryk, 'Sandomierz w czasach Długosza' (Sandomierz in the time of Długosz), in F. Kiryk, ed., *Jan Długosz. W pięćsetną rocznicę śmierci* (Jan Długosz five hundred years after his death), Olsztyn, 1983, p. 12.

[56] A. Penkalla,' Synagoga i gmina w Szydłowie' (Synagogue and community in Szydłów), *BŻIH* 1–2, 1982, pp. 59–60.

[57] Guldon, 'Źródła i metody', Table 2.

private towns (Janowiec, Pińczów). In the first half of the seventeenth century, we find new communities in five royal towns (Chęciny, Stopnica, Kozienice, Przedbórz, Opoczno) and five private towns (Raków, Tarłów, Iwaniska, Chmielnik, Opatów).[58]

Many Jews were killed during the 1654-60 war against Sweden. In 1655 the defence of Sandomierz was undertaken by nobles and a group of a few hundred young Jews. In revenge, Swedes decided to massacre Jews in the Sandomierz and Tarnobrzeg *kehilla*.[59] One year later Czarniecki's troops cut down Jews accused of co-operating with the Swedes. Hebrew sources list names of twenty-three victims – probably the best known. An elegy in honour of the murdered read:

> In the Sandomierz community, those who had been dressed in pure gold were maltreated in the streets; those whom silk covered were thrown on the scrap-heap; pure with abstention, whiter than milk, they turned red; purer than pearls, they were spattered with blood, trodden down in the mud and scattered in the streets.[60]

A similar fate met Jews in Przedbórz (50 families), Tarłów, Zwoleń, Klimontów, Chęciny (150 families), Secemin (50 families), Opatów (200 families), Wiślica (50 families), Chmielnik (100 families) and Pacanów. Only Pińczów gained from its owner's policy, as 150 families from Raków, 200 from Wodzisław and 200 from Szydłów found shelter there.[61] Even if we take into account the possibility of exaggeration, we have to admit that the demographic losses of the Jewish population were considerable.

After the war, from 1662 to 1676, the Jewish population paid poll tax in thirty-six out of eighty-three towns.[62] In the second half of

---

[58] K. Krzystanek, *Ludność żydowska w miastach lewobrzeżnej części województwa sandomierskiego w II połowie XVIII wieku* (The Jewish Population in towns on the west bank of the River Vistula in the province of Sandomierz in the second half of the eighteenth century), Kielce, 1987, chs. 1, 2.

[59] M. Bałaban, *Historia i literatura żydowska ze szczególnym uwzględnieniem historii Żydów w Polsce* (Jewish history and literature with special reference to Jewish history in Poland) III, Lwów, 1925, p. 270.

[60] D. Kandel, 'Rzeź Żydów sandomierskich w 1655 r.' (The massacre of Jews in Sandomierz in 1655), *Kwartalnik Poświęcony Przeszłości Żydów w Polsce* 1:2, 1912, pp. 111-17.

[61] L. Lewin, *Die Judenverfolgungen im zweiten schwedisch-polnischen Kriege*, Posen, 1901, pp. 13-16.

[62] Z. Guldon, 'Źródła i metody', Table 3.

POPULATION

Table 22.2
Jewish centres on the west bank of the Vistula in the province of Sandomierz in the fourteenth to the seventeenth centuries

Town	Date of incorporation	Oldest remark about		Jewish taxpayers 1662–76	
		Jews	community	Year	Number
1	2	3	4	5	6
Chęciny district					
Chęciny	1306–25	1564	1600	1662	157
Przedbórz	1333–70	1595	1634	1662	40
Radoszyce	1370	1615	–	1674	4
Secemin	1395	1649	–	1662	34
Sobków	1563	1662	–	1662	4
Włoszczowa	1539	1662	–	1662	10
Opoczno district					
Gowarczów	1430	1662	–	1662	33
Opoczno	1360	1501	1646	1662	32
Radom district					
Ciepielów	1548	1576	–	–	–
Gniewoszów	1693	–	–	–	–
Janowiec	1537	1571	1580	1662	58
Jedlińsk	1530	1674	–	1674	17
Kazanów	1556	1662	–	1662	16
Kozienice	1549	1607	1629	1662	78
Lipsko	1589	1662	–	1662	22
Nieznamirowice	1440	1676	–	1676	7
Przytyk	1488	1676	–	1676	8
Radom	1360	1568	(?)	–	–
Ryczywoł	1370	1677	1677	–	–
Sienno	1421	1576	–	–	–
Solec	1333–70	1660	–	1662	7
Szydłowiec	1401	1663	–	–	–
Zwoleń	1425	1554	1591	1662	102
Sandomierz district					
Bogoria	1616	1662	–	1662	28
Iwaniska	1500–50	1578	1629	1662	29
Klimontów	1604	1655	–	1662	129
Opatów	1278, 1328	1538	1633	1662	266
Ostrowiec	1597	1637	–	1662	81
Ożarów	1569	1616	–	1662	57
Połaniec	1264	1564	–	1662	19
Raków	1567	1607	1614	1662	104
Sandomierz	1286	1367	1418	1662	53

Table 22.2 continued

Town	Date of incorporation	Oldest remark about		Jewish taxpayers 1662–76	
		Jews	community	Year	Number
1	2	3	4	5	6
Staszów	1510–25	1578	–	–	–
Tarłów	1550	1571	1617	1662	95
Wiślica district					
Chmielnik	1551	1630	1630	1674	65
Kurozwęki.	1400	1578	–	1674	8
Nowe Miasto Korczyn	1258	1530	1569	1674	112
Oleśnica	1546	1676	–	1676	6
Opatowiec	1271	1578	–	–	–
Pacanów	1265	1578	–	1674	64
Pierzchnica	1359–97	1660–4	–	–	–
Pińczów	1428	1576	1592	1674	496
Stopnica	1362	1567	1616	1674	97
Szydłów	1329	1470	1470	1674	103
Wiślica	1345	1514	1542	1674	30

Table 22.3
Number of towns and Jewish centres on the west bank of the Vistula in the province of Sandomierz in the sixteenth to the eighteenth centuries

Tenure	Number of towns			Number of Jewish centres		
	2nd half 16th c.	2nd half 17th c.	End 18th c.	2nd half 16th c.	2nd half 17th c.	End 18th c.
Royal	18	18	19	8	14	19
Private	42	44	46	9	26	44
Church	20	21	20	1	–	12
TOTAL	80	83	85	18	40	75

the seventeenth century, a new Jewish community was formed in a royal town, Ryczywół.[63] We also find Jews in Szydłowiec[64] and in Gniewoszów, which was incorporated in 1693.[65] About 1690, Jews appeared again in Staszów.[66] Table 22.2 shows the growth of Jewish centres and communities in the area under discussion.

In the second half of the seventeenth century, poll tax was paid by 2,302 Jews, which one can interpret as the whole population numbering about 4,600 people. Jews at that time constituted 7 per cent of the total municipal population.[67]

At the end of the eighteenth century, larger or smaller centres of Jewish population existed in 75 out of 85 towns. Jews lived in all the royal towns, in 44 private towns and in 12 towns owned by the clergy (Table 22.3). Of the private towns, only Dębno and Białaczów were closed to them. Stanisław Małachowski, who restored Białaczów 'to laws and municipal status' in 1787, declared:

> It is well known what destruction Jews cause to burghers, whom, in turning [away], as my sincerest wish is for this settlement [to be] the state's pride with enrichment of the burghers, which could not in any way happen with joint residence with Jews, who would then not only buy property in this town, but also pay rent for a Catholic's or Dissident's [Protestant's] house, I therefore forbid Jews to be allowed to stay [here] (except for fairs and markets) any longer than three days.[68]

By the end of the eighteenth century, the number of Jewish communities had risen to 44.[69]

From 1765 to 1790 the number of Jews registered in the area under discussion fell from 28,000 to 19,000, that is by over 30 per cent.[70] It seems that this was largely due to the less reliable

---

[63] Horn, *Regesty dokumentów i ekscerpty* II, part 1, reg. 45.
[64] J. Morgensztern, ed., 'Regesty dokumentów z Metryki Koronnej i Sigillat do historii Żydów w Polsce, 1660–1668' (Summaries of documents from the Crown Registers and Sigillas for the history of Jews in Poland, 1660–1668), *BŻIH* 67, 1968, p. 77, para. 57.
[65] J. Wiśniewski, *Dekanat kozienicki* (The Kozienice Decanate), Radom, 1913, p. 69.
[66] Siek, *Opis historyczny*, p. 24.
[67] Guldon, 'Ludność żydowska', Table 2; idem, 'Źródła i metody', p. 255.
[68] *Dziennik Ekonomiczno-Handlowy*, 1792, p. 140.
[69] Krzystanek, *Ludność żydowska*, 1, 2.
[70] Guldon, 'Źródła i metody', Table 4.

character of the censuses from the end of the century. This is confirmed by the data from 12 urban centres of Jewish population in the province of Sandomierz. Thus in 1765 6,055 Jews were listed.[71] The 1787 church census specified only 2874 Jews (47.5 per cent of the earlier number), whilst the church census from the same year showed 4527 Jews (74.8 per cent of that number).[72] In 1790, 3383 Jews were registered,[73] i.e. 55.9 per cent of the 1765 situation (Table 22.4). As these figures show, the largest number of Jews were registered in the 1765 census, which gave far better results than the later statistical efforts of church and state.

Similar data were gathered in the district of Wiślica. For example, the number of Jews in Pińczów shows a decline in the period 1765 to 1790 from 2049 to 856 persons (see Table 22.4), whilst in the light of the registers from the period 1769–98, the number of Jewish houses in town grew from 155 to 180. In 1798, over 233 Jewish tenants lived in Pińczów, which gives us a total of 413 Jewish families.[74] So the 1790 census seems to be completely unreliable; the 1787 church census, which listed 1897 Jews (Table 22.4) was probably much nearer the truth. Whatever the case, theories about the large drop in Jewish population at the time of the Enlightenment, based on the registration of Jews, appear incorrect. But it is equally difficult to accept unconditionally the enormous growth in Jewish population in that period put forward in some literature on the subject. At the end of the eighteenth century, therefore, the Jewish population formed about 20 per cent of the total municipal population.[75]

Our knowledge of the social and occupational structure of the Jewish population in the second half of the eighteenth century is unsatisfactory. For this purpose, the 1765 census must be taken as the main authority. Thus, we find that in the 16 towns of the Province of Sandomierz, 68.8 per cent of heads of households were

[71] Mahler, *Jews in Old Poland* (see n. 8), Table 11.
[72] Kraków Diocese Census of 1787, ed. J. Kleczyński, *Archiwum Komisji Historycznej*, VII Kraków, 1894, pp. 322–4, and Pracownia Słownika Historyczno-Geograficznego Ziem Polskich w Średniowieczu Instytutu Historii PAN w Krakowie, kartoteka materiałów do słownika województwa sandomierskiego w dobie Sejmu Czteroletniego (Working group for the historical-geographical dictionary for the Polish lands in the Middle Ages at the Historical Institute of the Polish Academy of Sciences in Kraków; file of material for the dictionary on the Sandomierz province in the period of the Four Year Sejm).
[73] Guldon and Stępkowski, 'Spis ludności żydowskiej', Table 2.
[74] Inwentarz Pińczowa z 1769 roku (Pińczów Register from 1769), ed. Z. Guldon, Kielce, 1974, pp. 42–3; Archiwum Państwowe in Kielce, *Archiwum Ordynacji Myszkowskich*, MS 484, ff. 16–24.
[75] Guldon, 'Ludność żydowska', p. 27.

Table 22.4
Number of Jews in local communities in the districts of Sandomierz and Wiślica, 1765–90

Community centre	1765	1787 church census	1787 church census	1790
Sandomierz district				
Bogoria	124	125	36	68
Iwaniska	284	102	103	101
Klimontów	517	544	172	226
Opatów	1675	635	597	690
Ostrowiec	717	354	391	427
Ożarów	312	1005	193	259
Połaniec	443	155	153	175
Prosperów and Zawichost	103	186	152	179
Raków	371	209	112	228
Sandomierz	430	271	296	301
Staszów	607	394	398	465
Tarłów	472	547	271	264
TOTAL	6055	4527	2874	3383
%	100.0	74.8	47.5	55.9
Wiślica district				
Chmielnik	1132	782	–	573
Korczyn	882	474	–	517
Kurozwęki	66	90	–	64
Oleśnica	83	103	–	83
Pacanów	348	169	–	244
Pińczów	2049	1897	–	856
Stopnica	375	215	–	212
Szydłów	308	227	–	179
Wiślica	184	206	–	215
TOTAL	5427	4082	–	2943
%	100.0	75.2	–	54.2
TOTAL	11,482	8609	–	6326
%	100.0	75.0	–	55.1

engaged in crafts, 28.7 per cent in free professions, 6.8 per cent in trade, 5.1 per cent in tenancies and innkeeping, and 0.6 per cent in the carter's trade. But it is hard to reach any definite conclusion on the basis of such data, as the sample comprised only 706 persons, while the number the Jewish families in those towns totalled 2,361. Thus we have no information on the occupation of over 70 per cent of heads of families.[76] We can merely add that, according to the Pińczów registers, only 12 out of 188 families gave their occupation as trade. Yet the town register gives 161 out of 184 families stating their means of livelihood as trade.[77]

Different social categories were used in the 1789 state census. From the precise data that have survived from the Wiślica district, it appears that 31.5 per cent of Jews made a living from their own tenement houses and individual houses, 12.5 per cent from crafts, 14.5 per cent from trade and 6.4 per cent from innkeeping. As many as 35.1 per cent were servants and casual labourers.[78] These data are better in taking into account everyone on the register but, on the other hand, give us no information on the occupations of householders. Nevertheless, from the 1765 and 1789 censuses we get completely different pictures of the occupational structure of the Jewish population.[79]

As an interesting detail, we can record a professional mineral prospector from this region who looked for salt in Busko, Bejsce and Rączki, and for metals in Górno and Miedziana Góra (Copper Mountain). He was mentioned, though not by name, by Jacek Jezierski during the 1791 Diet. This fact was recalled by T. Korzon[80] and, recently, by Stefan Bratkowski, who asked: 'What was the name of that Jewish geologist, poor, cunning, and modest? We do not know – it has not, somehow, interested anyone so far.'[81] As can be shown from hitherto unpublished sources, the man in question was Jakub Izraelowicz from Przytyk close to Radom who, in the following words, told of his descent and youth:

---

[76] Mahler, *Jews in Old Poland*, p. 43.

[77] Z. Guldon and K. Krzystanek, 'Źródła do statystyki Żydów w województwie sandomierskim w II połowie XVIII wieku' (Sources for Jewish statistics in the province of Sandomierz in the second half of the eighteenth century, in Z. Guldon and M. B. Markowski, eds, *Źródła do dziejów Kieleczyzny w XVI-XX w.*, (Sources for the history of Kielce and its territories, from the sixteenth to the twentieth centuries), Kielce, 1987, Table 12.

[78] Z. Guldon and K. Krzystanek, *Ludność żydowska w miastach powiatu wiślickiego w końcu XVIII w.*, in *Studia Kieleckie* (Jewish population in towns of the district of Wiślica, Kielce Studies 3), Kielce, 1983, Table 3.

[79] Compare data on the Opatów Jews' economic activity in 1721; Z. Guldon and K. Krzystanek, eds, 'Instruktarz dla kahału opatowskiego z r. 1759' (Instruction for the Opatów *kehilla* from 1759), in F. Kiryk, ed., *Opatów: Materiały z sesji 700-lecia miasta* (Opatów: Proceedings from a Conference on the 700th Anniversary of the Town), Sandomierz, 1985, Table 1.

[80] T. Korzon, *Wewnętrzne dzieje Polski za Stanisława Augusta* (Domestic history of Poland during the reign of Stanisław August II), Warsaw/Kraków, 1897, p. 276.

[81] A. Bocheński, *Przemysł Polski w dawnych wiekach* (Polish industry in the old days), Warsaw, 1984, p. 317 (section written by S. Bratkowski).

In Baranów on the River Wieprz, he was born. His father was a priest, that is a Jewish elder. He left his father to go to Wilno, Kowno, Grodno, and other places, where he devoted his time to learning the Written Law and the Talmud. From youth he sought to investigate the secrets of nature, but opportunities did not match his aims. Ruled by curiosity, he made use of stones and pieces of earth, combining them with each other.[82]

The growth of Jewish centres and communities, and, above all, of the population itself points to an enormous Jewish demographic expansion, especially in the period between the mid seventeenth and the end of the eighteenth century. It found its expression in economic expansion, as can easily be demonstrated in the case of Opatów. In the period 1600 to 1619, trade between this town and Kraków was still dominated by Christian merchants, but by the years 1641–5, Jewish merchants already predominated, and still later they forced Christians out completely.[83]

We should add that, at the end of the sixteenth century and in the first half of the seventeenth century, a considerable role was played by Scottish and English merchants in this region. They appeared not only in towns closed to Jews (Iła, Kunów, Jedlińsk, Radom, Kielce), but also in those inhabited by Jews (Chęciny, Chmielnik, Opatów, Opoczno, Pińczów, Raków, Sandomierz).[84] Yet even before the mid-seventeenth-century war against Sweden, some Scots emigrated from the Sandomierz towns; for instance, in the period 1639–44, a few Scots renounced municipal rights, and returned to the Chęciny authorities their letters of exemption from customs.[85] In the second half of the seventeenth century, we find Scottish colonies in only a few Sandomierz towns.[86] Armenians, who appeared in Kielce, Opatów and Sandomierz, provided some

---

[82] Z. Guldon and L. Stępkowski, 'Jakub Izraelowicz z Przytyka – nieznany geolog z XVIII wieu' (Jakub Izraelowicz from Przytyk – an unknown geologist from the eighteenth century), *BŻIH* 3–4, 1987, pp. 123–5.

[83] Z. Guldon and L. Stępkowski, 'Udział Opatowa w wymianie towarowej w II połowie XVII wieku' (Opatów's contribution to commerce in the second half of the seventeenth century), in Kiryk, *Opatów*, pp. 116–18.

[84] Z. Guldon and L. Stępkowski, 'Ludność szkocka i angielska w Polsce w połowie XVII w.' (Scottish and English population in Poland in the mid seventeenth century), *KHKM* 30:2, 1982, pp. 208–9.

[85] Jagiellonian Library in Kraków, MS 5232, ff. 195ᵛ, 301–301ᵛ, 470, 478ᵛ.

[86] Even in 1676, Alexander Wolkisson from near Edinburgh accepted Sandomierz municipal rights; State Archive, Sandomierz, Sandomierz town files, MS 11, f. 123.

competition to Jewish merchants in the eighteenth century. They traded mainly in spices and Hungarian wine.[87]

Conclusions based primarily on fiscal sources, concerning the size and pace of Jewish demographic expansion, both in the whole area of the Nobles' Commonwealth (Table 22.1) and in the towns of the province of Sandomierz, may raise some objections. The growth of the Jewish population before the mid seventeenth century was largely due to immigration. In the mid seventeenth century, large demographic losses and Jewish emigration occurred. The last wave of immigration to the Nobles' Commonwealth is linked to the expulsion of Jews from Vienna in 1670. The next period witnesses Jewish emigration. The situation changes again after the first partition, largely owing to the policy of the Austrian authorities, to which we have already referred. What, then, explains the fivefold rise in Jewish population from the mid seventeenth to the end of the eighteenth centuries? The question remains whether this large rise is not – at least to some extent – the result of more complete and efficient registration of Jews, and whether there is any validity in earlier figures, based as they are on rare original sources. After all, the state censuses from the year 1787 registered only a quarter of the Jewish population. We have no idea of the situation in 1662, and the number of Jewish poll tax payers in the second half of the sixteenth century is incredibly low. Figures and hypotheses pulled out of the air and at variance with the tax system will not help much in this situation. We cannot even say unequivocally whether in the period of Enlightenment, when sources are so much richer, the number of Jews grew or fell.

Thus, the question of the usefulness of various types of sources for our investigations and the working out of an appropriate method remain the basic problems. Where fiscal sources are concerned, our possibilities appear somewhat limited. We must therefore turn from global to local research on the Jewish population in those centres where richer collections of source material have survived if we are to make further progress.

---

[87] E.g. in 1788 Jerzy Saul, 'Hungarian wine and spice trader', lived in Kielce; AGAD, *Archiwum Skarbu Koronnego* (Royal Treasury Records), section LVI, MS Ż-3, f. 27.

Glossary*

Chamber of deputies (Polish *izba poselska*) The lower house in the Sejm (q.v.), containing representatives from each voivodeship (q.v.; Polish *województwo*) in Poland (the Crown, q.v.) and the Grand Duchy of Lithuania. It was elected by the *szlachta* (q.v.) of each voivodeship, meeting in the local dietine (q.v.); Polish *sejmik*). It started to meet regularly after 1493 and, in accordance with the privilege *Nihil Novi* of 1505, the king promised that no new legislation would be introduced without the joint consent of the chamber of deputies and the Senate (q.v.).

Commonwealth (Polish *Rzeczpospolita*) The term *Rzeczpospolita* is derived from the Latin **respublica** and is sometimes translated as 'commonwealth' and sometimes as 'republic', often in the form 'Nobleman's Republic' (*Rzeczpospolita szlachecka*). After the union of Lublin in 1569, it was used officially in the form *Rzeczpospolita Obojga Narodów* (The Commonwealth of the Two Nations) to designate the new form of state which had arisen. In historical literature, this term is often rendered as 'The Polish-Lithuanian Commonwealth'.

Confederation (Polish *Konfederacja*) A union of nobles called together to defend the country or obtain certain defined political objectives. After 1652, but mainly in the eighteenth century, the indiscriminate use of the *liberum veto* (q.v.) regularly paralysed the Sejm and confederations, which were not subject to the veto, were the only means available for achieving political objectives in an emergency.

Corvée Compulsory labour service due from peasants to their

---

* Taken from A. Eisenbach's *The Emancipation of the Jews in Poland, 1780–1870* (Oxford, 1991). The publishers gratefully acknowledge Basil Blackwell & Co for permission to reproduce this glossary.

landlord. Remained in effect after the formal abolition of serfdom in the Grand Duchy of Warsaw in 1808, till 1864.

Crown (Polish *Korona*) The Polish part of the *Rzeczpospolita* (Republic or Commonwealth, q.v.), as distinct from the Grand Duchy of Lithuania, with which it was dynastically linked from the fifteenth century and constitutionally united in 1569 by the Union of Lublin. In addition to its ethnically Polish core territories, it also included royal Prussia and the Ukraine, which after 1569 was transferred from the Grand Duchy to the Crown.

Dietine (Polish *Sejmik*) A local assembly of the *szlachta* (q.v.), operating in each voivodeship (q.v.) of the Commonwealth. It elected deputies to the Sejm and provided them with instructions governing their conduct there. Dietines met much more frequently than the Sejm and by the end of the seventeenth century had much more importance in the regions than the Sejm. They were the basic forum for the political activities of the *szlachta* and, by the eighteenth century, had become subject to influence and manipulation by the magnates, who used them as a tool for their own political purposes.

Greater Poland (Wielkopolska) Western Poland, the area around Poznań.

Hasidism A Jewish mystical movement which grew up in the eighteenth-century Polish–Lithuanian Commonwealth. The Hasidiam (from *hasid* (Hebrew) 'a righteous man') sought direct communion with God through various means among others by singing and dancing and through communion with nature. Originally opposed by the bulk of the Orthodox establishment in Poland, who described themselves as *misnagdim* (lit. 'opposers', i.e. of Hasidism), the movement soon became particularly strong in central Poland – The Congress Kingdom, southern Poland (Małopolska or Galicia) and the Ukraine.

HaBaD An acronym derived from the Hebrew words *hokhma*, *bina*, *dina* (wisdom, understanding, knowledge). A sect of Hasidism which developed in the Grand Duchy of Lithuania. Its leading advocate was Rabbi Shneur Zalman of Liozna or Lady. He preached a more rationalistic and more ordered faith than the Hasidism of central and southern Poland. The Lubavich dynasty of rabbis, also called *HaBaD* hasidism are descended from Rabbi Shneur Zalman.

Haskalah (Hebrew: lit. 'wisdom' or 'understanding' but used in the sense of 'Enlightenment'.) A rationalistic movement which emerged in the Jewish world, under the impact of the European Enlightenment, in the second half of the eighteenth century. It first became important in Germany under the influence of Moses Mendelssohn and soon spread to the rest of European Jewry, first in the West and then, more slowly, in the East. The *Maskilim* (followers of the Haskalah), while retaining the Jewish religion, sought to diminish Jewish separateness from the nations among whom the Jews lived and to increase their knowledge of the secular world. The movement also fostered the study of biblical rather than Talmudic Hebrew and emphasized the poetic, critical and scientific elements in Hebrew literature. It aimed to substitute the study of modern subjects for those traditionally studied. In Eastern Europe, it opposed hasidism and what it regarded as the relics of Jewish fanaticism and superstition. It also sought Jewish emancipation and the adoption by Jews of agriculture and handicrafts.

Kahal, Kehilla (Hebrew: literally 'congregation') The lowest level of the Jewish autonomous institutions in the Polish–Lithuanian Commonwealth. Above the local Kehillot were regional bodies, and above these, a central body, the Va'ad arba aratsot (Council of the Four Lands) for the Crown (q.v.) and the Va'ad lita (Council of Lithuania). The Va'ad arba aratsot was abolished by the Polish authorities in 1764 but local autonomous institutions continued to operate until 1844 in those parts of the Polish–Lithuanian Commonwealth directly annexed by the Tsarist Empire and longer in the Congress Kingdom and the remaining parts of Poland.

Liberum veto The right of every deputy in the Sejm to overturn legislation of which he did not approve of for which his dietine (q.v.) had not provided him with instructions. The legal basis of this privilege seems to originate in the Statutes of Nieszawa (1454) which promised that no royal legislation would be introduced into a province without the consent of its local dietine. When dietine deputies began meeting regularly in the Sejm (q.v.), this was taken to mean that unanimity was required in the Sejm (q.v.), this was taken to mean that unanimity was required for all new legislation. In the sixteenth century and even into the seventeenth century decisions were still taken by majority vote, but in 1652 Władysław Siciński exercised his veto as an individual to 'explode' the Sejm and thenceforth there was continuous and irresponsible use of the veto, rendering normal parliamentary activity impossible. According to the practice, once a veto was used, the Sejm was suspended and all legislation hitherto introduced in the session was declared invalid.

Little Poland (Małopolska) Southern Poland. Also referred to under the Habsburgs as Galicia.

Nobleman's Republic See Commonwealth.

Revir A section of a town in which Jews were required to live.

Royal (free) town A town directly dependent on the king, and subsequently on the government of the Grand Duchy of Warsaw and the Congress Kingdom of Poland. Burghers in royal or 'government' towns had greater rights than those in town controlled by the nobility.

Sejm The central parliamentary institution of the Commonwealth (q.v.) and a chamber of deputies (q.v), both of which after 1501 had a voice in the introduction of new legislation. It regularly met for six weeks every two years, but could be called for sessions of two weeks in an emergency. When it was not in session, an appointed commission of sixteen senators, in rotation four at a time, resided with the king both to advise and to keep watch over his activities. Up to the mid-seventeenth century, the Sejm functioned reasonably well; after that, the use of the *liberum veto* (q.v) began to paralyse its effectiveness.

Senate The upper house of the Sejm. Its origin was the medieval Royal Council. It was composed of all the great officials of the government, the voivodes (q.v.) hetmans, marshals, treasurers, headed by the archbishop of Gniezno, who also served as *interrex* on the death of the king. The members of the senate were overwhelmingly drawn from the class of magnates (q.v. under *szlachta*) which came to dominate Polish society in the seventeenth and eighteenth centuries.

Soltys (German *Schultheiss*; Latin *scuiltetus*) During the period of extensive German colonization and immigration during the middle ages, the *soltys* was the agent who organized the establishment of new villages; as a reward, he was given one-sixth of the village's land, together with other privileges. This made these agents an extremely wealthy and influential group, posing a challenge to the *szlachta* (q.v.) itself. By the Statue of Warta (1423), the nobility was given the right to buy out the lands of the local *soltys*. This group thereafter disappeared as a social force, but the office of *soltys* remained as a local adminstrator acting for the landlord in a village.

Starosta A royal administrator, holder of the office of *starostwo*. From the fourteenth century, there were three distinct offices covered by this term – the *starosta generalny* (general starosta), in Wielkopolska (q.v.), Rus and Podolia (Ukraine) represented the crown in a particular region; the *starosta grodowy* (castle starosta) had administrative and judicial authority over a castle or fortified settlement and its surrounding region; and the *starosta niuegrodowy* (non-castle startosta) or *tenutariusz* (leasehold) administered royal lands leased to him.

Szlachta The Polish nobility. A very broad social stratum making up nearly 8 per cent of the population in the eighteenth century. Its members ranged from the great magnates, like the Czartoryskis, Potockis and Radziwills, who dominated political and social life in the last century of the Polish–Lithuanian Commonwealth, to small landowners (the *szlachta zagrodowa*) and even to landless retainers of the great houses. What distinguished this group from the remainder of the population was their noble status and their right to participate in political life, in the dietines, in the Sejm and in the electron of the king.

Tsaddik (Hebrew: lit. 'the just one' or 'a pious man') A leader of a hasidic sect (or communityu). Hasidism often credited their tsaddiks or *rebbes* with miraculous powers and saw them as mediators between God and man.

Voivode (Polish *wojewoda*) Initially this official acted in place of the ruler, especially in judicial and military matters. From the thirteenth century the office gradually evolved into a provincial dignity; between the sixteenth and eighteenth centuries, the voivode conducted the local dietine (q.v.), led the *pospolite ruszenie*, the *levée-en-masse* of the *szlachta* (q.v.) in times of danger to the Commonwealth (q.v.), and occasionally governed cities and collected certain dues. By virtue of his office, he sat in the senate.

Voivodeship (Polish *województwo*) A province governed by a voivoide (q.v.).

Wójt (German *Vogt*) During the medieval establishment of towns, he was the official who organized the new town and occupied the leading place in its local administration as the head of the town's courts. The office was hereditary and was provided with one-fifth of the dues and one-quarter of the penal fines collected by the town. After the rise of town councils, the office was bought out by the larger and richer towns. By the eighteenth century the *wójt* was bought out by the larger and richer towns. By the eighteenth century the *wójt* was generally the chief administrator of a group of villages.

This glossary is partly based on that in ed. F. K. Fedorowicz's *A Republic of Nobles: Studies in Polish History to 1864* (Cambridge, 1982).

Chronology

Before 963 to 992	Reign of Mieszko I	962	Otto I crowned Emperor
966	The Polish Court adopts Christianity		
972	Conquest of Western Peninsula by Mieszko I	987	Beginnings of the Capet dynasty in France
		988–989	Duke Vladimir of Ruthenia adopts Christianity
992–1012	Reign of Boleslaw the Brave		
1000	Emperor Otto III recognises Poland's independence; foundation of the archbishopric in Gniezno		
1004–1018	Boleslaw the Brave's war against the Germans Peace of Bautzen (Budišyn); Boleslaw the Brave's expedition against Kiev and the incorporation of the Czerwień castles into Poland		
		1024	Beginning of the Salic dynasty of the Franks in Germany
1025	Boleslaw I the Brave crowned King of Poland		
1025–1034	Reign of Mieszko II		
1033	Mieszko II renounces the royal crown		
1034–1058	Reign of Casimir I the Restorer		
1037	Casimir I the Restorer expelled from Poland; anti-feudal and anti-Christian rising of the people		
1038 or 1039	The Bohemian Duke Břetislav invades Poland Casimir I the Restorer returns to Poland; reconstruction of the State begins		
		1054	Beginning of the Eastern schism
1058–1079	Reign of Boleslaw II the Bold		
		1066	The Norman invasion of England
1076	Boleslaw II the Bold crowned King of Poland	1077	Henry IV in Canossa
1079	Revolt of the nobles and expulsion of Boleslaw II the Bold		
1079–1102	Reign of Władysław Herman	1096–1099	First Crusade
1102–1138	Reign of Boleslaw III the Wrymouth		
1109	Invasion of Poland by Emperor Henry V		
1121–1122	Western Pomerania reincorporated into Poland		
		1122	Condordat of Worms
1124–1128	Christianization of Western Pomerania Death of Boleslaw III the Wrymouth; beginning of Poland's territorial division with a Grand Duke as senior among the provincial rulers		
1138–1146	Reign of Władysław II as Grand Duke of Poland		
1146–1173	Reign of Boleslaw IV the Curly as Grand Duke		
		1147–1149	Second Crusade
		1152–1190	Reign of Emperor Frederick I Barbarossa
		1154	Beginning of the Plantagenet's rule in England (Henry II)
		1171	Conquest of Egypt by the Seljuks
1173–1177	Reign of Mieszko III the Old as Grand Duke		
1177–1194	Rule of Casimir II the Just as Grand Duke		
1180	Congress of Łęczyca, concessions by Casimir II the Just in favour of the clergy		

CHRONOLOGY 347

1181	Western Pomerania made dependent on the Empire		
1202–1227	Reign of Leszek the White as Grand Duke	c. 1200	Foundation of the University of Paris
		1202	Establishment of the Order of Knights of the Sword in Livonia
		1204	The Crusaders capture Byzantium
		1206	Establishment of the Mongolian State and beginnings of the Mongolian expansion
		1215	*Magna Carta Libertatum* in England
1226	Conrad of Mazovia brings the Teutonic Knights into Poland		
1227	Death of Leszek the White, decline of institution of Senior Duke		
		1228–1229	Sixth Crusade
1232–1234	Conquest of Little Poland and a part of Great Poland by the Silesian Duke Henry the Bearded		
		1240	Tartars capture Kiev and conquer Ruthenia
1241	First Mongol invasion of Poland; battle of Legnica, death of Henry the Pious	c. 1241	Establishment of the Hansa
1249–1252	Conquest of the Lubusz Land by the Margraves of Brandenburg	Middle 13th cent.	Foundation of parliaments in France and England
		1254–1273	The Long Interregnum in Germany
1291–1292	Conquest of Przemysł II as King of Poland		
1296	Death of Przemysł II		
1300–1305	Reign of Wacław II as King of Poland		
		1302	The States-General constituted in France
1306	Władysław I the Short conquers Little Poland		
1308–1309	The Teutonic Knights capture Gdańsk and Eastern Pomerania	1309–1377	The "Avignon captivity" of the Popes
1314	Władysław I the Short conquers Great Poland	1316–1341	Reign of Giedymin and unification of the Lithuanian State
1320–1333	Reign of Władysław the Short as King of Poland; end of territorial division		
1325	Polish–Lithuanian alliance against the Teutonic Knights		
		1328	Ivan Kalita gains the title of Grand Duke of Muscovy
1331	Battle of Płowce, victory of Władysław the Short over the Teutonic Knights		
1333–1370	Reign of Casimir III the Great, the last king of the Piast dynasty		
1335	Congress of Vyšehrad; John of Luxembourg renounces his claims to the Polish throne and Casimir III the Great – his rights to Silesia		
		1337	Outbreak of the Hundred Years' War
1340–1349	Poland occupies the greater part of Vladimir and Halicz Ruthenia		
		1342–1382	Reign of Louis d'Anjou as King of Hungary
		1346	Battle of Crécy
		1348	Foundation of the University of Prague
Middle of 11th cent.	The Statutes of Great Poland and Little Poland – first codification of the common law		
1355	Privileges for the gentry granted by Louis d'Anjou in Buda in return for the recognition of his recognition of his succession in Poland		
1364	Foundation of the University of Cracow		
1370–1382	Reign of Louis d'Anjou		
		1371	Beginning of the reign of the Stuarts in Scotland
		1377–1417	Western schism
		1380	Battle of Kulikovo Pole, victory of Demetrius Donskoi over the Tartars
1384	Jadwiga, daughter of Louis d'Anjou, becomes Queen of Poland		
1385	Polish–Lithuanian Union at Krewo		
1386	Baptism of the Lithuanian Grand Duke Jagiełło and his marriage to Jadwiga		

CHRONOLOGY

1386–1434	Reign of Władsylaw Jagiello; beginning of the Jagiellonian dynasty		
		1397	Union of Denmark, Norway and Sweden at Kalmar
1399	The Lithuanian Grand Duke Witold in the battle with Tartars on the Vorskla river		
1400	Restoration of the Cracow University		
		1409	Theses of Ian Hus
1410	Battle of Grunwald		
		1414–1418	Council of Constance
		1419–1434	Hussite wars
1420	Władyslaw Jagiello rejects the Bohemian crown offered to him by the Hussites		
1422–1433	The gentry obtain the charger *Newinen captivabinus nisi iure victum*		
		1429	Joan of Arc in Orléans
1434–1444	Reign of Władyslaw III		
1440	Władyslaw III ascends to the Hungarian throne; Casimir IV – to the Lithuanian throne; the Prussian Union formed		
1444	Battle of Varna and death of Władyslaw III		
1447–1492	Reign of Casimir IV in Poland		
		c. 1450	Discovery of print by Johannes Gutenberg
		1453	Constantinople captured by the Turks; end of the Hundred Years' War
1454	Incorporation of Prussia into Poland		
1454–1466	Thirteen Years' War with the Teutonic Knights		
		1455–1485	War of the Roses in England
		1462–1505	Reign of Ivan III and liberation of Russia from Tartar dependence
1466	Peace of Toruń with teutonic Knights		
1473	First printing shop in Cracow		
		1481	Inquisition established in Spain
1492–1501	Reign of John Albert	1492	Discovery of America; conquest of Granada the end of Spain's *reconquistà*
1492–1506	Reign lf Alexander in the Grand Duchy of Lithuania		
1496	Statues of Piotrków; the rights of peasants and burghers abridged		
1497	John Albert's defeat in Moldavia	1497–1498	Discovery of the sea-route to India (Vasco de Gama)
1501–1506	Reign of Alexander		
		1503–1513	Pope Julius II
1505	*Nihil Novi* Constitution		
1506–1548	Reign of Sigismund I the Old		
1514	Muscovite troops take Smoleńsk; Polish–Lithuanian victory at Orsza		
1515	Meeting in Vienna of Sigismund I the Old; Władyslaw Jagiello (son of Casimir IV) and Emperor Maximilian Habsburg: the Habsburg receive the guarantee to succeed to the Bohemian and Hungarian throne in case of extinction of the Jagiellonian dynasty		
		1517	Theses of Martin Luther
1518	Arrival to Poland of Bona Sforza, wife of Sigismund I the Old		
		1519	Charles V becomes Emperor
		1519–1521	Conquest of Mexico by Hernań Cortès
		1519–1522	Ferdinand Magellan's expedition round the world
1520	First royal edicts against dissenters	1521	The Edict of Worms outlaws Martin Luther as heretic
		1524–1525	Peasant war in Germany
1525	Secularization of the Teutonic Order in Prussia the Prussian Prince Albrecht pays homage to Sigismund I the Old		
1526	Extinction of the Mazovian line of Piasts;		
1526	The succession of the Habsburgs in		

CHRONOLOGY

1529	Sigismund II Augustus ascends to the throne of Lithuania		
		1531–1536	Conquest of Peru by Francisco Pizarro
		1534	Establishment of the Jesuit Order; separation of the English Church from Rome
1543	Nicolaus Copernicus *De revolutionibus orbium coelestium*		
		1545–1563	Council of Trent
		1547–1584	Reign of Ivan the Terrible in Russia
1548–1572	Reign of Sigismund II Augustus		
		1556–1598	Reign of Phillip II as King of Spain
		1558–1603	Reign of Queen Elizabeth in England
1561	Secularization of the Livonian Order; incorporation of Livonia and establishment of the Duchy of Courland		
1563–1570	The Seven Years Northern War		
1564	Jesuits brought into Poland		
1569	The Union of Lublin		
1570	Compact of Sandomierz – agreement of the Protestant denominations for the defense of religious freedom		
1573	The principle of the free election of kings adopted; religious peace guaranteed	1572	St. Bartholomew's Night in France
1573–1574	Reign of Henry de Valois		
		1574–1589	Reign of Henry III de Valois as King of France
1576–1586	Reign of Stephen Batory	1576	Outbreak of rising in the Netherlands
1577	War with Gdańsk		
1577–1582	War with the Grand Duchy of Muscovy for Livonia		
1578	Foundation of the Wilno Academy		
		1579	Establishment of the Republic of Provinces in the Netherlands
1587–1632	Reign of Sigismund III Vasa		
		1588	Victory of the English Navy over
		1589–1610	Reign of King Henry IV in France
1594–1596	Cossack uprising under Severin Nalevaiko		
1595	Foundation of the Zamość Academy		
1595–1596	Union of Brześć		
1600	Outbreak of the war with Sweden	1600	Establishment of the East India Company in England
		1603	Death of Elisabeth Tudor, beginning of the Stuart dynasty in England
1604–1606	Polish participation in the action of the False Demetrius		
1605	Victory over the Swedes at Kirchholm		
1606–1607	Rebellion of Mikołaj Zebrzydowski		
1609–1619	War with Russia		
1610	Stanisław Żółkiewski's victory over the Russian army at Kluszyn		
1611–1632	Reign of Gustavus Adolphus in Sweden		
1613	Beginning of the rule of the Romanovs in Russia		
1618	Beginning of the Thirty Years' War		
1620	Defeat of the Polish army in the battle with the Turks at Cecora	1620	Defeat of the Bohemians at Bílá Hora
1621	Defence of Chocim and peace with Turkey		
1627	Battle of the Polish and Swedish navies at Oliwa		
1629	Victory over the Swedes at Trzciana; truce with Sweden		
1632–1634	War with Russia	1632	Battle of Lützen and death of Gustavus Adolphus
1632–1648	Reign of Władysław IV Vasa		
		1642	Beginning of Revolution in England, Long Parliament
1648	Outbreak of the rising under Bohdan Chmielnicki in the Ukraine	1648	Peace of Westphalia
1648–1668	Reign of John Casimir		
		1649	Execution of Charles I Stuart
1651	Victory over Bohdan Chmielnicki's army at Beresteczko		

1652	Seym broken up by the first *Liberum veto*		
		1653–1658	Protectorate of Oliver Cromwell
		1654	Compact of Perejaslaw between Ukraine and Russia
1655–1660	Polish–Swedish war		
1657	Treaties of Wehlau and Bydgoszcz; Poland renounces the Prussian fief		
1658	Arians (Antitrinitarians) expelled from Poland; compact of Hadziacz		
1660	Peace with Sweden at Oliwa		
		1661–1715	Reign of Louis XIV
1665–1666	Rebellion of Jerzy Lubomirski		
1667	Truce of Andruszów		
1669–1673	Reign of Michael Korybut-Wiśniowiecki		
1672	Turkish invasion of Poland		
1673	Victory over the Turks at Chocim		
1674–1696	Reign of John III Sobieski	1682–1725	Reign of Peter the Great in Russia
1683	Siege of Vienna by the Turks and the Polish relief		
		1684	Creation of the first anti-Turkish League
1686	Peace with Russia (the Grzymułtowski treaty)		
1697–1733	Reign of Augustus II the Strong		
1699	Peace with Turkey at Karlovci	1699	The Habsburgs complete the conquest of Hungary
		1700–1721	The Northern War
		1701	Proclamation of the Kingdom of Prussia
		1701–1714	The Spanish war of succession
1702	Swedish invasion of Poland		
1704	The opponents of Augustus II proclaim an interregnum; election of Stanisław Leszczyński		
1709	Augustus II again recognised as King		
		1714	George I ascends to throne in England, beginning of the Hanover dynasty
1715–1716	The Confederation of Tarnogród	1716–1720	The affair of John Law in France
1717	The "Mute Seym"		
1733	Double election of Augustus III and Stanisław Leszczyński		
1733–1735	The struggle of Stanisław Leszczyński against Augustus III for the Polish throne		
1734–1763	Reign of Augustus III		
1740	The Collegium Nobilium established by	1740–1748	The Austrian war of succession and Silesian Wars
		1740–1786	Reign of Frederick II in Prussia and of Maria Theresa in Austria
		1742	Frederick II occupies Silesia
		1751	Volume I of the Encyclopaedia published in France
		1756–1763	The Seven Years' War
		1762–1796	Reign of Catherine II in Russia
1764–1795	Reign of Stanisław Augustus Poniatowski		
1764–1766	Constitutional reforms carried out by the "Convocation Confederation"		
1766–1768	Russian intervention on the side of reactionary opposition		
1767	The Confederation of the Dissenters and the Confederation of Radom	1767	James Watt's steam engine
1768–1772	The Confederation of Bar		
1772	First partition of Poland		
1773	Establishment of the Commission for National Education	1773	The Jesuit Order dissolved
1775	Establishment of the Permanent Council		
		1776	First workers' union organized in England
		1776–1782	The American War of Independence
		1787	Proclamation of the Constitution of United States of America
1788–1792	The Four Years' Seym		
1789	"The Black Procession" of burghers in Warsaw	1789	Outbreak of the Great Revolution
1790	"Warnings for Poland" by Stanisław Staszic		

CHRONOLOGY

1791	Constitution of the 3rd May		
1792	The Confederation of Targowica and war with Russia	1792	Overthrow of the monarchy in France
1793	Second partition of Poland		
1794	The Kosciuszko Insurrection		
1795	Third partition of Poland		

Index

Abraham ben Josef of Leszno 150, 157
Abraham from Kraków 276
Abraham Isak 242
Abraham Wiedeńczyk 284
Abrahamowicz, Jakub 291
Abram, son of Markus 276
Abram from Kraków 277
Agranat (judge) 220
Albinus, Maciej 33
Aleksander Jagiellończyk (king) 203
Alexandria 3
Altbauer, M. 14
Ambroży (Broży) (barber surgeon) 23
Amsterdam 61, 111, 115, 179
Andrychów 283
Anti-Jewish riots (programs, Cossack massacres) 17–18, 44, 59–60, 80, 100, 107
Anti-trinitarianism 23, 26, 27, 28, 30, 31, 34
Arenda system, arendors, inn-keepers (Jewish) 5, 73, 74–5, 77, 80, 82, 156, 157, 302, 319–21
Arians, Arianism 25, 27, 28, 32, 34
Arminians 2, 16, 37, 63–72 passim, 273, 339
Ark of the Covenant 29
Aron, son of Abraham 276
Aron from Kraków 277
Aron from Wiślica 279
Arson, accusaiton of 17, 18
Ash, Jehuda Lev, of Włodzimierz (Ludmir) 222, 227, 228
Asher ben Yehiel 231
Assaf, S. 174
August II (king) 123, 134, 161, 205, 330
August III Sas (king) 41, 134, 137, 257
Austria 73, 81, 271, 273, 284, 305, 308, 309

Ba'al-Shem-Tov 8, 190
Babylon 2, 3, 93
Bałaban, M. 48, 64, 133–8, 141, 144, 145, 151, 167, 174, 200, 217, 250, 251, 255, 256, 267, 280, 282, 291
Baranów 338
Barącz, S. 64, 65
Bardach, J. 63
Bardiów 271
Baron, S. W. 4, 109, 139, 323, 326, 327
Baruch Marek 150
Barukh, Eliyahu (Elihu Lewita) 128
Bejsce 338
Bełz 304
Berdyczów 261
Berlin 113
Bershadsky, S. A. 112
Będzin 272, 274, 285, 286
Będziński, Wolf, from Kraków 280
Biała 289
Biała Cerkiew 254
Breslau (Wrocław) 14, 15, 18, 115, 179, 271, 273, 276, 277, 283, 284, 286, 293, 294
  Duchy of 20, 21
  Synod of 19, 20
Breza, Wojciech 133
Brilling 115
Brody 187, 194, 261, 262, 289
Brzeg 271, 273
Brześć Kujawski 48, 273, 304
Brześć Litewski 100, 139, 268, 304, 309
Buczacz 285, 286, 290
Buczek, K. 308
Budny, Szymon 26, 27, 28, 32, 33
Budzin, Synod of 19
Budziński, Stanisław 29
Bujak, F. 30
Bunisiewicz, Izrael, from Buczacz 290
Burghers, and Jews 8, 21, 75–89 passim, 174–85 passim, 235–46 passim
Burzyński, A. 319
Burszta, J. 302, 319

353

Buski 254, 338
Butrymowicz, Mateusz 84, 85, 87
Bytom on the Odra river 15

Calvinism, Calvinists 26, 28
Capistrano, John 18
Charewiczowa, Ł. 66, 68
Chełm 304
Council of Four Lands 170, 172
Czarnobyl 168
Czortków 261, 327
Ćwik, W. 237

Daniel, Lewek 280
Danzig 1, 159, 179, 285, 286, 289, 293, 317
David HaKohen 227, 228
David, son of Sar Szalom 14
David from Lelów 279
Delumeau, J. 36
Dembiński, Stanisław 211
Deresiewicz, J. 236
Dernschwamm, Hans 24
Dębno 334
Dębowiec 289
Długi, Józef 277
Długosz, J. 22
Dobrowolski, K. 325
Dobrzyń 304
Domanowski 33
Dov Beer of Bolechów (Dov m'Bolechów) 110, 164
Dubno 110, 191, 262, 285
Dubnow, S. 2, 110, 135, 136, 137, 144, 145, 149, 151, 167
Działyński 158, 163

Eibenschütz, Jonatan 108, 150
Eidlish, Samuel 5
Eisenbach, A. 8
Elbląg 317
Elon, M. 171
Emden, Jakob 108, 150
England 1
Enlightenment 6, 8, 73, 76, 80, 84, 259, 336, 340
Esayash (Eliasz) 26, 27
Esterczykj, Wolf 280
Ettinger, S. 4
Europe 1, 5, 6, 18, 36, 60, 73, 94, 95

Fachinetti, Stanisław 290
Fajwisz 48
Falk, Joshua 221, 232
Feilchenfeld, Wolf 249

Fedorowicz, J. K. 1
Firlej, Jan 152
Firlej, Mikołaj 33, 176
Fisk, Jakub 229
Fishel Lewkowicz 161
Fiszer, Joachim 291
Forbes, Robert 292
Fortis, Izaak 161
France 1, 107
Francken, Chrystian 28, 31, 32
Frank, Jakub 8, 106
Frankfurt-am-Main 111
Frankists 8, 60, 106, 189
Fränkl, Jozue Janas 284
Franksztyn, *see* Ząbkowice Śląskie
Frederick Barbarossa 20
Frederick II (Prussian King) 151
Fuks, Leib 117
Fuks, M. 115

Galan 65
Galicia 191, 192, 194, 326
Garnysz, Maciej 80
Garliński 33
Gawurin, A. 145, 168
Germany, Germans 2. 3. 5. 18, 95, 114, 123, 128, 221, 257, 315
Gierowski, J. A. 125
Gieysztorowa, I. 329
Gilon, M. 128
Głogów (Ducy of) 15, 21
Gniewoszów 329, 332, 334
Gniezno 15, 258, 263, 273, 274, 306, 307
Goldberg, J. 115, 123, 130
Gorlice 285, 286, 289
Gowarczów 332
Góra Kalwaria 187
Górnicki, Ł. 25
Górno 388
Graetz, H. 145
Granowski, Kazimierz 153, 156, 158, 160, 163
Great Novogrod 25
Great Poland (province) 87, 96, 100, 137, 148, 167, 205, 237, 243, 259, 260–6, 275, 303, 304, 305, 307, 310, 329
Grodecki, R. 121
Grodno 139, 167, 168, 169, 172, 173, 255, 260, 338
Grodzisk Wielkopolski 254
Grodziski, Stanisław 143
Gródek 167, 168, 173
Guilds (trade craft) 41, 74–6, 242–3, 249–66 passim

INDEX

Guldon, Z. 323
Gumplowicz, L. 144, 199, 200
Gumplowicz, M. 120, 121
Gurewicz, A. J. 50
Guterman, Aleksander 126

Haagsen 327
Halicz region 37, 38
Haller, Józef 290
Halperin, I. 98, 105, 112–18, 126, 128, 130, 136, 139, 149, 150, 152, 166
Halperin, Z. 116
Hamburg 52
Hammeln, Glückel von 52
Hannover, Nathan 50, 55, 60, 105
Harkavy 112
Hasidic, Hasidim 60, 106, 186–95 passim
Haubenstock, Janina 9
Haubenstock, Józef 9
Hayszechger 327
Henry V (emperor) 20
Henryk of Legnica 20, 21
Henryk IV Prawy 20
Herburt, Mikołaj 70
Herzog, M. 188
Hesterczyk, Wolf 278
Hillel (prophet) 93
Hirsz Kiejdanower 49
Holland (the Netherlands) 117, 257
Horn, E. 64
Horn, M. 59, 64, 65, 67, 71, 323, 325
Horowic, Abraham Ben Sabbatay 50
Horowic family 48
Horowitz, Isaiah (Yezayash) 5, 60
Hungary, Hungarians 5, 14, 24, 37, 271, 273, 275, 278
Husiatyń 327

Icyk from Lesko 277
Ignacy (Kosy's student) 26
Iłża 338
Inflanty (Livonia) 304
Inowrocław 304, 305, 307
Istanbul 158
Italy 5, 257, 271
Ivan III 26, 35
Iwaniska 331, 332, 336
Iwaszko Czarny 35
Isaak (rabbi) 230, 231
Izaak ben Abraham of Troki (Karaite) 24, 25
Izaak from Chęciny 279
Izaak from Prague 276
Izaakowicz, Tsodek 291

Izaakowicz, Marek, from Lwów 54, 56
Izraelowicz, Abram 278
Izraelowicz, Jakub from Przytyk 338

Jabłonowski, Jan Stanisław 133
Jaffe, Mordekchay 51, 52, 56, 57, 58, 59
Jakub Nachman from Bełżyce 24, 29
Jakub from Olkusz 280
Jakub from Pacanów 279
Jakub (Abram's son-in-law) 277
Jakubowicz, Abram 289, 291, 294
Jakubowicz, Isaak from Kraków 58, 279
Jakubowicz, Moses 56
Jakubowicz, Wolf 278
Jampol 115
Jan, Kazimierz 60, 156, 241, 257, 291
Jan III Sobieski 66, 67, 69, 117, 123, 133, 144, 153, 156, 161, 184, 257, 291
Jan, Samuel 242
Jankiel (from *Pan Tadeusz*) 299
Janowiec on Wisła 331, 332
Janowski, Seweryn 216
Jarocin 264
Jarosław 97, 134, 140, 143, 258, 272, 274, 280, 285, 286, 291, 293
Jasioinówka 170
Jasło 15
Jaworów 254
Jedlińsk 332, 338
Jedwabne 262
Jekeles family 48
Jelenia Góra 271, 273
Jelén family 280
Jelén from Kraków 276, 277
Jerusalem 9, 33, 113, 114, 116, 118
Jesus 24, 26, 29, 30, 31, 32, 33
Jews in Poland
  as a separate estate 37, 45, 75, 199–200
  legal status 9, 13, 73–88 passim, 95
  legislation and jurisdiction 20–1, 37, 75, 79–80, 95, 100, 176, 199–218, 219–34 (J. LAW), 235–246 (in Wschowa)
  number and distribution 15–16, 64–6, 74, 95, 108, 237–8, 257, 265, 299, 303–15, 322–40 passim
  origins 13–14, 119
  private life 45–62 passim
  professional activity 14, 16–17, 37, 41, 44, 69, 71, 74, 80, 82, 249–66, 267–95, 318–21, 337
  relations with Poles (szlachta,

burghers, peasants) 17–19, 23–4, 73–88, 93–108 passim, 147–65 passim, 174–85 passim, 235–46 passim (in Wschowa), 254, 299–302, 318–21
  self-government (autonomy) 6, 9, 13, 21, 70, 93–131 passim (language of), 132, 147–73, 174–85 (in towns), 187–95 passim, 220
  taxation 39–41, 53, 67, 77, 79, 80, 87–8, 95, 98, 107–9, 135, 136, 138, 152–7 passim, 162, 170, 178–84, 191, 192, 225–9, 233, 322–6, 331, 334, 339
  trade, merchants 16, 41, 70–1, 74–5, 80, 82, 179, 267–95 passim
Jezierski, Franciszek 84
Jezierski, Jacek 85 88, 338
Jezierzany 327
Jezomierz 168
Józef from Kraków 279
Judah 93
Judaizers 23–35 passim
Juszczyk, J. 34

Kadłubek (master Vincenty) 17, 20
Kaiserslautern 32
Kalahora, Moses 48
Kalisz (city and/or Duchy of) 15, 20, 100, 273, 284, 304, 305, 306, 307
Kańczuga 272, 285, 291
Karaś, M. 121
Karbowa 273
Karo, Józef 5
Kaszewski, rev. 44
Katz, J. 117, 222, 225, 226, 227
Katzenellenbogen, Pinhas 115
Kaufmann 115
Kazanów 332
Kazimierz Jagiellończyk (king) 18, 21, 22, 95, 202, 203
Kazimierz Wielki (king) 3, 16, 21, 95, 201, 202, 203, 206, 210
Kehilla, Kahał, Community (elders of) 40, 47, 48, 49, 51, 54, 56–7, 59, 70, 75, 93–119 passim, 132–164 passim, 166–95, 204–6, 210, 214, 219, 234, 242–6
Kępno 261, 264
Kęty 289
Kiejdany 251
Kielce 338, 339
Kiev 2, 304
Kleczew 263
Kleczyński, J. 303, 307, 308
Klimontów 332, 336
Knyszyn 170
Kobylin 263, 264
Kochański, Łukasz, from Kochań 216
Kock 187
Kolberg, O. 000
Koloszvar 32
Kołłątaj, Hugo 83, 84, 87, 88
Koniecpol 273, 288
Konig 288
Koprzywnica 15
Korecka, Anna 26
Korzon, T. 322, 338
Kostrzewski, J. 119
Kosy, Teodozy 26
Kowno 338
Kozienice 187, 331, 332
Kożuchowski, David Teodor 56
Kórnik 261
Kraków (city/or province) 5, 6, 9, 14–18, 20, 21, 24, 30, 38, 44, 48, 51, 54, 56–8, 100, 103, 120, 121, 125, 136, 138, 143, 159, 160, 185, 202, 203, 206–8, 237, 249, 250, 253, 255, 256, 268–76, 278–94, 301, 304, 306, 308, 309, 311, 312, 314, 319, 320, 326, 338
  Kazimierz 18, 24, 44, 46, 48, 209, 256, 260, 261, 265, 273, 288, 294
  Kleparz 44
  Krowodrza 120
  Wawel 39, 209
  Salt mine 16, 20
  Synod of 27
Krauz, K. 290, 292
Krauz family 290
Krawiec, Walenty (Merchant) 26, 27
Krems 283, 284, 293
Krochmal, Menachem Mendel 61, 222, 223, 226–30, 232, 233
Kromieryż (Kremzir) 232, 271, 273
Krotoszyn 273
Królik, Michał 29
Książ 308
Kujawy 303, 305, 307
Kulczykowski, M. 282, 290
Kunów 338
Kupfer, F. 252
Kurozwęki 333, 336
Kurów 272
Kutno 264
Kutrzeba, S. 145, 147, 200, 201, 215, 217
Kutschera, H. von 119, 121
Kwilecki, Franciszek Antoni 240

INDEX

Laśkiewicz family 290
Latyczów 263
Lefin, Mendel 6
Legnica (city and/or Duchy of) 15, 21
Lehr-Spławiński, T. 119
Leipzig 283, 284
Lelów 272, 274, 308
Leningrad *see* Petersburg
Lesko 272
Leszczyński, A. 167–9, 252, 323
Leszno 237, 238, 243, 250, 260, 262–5, 284
Lewartów (Lubartów) 33
Lewek Szmulowicz 163
Lewek z Nikolsburga (Mikulova) 278
Lewin, I. 145, 160
Lewin, L. 250
Lewkowicz, Salomon 278, 279
Lewocza 271
Leżajsk 187
Linowski, Aleksander 87
Lipnik, Morawski 271, 273
Lipsko 332
Lithuania (Grand Duchy of) 1, 4, 6, 14, 26, 27, 32, 94, 96, 103, 104, 106, 121, 137, 148, 167, 168, 172, 251, 254, 259, 260, 262, 266, 284, 303
Little Poland (province) 74, 87, 96, 100, 137, 148, 154, 199, 205, 260–3, 266, 274, 275, 289, 300, 303, 304, 306, 307, 309, 311, 312, 315, 319, 320, 329
London 181
Lubaczów 289
Lubar 326
Lubartów 258, 261
Lubieniecki, A. 23
Lubieniecki, Krzysztof 33
Lublin (city and/or province) 15, 26, 27, 30, 46, 48, 97, 118, 133, 136, 159, 160, 237, 251, 253, 263, 2722, 274, 277, 280, 281, 285, 286, 304, 308, 309–12
Lubomirski family 161
Lubomirski, Antoni 176
Lubomirski, Stanisław 211, 212, 216
Lubowla 283, 288
Lubraniec 264
Luria, Shlomo (Maharshal) 5, 53, 59
Lusatia 14
Lwów (city and/or province) 15, 17, 38, 44, 46–8, 53, 58, 65, 66, 68, 100, 136, 160, 167, 182, 194, 215, 250, 253–6, 260–2, 268, 272, 274, 277, 280, 285, 286, 291, 301

Łańcut 289
Łaski, Jan 21
Łęczyca 273, 285, 286, 304, 306
Łokacze 140
Łomazy 187
Łowicz 273, 274, 285, 286, 294
Łuck 100, 261
Łuków 308, 315

Maciej (barber-surgeon from Sierpiec) 23
Maghreb 60
Mahler, R. 73, 151, 303, 307, 323
Maimon, Salomon 174
Mainz 13, 14, 94
Majer, Salomon (Slama) 287
Maimonides 220
Majorek (Majer) from Lublin 55
Malbork 304
Małachowski, Stanisław 87, 88, 334
Małecki, J. M. 283
Mandelsberg, Bella 118
Marcin (Jew) 290
Marek, Aleksander, from Kraków 276
Marek from Kraków 276, 279
Marek from Kraków (petty merchant) 278
Marek from Lelów 280
Marek from Prague 276
Margolith 110
Maria (Mother of God) 32, 33
Maria Kazimiera (queen) 137
Mark, B. 252
Marz, K. 115
Massachusetts 9
Matwijowski, L. 66
Maxymilian Habsburg, archduke 269
Mazowsze (Mazovia) 158, 263, 264, 266, 272, 286, 303–7, 309, 329
Mediterranean 3
Melles, Jakub 291, 292
Michał Korybut Wiśniowiecki (king) 142, 202, 256
Miechów 272
Miedziana Góra 338
Mielnik 170
Mieses, M. 34
Mieszko Stary (the Old) 16, 17
Międzybóż 261
Międzyrzecz Podlaski 159, 263
Międzyrzecz Wielkopolski 158, 159
Mikołaj of Kamieniec (Pilawa) 206
Mińsk 191, 192
Mińsk Litewski 273, 274, 304
Mittman, Samuel 290

Mława 23
Mojżesz, son of Izaak Fortis 161
Mojżesz from Kraków 277
Mojżesz from Przedbórz 279
Mojżeszowicz, Zelman 278
Moldavia 284
Montalto family 48
Moravia 5, 115, 223, 271, 273, 276, 277, 283
Mordekhai Hakohen 221
Mordys, Noach 291
Moscow 25, 26
Moses, son of Henoch 52
Moses 29, 30, 31
Moshe (Moses) Isserles 5, 6, 221, 222, 231
Mościska 272, 285, 286
Mośkowicz, Abraham, from Ryczywół 329
Mszczonów 187
Mścisław 138, 304
Muhammad 31
Muntenia 70
Muscovy (Grand Duchy of) 1, 2, 25, 27, 71
Mycielski, A. 242
Myślenice 272, 289

Nachmanowicz, Izaak 48, 58
Nachmanowicz family 48
Nasielsk 252, 261
Natan of Gaza 60
Nathan of Hannover 7
Nerbark 271
Neuser, Adam 32
New York 114, 188
Nieznamirowice 332
Nikitsky, A. J. 25
Nikolsburg (Mikulov) 271, 273
Nitsch, K. 120
Non-Adorationists 27, 32, 33
Nowe Miasto Korczyn 272, 274, 331, 333, 336
Nowogródek 33, 304
Nowy Sącz 258, 272
Nycz, M. 154, 157
Nysa 271, 273, 277, 283

Ochocki, J. D. 174
Olelkowicz, Micheł 25
Olesko 137, 183
Oleśnica 333, 336
Oleśno 289
Olewsk 168
Olkusz 272, 274, 285, 286

Olomuniec 273, 276
Opatowiec 330, 333
Opatów 175, 176, 178, 181, 183–5, 272, 274, 280, 281, 331, 332, 334, 336, 338, 339
Opoczno 272, 308, 331, 332, 339
Opole and Racibórz, Duchy of 28
Orla 170, 261
Osiek 272
Ossoliński, Józef 180
Ostrowiec 332, 336
Ostrowski, Jakub 27
Ostróg 57, 100, 262
Oświęcim 272
Ottoman Empire 24, 227
Owrucz 168
Ożarów 329, 332, 336
Oxford 9, 114

Pacanowski, Joachim 291, 292
Pacanów 272, 333, 334, 336
Paklepka, Stanisław 26, 27
Palestine 5
Pawiński, A. 36, 40, 322
Pawlikowice 31
Pawlikowski, Józef 85
Pawłowski, Józef 240
Pawołocz 263
Pazdro, Z. 215, 250
Perl, Josef, from Tarnopol 193, 194
Perles, J. 112
Petersburg (Leningrad) 250, 251
Pękalski, Tobiasz 142
Piast dynasty 14
Piattoli, Scipione 82, 87, 88
Piekarski, Hieronim 33
Pierzchnica 333
Pilica 272, 285
Pinkus, Gershel 242
Pinkus, Jakub, from Kraków 277
Pińczów 272, 279, 285–8, 291, 331, 333, 335–7, 339
Pińsk 139, 168, 169
Piotrków 273, 285, 286
Płock 15, 16, 23, 263, 264, 304
Podgórze 289
Podlasie 260–3, 266, 303, 304
Podole 189, 192, 261, 266, 304, 318
Podraza, A. 7
Pokorny 327
Polesie 26
Polish Brothers 30, 33
Połaniec 272, 332, 336
Połock 304
Pomorze 304

INDEX 359

Poniatowski, Michał Jerzy 308
Potocli family 70, 161
Potocki, Jędrzej 66
Potocki, Michał 38
Potocki, Stanisław 211
Poznań (city and/or province) 18, 46, 47, 57, 99, 100, 114, 115, 118, 133, 136, 154, 160, 167, 185, 237, 238, 240, 249, 260, 261, 264, 266, 268, 273, 274, 284, 301, 304, 305
Prague 271, 273
Privileges (granted to Jews) 3, 20–2, 46, 58, 66–7, 70, 75, 79, 95, 200–6, 213, 214, 239, 254
Prosperów 336
Prostic, Izaak, son of Aron 276, 278
Proszowice 308
Proszyński, Hieronim Władysław, from Proszna 216
Prościejów (Prostejov) 223, 271
Prussia 1, 73, 81, 112, 242, 273, 305
Prussia, Royal 303–5
Przebendowski, Jan Jerzy 143
Przedbórz 272, 274, 285, 286, 331, 332, 334
Przemyśl (city and/or province) 13, 38, 39, 124, 160, 250, 254, 260, 261, 272, 274, 280, 285, 286, 291
Przeworsk 289
Przyczyna (Górna and Dolna) 237
Przytyk 332

Rabinowicz, Marek 37
Rachela (from the play *Wesele*) 299
Radom 308, 326, 329, 332, 338
Radomsko 289
Radoszyce 272, 332
Radziwiłł family 180
Radzymin 272
Rajgród 170
Raków 28, 331, 334, 336, 339
Rawa 273, 286, 304
Rączki 338
Rebel, Tomasz 290
Re'em 127
Reformation 23–6, 33, 102
Rhineland 3, 13, 14, 94
Riga 291
Ritual slaughter 188–95 passim, 225, 241
Rolbiecki, G. J. 236
Roman Empire 94
 of the German Nation 20
Rome 114
Ronemberg, Szymon 31, 33

Rorajski, Jan 216
Rostworowski, E. 154, 155
Rożanka, Janusz 276
Rudnicki, Krzysztof 33
Russia, Russian Empire 9, 107, 112, 257, 284, 305, 315
Ruthenia, Ruthenians 16, 17, 65, 133, 137, 138, 160, 250, 272, 285, 286, 294, 304
 Halicz and Włodzimierz 15–17
 Red 100, 252, 253, 260–2, 266, 318, 323, 326
Rutkowski, J. 301, 316
Rybarski, R. 138, 153, 154, 155, 269, 321
Ryczywół 332, 334
Rymanów 285, 286
Rzeszów 159, 160, 258, 261, 272, 274, 285, 286, 291
Rzewuski, Stanisław Mateusz 44

Sabbatarianism 2
SachAria (Zachariasz) 257
Safarowiczawa, H. 121
Salomon, Efraim ben Aron, from Łęczyca 51, 59
Salomon Ibn Aderet 227
Sambor 285, 286
Samuel from Lesko 277
Samuel from Kraków 24
Sandomierz (city and/or province) 14, 15, 100, 138, 272, 274, 286, 304, 307–12, 319, 322–40 passim
Sanguszko, Paweł Karol 178, 183, 185
Sanok 289
Sasportas, Jacob 60
Schipper, I. 4, 120, 121, 139, 141, 144, 151, 160, 267–9, 276, 280, 282, 293, 323, 324–7
Schorr Liberals, Moses 256
Schorr, M. 124, 131, 135, 140, 144, 145, 147, 148, 151, 157, 200, 249, 250
Schrenk 288
Scots 37, 181, 339
Secemin 272, 332, 334
Sedlnicki, Karol Odrowąż 127, 150
Seidel, Marcin, from Oława 30, 31
Sejm (Diet) 2, 101, 159–63
 Convocation (1764) 164, 235, 238
 Four Years' 8, 73–88 passim, 179
 Grodno of 1793 86
 of 1768 76, 78
Sejmiki (Dietines) 2, 36–44 passim, 95;
 Sejmiki żydowskie (Jewish Dietines) 140–1, 149

Seligowicz, Eliasz 48
Sędziwój of Czechło 22
Shabatai Tsvi of Smyrna 8, 60, 189
Siemiatycze 169, 170, 171
Sienno 332
Sieradz 273, 286, 304, 306
Sieradz-Łęczyca province 303, 304, 305, 307
Sierpiec 23
Siewiersk 308, 309
Siewierz 26
Silesia 149, 242, 271, 273, 283, 284, 286, 289, 309
Simon of Poland 117
Skoki 263
Skoroszewski, Marcin 216
Słuck 139
Smalc, Walenty 33
Smoleński, W. 175
Sobków 332
Sochaczew 264
Socyn, Faust 30-2
Sokal 262, 285, 286
Sokolniki 15
Sokołów 251, 260, 261
Solec 183, 332
Sommerfeldt, J. 300
Spain 3, 94, 220
Speyer 94
Spisz 271, 273, 288
Stanisław August Poniatowski (king) 4, 73, 77, 81, 108, 165, 202, 240, 241, 258, 259, 265
Stanisławów 66, 70
Staszic, S. 84
Staszów 289, 330, 332, 334, 336
Stawiska 173, 262
Stefan Batory (king) 201
Stężyca, region 310, 312
Stopnica 272, 285, 286, 331, 333, 336
Strzemski, M. 145
Sudyłków 261
Suleiman II 24
Suliński, Mikołaj, of Sulanki 216
Sułkowski, Z. 323, 325
Swarzędz 183
Sweden 107, 257, 315, 331, 339
Sylwanus 32
Szczebrzeszyński, Franczek 277
Szczęsny, Jakub 278
Szczucki, L. 31
Szkłow 262
Szoman, Jerzy 31
Szydłowiec 332, 334
Szydłowski, Jan Jakub 143

Sztsłów 272, 274, 331, 333, 334, 336
Śniadowo 262
Śrem 261
Świerczowski Zymunt from Świerczów 216
Świetlik Lewek 280
Święcicki, Jan Baptysta 33

Tapiński, Wasyl 33
Tarło, Jan 138
Tarłów 331, 333, 334, 336
Tarnobrzeg 331
Tarnogród 258, 285, 286, 288
Tarnopol 254, 285
Tarnów 254, 261, 272, 274
Taszycki, W. 121
Tazbir, J. 39
Tęczyński, Andrzej 211, 215
Tęczyński, Jan 211, 216
Toruń 273, 274, 275, 285, 286
Toszka, Jeleń 277
Towns, burghers 15, 17, 33, 37, 39, 41, 44, 68, 71, 74–83, 87, 88, 95, 97, 106, 108, 174–85 (private towns) passim, 235–46 (town of Wschowa) passim, 254, 257, 311, 329
Transylvania 27, 32, 315
Trąba, Mikołaj 20
Trembowla 38
Troki 304
Trzebicki, Andrzej 292
Tsodek, Zelig 292
Turkey 24, 71, 103, 257, 286, 315
Tyczyn 286
Tykocin 113, 159, 160, 166–73 passim, 261, 262, 263, 266
Tymf, Tomasz 291
Tyniec (Silesian) 15

Ukraine, Ukrainians 2, 7, 8, 261, 262, 263, 266, 315, 318
Unitarianism, Unitarians 27, 28, 30, 31, 32, 103
USA 109, 113
Usury 16, 17, 19, 70, 321

Vehe-Glirius, Mathias 32, 33
Venice 271, 273
Verona 127
Vienna 226, 230, 231, 271, 273, 276, 339

Wadowice 289
Wahl family 48
Wallachians 37

INDEX

Warsaw 79, 80, 82, 85, 87, 113, 161, 235, 237, 269, 2722, 274, 285, 286, 291, 293
Weigl, Melchior 24
Weiglowa, Katarzyna 24, 25
Wein, A. 252
Weinreich, V. 188
Weinryb, B. D. 4, 325
Wettstein, F. H. 249
Węgrów 159, (Synod of) 32
Wieledniki 262, 263
Wieliczka *see* Kraków, Salt mine
Wieluń 273, 304, 306
Wiktor from Wodzisław 279
Wilkowski, Kasper 28, 33
Wiolno 46, 113, 114, 139, 191, 255, 268, 304, 338
Wischnitzer, Mark 251
Wiślica 272, 308, 331, 333–7
Wiśnicz 272, 285, 286, 289
Wiśniowiecki, Janusz 211
Witebsk 138, 304
Witkowo 263
Witrelin, Aleksander 30
Władysław IV (king) 213, 241, 254, 255
Włoch, Józef 280
Włodzimierz Wołyński 140
Włoszczow a332
Wodzimin 273
Wodzisław 272, 274, 284, 285, 286, 291, 334
Wolbrom 284, 285, 286, 294
Wolf, Szymon, son of Abraham 278, 279, 280
Wołozko 26

Wołyń (Volhynia) 26, 100, 130, 134, 137, 2148, 160, 168, 169, 192, 261, 262, 266, 304, 318, 326
Worms 14, 94
Wrocła*see* Breslau
Września 263
Wschowa (Stara and Nowa) 235–46 passim, 273
Wujek, Jakub 125
Wyrobisz, A. 178
Wyrozumski, J. 3

Yaffe, Mordekhai 6, 222
Yakov of Janov 6
Yehud Ha-Kohen 13
Yeshivot 5, 50, 51, 98, 105

Zabłudów 142, 167, 168, 172, 173, 261
Zachariasiewicz 65
Zakrzewska-Dubas, M. 64–6
Zaleszczyki (district) 327
Zambrów 170
Zamorski, K. 319
Zamość 64, 183
Zator 272
Ząbkowice Śląskie (Franksztyn) 271, 273
Złoczew 157
Złotnik, Jonas 280
Zwoleń 331, 332, 334
Zygmunt August (king) 23, 45, 211, 213, 216
Zygmunt I (king) 96, 213
Zygmunt II (king) 68, 70, 152, 213, 254, 255

www.ingramcontent.com/pod-product-compliance
Lightning Source LLC
Chambersburg PA
CBHW072119290426
44111CB00012B/1711